Thomson's D[...]
Liability

This edition is dedicated to the memory of Joseph McGeachy Thomson, 1948–2018.

Thomson's Delictual Liability

Sixth Edition

Gordon Cameron

Formerly Senior Lecturer in the School of Law at the University of Dundee.

Bloomsbury Professional

LONDON • DUBLIN • EDINBURGH • NEW YORK • NEW DELHI • SYDNEY

BLOOMSBURY PROFESSIONAL
Bloomsbury Publishing Plc
50 Bedford Square, London, WC1B 3DP, UK
1385 Broadway, New York, NY 10018, USA
29 Earlsfort Terrace, Dublin 2, Ireland

BLOOMSBURY and the Diana logo are trademarks of Bloomsbury
Publishing Plc

First published in Great Britain 2021

British Library Cataloguing-in-Publication Data

A catalogue record for this book is available from the British Library.

ISBN:	PB	978 1 52651 878 1
	Epub	978 1 52651 879 8
	Epdf	978 1 52651 880 4

Typeset by Evolution Design & Digital Ltd (Kent)
Printed and bound by CPI Group (UK) Ltd, Croydon, CR0 4YY

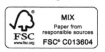

To find out more about our authors and books visit www.
bloomsburyprofessional.com. Here you will find extracts, author
information, details of forthcoming events and the option to sign up for
our newsletters

Preface

It is an honour to be entrusted with the first posthumous edition of this book. Joe's knowledge of the subject was extensive and keenly perceived. There cannot be many among those whose work or studies involve Scots private law who do not owe something of their understanding of delict to him.

The seven years that have passed since the last edition have seen much change in delict, mostly for the better. I have retained as much text from the previous edition as possible, working new developments into the existing structure and adjusting the analysis where needed. This proved a more difficult task than I had anticipated and there are elements in the book where I felt some restructuring was called for. I have done what I can to retain Joe's discursive approach and accessible style. The book was always intended to stimulate a deeper interest as well as to inform.

I record my thanks to those who have provided welcome assistance: Dr Stephen Bogle and Dr Bobby Lindsay of the Law School at the University of Glasgow and Rhona McLean, solicitor at Revenue Scotland. Thanks also to my wife Lesley who kept the domestic ship afloat and the dog walked during a period in which she might reasonably have expected more input from myself. Thanks also to staff at Bloomsbury who coped admirably with my cutting and pasting and muddling up footnotes and finally thanks to the University of Dundee for allowing me continuing access to software and databases.

For those readers who would like to know more about the original author I highly recommend two tributes published in the *Juridical Review*, 2019. 'An Academic Portrait of JM Thomson, Teacher, Scholar and Connoisseur' by Scott C Styles at pp 2–17 and 'Joe Thomson and Contract Law in Scotland' by Hector MacQueen at pp 18–32.

Gordon Cameron
Kirkcaldy
9 September 2021

Contents

Table of Statutes

[All references are to paragraph number]

Table of Statutory Instruments

[All references are to paragraph number]

Table of Cases

xx   *Table of Cases*

C

H

K

S

Introduction

The essence of the modern Scots law of delict is the obligation of a person, A, to compensate another person, B, for the losses B has sustained as a result of harm caused to B by the wrongful actions of A. This obligation to pay compensation is called reparation. The obligation to make reparation when loss has been suffered as a result of a person's wrongful actions is obediential; it arises *ex lege* regardless of the will of the wrongdoer. In this respect, delictual obligations differ from contractual obligations which arise as a result of the agreement of the parties to a contract. However, a delictual obligation is similar to the obligation to reverse an unjustified enrichment, since the latter obligation also arises *ex lege*. But unlike unjustified enrichment the delictual obligation to make reparation arises only when the loss has arisen as a result of the wrongful act of the person who caused the harm. It is only when a person has been at fault that the obligation to make reparation arises. In Scots law we use the term '*culpa*' to describe fault. *Culpa* covers both intentional and unintentional conduct which causes harm to another but before there is liability the law must regard the conduct as wrongous. This is encapsulated in the brocard *damnum injuria datum*, ie harm caused by wrongous conduct.

Some examples will make the point clearer. If A intentionally assaults B, causing him harm, A is under a delictual obligation to compensate B for the losses he has sustained from his injuries: A's conduct is culpable, because he deliberately intended to harm B by assaulting him, which the law regards as a wrongous act. If A drives his car carelessly on a public highway and as a result injures B, a pedestrian, then A is under a delictual obligation to compensate B for the losses he has sustained from his injuries: A's conduct is culpable because of his careless driving which the law regards as a wrongous act. Thus, we can say that modern Scots law begins from the premise that there is an obediential obligation on a person to make reparation to another who has sustained losses as a consequence of suffering harm as a result of the *culpa* or fault of the wrongdoer, ie the wrongdoer's intentional or unintentional, but careless, conduct, which caused the harm. Its function is corrective justice – to put the victim, so far as an award of damages can, into the position he would have been if the wrong had never taken place.

It is not the case that a person who suffers loss from harm caused by another's intentional or unintentional, but careless, conduct will always be entitled to reparation. The act which causes the harm must be regarded by the law as wrongful (*injuria*). For policy reasons, certain acts are not regarded as wrongful in this sense. So, for example, as we shall see,[1] A is free to undercut the prices of his competitor, B, even if B suffers economically; nor does it matter if A deliberately undercuts B's prices with the intention of putting B out of business. The reason for this is that, in our society, competition is to be encouraged even if persons suffer economically as a result. This is an example of *damnum absque injuria*, ie harm without wrongful conduct The encouragement of competition, however does not go so far as to allow two parties to conspire to drive a third out of business. Conspiracy is a delict.[2]

Before there is an obligation to make reparation, the victim must suffer harm. But, in addition, this harm must arise from an intrusion by the wrongdoer upon a right of the victim which is recognised by the law as reparable. One of the fascinating aspects of the law of delict is to see when the courts are prepared to recognise rights as reparable and when they are not.

For example, the law has long recognised as reparable a person's right to physical integrity so that if there is an intrusion of that right as a result of wrongful conduct, the wrongdoer must make compensation for pain and suffering, ie non-patrimonial loss and any patrimonial, ie economic, loss arising from the injuries sustained, such as loss of earning capacity. But the Scots law of delict has, hitherto, not recognised as a reparable right a person's privacy per se[3] although it has, for example, protected a person's confidential information.[4]

An area which has caused controversy is whether the law should recognise as a reparable right economic loss sustained by a person where the economic loss does not derive from injury to that person's body or damage to his property.[5] So, for example, if A carelessly damages an electric cable owned by B with the result that there is a loss of power to C's factory, should C be able to obtain compensation for his loss of production (pure economic loss) if the power cut did not cause any physical damage to the machinery in his factory? B, of course, can seek reparation from A in respect of the physical damage to B's cable.

1   See para 2.1 below.
2   See paras 2.6–2.8 below.
3   Although it appears to be on the verge of doing so. See discussion at para 1.9
    below. *C v Chief Constable Police Scotland* [2020] CSIH 61, 2020 SLT 1021.
4   Breach of confidence is discussed at paras 1.11–1.12 below.
5   This matter is discussed at length in Chapter 4.

Scottish lawyers maintain that Scots law is based on principle
rather than remedies. It is probably true to argue that the
modern Scots law of delict is based on the general principle of an
obediential, *ex lege* obligation to make reparation for loss sustained
as a result of wrongful conduct. This was not always the case and
is, indeed, a comparatively recent development. In medieval
times, before there was a centralised system for the prosecution
of criminal offences, there was a close relationship between what
would now be considered delictual actions and the enforcement
of the criminal law. What we discover is that there were specific
remedies to deal with situations which were common in those
turbulent times. *Stair* lists the following:[1]

> 'besides those of a special name and nature, which are chiefly
> these, assythment, extortion, circumvention, spuilzie, intrusion,
> ejection, molestation, breach of arrestment, deforcement,
> contravention, forgery, which comes in more properly in the
> process of improbation'.

Three of these deserve further consideration to illustrate the close
relationship which existed at that time between delictual liability
and the enforcement of the criminal law.

Assythment was concerned with the regulation of acts which
caused death and was an attempt to avoid blood feuds. The
remedy of assythment was an action for a sum of money:

> 'to be payit be the commirtaris of slaughter, to the kin, bairnis
> and friends of any person that is slane ... gevin to thame in
> contentatioun of the hurt, damnage and skeith sustenit be thane
> throw the wanting of the person who is slane, and for the skaith
> incurrit be thame thairthrow, and for the pacifying of their
> rancor'.[2]

Several features of the action should be noted. There had to be
a crime which caused death or physical injury to the victim.
The action could be brought by any person, however remote,
who was a relative of the deceased or injured person. The
damages depended on the wrongdoer's means, ie they were
not simply compensatory, and, finally, no assythment was due
if the wrongdoer was executed. Assythment arose either if the
wrongdoer was convicted and because of his position received a

lesser penalty than was due or if there was no conviction and the family of the deceased issued a document known as a letter of slains acknowledging receipt of assythment and petitioning the Crown not to proceed with a prosecution. The latter situation was more important because it short-circuited the need for a criminal trial. With the establishment of a centralised system of public prosecution it became contrary to public policy that the victim or his family should be able to circumvent the normal prosecution process by issuing letters of slains. In practice, actions for assythment died out though they were still theoretically possible if the wrongdoer had been prosecuted but had not suffered the due pains of the law. At the same time, the common law developed an action under which the spouse and ascendants and descendants of a person who had been killed as a result of the defender's *culpa* could obtain reparation in respect of the death, ie they could bring an action in delict.

1   *Institutions* IX, 5, 6.
2   Balfour *Practicks* p 516.

An attempt to revive an action of assythment was made in *McKendrick v Sinclair*.[1] A workman was killed by an electric shock allegedly due to the negligence of his employer. He had financially supported his sister and two brothers. They could not bring an action in delict because at common law brothers and sisters of the deceased had no title to sue.[2] However, the Lord Advocate was not prepared to prosecute the defender or to concur if the relatives had sought a private prosecution. The old practice of letters of slains was inappropriate as the employer denied liability for culpable homicide. Accordingly, assythment would only have been available on the old authorities if there had been a conviction. As this was not the case, the action failed since it did not fall within the recognised parameters of the remedy.[3] Lord Simon of Glaisdale was prepared to dismiss the action on a more radical ground: that in spite of being a common law remedy assythment had fallen into desuetude, ie had become obsolescent:

> 'This Brunnhilde [assythment] would awake in our uncongenial modern Niebelheim. This Rip van Winkle would find *Eisten's* case firmly embodied in the law, that private prosecutions are extinct, that capital punishment for homicide has been abolished, and that damages are related to loss to the pursuer and not to the means of the defender. Even if this Sleeping Beauty were so attractive as to tempt your Lordships to favour her with your kisses she could not live happily ever after.'[4]

Assythment was finally laid to rest when it was abolished by section 8 of the Damages (Scotland) Act 1976 which extended title to sue in respect of the death of a relative to include the deceased's brothers and sisters[5] thus closing the lacuna revealed in the *McKendrick* case.

1   1972 SC (HL) 25, 1972 SLT 110.
2   *Eisten v North British Railway Co* (1870) 8 M 980.
3   *McKendrick v Sinclair* 1972 SLT 110 at 113 per Lord Reid and at 120 per Lord Kilbrandon, 1972 SC (HL) 25.
4   1972 SLT 110 at 117.
5   For discussion of the right to sue in respect of the death of a relative, see Chapter 13. The 1976 Act has been repealed and replaced by the Damages (Scotland) Act 2011.

The second old remedy we should consider is contravention of lawburrows. This was a method of primitive law enforcement in the absence of an effective police force and system of public prosecution of criminal offences. If a person had reasonable grounds to believe that he or his family or their property was in danger from another person, he could apply to a court to have that person find caution (ie to lodge a sum of money in court) not to harm him or his family or their property. This was known as lawburrows. In other words, the defender was ordered not to molest the pursuer or the family or their property on pain of losing caution, ie the money lodged in court. If the defender contravened the non-molestation order, he could be sued in an action of contravention of lawburrows for forfeiture of the caution.[1] With the advent of effective law enforcement agencies, the use of lawburrows declined, though there is no doubt that the action is still technically competent.[2]

Other old delicts which technically continue to form part of the law, but which are seldom if ever litigated include seduction and entrapment. Seduction is a ground of action where the consent of a woman to sexual intercourse is obtained by deception or abuse of position, typically where the male protagonist has made a promise of marriage which he has no intention of keeping.[3] Entrapment arises where a person has fraudulent been enticed into a void marriage. This would happen where the other party is already married.[4] The basis for both these delicts is fraud.

Finally, there was the action of spuilzie. This action arose when the defender interfered with the possession of another's moveable property, for example, stole cattle or sheep. The pursuer was the owner or the lawful possessor of the property.[5] The action was to have the property returned, or its value. But the quasi-criminal nature of the action is illustrated by the fact that the pursuer was entitled to violent profits, ie all the profits which the pursuer might have made from the property while in possession of the defender. In many situations, spuilzie has been overtaken by the general principle of liability for wrongful conduct.[6]

1   Lawburrows Acts 1429 and 1581.
2   On lawburrows generally, see 13 *Stair Memorial Encyclopaedia* paras 901–926; *Morrow v Neil* 1975 SLT (Sh Ct) 65; *Liddle v Morton* 1996 SLT 1143. In the modern context pursuers are more likely to seek non-harassment orders. See para 1.7 below.
3   See, eg, *Murray v Fraser* 1916 SC 623.
4   See, eg, *Burke v Burke* 1983 SLT 331 OH.
5   *FC Finance Ltd v Brown & Son* 1969 SLT (Sh Ct) 41.
6   See, eg, *Harris v Abbey National plc* 1997 SCLR 359 (liability based on gratuitous deposit of property rather than spuilzie).

We have seen, then, how these specific remedies had important quasi-criminal aspects. While it is clear that lawburrows and spuilzie remain, theoretically at least, part of Scots law, in practice they have largely been overtaken by the development of effective law enforcement agencies and the general principle of liability to make reparation for loss caused as a result of the defender's wrongful conduct. *Stair* laid the basis for the general principle of delictual liability when he recognised that to cause damage by delinquence gave rise to an obediential obligation to make reparation for the damage caused: *damnum injuria datum*. This was a general innominate remedy based on the defender's *culpa* which included deliberate as well as careless conduct. *Stair* treated the nominate Scottish remedies as simply aspects of the general obligation to make reparation for loss caused by a wrong.[1] This general obligation was accepted by the later institutional writers.[2] In attempting this synthesis, reliance was, of course, placed on Roman law and in particular liability under the Lex Aquilia which included liability for unintentional, but careless, conduct.

Although the modern Scots law of delict can be traced back to the institutional writers, their treatment is not extensive. Instead, the principles of the law of delict are largely the creation of the courts. The judges have had to develop the law to take account of the increase of potential injury to persons and damage to property created by industrialisation, mass production and distribution of goods, easier access to information, and the motor car. At the same time, they have also appreciated that there must be limits on a person's liability, particularly for unintentional conduct, if that person is to continue to engage in conduct which is socially and economically desirable, even if it is potentially harmful. The traditional Scots law solution has been to restrict liability by insisting that it is only triggered by the defender's fault and by refusing to recognise certain kinds of harm as reparable rights. This book is largely concerned with the rules of common law and statute which have developed to achieve this balance. However, in some areas it has been considered socially and economically desirable that persons should recover compensation for losses resulting from physical injury or damage to property without the need to establish fault on the part of the defender. Accordingly, legislation has been necessary to introduce into Scots law what is known as strict liability, ie where a person can be liable in delict for harm for which they are deemed responsible without the need for the person who suffers loss from the injury or damage to establish fault.[3] An example of strict liability at common law is vicarious liability whereby employers may be held liable for the delicts of their employees while not being at fault themselves.[4] In a modem context, it is therefore important to discuss the principles of strict liability in relation to the breach of statutory duties imposed by some, at least, of the most important statutes.

1   *Stair* I, 9, 2.
2   See, for example, Erskine *Institute* III, 1.
3   For example, liability for defective products falls on the manufacturer or importer, see Chapter 8 below; liability for some injuries or damage caused by animals falls on the keeper of the animal, see Chapter 9 below.
4   See Chapter 12 below.

The Human Rights Act 1998 makes the European Convention on Human Rights directly effective in Scots – and English – domestic law. As a consequence, the Convention is having a profound effect on how the law is being developed by the courts in such areas as privacy[1] the delictual liability of state agencies[2] and the law of defamation.[3] Moreover, where a public authority has infringed a Convention right, the victim may be entitled to damages under the 1998 Act,[4] whether or not the violation of the Convention right amounts to a delict. It should be noted that damages are only available against a public authority, not a private individual. Detailed discussion of damages for breach of Convention rights is outwith the scope of this book.

It is the author's primary intention to concentrate on the common law principles which underlie delictual liability, ie intentional and unintentional wrongdoing. There have been times when these principles have become difficult to explain in a coherent fashion. While it has always been accepted that the imposition of a duty of care in novel situations involves the courts making decisions on grounds of legal policy,[5] once that decision was made, precedent could be applied more or less mechanically to determine whether or not a duty would be recognised in the instant case. A developing tendency to apply a 'fair, just and reasonable' test, whenever the question of duty arose had the potential to undermine principle and reduce every determination to the level of policy. [6] That situation has largely been averted by the Supreme Court in *Robinson v Chief Constable of West Yorkshire*.[7] A return to orthodoxy is well under way.

The book begins with a study of delictual liability for intentionally harmful conduct; the second part contains an analysis of the general principles of liability for unintentional, but careless, conduct; the third part considers delictual liability in the context of some important social and economic relationships. Included in this part is a chapter on defamation and malicious publication which are now on a statutory footing. The book ends with a chapter on damages.

1   For discussion, see beyond paras 1.8 ff.
2   See Chapter 11 below
3   See Chapter 15 below.
4   Human Rights Act 1998, s 8(3).
5   See Chapter 4 below.
6   See Joe Thomson 'Principle as Policy' (2003) 56 CLP 123.
7   [2018] UKSC 8, [2018] 2 WLR 595.See para 3.10 below.

Part I

INTENTIONAL DELICTS

CHAPTER 1

Intentional wrongs

A. INTRODUCTION

1.1 As we have seen,[1] *culpa* includes (a) deliberate conduct intended to harm the victim or the victim's property and (b) unintentional, but careless, conduct which has harmed the victim or the victim's property. In the case of unintentional conduct, the range of victims is prima facie indeterminate, ie it could potentially include any person who has been harmed by the conduct. Because of this, the law has had to invent devices for limiting the number of persons who are entitled to sue in delict if they suffer harm as a result of another's careless conduct. The most important of these devices is the concept of a duty of care:[2] it is only a person to whom the defender owes a duty of care who can sue in delict for harm arising from the defender's careless conduct.[3]

Where an act is done deliberately to harm a particular person, there is not the same degree of difficulty since the potential pursuer is normally determinate:[4] the pursuer is the person whom the defender *intended* to harm by his conduct and there is no need to invoke the concept of a duty of care. Intentional delicts in relation to personal and bodily integrity and personality rights are discussed in this chapter.

1 Introduction above.
2 There are other devices such as remoteness of injury and causation: see paras 5.4, 5.10 and Chapter 6.
3 The duty of care is discussed at Chapter 3 below.
4 There can be cases where this might not be so: A may intend to harm B by blowing up B's house but injure C instead; while it is thought that A will be liable to C, such cases are rare in practice.

B. PERSONAL AND BODILY INTEGRITY

(1) Assault

1.2 'Everyone who lives under the protection of the law has an absolute right to the safety of his person; and wherever this right is invaded there is in Civil law a provision for redress of injury, as well as in penal law a punishment for the crime.'[1] An assault may amount to a breach of Article 3 of the European Convention of Human Rights: 'No one shall be subjected to torture or to inhuman or degrading treatment or punishment.' Where this is so, it is competent to seek damages at common law for assault and compensation for a breach of Article 3 in the same action.[2]

A physical assault is a common law crime provided there is the necessary evil intent on the part of the perpetrator *(dolus)*. Assault also constitutes a civil wrong and civil liability is not dependent on criminal proceedings having been brought. The standard of proof in a criminal case is 'beyond reasonable doubt' whereas in civil law the lower standard 'on the balance of probabilities' applies and so a civil action may succeed where a prosecution has resulted in findings of 'not guilty' or 'not proven'. For example, the pursuer was awarded damages in *Mullan v Anderson (No.2)*[3] after a prosecution for a knife attack failed. A victim of rape succeeded in a civil claim after a not proven verdict in the criminal court.[4] Where prosecutions are successful, victims are commonly awarded compensation under the Criminal Injuries Compensation Scheme.[5]

1   Bell *Principles* para 2028.For a detailed treatment of this delict see Elspeth Reid, *Personality, Confidentiality and Privacy in Scots Law*, 2010 (W Green & Son, Edinburgh), Chapter 2.
2   *Ruddy v Chief Constable of Strathclyde* [2012] UKSC 57 (alleged assault by police on the pursuer when he was arrested and detained in custody).
3   1997 SLT 93.
4   *DC v DG & DR* [2017] CSOH 5. See also *AR v Coxen* 2018 SLT (Sh Ct) 335.
5   Criminal Proceedings (Scotland) Act 1995 ss 249–253.

1.3   The essence of assault is non-consensual and unwarranted interference with the person. Deliberate conduct is required. The intention to inflict hurt or injury is perfectly apparent in most assaults, but even where harm is not the object of the conduct the defender will nevertheless be liable if they acted in the knowledge that harm was likely to occur, or acted recklessly, disregarding the possibility of harm.[1] So where A playfully attacked B in order to make B engage in sport, it nevertheless constituted an actionable wrong even although it was done 'for a lark'.[2] Pure accidents such as people colliding in a busy street, are not actionable as assaults,[3] but may give rise to a claim grounded in negligence.[4] The delict of assault in Scots law developed from the civilian *actio injuriarum* which did not require proof of physical injury, but compensated insult and affronts to dignity. If the assault does not result in serious physical harm however, the damages awarded will not be substantial despite the insult caused to the victim.[5] The flow of complaints based on affront without any physical invasion has not persisted to the present day.[6] It remains the case that apprehension of the threat of immediate bodily harm will found a claim for damages even though the threat is not carried out.[7]

Consent of the victim prevents delictual liability for assault from arising. This explains why there is no liability for assault in sports involving physical contact: boxing, rugby, soccer etc. But the players give consent only to the physical contact inherent in the sport, so that there will be liability if injury is sustained as a result of conduct outwith the rules of the game; if, for example, a rugby player punches, as opposed to tackles, an opponent or where a prop forward bites the ear off their opposite number in the scrum. In the context of non-contact sports, presence on a golf course does not indicate consent to being struck by a wayward golf ball.[8]

Where this principle is important is in respect of medical procedures. The basis for medical intervention is the informed consent of the patient.[9] Litigation is more likely to arise as a claim for damages grounded on negligence where injury or deterioration in health occurs, but if a doctor or dentist carries out a medical procedure on an adult[10] without the patient's consent, then the doctor or dentist is liable to make reparation.[11] Although this will usually not be a crime because of the absence of evil intent on the part of the doctor or dentist, it is still a delict. The patient can obtain reparation not only for any resulting patrimonial loss but also for *contumelia*, ie the insult suffered as a result of the non-consensual invasion of bodily integrity. The fact that the procedure was carried out for the patient's benefit is irrelevant.[12]

1   E Reid, *Personality, Confidentiality and Privacy in Scots Law*, para 2.10.
2   *Reid v Mitchell* (1885) 12 R 1129.
3   See, eg, *Hall v Watson* (1896) 12 Sh Ct Rep 117.
4   See, eg, *Robinson v Chief Constable West Yorkshire* [2018] UKSC 4.
5   See, eg, *Downie v Chief Constable of Strathclyde Police* 1997 SCLR 603 (the pursuer was awarded £1,500 in respect of an assault by two policemen; the victim had recovered without the need of medical treatment).
6   For discussion see E Reid, *Personality, Confidentiality and Privacy in Scots Law*, paras 2.19ff.
7   See, eg. *Ewing v Earl of Mar* (1851) 14 D 314.
8   *Lewis v Buckpool Golf Club* 1993 SLT (Sh Ct) 43. For other golf injury cases, see eg, *Lamond v Glasgow Corporation* 1968 SLT 291; *Phee v Gordon* 2013 SC 379; *McMahon v Dear* [2014] CSOH 100. For discussion see Daniel J Carr, 'Personal Injury and the Game of Golf', 2015 19 ELR 259.
9   *Montgomery v Lanarkshire Health Board* [2015] UKSC 11, 2015 SLT 189; see para 7.4 below.

10 A person under the age of 16 will have legal capacity to consent if the doctor or dentist is of the view that the young person is capable of understanding the nature and probable consequences of the medical treatment or procedure: Age of Legal Capacity (Scotland) Act 1991, s 2(4).

11 In an emergency, if the patient is, for example, unconscious, a doctor may proceed without the patient's consent if it is *necessary* for the patient's wellbeing to do so.

12 'Even when his or her own life depends on receiving medical treatment, an adult of sound mind is entitled to refuse it': *St George's Healthcare NHS Trust v S; R v Collins, ex parte S* [1998] 3 WLR 936, [1998] 3 All ER 673, CA at 685 per Judge LJ.

1.4 There is a complete defence to an action of assault if it was the result of an unavoidable accident. Actions can be defended where the conduct complained of was justified. Self-defence provides justification, but the defender's belief that he or she was under threat of imminent attack must be reasonably held.[1] In a case where physical contact has taken place the defender's conduct must be reasonable. The defence will not succeed where the defender had the opportunity to disengage.[2]

There are circumstances where the use of force is justified. Most commonly, this arises in the course of police duties but there are other public officials for whom some degree of force may be justifiable. The level of force used must, however, be warranted in the circumstances.[3] Where a police officer uses excessive force or uses force in circumstances where there is no lawful basis for its use, they act beyond the scope of their duty and lose the protection from liability afforded by the defence.[4] 'Reasonable chastisement' used to provide justification for beating children, but that rule has been abolished.[5] There is no longer an extra defence available to a person who has assaulted a child.

If the assault took place as a result of the pursuer's provocation, the damages can be reduced. 'No verbal provocation whatever can justify a blow ... But ... verbal provocation is a good ground for mitigating damages ...'.[6] The rationale is that since reparation for intentional wrong is based on *culpa*, the pursuer must come to the court with clean hands; if the pursuer's hands are not clean, the pursuer's damages can be reduced.[7]

Finally, an assailant is not entitled to think the victim is in good health. The thin skull rule operates. The defender will be liable to the full extent of damage suffered even though injury is exacerbated by the pursuer's health condition.[8]

1 *Ashley v Chief Constable of Sussex Police* [2008] 1 AC 962; it is a defence to a criminal assault that the accused had acted in an honest but mistaken belief

that he was under threat of imminent attack. While *Ashley* is an English case, it is thought that it would be followed in Scotland.

2   *Marco v Merrens* 1964 SLT (Sh Ct) 74. The defender had hit the pursuer over the head with a bottle while they were fighting over a girl.

3   As in the case of the prison officer who parted the buttocks of a prisoner to view his anus during a strip search. *Tolmie v Dewar* 2003 SC 265, 2003 SLT 215. This conduct was justified and fell within the ambit of the applicable regulations, Prisons and Young Offenders Institutions (Scotland) Rules 1994 r 88(2)(c).

4   *Mason v Orr* (1901) 4F 220. See also *Downie v Chief Constable Strathclyde Police* 1998 SLT 8, 1977 SCLR 603.

5   Children (Equal Protection from Assault) (Scotland) Act 2019.

6   *Anderson v Marshall* (1835) 13 S 1130 at 1131 per the Lord President (Hope). See also *Ashmore v Rock Steady Security Ltd* 2006 SLT 207.

7   *Ross v Bryce* 1972 SLT (Sh Ct) 76. In *Ashmore v Rock Steady Security* 2006 SLT 207, the Lord Ordinary (Emslie) thought that, because of his provocation, the pursuer's damages should be reduced by 20 per cent: the pursuer had been punched by a security guard at a club.

8   *MacGregor v Shepherd* 1946 SLT (Sh Ct) 42.

(2) Unjustified detention

1.5 'Next to life is liberty; and the delinquence against it are restraint and constraint. And though liberty itself be inestimable, yet the damages sustained through these delinquencies are reparable.'[1] A slight infringement of liberty is prima facie actionable: so, for example, where a lady was alleged to have been detained against her will for a quarter of an hour by the manager of a hydropathic establishment, her action in delict was held to be relevant.[2] As a general principle, no one can be detained against his or her will without lawful justification; if this occurs, there is liability in delict. The loss suffered is both the loss of liberty and the affront caused to the pursuer. However, detention can be justified at common law if, for example, a store detective arrests a person suspected of shoplifting and detains that person for a reasonable time until the police arrive.[3]

In practice, cases of wrongful detention by ordinary members of the public are rare; instead, they arise when the person has been held under what purports to be lawful legal process. Commonly this means detention on mental health grounds[4] or by police officers in the course of their duty. Even so, an action in delict may still arise, but the onus rests on the pursuer to show that the exercise by the authorities of their powers was neither reasonable nor necessary and accordingly unjustified.[5]

Where a person is wrongfully imprisoned by a court, superior court judges are immune from liability. Inferior judges, such as justices of the peace or magistrates, can be liable if the sentence is imposed maliciously and without probable cause.[6] If, for example, a magistrate lacks jurisdiction, he will be acting *ultra vires* but there is no liability for a bona fide error in relation to the statutory interpretation of his jurisdiction. Before he can succeed, the pursuer must also prove that the magistrate was acting maliciously.[7] Where there has been a miscarriage of justice by the superior courts, the Secretary of State may make an *ex gratia* award of compensation to the victim. There are strong policy reasons against encouraging civil claims for malicious prosecution and so the requirements for establishing a case are exacting, malice must be shown. It is arguable however that the same requirement for a case of wrongful arrest, that is unlawful detention brought against the police sets the bar too high. Malicious prosecution and unlawful detention are separate delicts although they are not always clearly differentiated.[8]

1   *Stair* I, 9, 4. For fuller coverage of this topic see E Reid, *Personality, Confidentiality and Privacy in Scots Law*, Chapter 5.
2   *Mackenzie v Cluny Hill Hydropathic Co* 1908 SC 200, 15 SLT 518. In the course of his judgment, Lord Low said: 'It is averred that the manager detained this lady for fifteen minutes … and refused to let her go until she made an apology. If that be true it was an outrage …': 1908 SC 200 at 206.
3   Where, as in the example, the arrest is made without a warrant, the defender must establish that the suspicions were justified: *Pringle v Bremner and Stirling* (1867) 5 M (HL) 55; *Dahl v Chief Constable, Central Scotland Police* 1983 SLT 420, OH. If an arrest is made under authority of a warrant, it is presumed that the detention was lawful and the onus rests on the pursuer to show that the detention was not justified.
4   Under the Mental Health (Care and Treatment) (Scotland) Act 2003 or by police officers in the course of their duty.
5   See, for example, *Henderson v Chief Constable, Fife Police* 1988 SLT 361, OH. (Staff staged a 'work-in'. They were arrested. When they were put in police cells, a man was handcuffed and a woman told to remove her brassiere. The use of handcuffs was conceded to be unjustified. While it was normal practice to ask women to remove underwear to prevent suicide attempts, this was not justified in this case as the woman had co-operated, made no attempt to escape and was not a danger to herself or others
6   Criminal Procedure (Scotland) Act 1995, s 170(1). The Lord Advocate no longer enjoys immunity. *Whitehouse v Lord Advocate* 2020 SC 133.
7   *McPhee v Macfarlane's Exor* 1933 SC 163, 1933 SLT 148. Similarly, malice must be proved if a pursuer seeks reparation on the grounds of malicious prosecution: *McKie v Strathclyde Joint Police Board* 2004 SLT 982.
8   *Whitehouse v Gormley* [2018] CSOH 93. For further discussion see B Lindsay, 'Relegated No Longer? The Role of Malice in the Delictual Protection of Liberty' 2019 23 ELR 75.

1.6   The right to liberty is enshrined in Article 5(1) of the European Convention of Human Rights: 'Everyone has the right to liberty and security of person.' This is a fundamental right. No one is to be deprived of their liberty unless it falls within one of six exceptions expressly listed in Article 5: these deal with lawful arrest and detention for various purposes and are to be narrowly interpreted. Otherwise, the right is absolute and unqualified. The revulsion of detention without charge or trial trumps all other interests even the interests of national security.[1] But while the right to liberty cannot be restricted, liberty of movement can be restricted in the interests of public safety or to maintain public order. The paradigm case of deprivation of liberty is literal imprisonment where the prisoner 'has no freedom of choice about anything. He cannot leave the place to which he has been assigned. He may eat only when and what his gaoler permits. The only human beings he may see or speak to are his gaolers and those whom they allow to visit. He is entirely subject to the will of others'.[2]

But outwith the paradigm, it is a question of degree on whether a restriction on freedom of movement has become a deprivation of liberty within Article 5. In *Austin (FC) v Commissioner of Police of the* Metropolism,[3] a demonstrator was held in a police cordon for seven hours. The cordon was necessary to prevent violence. The measures were done in good faith,[4] were proportionate and enforced for no longer than reasonably necessary: therefore, they were not arbitrary. In these circumstances, the restriction on freedom of movement as a result of the cordon did not amount to an arbitrary deprivation of liberty and therefore did not amount to a breach of Article 5.[5] Because there was no breach of Article 5, the appellant had been lawfully detained at common law to prevent a breach of the peace and therefore no wrong had been committed. It should be noted that in Article 5 actions there is no requirement on the pursuer to aver or prove malice.[6]

Article 5(4) provides: 'Everyone who is deprived of his liberty by arrest or detention shall be entitled to take proceedings by which the lawfulness of his detention shall be decided speedily by a court and his release ordered if the detention is not lawful.' Where a person is sentenced to life imprisonment, the judge must impose a minimum sentence or 'tariff' to be served for the purposes of retribution or deterrence. Once the tariff has expired, the prisoner may apply to the Parole Board which can order his release if satisfied that the prisoner is no longer a danger to the public, ie that he has been rehabilitated. Where the prisoner's right to apply to the Parole Board has been delayed, his detention after the tariff has expired is not unlawful and he has no claim for damages at common law for wrongful imprisonment.[7] Nor will there normally be a breach of Article 5(4) or Article 5(1), although the prisoner may receive compensation if he can prove that the Parole Board would have released him earlier.[8] Where there was a failure to provide programmes or courses to help the prisoner's rehabilitation, the House of Lords held there was no breach of Article 5(4) or Article 5(1).[9] However, the European Court of Human Rights has taken the view that failure to provide rehabilitative courses can amount to a breach of Article 5(4), which would render the detention arbitrary and result in a breach of Article 5(1).[10] There is clearly a tension between the approaches. In spite of the decision in the House of the House of Lords being binding upon him, in *Arthur Duncan Petitioner*[11] the Lord Ordinary (Glennie) held that a failure to provide rehabilitative programmes could amount to a breach of Article 5(4) and consequently Article 5(1).[12]

1 *Secretary of State for the Home Department v JJ and others* [2008] 1 AC 385.
2 Ibid per Lord Hoffmann at para 37.
3 [2009] UKHL 5.
4 Cf if they had been used to punish the demonstrators or treat them a lesson; ibid per Lord Neuberger at para 63.
5 Ibid per Lord Hope at paras 33, 34 and 37. This approach was indorsed by the European Court of Human Rights; *Austin v United Kingdom* (2012) 55 EHRR 14.
6 See, eg, *McCaffer v Lord Advocate* 2015 SLT (Sh Ct) 44 per sheriff Deutsch at para 48.
7 *R (on the application of Faulkner) (FC) (Appellant) v Secretary of State for Justice* [2013] UKSC 23.
8 Ibid. Where a prisoner has received a determinate sentence but has been detained for breaking the conditions of the licence under which he was freed after serving part of his sentence, a delay in his right to take his case to the Parole Board does not constitute unlawful detention or a breach of Article 5: *Brown v Parole Board of Scotland* [2013] CSOH 200.
9 *R (James) v Secretary of State for Justice* [2010] 1 AC 553.
10 *James v the United Kingdom* (2013) 56 EHRR 12.
11 [2014] CSOH 24.
12 Living arrangements made for mentally incapacitated persons may amount to a deprivation of liberty and a breach of Article 5: *Chester West and Chester Council v P* [2014] UKSC 19.

(3) Harassment

1.7 Every individual has a right to be free from harassment.[1] Where a person pursues a course of conduct which amounts to harassment, the victim can bring a civil claim against him:[2] this is known as an action of harassment.[3] Before the pursuer will succeed it must be established that the defender intended his behaviour to amount to harassment, or his behaviour occurred in such circumstances that a reasonable person would conclude that it amounted to harassment.[4] The course of conduct can include speech and must have occurred on at least two occasions.[5] The exception is in cases of domestic abuse where a single instance will suffice.[6]

Harassment is *not* defined in the legislation but 'includes causing the person alarm or distress'.[7] In the context of alleged harassment at work, when 'the quality of the conduct said to constitute harassment is being examined, courts will have in mind that irritations, annoyances, even a measure of upset arise at times in everybody's day-to-day dealings with other people. Courts are well able to recognise the boundary between conduct which is unattractive, even unreasonable, and conduct which is oppressive and unacceptable'.[8] An employer is vicariously liable for harassment carried out by an employee on a fellow employee or a third party.[9] If the action is successful, the court can award damages:[10] these can include compensation for anxiety and financial loss caused by the harassment.[11] The court can also grant interdict or a non-harassment order.[12] Breach of a non-harassment order is a criminal offence.[13] It is a defence to an action of harassment that the course of conduct was authorised by law or was pursued for the purpose of preventing or detecting crime or was reasonable in the particular circumstances of the case.[14]

1 Protection from Harassment Act 1997, s 8(1). It is arguable that conduct which deliberately caused fear and alarm, even in the absence of physical harm, was delictual at common law: *Ward v Scotrail Railways Ltd* 1999 SC 255. Such conduct could certainly be controlled by an interdict (molestation) and, in theory, should have been sufficient cause for a claim in damages. However, in *G v S* 2007 SCLR 137, Lord Turnbull observed at 142 para 18 that '… a claim for damages arising out of anxiety would not normally sound in damages. It is only the statutory provision in section 8(6) of the [1997] Act which permits this'. It has been held in England that the infliction of humiliation and distress by conduct calculated to humiliate and distress, without more, does not give rise to liability at common law: *Wainwright v Home Office* [2003] All ER (D) 279.
2 Individual instances of harassment will make up a course of conduct, but it is the course of conduct which has to have the quality of amounting to harassment rather than the individual instances of conduct. See *Iqbal v Dean Manson, Solicitors* [2011] EWCA Civ 123; *Marinello v City of Edinburgh Council* [2011] CSIH 33.
3 Protection from Harassment Act 1997, s 8(2).
4 PHA 1997, s 8(1)(a), (b).
5 PHA 1997, s 8(3). Thus, a single assault will not amount to harassment unless it is the cumulation of a course of conduct which amounts to harassment: *Vaickuviene v Sainsbury* [2013] CSIH 67.
6 PHA 1997 s 8A.
7 PHA 1997, s 8(3). See, eg, *Green v Chalmers* 2017 SLT (Sh Ct) 69.

8   *Majrowski v Guy's and St Thomas's NHS Trust* [2007] 1 AC 224 per Lord Nicholls at para 30.
9   Ibid. PHA 1997, s 10(1) adds a new s 18B to the Prescription and Limitation (Scotland) Act 1973 where it is clear that Parliament anticipated that an action could be brought against the employer of a person alleged to have harassed the complainer. Lord Hope's reasoning in *Majrowski* is a remarkable example of literal construction of a statute overriding policy considerations: ibid at para 43. See also *Vaickuviene v Sainsbury* [2013] CSIH 67 discussed beyond para 12.14.
10 PHA 1997, s 8(5)(a). But an action of damages for non-harassment is not an action for personal injuries: *G v S* 2007 SCLR 137.
11 PHA 1997, s 8(6).
12 PHA 1997, s 8(5)(b). Although an interim interdict is competent, an interim non-harassment order is not: *Heenan v Dillon* 1999 Fam LR 62. On non-harassment orders, see, for example, *McCann v McGurran* 2002 SLT 592; *McGuire v Kidston* 2002 SLT (Sh Ct) 66.
13 PHA 1997, s 9.
14 PHA 1997, s 8(4). To succeed, the defender must show that he had acted rationally: *Hayes v Willoughby* [2013] UKSC 17.

C. PRIVACY

(1) Introduction

1.8   The protection of privacy is a developing area of the law, prompted by the coming into force of the Human Rights Act 1998 and the need to give effect to Article 8 ECHR. In *Wainwright v Home Office*,[1] the House of Lords maintained that there was no liability at common law for invasion of privacy. The plaintiffs, a mother and son with physical and mental learning difficulties, claimed that they had suffered mental harm as a consequence of a strip search in humiliating circumstances when visiting a relative in prison. The 1998 Act did not apply at the time these events occurred, but subsequently, the ECHR at Strasbourg held unanimously that the claimants' Article 8 right had been breached.[2] Clearly the courts need to comply with Article 8 but, in England, the House of Lords was not prepared to do so by recognising a common law tort of invasion of privacy and, if brought in tort, it remains the case that the Wainwright's action would not succeed. The developments that have taken place cover private information. The law on protecting privacy more broadly remains to be developed.[3]

The courts in England have adapted and extended the equitable doctrine of breach of confidence to cover the dissemination of private information thus giving effect to Article 8 rights. This has given rise to two grounds of action, breach of confidence and the tort of misuse of private information. The former protects confidential information, the latter, private information. The question of how distinct these grounds turn out to be in practice remains to be seen. Since information may be both confidential and private it is hardly surprising that the case law shows overlap between the two grounds of action.[4] Indeed, claims may include other grounds such as breach of the Data Protection Act 1998[5] or breach of copyright.[6]

1   [2003] UKHL 53, [2004] 2 AC 406.
2   *Wainwright v United Kingdom* (12350/04) (2007) 44 EHRR 40.
3   E Reid, *Personality, Confidentiality and Privacy in Scots Law* Chapter 17.
4   See, eg, *McKennitt v Ash* [2006] EWCA Civ 1714, [2008] QB 73; *HRH Prince Charles v Associated Newspapers* [2006] EWCA Civ 1776, [2008] Ch 57.
5   See, eg, *TLT v Secretary of State for the Home Department* [2016] EWHC 2217 QB; *ST v L Primary School* [2020] EWHC 1046 QB.
6   See, eg, *HRH Duchess of Sussex v Associated Newspapers* [2021] EWHC 273 Ch, [2021] 4 WLR 35].

1.9   The vast majority of litigation on privacy is in the English jurisdiction and while there was discussion at one time that Scots law could develop its own approach, it seems that English and Scots law on this point are converging.[1] In Scotland, breach of confidence is established as a delict.[2] The approach taken in privacy cases is no different from 'misuse of private information' indeed, in *C v Chief Constable of Police Scotland*[3] the Lord Ordinary (Bannatyne) went further than the English courts in appearing to recognise a common law right to privacy. While there was no reclaiming motion on this point, Lady Dorian and Lord Menzies in the Inner House cast doubt on whether the development of the law had reached this point.[4]

it is likely that breach of confidence will continue to ground actions brought in respect of dissemination of information that is not in the private domain, commercially sensitive information for example,[5] while those whose complaint arises from dissemination of personal information will ground their claims on misuse of private information.

1   For discussion see E Reid, *Personality, Confidentiality and Privacy in Scots Law* paras 12.24–12.27.
2   *Lord Advocate v Scotsman Publications Ltd* 1988 SLT 490 at 502–503 per Lord Justice Clerk (Ross), at 508–509 per Lord Dunpark and at 514 per Lord McDonald; 1989 SLT 705, HL at 708 per Lord Keith of Kinkel.
3   [2019] CSOH 48.
4   [2020] CSIH 61, 2020 SLT 1021 at paras 75–86 and 124.
5   See E Reid, *Personality, Confidentiality and Privacy in Scots Law*, Chapter 13.

1.10 Remedies are interdict (injunction in England) and damages.[1] The super-injunctions that are sometimes awarded in England, under which the identity of claimants may not be reported, have not been sought in Scotland.[2] In *Gulati v MGN*, a framework for calculating damages was established.[3] It should be noted that while aggravated damages may be awarded in England[4] Scots courts can achieve the equivalent effect through increased awards of solatium.[5]

1 The general criteria for granting interdict must, of course, be present: see, e.g., *Waste Systems International Inc v Eurocare Environmental Services Ltd* 1999 SLT 198, OH.
2 See, eg, *PJS v News Group Newspapers* [2016] UKSC 26, [2016] AC 181.
3 [2015] EWHC 1428 (Ch).
4 See, eg, *Richard v BBC* [2018] EWHC 1837 (Ch), [2019] Ch 169.
5 See J Bailey, 'Aggravated Damages or Additional Solatium: A Distinction Without a Difference?' (2018) 22 ELR 29.

(2) Breach of confidence

1.11 Breach of confidence involves the wrongful dissemination of confidential information in breach of a duty of confidence. This duty arises from the defender's knowledge of the confidential nature of the information. Traditionally, the duty depended on a relationship of confidence between the parties. This could be a personal relationship such as that between married partners,[1] a professional relationship such as between doctor and patient or solicitor and client,[2] or a commercial relationship such as that between employer and employee. A prior relationship of confidence is no longer a requirement for liability.[3] A duty of confidentiality will arise where the person receiving the information knows or ought to know that it is fairly and reasonably to be regarded as confidential.[4] Such knowledge may follow from the pursuer's reasonable expectation of privacy,[5] or from the way in which the information has been obtained.[6] The requirements for breach of confidence can be summarised as: information of a confidential nature; communicated in circumstances importing a duty of confidence; used in an unauthorised way.[7]

1 *Duchess of Argyll v Duke of Argyll* [1967] Ch 302.
2 See, eg, *Cornelius v De Taranto* [2002] EMLR 6.
3 *Campbell v Mirror Group Newspapers Ltd* [2004 UKHL 22, [2004] 2 AC 457.
4 See generally, E Reid, *Personality, Confidentiality and Privacy in Scots Law*, Chapter 14.
5 'A duty of confidence will arise whenever the party subject to the duty is in a situation where he knows or ought to know that the other person can

reasonably expect his privacy to be protected.' *Campbell v MGN Ltd* per Lord Hope [2004] UKHL 22 at para 85.
6   *Douglas v Hello! Ltd No 6* [2006] QB 125.
7   *Coco v AN Clark (Engineers) Ltd* [1969] RPC 41 per Megarry J at 47–48.

1.12   Out of breach of confidence the courts have fashioned a tort (or delict) of misuse of private information. The major development took place in *Campbell v MGN* in which supermodel Naomi Campbell successfully raised an action when photographs of her emerging from a rehabilitation clinic were published in the press.[1] An analogy was drawn with medical treatment which is always confidential and, by a 3:2 majority, the House of Lords held that the claimant's interest in protecting her privacy was not outweighed by the public interest in being informed that she had lied about not taking drugs. In *Campbell*, the need for information to come from a prior relation of confidence was dispensed with. The critical point was the claimant's reasonable expectation of privacy. The other significant case for the development of misuse of private information is *McKennitt v Ash*.[2] This was a breach of confidence case brought by well-known Canadian folk singer Loreena McKennitt against the further publication of a book containing confidential information gleaned from a long friendship. This case would have succeeded under the traditional formulation of breach of confidence, but Buxton LJ confirmed it as a case to be determined with reference to Articles 8 and 10 ECHR and posed the test for liability in the form of two questions.[3] Is the information private in the sense that it is protected by Article 8? If so, must the interest of the claimant yield to the defendant's right of freedom of expression under Article 10?

1   [2004 UKHL 22, [2004] 2 AC 457.
2   [2006] EWCA Civ 1714, [2008] QB 73.
3   [2008] QB 73 at para 11.

(3) Misuse of private information

1.13   Article 8 ECHR states:

'1. Everyone has the right to respect for his private and family life, his home and his correspondence.

2. There shall be no interference by a public authority with the exercise of this right except such as in accordance with the law and is necessary in a democratic society in the interests of national security, public safety or the economic well-being of the country, for the prevention of disorder or crime, for the

protection of health or morals, or for the protection of the rights and freedoms of others.'

Article 10 ECHR states:

'1. Everyone has the right to freedom of expression. This right shall include freedom to hold opinions and to receive and impart information and ideas without interference by public authority and regardless of frontiers …

2. The exercise of these freedoms, since it carries with it duties and responsibilities, may be subject to such formalities, conditions, restrictions or penalties as are prescribed by law and are necessary in a democratic society, in the interests of national security, territorial integrity or public safety, for the prevention of disorder or crime, for the protection of health or morals, for the protection of the rights or reputation of others, for preventing the disclosure of information received in confidence, or for maintaining the authority and impartiality of the judiciary.'

Neither right is absolute. Note that Article 8 is subject to the rights and freedoms of others including the right to freedom of expression. Similarly, Article 10 is subject to restrictions imposed for the protection of the rights of others including the right to privacy and to prevent disclosure of confidential information. Where these two rights conflict, that is where the pursuer's right to privacy clashes with the defender's right to freedom of expression, neither right takes precedence.[1] A balancing process is called for, but first it is necessary to determine that the pursuer's Article 8 right is engaged; this is done with reference to the pursuer's reasonable expectation of privacy given the circumstances.

1   *In Re S* [2004] UKHL 47, [2005] 1 AC 593.

1.14 The reasonable expectation of privacy test is objective requiring the court to determine the expectations of a reasonable person in the position of the pursuer, taking into account all the facts. The best guide, of course, is case law. Prominent examples where a reasonable expectation of privacy has been found include intimate or sexual information,[1] photographs of the children of celebrities[2] and criminal investigations prior to the point at which the suspect is charged with an offence.[3]

By contrast, no reasonable expectation of privacy arose when a man, thinking he was communicating online with a 13-year-old boy, sent a picture of his erect penis. His communicant was, in fact, a member of a 'paedophile hunter' group who passed a record of the communications to the police. The individual could have had no reasonable expectation of privacy in regard to the recipient with whom he had no relationship; moreover, it was held that communications of such a reprehensible nature do not attract the protection of Article 8(1).[4]

In *C v Chief Constable Police Scotland*,[5] ten police officers who were the subject of disciplinary proceedings were held to have had no reasonable expectations of privacy in regard to WhatsApp messages posted between them as a group. The messages were used in the proceedings against them. While the Lord Ordinary accepted that ordinary members of the public might have reasonable expectations of privacy when using WhatsApp, an objective assessment on the facts included considering the content of the messages and the attributes of those involved.[6] Since these were serving police officers under a sworn duty to report conduct falling below standards of professional behaviour, they could have had no reasonable expectation of privacy concerning messages described as sexist and degrading, racist, anti-semitic, homophobic and mocking of disability. Messages showing crime scene photographs of current investigations, moreover, showed a flagrant disregard for police procedures.

1 *Mosely v News Group Newspapers Ltd* [2008] EWHC 177 (QB); *PJS v News Group Newspapers Ltd* [2016] UKSC 26, [2016] AC 181; *BVC v EWF* [2019] EWHC 2506 (QB), [2019] 9 WLUK 322; *Reid v Price* [2020] EWHC 594 (QB).
2 *Murray v Express Newspapers plc* [2009] Ch 481; *Weller v Associated Newspapers* [2016] 1 WLR 1541.
3 *Richard v BBC* [2018] EWHC 1837 (QB); *ZXC v Bloomberg LP* [2020] EWCA Civ 611, [2021] QB 28 (appeal outstanding at the time of writing).
4 *Sutherland v HMA for Scotland* [2020] UKSC 32, [2021 AC 427.
5 [2020] CSIH 61, 2020 SLT 1021.
6 2019 CSOH 48, 2019 SLT 875. This approach was approved in the Inner House.

1.15 Only where the Article 8 right is engaged will the court proceed to balance the rights of the parties. The factors to be taken into account include: the contribution of the information to a debate of public interest; the public status of the pursuer and their prior conduct; the method of obtaining the information and its veracity; the content, form and consequences of the publication; and the 'chilling effect' of inhibition of freedom of expression.[1] Ultimately, if one party's Article 8 right is to be infringed, this can only be allowed to proceed without remedy where the infringement is justified. Equally, any inhibition placed on the other party's Article 10 right requires justification.[2]

An argument that dissemination of information contributes to a debate of public interest is greatly assisted where there is some genuine public interest independent of the actual information provided and which is more profound than the taste of the public for idle tittle tattle concerning the private lives of people in the public eye. This may be illustrated by contrasting two Article 8 actions brought by Princess Caroline of Hanover. She succeeded in the first action which concerned the publication of covertly taken photographs of herself and family going about their private business. There was no real context for the publication beyond the interest of the public in viewing a famous person's private activities.[3] In the second action she failed to prevent publication of photographs of a family skiing holiday and of her father Prince Rainier of Monaco, On this occasion there was a context which was a genuine public interest in the state of health of Prince Rainier.[4] In *Ferdinand v MGN*[5] the claimant's status as England Football Captain made him a role model creating a genuine public interest the way he conducted himself in his affairs that outweighed his own interest in keeping extra-marital exploits under wraps.

Sir Cliff Richard succeeded in his action against the BBC despite the public interest in uncovering historic child sex abuse.[6] The circumstances were that a journalist had received a tip off that an accusation had been made against the singer. The journalist then exerted pressure on the South Yorkshire police who informed the BBC when Sir Cliff's home was to be searched. The BBC sensationalised the story, the search was filmed from a helicopter and broadcast live. No charge was ever brought against Sir Cliff. Given the seriousness of the consequences for the claimant the coverage could not be justified and damages were awarded. There are, of course, cases in which no justification is offered by the defender.[7]

1   *Axel Springer AG v Germany* [2012] EMLR 15, (2012) 55 EHRR 6. These factors are worked through meticulously in the judgment of Mann J in *Richard v BBC* [2018] EWHC 1837 (QB).
2   The balancing process is discussed in E Reid, *Personality, Confidentiality and Privacy in Scots Law* paras 15.1–15.32.
3   *Von Hanover v Germany* (59320/00) (2005) 40 EHRR 1 See also *Weller v Associated Newspapers* [2016] 1 WLR 1541.
4   *Von Hanover v Germany* (40660/08) (2012) EHRR 15.
5   *Ferdinand v MGN* 2011 EWHC 2454 (QB)
6   *Richard v BBC* [2018] EWHC 1837 (QB)
7   See, eg, *Reid v Price* [2020] EWHC 594 (QB).

CHAPTER 2

The economic wrongs and fraud

A. THE ECONOMIC WRONGS

(1) Introduction – the general principle

2.1 In a free market, competition is regarded as essential and in the public interest. This can result in one business being successful while another goes to the wall. The common law therefore took the view that A was entitled to harm B economically provided A used lawful means, for example undercutting the price of his product, in order to do so. Towards the end of the nineteenth century and during the twentieth century, the courts recognised a range of actionable wrongs which set parameters beyond which parties could not wield their economic and social power.[1] Since then, important statutory provisions and principles of EU law have been introduced directly to regulate competition, for example the Office of Fair Trading. Competition law is outwith the scope of this book. Nevertheless the economic wrongs remain important. The theoretical nature of these wrongs was radically redrawn by the House of Lords in *OBG v Allan*[2] (*OBG*) and *Customs and Excise Commissioners v Total Network SL*[3] (*Total*). This chapter proceeds on the principles laid down in these cases and will not discuss the earlier, now discredited, law.[4]

The basic principle is still that laid down by the House of Lords in *Allen v Flood*.[5] In this case boilermakers objected to the practice of employing shipwrights to repair ironwork on board ships. The plaintiffs were shipwrights who were employed to repair woodwork on certain ships. Members of the boilermakers' union discovered that they had previously been employed by another employer to repair ironwork on ships. Incensed, a trade union representative approached the current employer of the shipwrights and informed him that unless he dismissed the plaintiffs, his other employees would strike. This was done maliciously, to punish the plaintiffs. The employer dismissed the plaintiffs who brought the action against the trade union representative.

Three points should be noticed. First, the case proceeded on the basis that there was no conspiracy, ie no agreement among the boilermakers that they would strike; it was simply the individual trade unionist who said that there would be a strike. Second, if there had been a strike, the employees would have terminated their contracts of employment lawfully. Third, when the employer dismissed the plaintiffs he did so by lawfully terminating their contracts. In other words, the individual trade unionist used lawful means (the threat of a lawful strike) to compel the employer to use lawful means (the lawful dismissal) to harm the plaintiffs economically (the loss of their employment). In these circumstances, the House of Lords held that no wrong was committed even though the defendant had acted maliciously.

Accordingly, *Allen v Flood* is authority that an individual, A, can wield economic pressure to force B to act to his own or another's economic harm provided the means used by A are lawful. If, as in this case, the means used are lawful, no wrong is committed even if A acts maliciously to harm B or another person rather than to further A's economic interests. This result, while harsh, is an inevitable consequence of a free market economy. But if the means used are *not* lawful, delictual liability may be incurred. It is to these circumstances that we shall now turn.

1   For an excellent account of these wrongs, see Greg Gordon, SULI *Delict*, Chapter 15.
2   [2008] 1 AC 1.
3   [2008] 1 AC 1174.
4   For the previous law, see the 3rd edn of this book, Chapter 2.
5   [1898] AC 1, HL.

(2) Inducing breach of contract

2.2   If A induces B to break his contract with C, C can sue B for breach of contract. Alternatively, C may be able to sue A in *delict* for inducing B to break his contract with C. This actionable wrong was recognised as part of Scots law in *British Motor Trade Association v Gray*.[1] There Lord Russell approved counsel's concession that:

'by the law of Scotland an actionable wrong is committed by one who intentionally and without lawful justification induces or procures someone to break a contract made by him with another, if damage has resulted to that other, provided the contract creates contractual relations recognised by law'.[2]

In *OBG* the House of Lords emphasised that inducement of breach of contract is an example of accessory liability in the sense that A is only liable if B breaks his contract with C as a consequence of A's acts: A's liability in *delict* for inducement of breach of contract is therefore *accessory* to B's breach of his contract with C.

The wrong can be represented by the following diagram.

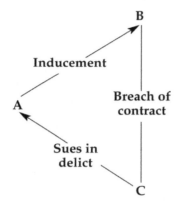

---

1   1951 SC 586, 1951 SLT 247. For a recent example see *Aviva Insurance v Oliver* [2019] EWHC 2824 (Comm).

2   1951 SC 586 at 603.

2.3   In *Global Resources Group v MacKay*,[1] Lord Hodge, following the analysis in *OBG,* said that inducement of breach of contract has five characteristics:

(1)   B must *breach* the contract with C: interference with B's performance of the contract which does not result in a breach of contract by B will not suffice.

(2)   A must *know* that his acts will result in B breaching his contract with C. Therefore, A must be aware of the existence of the contract between B and C. It is not enough that A was reckless as to whether or not a contract existed between B and C.[2] But if A consciously decided not to inquire into the terms of the contract between B and C in the knowledge of the existence of the contract and that his actions were likely to induce a breach of that contract, that knowledge and the deliberate turning of a blind eye would probably be sufficient.

(3)   A must *intend to induce the breach of contract* either as an end in itself or as the means by which he achieves some further end.[3] There is no need for A to intend to harm C. If for example A induces B to break his contract of hire with C and come to work for A at a bigger fee, A is liable even if A did not intend to harm C; the breach of contract was the means by which A achieved his objective of obtaining B's services. However there is no liability merely because it is reasonably foreseeable that A's acts might cause B to break his contract with C. If A, an artiste, under a contract to sing for an impresario, B, cancels the concert, she would not be liable to the musicians B has hired to play at the concert for inducing B to break his contracts with them. While it is foreseeable that by cancelling the concert, B might be in breach of his contracts with the musicians, A did not intend B's breach of contract with the musicians to be an end in itself or a means to an end when she cancelled the concert.[4]

(4)   A must *in fact induce* B to break the contract by persuading, encouraging or assisting him to do so.[5] It is not necessary that A's inducement takes the form of unlawful means, for example threatening to assault B: A will still be liable to C if the means used are lawful and, indeed, beneficial to B, for example giving B a gift to break his contract with C. If A stands by and knowingly lets parties break their contracts this is not inducement even if it was in A's economic interests that they should do so.[6] C must suffer loss as a result of the inducement but proof of specific damage is not required and once inducement of the breach is established, some damage will readily be inferred by the court.[7]

(5)   A will have a defence if the inducement of the breach is justified, for example inducing female artistes to break their contracts of employment to obtain better wages so that they do not have to resort to prostitution.[8]

1   2008 SLT 104 at 106–107.

2   *Rossleigh Ltd v Leader Cars Ltd* 1987 SLT 355, OH. Cf the position in England where constructive knowledge is sufficient, ie turning a blind eye: *Emerald Construction Co Ltd v Lowthian* [1966] 1 All ER 1013, [1966] 1 WLR 691, CA; *Inshore Services (International) v NFFO Services* [2001] EWCA Civ 1722.

3   *BGC Capital Markets (Switzerland) LLC v Rees* [2011] EWHC 2009 (QB). (Defendants only engaged a broker when they believed that it was lawful to employ him. In fact broker was in breach of his contract with his former employer when he did so. No liability, as defendant did not intend to cause a breach of contract.) A defendant was not liable having taken legal advice on

whether a contract would be breached. The wrong advice was given. *Allen v Dodd & Co Ltd* [2020] EWCA Civ 258, [2020] QB 781.

4   In *OBG* the House of Lords held that the decision of the Court of Appeal in *Millar v Bassey* [1994] EMLR 44 was wrong.

5   The inducement must be directed at B, the person in the contractual relationship with the victim, C: *Middlebrook Mushrooms Ltd v Transport and General Workers' Union* [1993] ICR 612, CA.

6   'Failing to stop a breach is not enough': *Calor Gas Ltd v Express Fuels (Sc) Ltd* 2008 SLT 123 per Lord Malcolm at 135.

7   *British Motor Trade Association v Gray* 1951 SC 586, 1951 SLT 247. When a film franchise induced the organiser of a fan convention to breach a contract with an independent film company which was to film and broadcast the event, the court assessed damages based on the lost chance of making a profit. *Quantum Digital v Lucasfilm Ltd* [2018] EWHC 624 (QB).

8   *Brimelow v Casson* [1924] 1 Ch 302.

(3) Intentional infliction of harm by unlawful means

2.4   In *OBG* the House of Lords recognised the existence of an actionable wrong of causing loss by unlawful means. The classic form of this wrong involves three parties. A with the intention of harming C uses unlawful means against B in order to cause economic harm to C.[1] In this situation, A's delictual liability is primary: it is not dependent on B committing a wrong, such as a breach of contract, against C. Consider the following examples:

(i)   A steals B's tools which prevents B fulfilling a contract with C. A is not liable to C for inducing B to break his contract with C as A has not induced the breach but has prevented B's performance. But B has used unlawful means, ie theft against B and will therefore be liable for causing loss to C by unlawful means provided it can be established that A intended to harm C.

(ii)   A breaks his contract with B. As a consequence, B is unable to perform his contract with C. A is not liable to C for inducing B to break his contract with C as A has not induced the breach but has prevented B's performance. But A has used unlawful means ie his own breach of contract with B and will therefore be liable to C for causing loss to C by unlawful means provided that it can be established that A intended to harm C.

(iii)   A induces B to break his contract with C. As a consequence C is unable to fulfil his contract with D. A is liable to C for inducing B to break his contract with C whether or not he intended to harm C. But A has used unlawful means, ie inducing a breach of contract between B and C and will therefore be liable to D for causing loss to D by unlawful means provided it can be established that A intended to harm D.

(iv)   A threatens to break his contract with B unless B ceases to trade with C. B yields to the threat and stops trading with C. As a consequence C sustains a loss. C has no redress against B as it is lawful to cease trading with a customer. But A's threat to break his contract with B is a threat to use unlawful means against B: this is intimidation and amounts to unlawful means. Therefore A has used unlawful means, intimidation of B, and will therefore be liable to C for causing loss to C by unlawful means provided it can be established that A intended to harm C.[2]

1   See *Global Resources v McKay* 2009 SLT 104.
2   Before *OBG*, intimidation was treated as a separate actionable wrong: on intimidation see the 3rd edn of this book at pp 44–46.

2.5   The characteristics of the actionable wrong are:

(1)   A must use *unlawful means* against B. In *OBG* Lord Hoffmann[1] held that unlawful means were restricted to conduct which amounted to a civil wrong against B and which affected B's freedom to deal with the claimant, C. Thus the theft in: (i) qualifies, as B can sue A for restitution of his tools and/or recompense and the absence of his tools interfered with his freedom to perform his contract with C; in (ii) A's breach of contract with B qualifies, as it is actionable by B and interfered with his freedom to perform his contract with C; in (iii) A's inducement of a breach of contract between B and C qualifies, as it is actionable in delict by C and interfered with C's freedom to perform his contract with D. In (iv) B cannot sue A because he has sustained no loss. However in *OBG*, Lord Hoffmann held that A's conduct would be treated as unlawful means if absence of loss was the only reason B could not sue. So in (iv) A's threat to breach his contract with B qualifies as B could have sued A for breach of contract if he had not succumbed to the intimidation and the threat interfered with his freedom to trade with C. But if C had an exclusive license from B to use B's intellectual property and A infringed B's intellectual property rights, while this is a criminal offence and will cause economic loss to C the infringement would not constitute unlawful means because it does not interfere with B's freedom to deal with C.[2]

On the other hand, Lord Nicholls thought that unlawful means should embrace all acts which a person is not permitted to do whether by civil or criminal law provided the acts against B were instrumental in causing economic harm to C.[3] As we shall see, there has been support for Lord Nicholls' test in the context of unlawful means conspiracy[4] but it is thought that Lord Hoffmann's concept of unlawful means is more likely to ensure that the scope of this actionable wrong is kept within reasonable bounds.

(2) A must *intend* to harm C. The intention appears to be subjective. Harm to C does not have to be A's predominant intention. It is enough that A intentionally causes harm to C as a means to protect or promote his own economic interests. As in the case of inducement of breach of contract, there is no liability if economic harm to C is merely a foreseeable consequence of A's conduct but was not intended by A to further A's ends. So if A, a singer, cancels a concert in breach of her contract with an impresario, B, she would not be liable for any loss sustained by the musicians B had hired: but if A cancelled because she thought that the musicians had been insufficiently deferential to her during rehearsals and that they should be taught a lesson, then there would be liability.

(3) While there is no authority directly in point, it appears that a defence of justification might be possible.

We have been considering the classic three-party situation, where A uses unlawful means against B in order to cause economic harm to C. There are *dicta* that the wrong may take a two-party form, *viz* A uses unlawful means against B in order to harm B.[5] It is difficult to see how this form of the wrong can arise other than in the context of intimidation, ie where A threatens B with unlawful means unless B causes himself economic harm. It has been affirmed in the Supreme Court that the unlawful means must have affected a third party's freedom to deal with the claimant which would appear to settle the matter.[6]

1   [2008] 1 AC 1 at para 45. Lord Brown and Baroness Hale agreed with Lord Hoffmann.
2   This was the result reached in *RCA v Pollard* [1983] Ch 335. In *McLeod v Rooney* [2009] CSOH 158 the defender (A) ran a company's business (B) in such a way that the company's value was greatly reduced resulting in the shareholders (C) selling their shares to A at a low price. Even though B had suffered economic loss by A's breach of contract, C could not sue A for intentional harm inflicted by unlawful means as A's conduct did not interfere with B's freedom to deal

with C while they were shareholders. C might have had a claim for damages on the ground of an unlawful means conspiracy: see para 2.8 beyond.

3   [2008] 1 AC 1 at para 162. Lord Nicholls' test has difficulty in accommodating bootlegger cases such as *RCA v Pollard* [1983] Ch 335. Lord Walker did not support Lord Nicholls preferring an 'incremental approach' to unlawful means: *OBG* at para 270.

4   See paras 2.8 beyond.

5   See *OBG* per Lord Hoffmann at para 61; per Lord Nicholls at para 161.

6   *Secretary of State for Health v Servier Laboratories* [2021] UKSC 24.

(4) Conspiracy

2.6   *Allen v Flood*[1] was concerned with the situation where A uses lawful means to harm B economically. There it was held that A was not liable in delict to B, even if his predominant motive or intention was to harm B rather than further A's legitimate business interests. Only three years later, in *Quinn v Leathem*,[2] the House of Lords held that if A and B combine together with the intention to harm C, then A and B are liable in delict for harm caused to C as a result of their combination or conspiracy against him. The rationale of the wrong of conspiracy is that while a person can be expected to withstand the harmful but lawful acts of another, he cannot be expected to withstand the harm caused by a combination or conspiracy of persons to harm him.[3] This rationalisation has been doubted, for a multinational conglomerate or oil company may exercise far greater economic power than a combination of small businesses.[4]

The essence of conspiracy is therefore a combination of persons, who come together with the intention of harming the pursuer economically. There are two types of conspiracy: (a) where the means used by the conspirators are lawful in the sense that they would not be actionable if carried out by one person alone (lawful means conspiracy); (b) where the means used by the conspirators are unlawful in the sense that *either* they would be actionable if carried out by one person alone, for example if the means constitute a delict or breach of contract, *or* they involve a crime or a breach of statute which does not provide a civil remedy for breach (unlawful means conspiracy).

1   [1898] AC 1, HL. Discussed at para 2.1 above.

2   [1901] AC 495, HL.

3   *Mogul Steamship Co Ltd v McGregor, Gow & Co* (1889) 23 QBD 598, CA, at 616 per Bowen LJ.

4   *Lonrho Ltd v Shell Petroleum Co Ltd (No 2)* [1982] AC 173, [1981] 2 All ER 456, HL, at 464 per Lord Diplock; see also *Crofter Hand Woven Harris Tweed Co Ltd v Veitch* 1942 SC (HL) 1 at 8 per Viscount Simon LC.

(a) Lawful means conspiracy

2.7 A combination of persons will be liable in conspiracy if they come together with the predominant motive or intention of harming the pursuer rather than furthering their own legitimate interests. Thus, if A and B come together with the predominant motive or intention to harm C, A and B are liable in conspiracy even if their actions, for example undercutting C's prices, would not be actionable in delict if carried out by A or B alone. It is the *combination* of A and B together *and* their predominant motive or intention of harming C which renders their conspiracy wrongful. If the predominant motive or intention of A and B is not to harm C but to further their own legitimate interests, the conspiracy is not wrongful even though C suffers economic loss as a result of the actions of A and B, always provided these actions are lawful. Where lawful means are used, a conspiracy is wrongful only if the predominant motive or intention of the conspirators is to harm the pursuer.

These principles were laid down in the leading case of *Crofter Hand Woven Harris Tweed Co Ltd v Veitch*.[1] Mill owners on the Island of Lewis who made and sold tweed cloth from yarn spun on the island were unable to agree a 100 per cent union membership agreement (closed shop) with the TGWU because of competition from rival producers on the island (the pursuers) who obtained cheaper yarn from the mainland, wove it into cloth and sold it at a lower price than the mill owners. The TGWU and the mill owners came together. They instructed the members of the TGWU who were employed at the port to refuse to handle the yarn being imported by the pursuers to the island from the mainland. The case proceeded on the basis that the dockers were not in breach of their contracts of employment with the port authority in refusing to handle the imported yarn because they were never asked by their employer to do so. The question was whether the combination amounted to an actionable conspiracy. This complex factual situation can be shown thus:

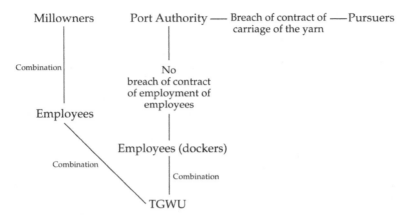

The House of Lords held that since no unlawful means were used because the dockers were not in breach of their contracts of employment, ie there was no conduct which would be actionable if done by one person alone, the conspiracy would be wrongful only if the pursuers could establish that the predominant motive or intention of the conspirators was to harm the pursuers. In this case, the predominant motive or intention was to further the union's legitimate interests, ie 100 per cent union membership. Harm to the pursuers was not their primary intention: it was only incidental to achieving their goal. Accordingly, the defenders were not liable.

It can, of course, be a very difficult issue of fact to establish whether the predominant purpose of the conspiracy is to harm the pursuer or whether the damage done to the pursuer is simply incidental to the furtherance of the conspirators' legitimate interests, be they commercial[2] or trade union interests as in the *Crofter* case. In *Scala Ballroom (Wolverhampton) Ltd v Ratcliffe*[3] it was held to be legitimate for trade union officials to organise a boycott among their members from playing at a dance hall which operated a colour bar; although this objective did not bring any financial benefits to the members of the union, it was genuinely thought by them to be in the interests of the union.

To summarise: when the combination uses lawful means, ie means which would not be actionable if done by one person alone, then the conspiracy is not delictual unless the predominant motive or intention of the conspirators is to injure the pursuer. The onus rests on the pursuer to prove that the predominant purpose of the conspiracy was to harm the pursuer economically. Moreover, the pursuer must prove economic loss.[4]

1   1942 SC (HL) 1, 1943 SLT 2.
2   As in *Mogul Steamship Co Ltd v McGregor, Gow & Co* (1889) 23 QBD 598, CA.
3   [1958] 3 All ER 220, [1958] 1 WLR 1057, CA.
4   In *Lonrho plc v Fayed (No 5)* [1994] 1 All ER 188, [1993] 1 WLR 1489, CA, the
     Court of Appeal accepted that the defendants could be liable in conspiracy
     even if the statements they had made about the plaintiff were true, ie when
     they would have had a defence to an action of defamation. Since the means
     were lawful, their predominant motive would have had to have been harm to
     the plaintiff. Only damages for patrimonial loss would be recoverable; cf loss
     of reputation. On defamation, see Chapter 15 below.

(b) Unlawful means conspiracy

2.8   In considering unlawful means conspiracy, two situations have to be discussed. First is the case where the means used are unlawful in the sense that they would be actionable as a breach of contract or delict if committed by one person alone. So, for example, if the boycotting of the imported yarn in the *Crofter* case had involved a breach of the dockers' contracts of employment (unlawful means), the union would have been liable to the pursuers for inducement of a breach of their contract with the port authority to carry the imported yarn. Where the means are delictual or amount to a breach of contract, the pursuer will usually sue on the substantive delict or breach of contract without relying on the conspiracy.

Second, the means may be unlawful but not actionable as a breach of contract or a delict if committed by one person alone. This will usually arise where the means used involve a breach of a statutory provision.[1] While breach of some statutes gives rise to an action in delict,[2] not all breaches of statute give a person who suffers harm as a result the right to sue in delict. In particular, the pursuer will not generally have title to sue in delict unless the statute was specifically designed to protect the interests of a class of persons to which the pursuer belongs.[3] In this situation, since the means used do not constitute a substantive delict, conspiracy may be the only form of redress.

The criteria for an actionable unlawful means conspiracy were the subject of two decisions of the House of Lords concerned with Lonrho. The first is *Lonrho Ltd v Shell Petroleum Co Ltd (No 2)*.[4] Lonrho owned a pipeline running from Beira in Mozambique to a refinery in Southern Rhodesia. The pipeline was operated under an agreement between Lonrho and oil companies including Shell. When Southern Rhodesia declared unilateral independence, the British government made a sanctions order under the Southern Rhodesia Act 1965. As a result of the sanctions order, oil was no longer shipped to Beira, the pipeline ceased to be used and Lonrho lost profits. Before unilateral independence was declared, the oil companies gave assurances to the Rhodesian government that they would supply petroleum products to Rhodesia through South Africa. After independence had been declared, the defendants supplied the oil to Rhodesia in breach of the sanctions order. In an action of conspiracy against the defendants, Lonrho argued that the breach of the sanctions order enabled unilateral independence to last longer and thereby led to a loss of its revenue as a result of the prolonged non-use of its pipeline.

While the supply of the oil was a breach of the sanctions order, this was simply a criminal offence. In other words, the sanction order was not imposed for the benefit of persons like Lonrho who had traded with Rhodesia before independence. There was therefore no substantive delict arising from the defendants' breach of the order. The only delictual claim had to be based on conspiracy. Both the Court of Appeal and the House of Lords held that the conspiracy was not actionable because Lonrho had failed to establish that the defendants had *intended* to harm Lonrho when they breached the sanctions order. In the course of his speech in the House of Lords, Lord Diplock expressed the view that he did not wish to extend the wrong of conspiracy beyond its existing limits.[5] Since the previous cases had been concerned with lawful means conspiracy where there is no liability unless the predominant motive or intention of the conspirators was to harm the pursuer, Lord Diplock's *dicta* were subsequently taken as authority that there was also no liability for an unlawful means conspiracy unless the primary aim of the combination was to harm the pursuer.[6]

The issue was purportedly clarified by the House of Lords in the second Lonrho case, *Lonrho plc v Fayed*.[7] Here Lonrho argued that the defendants had committed an unlawful means conspiracy against them, an alleged fraudulent misrepresentation to the Secretary of State constituting unlawful means. The House of Lords held that Lord Diplock's analysis in *Lonrho Ltd v Shell Petroleum Co Ltd (No 2)*[8] was not intended as a definitive account of the law relating to unlawful means conspiracy.[9] While accepting that a lawful means conspiracy was wrongful only if the predominant motive or intention of the conspirators was to harm the pursuer, an unlawful means conspiracy was actionable if the pursuer could establish that the conspirators had *an* intention to harm the pursuer even though that was not their *predominant* motive or intention. This intention could not be proved merely by showing that the defenders had used unlawful means: otherwise, Lonrho should have succeeded in the *Shell Petroleum* case.

In the *Total* case[10] the House of Lords unanimously rejected the argument that the concept of unlawful means should be the same for the purpose of unlawful means conspiracy as for intentional infliction of harm by unlawful means. While it might be necessary to restrict unlawful means[11] to actionable civil wrongs to limit the scope of the latter wrong, criminal conduct which was not actionable as a substantive delict could nevertheless amount to unlawful means for the purpose of unlawful means conspiracy. This view has been affirmed by the Supreme Court holding that unlawful means was constituted by conduct in contempt of court.[12] It should be noticed that *Total* only involved two parties, the Revenue and the conspirators: a third party was not involved. It remains to be seen whether the narrower concept of unlawful means would be used if the conspirators had acted against a third party in order to further their ends against the pursuer. For the present, *Total* confirms that if the conspirators have an intention to harm the pursuer, an unlawful means conspiracy is an actionable wrong even if the unlawful means used would not be actionable if done by one person alone.

To summarise: if the means used are lawful, a conspiracy is actionable only if the *predominant* motive or intention of the conspirators is to harm the pursuer; if the means used are unlawful, a conspiracy is actionable if *an* intention of the conspirators was to harm the pursuer even though that was not their primary purpose.[13] Unlawful means include means which are delictual if done by one person alone or which constitute a breach of contract or amount to a breach of criminal law even though this would not give rise to a delictual action if done by one person alone.

1 But in the leading case of *Customs and Excise Commissioners v Total Network SL* [2008] 1 AC 1174 the wrongful means was the common law crime of cheating the public revenue.

2 See Chapter 11 below.

3 *RCA Corpn v Pollard* [1983] Ch 135, [1982] 3 All ER 771, CA.

4 [1982] AC 173, [1981] 2 All ER 456, HL.

5 [1981] 2 All ER 456 at 464.

6   *Allied Arab Bank Ltd v Hajjar (No 2)* [1988] QB 944, [1988] 3 All ER 103; *Metall und Rohstoff AG v Donaldson Lufkin and Jenrette Inc* [1990] 1 QB 391, [1989] 3 All ER 14, CA.

7   [1991] 3 All ER 303, HL.

8   [1982] AC 173, [1981] 2 All ER 456, HL.

9   *Lonrho plc v Fayed* [1992] 1 AC 448, [1991] 3 All ER 303 at 312 per Lord Bridge; Lord Bridge had been a member of the House of Lords in *Lonrho Ltd v Shell Petroleum Co Ltd (No 2)* [1982] AC 173, [1981] 2 All ER 456, HL.

10   [2008] (QB)1 AC 1174. See also *Croesus Financial Services v Bradshaw* [2013] EWHC 3685.

11   The issue may be revisited. *Secretary of State for Health v Servier Laboratories* [2021] UKSC 24 per Lord Sales [102].

12   *JSC BTA Bank v Krapunov* [2018] UKSC 19, [2020] AC 727. Two conspirators concealed assets on which the claimant bank had had freezing orders placed and, moreover, acted in breach of a receivership order.

13   In *Constatin Medien AG v Ecclestone* [2014] EWHC 387 (Ch), [2014] 2 WLUK 636 the claim failed. Although a corrupt deal had been entered into, there was no intention to cause loss and indeed no loss had been caused to the claimant.

(5) Postscript

2.9   The economic wrongs were developed in the context of industrial conflict between employers and trade unions. Most forms of effective industrial action will involve the commission of one or more of the economic wrongs. In order to obtain a balance between the power of capital and labour for the purpose of collective bargaining, legislation has been passed to give immunity to trade unions and trade unionists from civil liability in respect of some, at least, of these wrongs. Immunity arises only if the acts which prima facie constitute an economic wrong are carried out in contemplation or furtherance of a trade dispute. There are now stringent balloting requirements of the members of a trade union which must be satisfied before the statutory defences are applicable; and the defences do not apply to some forms of secondary industrial action. The law has now been consolidated in the Trade Union and Labour Relations (Consolidation) Act 1992 (as amended) and the reader seeking an account of the law relating to industrial action is referred to the textbooks on labour law.

B.   FRAUD

2.10   Fraud is the paradigm of an intentional delict in Scots law. It has been defined as 'a machination or contrivance to deceive'.[1] Fraud will usually cause pure economic loss to the pursuer. As we shall see, this provides a stark contrast to the situation where unintentional conduct results in pure economic loss; there the courts have traditionally been unwilling to allow damages in negligence for pure economic loss. But fraud is not restricted to economic loss. If A lies to B when A tells B that B's wife and children have been seriously injured, with the result that B suffers distress or a psychiatric disorder, B can recover damages from A for fraud.[2]

Much confusion has arisen in this area because the fraudulent conduct will often take the form of a misrepresentation which induces the misrepresentee to enter into a contract with the misrepresentor. In these circumstances, the misrepresentee may have two sets of remedies, ie contractual and delictual. If the fraudulent misrepresentation prevented the formation of the contract, the contract is null;[3] if, however, a contract is concluded but the misrepresentee was induced by the fraudulent misrepresentation to contract under essential error, the contract may be reduced provided *restitutio in integrum* is possible.[4] But, in addition, the misrepresentee can sue in *delict* for damages. Thus, if A lies to B to induce B to enter a contract with A, B will have contractual remedies against A, for example reduction, and the right to sue A for damages in delict. If A lies to B who as a result enters into a contract with C, B will have no contractual remedies against C (unless A was acting as C's agent) but B will be able to sue A in delict.

Although the institutional writers had a flexible view of the concept of fraud, as a result of developments in the nineteenth century fraud as a wrong was confined to a relatively narrow range of situations where the defender *intended* to harm the pursuer. In effect, the Scots wrong of fraud was equated with the English tort of deceit.[5]

Before delictual liability arises for fraud, there must be a positive act by the defender which causes loss to the pursuer. This will often take the form of a misrepresentation by words. But positive conduct can amount to a fraudulent misrepresentation, for example supplying reconditioned as opposed to new cash registers[6] or selling reproduction furniture 'got up' to look like antiques.[7] As a general rule, non-disclosure does not amount to a misrepresentation unless there is a fiduciary relationship between the parties or the contract is a contract *uberrimae fidei*.[8]

Before there is liability for fraud, the pursuer must establish that the defender had the requisite mental element, *mens rea*.

In other words, the pursuer has to show that at the time of the misrepresentation the defender's state of mind was such that he did not, or could not, believe his statement was true. It is, of course, extremely difficult to prove this mental element. In *Zurich v Gray and Kellas*[9] Lord Brodie observed[10] 'Fraud is not something to be lightly inferred. Nor should it be lightly averred. It is for the party alleging fraud to prove it and, in order to do so, to set out in specific terms the basis upon which the court will be invited to infer that the party against whom fraud is alleged did not honestly believe that the representation was true.' Consequently, the law has developed liability for negligent – as opposed to fraudulent – misrepresentation where the defender's conduct can be tested objectively.[11]

What, then, will constitute the *mens rea* of fraud? The first situation is where the defender makes a statement which he knows is false. For example, A tells B there is a gold seam in A's garden when A knows that no seam is there. In these circumstances, A is lying. The second situation is where the defender makes a statement which he does not positively *know* is false but which he positively *believes* to be false. For example, A tells B there is a gold seam in A's garden; A has not dug up his garden and therefore does not know that there is no gold seam but A believes no gold seam is there. If in fact there is no gold seam, then A can be sued by B for fraud. B will have great difficulty in proving that A believed his statement was false if A maintains he believed it was true. However, the court will infer fraud if the statement was destitute of all reasonable grounds for believing it was true or the least inquiry would immediately correct.[12]

The final situation is where the defender makes a statement which he does not positively know is false and does not positively believe is false but is recklessly indifferent to whether it is true or false. If the matter is of no importance to speaker and listener, this is not dishonesty. But if it is a matter of importance between them, it is fraud since the speaker has attempted to induce a belief in the listener, ie that the statement is true, which the speaker does not actually entertain.[13] For example, A tells B there is a gold seam in A's garden. A has done tests which establish that the strata are not inconsistent with a gold seam but A, nevertheless, has serious doubts whether a gold seam is actually there. Assuming B has an interest in the statement, although A does not positively know that the statement is false and does not positively believe that it is false, if he does not care whether it is true or false, he is liable in fraud to B if in fact there is no gold seam in the garden.[14] Proof of the requisite *mens rea* in this situation will be difficult but again will be inferred if the statement was destitute of all reasonable grounds for believing it was true or the least inquiry would immediately correct.

To summarise,[15] *mens rea* for the purposes of fraud arises if the misrepresentor:

(1)   positively knows the statement is false;[16] or

(2)   positively believes the statement is false even though he does not positively know it is false: liability if in fact untrue;

(3)   does not positively believe the statement is true even though he does not positively know or believe it is false: liability if in fact untrue, provided both parties have an interest in what has been said.

There can, therefore, be no liability in fraud if the defender positively believes that the statement is true. In these circumstances, if he did not take reasonable care in making the statement, there may be liability for negligent misrepresentation.[17]

Because fraud is an intentional delict, the pursuer is entitled to recover damages for all the losses directly arising from the fraud – even if the losses are not reasonably foreseeable by the defender. Suppose, for example, A bought shares from B for £100K. A was induced by B to purchase the shares as a result of B's fraudulent misrepresentation as to the value of the shares. In fact their value is only £80K. However, unknown to A and B, at the time of the transaction the shares were in fact overvalued at £80K because of a fraud by C. When C's fraud is subsequently discovered, the shares fall in value to £30K. A can recover the full extent of his loss, ie £70K as opposed to £20K, from B since A has been the victim of a fraudulent misrepresentation: B is liable for all A's losses directly arising from B's fraud, even though they were unforeseeable and, indeed, the result of the actions of a third party. In other words, A is put back into the position he would have been if he had not entered the transaction.[18] It is not possible to exclude liability for fraud by an exemption clause.[19]

1   Erskine *Institute* III, 1, 16.

2   *Wilkinson v Downtown* [1897] 2 QB 57; *Wainwright v Home Office* [2003] UKHL 53, [2004] 2 AC 406, [2003] 3 WLR 1137, [2003] 4 All ER 969, HL. Cf *Powell v Boladz* [1998] Lloyd's Rep Med 116, CA (defendant had no intention to harm plaintiff by falsifying medical records).Similarly, if A obtained sexual intercourse with B as a result of fraudulent misrepresentation.

3   *Morrisson v Robertson* 1908 SC 332, 15 SLT 697; *Shogun Finance Ltd v Hudson* [2004] 1 All ER 215.

4 *Spence v Crawford* 1939 SC (HL) 52, 1939 SLT 305; *MacLeod v Kerr* 1965 SC 253, 1965 SLT 358. See generally MacQueen and Thomson *Contract Law in Scotland* (3rd edn 2012), Chapter 4.
5 On these developments see, generally, 11 *Stair Memorial Encyclopaedia* paras 701–789.
6 *Gibson v National Cash Register Co Ltd* 1925 SC 500, 1925 SLT 377.
7 *Patterson v H Landsberg & Son* (1905) 7 F 675, 13 SLT 62.
8 For example, a contract of insurance.
9 [2007] CSOH 91.
10 At para 24. See also *Grant Estates Ltd v Royal Bank of Scotland* [2012] CSOH 133 per Lord Hodge at paras 85 ff. In *The Royal Bank of Scotland v Holmes* 1999 SLT 563, Lord Macfadyen stated at 569 that it was essential to have clear and specific averments on three matters, *viz*: the act or representation founded upon, the occasion on which the act was committed or the representation made, and the circumstances relied on as yielding the inference that that act or representation was fraudulent.
11 On these developments, see paras 4.10 ff below.
12 *Western Bank of Scotland v Addie* (1867) 5 M (HL) 80.
13 *Lees v Tod* (1882) 9 R 807.
14 *H & J M Bennet (Potatoes) Ltd v Secretary of State for Scotland* 1986 SLT 665, OH (revsd on another point 1988 SLT 390).
15 The *locus classicus* is to be found in *Derry v Peek* (1889) 14 App Cas 337, HL, at 374 per Lord Herschell.
16 See, for example, *Henry Ansbacher & Co Ltd v Binks Stern* [1998] Lloyd's Rep Bank 1, (1997) *Times*, 26 June 1997, CA.
17 However, where a solicitor discovers that his client was engaged in fraudulent dealings, he will be liable as an accessory of his client's fraud if he does not dissociate himself from the fraud and alert his client's potential victim. Liability for being an accessory to fraud does not require subjective dishonesty, but rests on the solicitor's failure to come up to the objective standard of honest behaviour which the law requires, ie because the solicitor is in bad faith. See *Frank Houlgate Investment Company Ltd v Biggart Baillie LLP* [2013] CSOH 80.
18 *Smith New Court Securities Ltd v Scrimgeour Vickers (Asset Management) Ltd* [1997] AC 254, [1996] 4 All ER 769, HL. The House of Lords indicated that B would not be liable for all A's losses if C's fraud had occurred after the transaction on the basis that the causative influence of B's fraud on A's losses vis-à-vis C's fraud had faded: *sed quaere*? In *Barry v Sutherland* 2002 SLT 413, the pursuers bought a pub as a result of the seller's fraudulent misrepresentation concerning the business accounts. The Lord Ordinary (Eassie) held that the pursuers were able to recover damages for trading losses they had incurred when running the business: they were not restricted to compensation for the difference in the price paid as opposed to the true price of the pub. In other words, they were entitled to recover for the losses which directly flowed from entering into the sale and running the business.
19 Hence the necessity to plead fraud in *H & J M Bennet (Potatoes) Ltd v Secretary of State for Scotland* 1986 SLT 665, OH.

C.   GOODWILL – PASSING OFF

2.11   The goodwill and reputation of a business can be a very valuable asset. Important elements of goodwill are the marketing devices used to enable customers to recognise the product and distinguish it from the products of competitors. These devices include trade names, personal and geographical names associated with a product, for example Rennie Mackintosh jewellery[1] or Glenfiddich whisky,[2] and the 'get up' of the product, for example a distinctive container.[3] If a competitor markets a product using a similar name or get up, this may cause confusion among actual or potential customers resulting in damage to the goodwill of the original trader through loss of custom or loss of reputation if the rival product is inferior. In order to protect a trader's goodwill, the delict of 'passing off' has been developed.

Goodwill consists of the features of a business which attract customers to trade with that business. Before there is an action for passing off it must be established that there is a close association between the trader and the particular device which identifies the product or services for existing or potential customers, ie that the device is part of the goodwill of the trader. It may be very difficult, particularly in relation to ordinary words, as opposed to invented words, to show that the word is a marketing device peculiar to the goodwill of a particular trader. Some words, such as 'hoover', may become part of ordinary usage and lose their distinctive quality of being associated with a particular manufacturer. On the other hand, other words, such as 'Scotch', while describing a geographical situation, may, as in relation to whisky, acquire a secondary meaning peculiar to a particular product. Similar difficulties can arise if a trader claims that the shape of a product is sufficiently distinctive to constitute a protectable device; but a lemon-shaped container of lemon juice has been held to have a secondary meaning associated with a particular product.[4] Once it is established that the device is part of his goodwill, the law will protect the goodwill of the trader from being undermined by a competitor passing off his own product by using a similar name or get up.

1   *Carrick Jewellery Ltd v Ortak* 1989 GWD 35-1624, OH.
2   *William Grant & Sons Ltd v William Cadenhead Ltd* 1985 SC 121, 1985 SLT 291.
3   *John Haig & Co Ltd v Forth Blending Co Ltd* 1954 SC 35, 1954 SLT 2, OH (dimple bottle); *Reckitt and Colman Products Ltd v Borden Inc* [1990] 1 All ER 873, HL (Jif plastic lemon).
4   *Reckitt and Colman Products Ltd v Borden Inc* [1990] 1 All ER 873, HL.

2.12   The criteria of the wrong were articulated by Lord Diplock in the leading case of *Erven Warnink BV v J Townend & Sons (Hull) Ltd*.[1] Passing off consists of:

'(1) a misrepresentation (2) made by a trader in the course of trade, (3) to prospective customers of his or ultimate consumers of goods or services supplied by him, (4) which is calculated to injure the business or goodwill of another (in the sense that this is a reasonably foreseeable consequence) and (5) which caused actual damage to a business or goodwill of the trader by whom the action is brought or (in a *quia timet* action) will probably do so'.[2]

The essence of the wrong is that by using the same or similar device which forms part of the goodwill of the pursuer, the defender misrepresents his product as that of the pursuer, thus causing actual or potential damage to the pursuer's business. There is little difficulty if the exact device is used: but an action of passing off will lie even where there are differences provided there is likelihood of confusion among a substantial number of the pursuer's customers or potential customers. If there is no likelihood of confusion, then there is no passing off even if, for example, the same name is used.[3] Thus in *Dunlop Pneumatic Tyre Co v Dunlop Motor Co*[4] it was held that the pursuers, a large manufacturer of tyres, would not be confused with a small family-owned garage of a similar name in Kilmarnock. There is less likelihood of confusion where the products do not belong to a 'common field of activity'. In *Scottish Milk Marketing Board v Dryborough & Co Ltd*,[5] for example, the pursuer, who marketed 'Scottish Pride' butter, failed to interdict the defender from selling 'Scottish Pride' lager since it was unlikely that the products – being so different – would be confused. Although confusion is more likely to be established where there is a common field of activity, a common field of activity is not essential where the device to be protected is, for example, a household name.[6] If there is sufficient likelihood of confusion, it may not be permissible for the defender to use his own name.[7]

In *John Haig & Co Ltd v Forth Blending Co Ltd*,[8] the pursuers established that a particular type of bottle (Dimple) was distinctive to their product's get up and successfully interdicted a rival from using a similarly shaped bottle despite its having a different label and stopper. The court was satisfied that when in use in a bar, there was a sufficient degree of likelihood of confusion to constitute passing off.

It has been held that manufacturers of Scotch whisky may interdict persons from exporting Scotch whisky which they know will be mixed with local spirit abroad and passed off in the foreign country as the genuine article.[9] Similarly, passing off actions will lie where a spirit not distilled in Scotland is marketed as Scotch.[10] In *Lang Bros Ltd v Goldwell Ltd*[11] the defender manufactured 'Wee McGlen', a whisky Mac, a blend of Scotch whisky and ginger wine which was made in England. This get-up consisted of various words and phrases as well as a caricature of a betartaned Scotsman. The Lord Ordinary (Wheatley), a well-known teetotaller, held that the action was relevant. The get up could mislead the public into thinking that the whole product, ie the ginger wine as well as the whisky, was made in Scotland. This misrepresentation as to the origin of the ginger wine could endanger the reputation and goodwill which attaches to Scotch whisky because of its origins. This decision seems to push the wrong to its limits since the defender was not misrepresenting his product as Scotch whisky, nor was the get up proved to be part of the exclusive goodwill of the pursuer.[12]

At one time it was thought that passing off was simply a particular aspect of the delict of fraud. This is no longer thought to be sound – at least if the only remedy sought is interdict as opposed to damages. Although the misrepresentation which constitutes passing off must be 'calculated to injure' the pursuer's business or goodwill, it is enough if this is a reasonably foreseeable consequence of the misrepresentation.[13] In other words, the 'calculated to injure' element is objectively ascertained.

The primary remedy is interdict. Damages may be restricted to cases of actual fraud. It is extremely difficult to assess and quantify damages in respect of loss of custom, potential custom and goodwill.[14]

1 [1979] AC 731 at 742, [1979] 2 All ER 927, HL. This approach was applied by the Second Division of the Inner House of the Court of Session in *Lang Bros Ltd v Goldwell Ltd* 1980 SC 237, 1982 SLT 309.
2 For a slightly different formulation, see also the speech of Lord Fraser of Tullybelton in *Erven Warnink BV v J Townend & Sons (Hull) Ltd* [1979] AC 731 at 755 and 756, [1979] 2 All ER 927, HL.
3 *Harrods Ltd v Harrodian School* [1996] RPC 697, (1996) *Times*, 3 April 1996, CA.
4 1907 SC (HL) 15, 15 SLT 362. But in *Property Care Ltd v White Thomson Preservation Ltd* [2008] CSIH 44, 2008 GWD 28–440, Extra Div, the similarity in trade, in trading area and names between the parties was held sufficient to cause confusion among customers.
5 1985 SLT 253, OH.
6 In *Lego System A/S v Lego M Lemelstrich Ltd* [1983] FSR 155, a toy manufacturer successfully obtained an injunction preventing the manufacturers of irrigation equipment from using the name 'Lego' on the basis that their goodwill might be affected if they entered the same type of business as the defendant sometime in the future.
7 *Parker-Knoll Ltd v Knoll International* [1962] RPC 265, HL.
8 1954 SC 35, 1954 SLT 2, OH.

 9 *John Walker & Sons Ltd v Douglas Laing & Co* 1993 SLT 156, OH.
10 *John Walker & Sons Ltd v Douglas McGibbon & Co Ltd* 1972 SLT 128, OH; *John Walker & Sons Ltd v Henry Ost & Co Ltd* [1970] 2 All ER 106, [1971] 1 WLR 917. Nevertheless, the author has noted that 'House of Lords' whisky, which used to be sold in the Crush Bar at Covent Garden, was manufactured in England!
11 1980 SC 237, 1982 SLT 309.
12 See, further, H L MacQueen 'Wee McGlen and the Action of Passing Off' 1982 SLT (News) 225.
13 *Erven Warnink BV v J Townend & Sons (Hull) Ltd* [1979] AC 731 at 742 per Lord Diplock.
14 On passing off generally, see 18 *Stair Memorial Encyclopaedia* paras 1451–1500.

Part II

UNINTENTIONAL DELICT – GENERAL PRINCIPLES OF LIABILITY

CHAPTER 3

The duty of care

A. INTRODUCTION

3.1 The first part of this book examined the intentional wrongs. *Culpa* or fault is the basis of delictual liability and is present in those delicts because the defender intended to carry out the wrongful actions. Moreover, and this is important, the range of potential pursuers in those delicts is automatically restricted to those persons whom the defender intended to harm or to be affected by his conduct. In Scots law the concept of *culpa* also covers conduct which is merely careless, ie where the defender causes harm to the pursuer *unintentionally*. Immediately a difficulty arises. If A acts in a careless manner, ie his conduct fails to meet the standard of care demanded by society of a person in his position, then prima facie A is liable to anyone who suffers harm as a result of such conduct.[1] In order to *limit* A's potential liability in delict to an indeterminate class of persons, the law has had to develop devices which restrict the number of persons who can claim damages for harm incurred by A's unintentional, but careless, conduct.

While there are many ways to restrict A's potential liability,[2] modern Scots law has accepted as a general principle that A will be liable for careless conduct only if he owed a duty of care to the person harmed by his actions. This duty of care must pre-exist the careless conduct. Whether a duty of care is owed by A to a particular person or class of persons is ultimately a question of law to be determined by the courts. In deciding whether to recognise the existence of a duty of care in particular circumstances, the courts are influenced by issues of policy as well as legal principle. By recognising – or refusing to recognise – the existence of a duty of care, the courts in effect set the parameters of delictual liability for unintentional, but careless, conduct.

Brodie identifies three main principles, guides or tests as to the existence of a duty. These are: (1) the neighbour principle; (2) the *Hedley Byrne* reliance/ assumption of responsibility principle; and (3) the incremental or pragmatic approach to the imposition of a duty in circumstances where none has been recognised before, that is, where there is no governing precedent. These three principles are considered in turn below.

1   Cardozo J's phrase 'liability in an indeterminate amount for an indeterminate time, to an indeterminate class' elegantly summarises the point: *Ultramares Corpn v Touche* (1931) 255 NY 170 at 179.
2   For example by developing a doctrine of proximate causation before A will be liable.
3   D Brodie, *Reparation: Liability for Delict* A11-002 (Westlaw).

B.   *DONOGHUE V STEVENSON*: THE NEIGHBOURHOOD PRINCIPLE

3.2   The starting point of any discussion of the duty of care in Scots law is the famous case of *Donoghue v Stevenson*.[1] One Sunday evening, Mrs Donoghue went to visit a friend in Paisley.[2] They went to Wellmeadow café at Wellmeadow Place, Paisley. The café was owned by Mr Minchella. They decided to have 'iced drinks', ie ice cream over which was poured lemonade. Mrs Donoghue's friend bought the ice cream and a bottle of 'ginger'.[3] The case proceeded on the assumption that Mrs Donoghue's friend had, in fact, bought ginger beer which would have been in an opaque bottle. The friend poured some of the ginger beer over Mrs Donoghue's ice cream; but when, later in the evening, the friend poured the rest of the ginger beer over Mrs Donoghue's melting ice, out floated the decomposing remains of a snail. The sight of the snail and her consumption of the snail-tainted iced drink resulted in Mrs Donoghue becoming ill. Mrs Donoghue sued Stevenson, the manufacturer of the ginger beer, in delict. The question before the courts was whether the manufacturer was liable to Mrs Donoghue in delict even if she could prove the facts alleged and Stevenson had, in fact, been careless.

A most important point to notice is that there was no contractual nexus between Mrs Donoghue and Stevenson. The facts of the case can be shown thus:

Mrs Donoghue's friend could sue Minchella for breach of the contract of sale on the grounds that the ginger beer was not of merchantable (ie satisfactory) quality. However, the friend's damages would be minimal since the friend did not suffer any ill-effects.[4] Mrs Donoghue could not sue Minchella because she was not a party to the contract. Minchella could also have sued Stevenson in contract if he had suffered any loss. But Mrs Donoghue had no contractual remedy. Therefore, the issue before the House of Lords was whether *in the absence* of any contractual nexus between them, Mrs Donoghue, the ultimate consumer of the product, could sue the manufacturer in delict.

1   1932 SC (HL) 31, 1932 SLT 317. The literature on this case is voluminous but see, in particular, A F Rodger 'Mrs Donoghue and Alfenus Varus' (1998) 41 CLP 1.

2   The sex of the friend changes as the case proceeds through the courts!

3   In the parlance of the West Coast of Scotland at the time, 'ginger' was a generic term covering all kinds of aerated drinks.

4   For that reason it would have been pointless for the friend to have assigned his or her rights under the contract to Mrs Donoghue.

3.3   It was held by a majority of the House of Lords[1] that Mrs Donoghue was entitled to sue Stevenson in delict because he owed her a duty of care: if he had *in fact* broken his duty towards her by his careless conduct and she had suffered harm, then she would succeed.[2] In other words, the relationship between the pursuer and defender was sufficiently proximate that the majority was prepared to hold that Stevenson owed Mrs Donoghue a duty of care for the purpose of liability in delict. Lord Atkin concluded:[3]

' … a manufacturer of products, which he sells in such a form as to show that he intends them to reach the ultimate consumer in the form in which they left him, with no reasonable possibility of intermediate examination, and with the knowledge that the absence of reasonable care in the preparation or putting up of the product will result in an injury to the consumer's life or property, owes a duty to the consumer to take that reasonable care'.

Lord Macmillan had

'no hesitation in affirming that a person, who for gain engages in the business of manufacturing articles of food and drink intended for consumption by members of the public in the form which he issues them, is under a duty to take care in the manufacture of these articles. That duty, in my opinion, he owes to those whom he intends to consume his produce … '[4]

At its most specific level *Donoghue v Stevenson* is authority that a manufacturer of food and drink which he intends to be used by the ultimate consumer without the opportunity of inspection or interference before use owes a duty of care to the ultimate consumer to prevent him sustaining harm to his person or property as a result of the manufacturer's carelessness when manufacturing the product. In other words, the relationship between manufacturer and ultimate consumer was sufficiently proximate in these circumstances that the court was prepared to impose a duty of care on the manufacturer towards the ultimate consumer. Four years later, the Privy Council refused to interpret *Donoghue v Stevenson* in such a narrow way and held that the manufacturer of underpants owed a duty of care to the ultimate consumer even though the product was not for internal consumption, the underpants had been removed by the retailer from packets in which they had been delivered and they could have been – but had not been – washed by the ultimate consumer before use.[5] *Donoghue v Stevenson* thus becomes authority for the more general principle that a manufacturer of *any* product owes a duty of care to the ultimate consumer not to cause harm to his person or property as a result of a latent defect in a product which could not be discovered by inspection before use and was intended by the manufacturer to be used by the ultimate consumer in the same condition as it left the manufacturer. If by his careless conduct the manufacturer breaches this duty, causing harm to the ultimate consumer's person or property, then he is liable in delict to make reparation for the harm sustained by the consumer.

1   Lord Atkin, Lord Thankerton and Lord Macmillan; Lord Buckmaster and Lord Tomlin dissented.
2   After the decision of the House of Lords on the relevancy point, the case was settled and did not go to proof.
3   1932 SC (HL) 31 at 57.
4   1932 SC (HL) 31 at 71. On the genesis of Lord Macmillan's speech, see A F Rodger (1992) 168 LQR 236.
5   *Grant v Australian Knitting Mills Ltd* [1936] AC 85, PC. The plaintiff suffered dermatitis because free sulphites used in the manufacturing process had not been washed out of the garments before they were marketed. The fact that, unlike Mrs Donoghue, the plaintiff could have sued the retailer for breach of contract did not prevent recovery against the manufacturer in delict.

3.4   Even at this more general level, there are two important limitations on the extent of the duty of care laid down in *Donoghue*:

(1)   The duty only extends to *latent* defects; the bottle of ginger beer was opaque and the snail could not be seen before the contents were used.[1] If the defect is patent, ie obvious, and the consumer chooses to use it, the manufacturer may escape liability because the chain of causation is broken[2] or the damages will be reduced by the ultimate consumer's contributory negligence.[3]

(2)   The duty is to prevent harm to the ultimate consumer's person or property. If A is physically injured by a defective product, carelessly manufactured by B, A can sue B for damages for pain and suffering (solatium). A can also sue B for economic loss which derives from his injuries (derivative or parasitic economic loss), for example loss of wages when in hospital, loss of wages in the future if A is permanently incapacitated and so forth.[4] If A's property is damaged by a defective product carelessly manufactured by B, then A can recover damages from B in respect of the damage to his property: for example if A's dog dies as a result of contaminated dog food or a defective vacuum cleaner damages A's carpet. But A is not able to sue B in delict if the only property damaged is the defective product itself. A cannot sue B in delict for the cost of repairing a defective car or for replacing a defective vacuum cleaner which blew up without harming A's person or damaging any property other than the vacuum cleaner itself. In these situations, A has suffered *pure,* as opposed to derivative or parasitic, economic loss, ie the cost of repair or replacement or the difference in value between the property with and without the defect. As we shall see, the courts are reluctant to allow a person to recover damages for pure economic loss in *delict*; A's remedy lies in *contract* against

the person who sold him the goods, not the manufacturer.[5] Similarly, if the defect is discovered before there has been any harm done to A's person or property, the cost of repairing the defect is pure economic loss and cannot be recovered in delict.[6]

1   Similarly, the defect in the underpants in *Grant* was latent.

2   On causation, see Chapter 6 below. Where the defect was originally latent, the chain of causation is not necessarily broken if the defect later comes to the attention of the consumer or the fact that a third party had the opportunity or indeed an obligation to inspect the product. In the latter circumstances, the manufacturer and the third party can be jointly and severally liable: see *Grunwald v Hughes* 1964 SLT 94, OH, 1965 SLT 209; *Clay v A J Crump & Sons Ltd* [1964] 1 QB 533, [1963] 3 All ER 687, CA.

3   On contributory negligence, see paras 6.12-6.13 below.

4   On damages generally, see Chapter 16 below.

5   Of course A may not have a contract; for example, if the goods were a gift. But the purchaser could assign his contractual rights against the seller to A.

6   On economic loss, see further para 4.16 ff below. There is no such restriction in the case of the intentional delicts.

3.5   *Donoghue* is, therefore, an important decision in relation to product liability. But what makes the case remarkable is that two of the judges attempted to lay down criteria to determine the existence of a duty of care which would be applicable whenever an action for reparation as a result of unintentional, but careless, conduct arose. Lord Macmillan sets the scene:[1]

> 'The law takes no cognisance of carelessness in the abstract. It concerns itself with carelessness only where there is a duty to take care and where failure in that duty has caused *damage*.[2] In such circumstances carelessness assumes the legal quality of negligence and entails the consequences in law of negligence. What then are the circumstances which give rise to this duty to take care? In the daily contacts of social and business life, human beings are thrown into, or place themselves in, an infinite variety of relations with their fellows; and *the law can refer only to the standards of the reasonable man in order to determine whether any particular relationship gives rise to a duty to take care as between those who stand in relation to each other.* The grounds of action may be as various and manifold as human errancy; and the conception of legal responsibility may develop in adaption to altering social conditions and the changing circumstances of life. *The categories of negligence are never closed.* The cardinal principle of liability is that the party complained of should owe to the party complaining a duty to take care, and that the party complaining should be able to prove that he has suffered damage in consequence of a breach of that duty.'

Lord Macmillan is arguing that given changes in society, the courts, using as a yardstick the values of the reasonable man, may consider that new relationships are sufficiently proximate to impose a duty of care, breach of which gives rise to delictual liability for unintentional, but careless, conduct. *Donoghue v Stevenson* thus introduces a dynamic into the law which can extend the parameters within which there is delictual liability for careless conduct; this is done by the court deciding that a duty of care exists between parties in new social or economic relationships. Conversely, the court can refuse to extend the boundaries of delictual liability for careless conduct by deciding that a duty of care does not exist between parties in the circumstances of the case. In determining whether to impose a duty of care, the courts will clearly be influenced by policy considerations as well as legal principle.

1   *Donoghue v Stevenson* 1932 SC (HL) 31 at 70 (italics added).
2   *Rothwell v Chemical and Insulating Co Ltd* [2007] UKHL 39, [2008] 1 AC 281. This case is discussed in detail at **3.16** below.

3.6   In *Donoghue v Stevenson,* Lord Atkin attempted to provide a criterion for the existence of a duty of care which, at first sight, appears to be more objective. In a famous passage, he said:[1]

> 'The liability for negligence, whether you style it such or treat it as in other systems as a species of "*culpa*", is no doubt based upon a general public sentiment of moral wrongdoing for which the offender must pay. But acts or omissions which any moral code would censure cannot, in a practical world, be treated so as to give a right to every person injured by them to demand relief. *In this way rules of law arise which limit the range of complaints, and the extent of their remedy.* The rule that you are to love your neighbour becomes in law, you must not injure your neighbour; and the lawyer's question, Who is my neighbour? receives a *restricted* reply. You must take reasonable care to avoid acts or omissions which you can *reasonably foresee* would be likely to injure your neighbour. Who, then, in law, is my neighbour? The answer seems to be – persons who are so *closely and directly* affected by my act that I ought reasonably to have them in contemplation when I am directing my mind to the acts or omissions which are called in question.'

For Lord Atkin a duty of care arises when it is reasonably foreseeable by the defender that a person in the position of the pursuer would be closely and directly affected by the defender's acts or omissions. This neighbourhood principle can explain why a duty of care arises in many situations. A driver owes a duty of care to other road users because it is reasonably foreseeable that if he drives carelessly, he may harm other road users. The occupier of property owes a duty of care to those who enter her property because it is reasonably foreseeable that they may be injured if the occupier is careless in the way she maintains the property. An employer owes a duty of care to his employee because it is reasonably foreseeable that if he is careless in the way he runs his system of working the employee may be harmed. A manufacturer of a product owes a duty of care to the ultimate consumer because it is reasonably foreseeable that the ultimate consumer may be injured or his property may be damaged if the product is defective.

1   1932 SC (HL) 31 at 44 (italics added).

C.   *HEDLEY-BYRNE V HELLER*: THE RELIANCE/ ASSUMPTION OF RESPONSIBILITY PRINCIPLE

3.7   It will be noticed in the above discussion that the duty of care is to prevent *physical* harm to the pursuer or physical damage to his property and, where breached, will enable the pursuer only to recover economic loss which is *derivative* from the injuries or damage sustained. But in situations where the pursuer does not suffer physical harm or damage to property, for example pure economic loss, the courts tend to be reluctant to impose a duty of care even though the loss to the pursuer would have been reasonably foreseeable by a person in the position of the defender. In other words, the reasonable foreseeability criterion, while a necessary condition for the existence of a duty of care, might not be sufficient to persuade the court to impose a duty of care in areas where no precedent for such a duty exists. The courts refused to impose duties of care where losses were purely economic until 1963 when the House of Lords recognised a duty of care in the context of careless misstatement.

The criteria for the existence of such a duty were laid down by the House of Lords in *Hedley Byrne & Co Ltd v Heller & Partners Ltd*.[1] The plaintiffs, through their bankers, asked E's bankers, the defendants, whether E was a respectably constituted company. E's bankers replied that E was. On reliance of this statement, the plaintiffs became E's advertising agents. E later went into liquidation. As a result, the plaintiffs suffered pure economic loss. The facts of the case can be shown as follows:

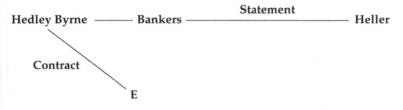

It will be clear that there was no contract between Hedley Byrne and Heller. The question was whether the plaintiffs could sue the defendants in delict. The House of Lords held that the defendants owed a duty of care to the plaintiffs if the defendants had undertaken responsibility for the accuracy of the statement and knew or ought to have known that the plaintiffs would rely on that statement. If the duty was broken as a result of the statement being made carelessly, the defendants could be liable for the plaintiffs' pure economic loss. In the course of his speech, Lord Devlin stated[2] that before there was liability, the plaintiffs had to show that the defendants owed the plaintiffs 'a special duty' to take care. The categories of relationships where this duty arose included not only contractual relationships (ie, where there was a contract between the parties) or fiduciary relationships (for example, principal and agent, trustee and beneficiary), but also relationships which were the 'equivalent to contract'. One example of this would be where the defender had voluntarily assumed responsibility for the accuracy of the statement and knew or ought to have known that the pursuer would rely on the information. The paradigm situation is where the defender is a professional businessman, for example a banker, solicitor or accountant, who in the absence of a contract between them, gives advice to the pursuer in the course of the defender's business, knowing that it will be relied on by the pursuer.[3]

1   [1964] AC 465, [1963] 2 All ER 575, HL.
2   [1964] AC 465, [1963] 2 All ER 575, HL.
3   See discussion at paras 4.16ff.

3.8 The *Hedley-Byrne v Heller* duty of care has been refined subsequently by the House of Lords in the case of *Henderson v Merrett Syndicates*.[1] To summarise: in Lord Goff's opinion a general duty of care to prevent pure economic loss would arise if:

(1)   the defender has voluntarily assumed responsibility for the economic interests of the pursuer;

(2)   the defender knows that the pursuer is relying on the defender's professional expertise; and

(3)   the terms of any contract linking the pursuer and defender do not negative delictual liability.

These cases are further discussed below. The point to note at this stage is that an assumption of responsibility may give rise to a duty of care and, while originally formulated in the context of economic loss, the presence or absence of an assumption of responsibility has been a factor of major significance in many difficult cases involving death or personal injury.[2] The test is therefore of general application.

1   [1995] 2 AC 145, [1994] 3 WLR 761.
2   See, eg, *Barrett v MOD* [1995] 1 WLR 1217; *Costello v Chief Constable of Northumbria* [1999] 1 All ER 550; *Michael v Chief Constable of South Wales* [2015] UKSC 2, [2015] AC 1732.

D.   *CAPARO V DICKMAN*: THE INCREMENTAL APPROACH

3.9   The defendant in *Caparo Industries plc v Dickman*[1] was the auditor of a company who carelessly carried out an audit showing that the company was in a better financial position than was in fact the case. It was reasonably foreseeable (a) that potential investors in reliance on the audit would invest in the company to their loss; and (b) that existing shareholders, in reliance on the audit, would purchase more shares in the company to their loss. This, in fact, happened. Although the auditor had a contract with the company, he did not have a contract with existing and potential shareholders. Although the losses which had been incurred were reasonably foreseeable, the House of Lords held that the auditor did not owe a duty of care to the shareholders or potential shareholders to prevent them suffering pure economic loss as a result of the careless audit. The reasons were that their relationships were not sufficiently proximate and that it was not fair, just and reasonable to impose a duty of care. Lord Bridge explained:[2]

'The salient feature of all these cases [ie where a *Hedley Byrne v Heller* duty of care was recognised] is that the defendant giving advice or information was fully aware of the nature of the transaction which the plaintiff had in contemplation, knew that the advice or information would be communicated to him directly or indirectly and knew that it was very likely that the plaintiff would rely on that advice or information in deciding whether or not to engage in the transaction in contemplation. In these circumstances the defendant could clearly be expected ... specifically to anticipate that the plaintiff would rely on the advice or information given by the defendant for the very purpose for which he did in the event rely on it. So also the plaintiff ... would in that situation reasonably suppose that he was entitled to rely on the advice or information communicated to him for the very purpose for which he required it. The situation is entirely different where a statement is put into more or less general circulation and may foreseeably be relied on by strangers to the maker of the statement for any one of a variety of different purposes which the speaker has no specific reason to anticipate. To hold the maker of the statement to be under a duty of care in respect of the accuracy of the statement to all and sundry for any purpose for which they may choose to rely on it is not only to subject him, in the classic words of Cardozo CJ to "liability in an indeterminate amount for an indeterminate time to an indeterminate class",[3] it is also to confer on the world at large a quite unwarranted entitlement to appropriate for their own purposes the benefit of the expert knowledge or professional expertise attributed to the maker of the statement.'

Accordingly, the House of Lords held that an auditor did not owe a duty of care to a member of the public at large who relied on the audit to purchase shares or increase an existing shareholding in the company: such a duty would arise only if the auditor knew that his statement would be communicated to the plaintiff and relied upon by the plaintiff in a particular transaction of a particular kind.[4]

1   [1990] 2 AC 605, [1990] 1 All ER 568, HL.
2   [1990] 1 All ER 568 at 576.
3   *Ultramares Corpn v Touche* (1931) 255 NY 170 at 179.
4   In *Nordic Oil Services Ltd v Berman* 1993 SLT 1164, OH, the Lord Ordinary (Osborne) held that directors of a company did not owe a duty of care to creditors of the company to prevent them suffering economic loss as a result of the acts or omissions of the company.

3.10 *Caparo* is a highly significant case. It reinforces the point that duties are not owed to the world at large and are owed only in respect of harm that ought reasonably to be within the contemplation of the defender. In short, it places a strong emphasis on the need for proximity. Lord Bridge observed:[1]

'It is never sufficient to ask simply whether A owes B a duty of care. It is always necessary to determine the scope of the duty by reference to the kind of damage from which A must take care to save B harmless. 'The question is always whether the defendant was under a duty to avoid or prevent that damage, but the actual nature of the damage suffered is relevant to the existence and extent of any duty to avoid or prevent it.'

Caparo also has a broader significance in establishing an incremental approach to the expansion of duties of care into new circumstances. In 1978, in *Anns v Merton LBC*,[2] the process for recognition of a duty of care was presented in the House of Lords as a simple formulation in which proximity and foreseeability of harm would give rise to a *prima facie* duty which could then be supported or refuted by considerations of policy. This approach made no distinction between pure economic and other forms of loss and was criticised as it potentially widened the scope of liability beyond the bounds thought appropriate. Another difficulty is the emphasis it placed on policy at the expense of principle. The reaction to this formulation has become known as 'the retreat from *Anns*'. In *Caparo* Lord Bridge affirmed the view that,

> 'rather than a massive extension of a prima facie duty of care restrained only by indefinable considerations which ought to negative, or reduce or limit the scope of the duty or the class of persons to which it is owed," the law should "develop incrementally and by analogy with existing categories'.[3]

Following *Caparo*, reasonable foreseeability of harm, proximity and the fair, just and reasonable test for imposition of a duty, became characterised as a three-fold or tripartite test. This view of the law has since been emphatically rejected in the Supreme Court. As Lord Reed observed:[4]

> '[T]hat understanding of the case mistakes the whole point of *Caparo*, which was to repudiate the idea that there is a single test which can be applied in all cases in order to determine whether a duty exists, and instead to adopt an approach based, in the manner characteristic of the common law, on precedent, and on the development of the law incrementally and by analogy with existing authorities.'

This statement clarifies the law. It affirms the orthodox view, that the recognition or denial of duties of care will be governed by precedent. Policy considerations will already have been taken into account in existing case law on duties. Only in novel circumstances, that is, in the absence of authority, will courts consider whether the imposition of a duty would be fair, just and reasonable. The important point is that the concept of a duty of care is used as a *threshold* device, enabling the courts to extend the scope of delictual liability or to refuse to do so, depending on policy considerations.[5] The duty of care allows the courts, if they so wish, to give an inch without fear that potential pursuers will take the proverbial mile.

The position has been admirably summarised by the Hon Justice Michael Kirby when he said extra-judicially:[6]

> 'Novel cases therefore require judges with the responsibility of decision to evaluate the choices they make by reference to considerations of legal policy. Will the imposition of a duty of care for negligence impose indeterminate liability on too many people? Will it expose people unreasonably to liability to others? Will it result in intolerable economic burdens upon citizens? Will it have adverse implications for the availability of liability insurance? Will it offend legitimate freedom of action by people in the position of the defendant? Will it drive some useful participants out of a valuable economic market? Will refusing it leave a vulnerable party without recompense reasonable to the circumstances?'

1 [1990] 2 AC 605 at 627.
2 [1978] AC 728, [1977] 2 WLR 1024 discussed at para 4.27 below.
3 *Sutherland Shire Council v Heyman* (1985) 60 ALR 1 per Brennan J at 43–44 cited in Caparo [1990] 2 AC 605 at 618.
4 *Robinson v Chief Constable of West Yorkshire* [2018] UKSC 8, [2018] 2 WLR 595 per Lord Reed at para 21. Note that Lord Reed uses the word 'authorities' in place of 'categories'. There is some significance in the alteration, the idea of categories of negligence being somewhat problematic.
5 See, eg, *D v East Berkshire Community Health NHS Trust* [2005] 2 AC 373 where the House of Lords held that it was not fair, just and reasonable to impose a duty of care on a local authority towards the parents of a child whom they suspected of being a victim of child abuse: but it was fair, just and reasonable that a duty of care was owed to the *child* in relation to their investigations.
6 'Judicial Activism' (2004) 55 Hamlyn Lectures.

E. GENERAL MATTERS

(1) Proximity: neighbours in law

3.11 In *Donoghue*, Lord Atkin posed the question, 'Who, then in law, is my neighbour?' and answered it thus: 'persons who are so closely and directly affected by my act that I ought reasonably to have them in contemplation when I am directing my mind to the acts or omissions which are called into question'.[1] Lord Atkin's answer serves well enough in commonplace situations where there is a risk of physical injury to persons in the vicinity if sufficient care is not taken. Where circumstances are unusual, where losses are purely economic or where harm is caused by the criminal act of a third party for instance, the need to avoid indeterminate liability plus the commitment to incremental development mean that the issue of proximity comes necessarily to the fore. Proximity addresses the issue of how a boundary is to be drawn around those persons who ought reasonably to be within my contemplation. Which persons should be excluded? Proximity may be constituted by factors that serve to bring the parties together so that it appears fair to hold that one ought to have been in the contemplation of the other. Relevant factors will vary according to the circumstances at hand.

It can be seen that questions of fairness, justice and reasonableness may be integral to assessing proximity as well as providing a basis for recognition or denial of a duty in novel circumstances. As Lord Hoffman explained:[2]

> '[T]he requirement that the imposition of a duty should be fair, just and reasonable may sometimes inform the decision as to whether the parties should be considered to be in a relationship of proximity and may sometimes provide a special reason as to why no duty should exist, notwithstanding that the relationship would ordinarily qualify as proximate. In these proceedings the defendant does not allege any such special reason but the concept of fairness and justice obviously looms large in the question whether it is fair, just and reasonable that the author of a geological survey should be treated as having a relationship of proximity to the population of Bangladesh.'

The context for these remarks was *Sutradhar (FC) v National Environmental Research Council*.[3] The defendant carried out tests on ground water systems in Bangladesh for the purpose of discovering whether the water might contain toxic trace elements. At the time standard procedures for testing ground water did not include tests for arsenic. The defendant was not asked and did not test for arsenic. Their report made it clear that they had not done so. Four million shallow hand pumped wells were installed to supply drinking water. The water was contaminated with arsenic. The claimant was one of the thousands to suffer from arsenic poisoning. The House of Lords held that the defendant did not owe the claimant a duty of care on the ground that there was no proximity between the parties.

As Lord MacMillan famously remarked in *Bourhill v Young*:[4] 'The duty to take care is not owed to the world at large, but to those to whom injury may reasonably and probably be anticipated if the duty is not observed.' Duties can only be owed to identifiable persons or to persons within a reasonably well-defined class. In the absence of specific factors pointing to proximity, a population of 140.9 million is clearly too large a group to be owed a duty of care.

1   See para 3.6 above.
2   *Sutradhar (FC) v National Environmental Research Council* [2006] UKHL 33, [2006] 4 All ER 490 HL at para 32.
3   Ibid.
4   1942 SC (HL) 78 at 88.

(2) Proximity: Scope of the duty of care

3.12 A proximate relationship between the parties is essential before a duty of care will arise. The concept of proximity, however, embraces not just the relationship, but the harm against which there is a duty to guard, in other words the scope of the duty. Lord Hope put the point clearly:[1]

> 'If commonplace situations of that kind [injuries in the course of employment and road traffic accidents] had to be analysed, the conclusion would be that the duty is owed not simply because loss, injury or damage is reasonably foreseeable. It is because there is a relationship of proximity between the employer and his employees and the driver and other road users. This is sufficient in law to give rise to a duty of care. *The duty is created by the relationship, and the scope of the duty is determined by what in the context of that relationship is reasonably foreseeable.*'

Duties are limited in their scope. The leading case is *Muir v Glasgow Corporation*.[2] Members of the Milton Free Church were having a Sunday school picnic in King's Park, Glasgow. Although it was a June afternoon, it began to rain. Mrs Alexander, the manageress of a tearoom/sweet shop in the park, gave permission to the party to have their tea there. Access to the tearoom was through a narrow passage where the sweet shop was situated. Some of the children were queuing in the passage to purchase sweets from the shop. When two members of the party carried a tea-urn full of boiling water through the passage to gain entry to the tearoom, the tea-urn dropped, scalding several children. It was never established how the urn was upset. We can illustrate the case as follows:

Clearly the persons carrying the urn owed a duty of care to the scalded children but no action in delict was brought against them either because of difficulty in establishing the cause of the accident or, more likely, because they had no assets or insurance. Instead, an action was brought against the Glasgow Corporation on the basis that, as Mrs Alexander's employer, the corporation was vicariously liable for any delicts she committed in the course of her employment.[3] It was accepted that as manageress of the tearoom Mrs Alexander owed a duty of care to any persons she allowed to enter the premises. But, in order to succeed, the pursuer had to show that by allowing the urn to be carried through the passage crowded with children, Mrs Alexander was in breach of the duty of care she undoubtedly owed to them. The House of Lords took the view that Mrs Alexander could only be liable for those consequences of her actions which a reasonable person in her position would have had in contemplation in the circumstances of the case. Lord Thankerton said:[4] '... it has long been held in Scotland that all that a person can be held bound to foresee are the reasonable and probable consequences of the failure to take care, judged by the standard of the ordinary reasonable man [sic]'. Lord Wright considered[5] that:

> 'It is not, of course, a question of what she [Mrs Alexander] actually thought at the moment, but what the hypothetical reasonable person could have foreseen. That is the standard to determine the scope of her duty. This involves the question: Was the operation of carrying the tea-urn something which a reasonable person in Mrs Alexander's position should have realised would render the place in which it was performed dangerous to the children in the circumstances? This is the crucial issue of fact and the acid test of liability.'

The House of Lords held that the answer to this question was no. Mrs Alexander was entitled to assume that the tea-urn would be carried by responsible persons and that if carried with reasonable care would cause no harm to the children. A reasonable person in her position would not, therefore, have foreseen as a possibility, let alone a probability, that the urn would slip and the children would be scalded. Thus, because injury to the children could not have been foreseen as a *reasonable* and *probable* consequence of allowing the urn to be carried through the passage, Mrs Alexander had not broken the duty of care she owed the children.[5] The event that transpired was outwith the scope of her duty.

1   *Mitchell v Glasgow City Council* [2009] UKHL 11 at para 16. See also Lord Bridge, text at n 1, 3.10 above.
2   1943 SC (HL) 3, 1944 SLT 60.
3   On vicarious liability, see para 12.5 ff below.
4   1943 SC (HL) 3 at 8.
5   1943 SC (HL) 3 at 15.
5   Lord Wright thought it would have been different if, for example, Mrs Alexander had allowed lions or tigers to be taken through the passage: 1943 SC (HL) 3 at 16.

3.13   *Muir v Glasgow Corpn* is, therefore, authority that the scope of a duty of care is limited to the *reasonable* and *probable* consequences of the defender's conduct. The test is the reasonable foresight of the hypothetical reasonable person in the position of the defender as opposed to what the defender actually foresaw. But since the hypothetical reasonable person is, in effect, the court, it will be obvious that the scope of the duty of care in a particular case is, to some extent at least, determined by the judges.[1]

Thus, for example, in *Malcolm v Dickson*[2] a painter who was working on a house set the house on fire. A guest who was staying there attempted to save some of the property. As a result of his exertions, the guest collapsed and died. The court held that the painter had not broken the duty of care he owed to the deceased because it could not have been anticipated by a reasonable person in the defender's position that an occupant of the house would die trying to salvage furniture. As Lord Patrick said:[3]

'It would not occur to the ordinary reasonable man that a reasonable and probable consequence of his being careless in burning paint from a window frame would be that some intervener would suffer a substantial injury through over-exertion, strain and excitement in carrying furniture from the house.'

It is important to note in this case that the deceased died from a heart attack. If he had died as a result of the fire, for example suffocated by smoke, it is submitted that there would have been a breach of the duty of care because it is foreseeable as a reasonable and probable consequence of carelessly setting a house on fire that an occupant might die from the smoke.

Since policy considerations are inevitably involved in determining what the hypothetical reasonable person can be deemed to have foreseen, it should occasion little surprise that, as a general rule, the courts take the view that when a person causes an accident, it is a reasonable and probable consequence of his carelessness that a rescuer may appear on the scene and be injured.[4]

1   In *Mullin v Richards* [1998] 1 All ER 920, CA, the Court of Appeal held that a reasonable 15-year-old schoolgirl could not foresee as a probable consequence of play fighting with plastic rulers that her friend (the plaintiff) could lose her eye as a result of the plastic snapping. See, too, *McDougall v Strathclyde RC* 1996 SLT 1124 (PE instructor not in breach of his duty to assist a pupil when pupil chose to perform an exercise not previously performed without supervision during teacher's absence to assist another pupil: not reasonably foreseeable as a probable consequence of instructor's absence that pupil would try out the difficult exercise); *Kemp v Secretary of State for Scotland* 2000 SLT 471 (in determining whether a kerb they were obliged to maintain was a hazard to pedestrians, a local authority was not entitled to assume that all pedestrians using the footpath would behave with reasonable care at all times. While they were not bound to foresee every extremity of folly, it was foreseeable, at least in Scotland, that some pedestrians would use the road while under the influence of drink. In these circumstances it was reasonably foreseeable as a probable consequence of failing to light the raised kerb that a pedestrian who had had a drink might fall over it: pursuer held one-third contributorily negligent); *McGinnes v Endeva Service Ltd* 2006 SLT 638 where the Lord Ordinary (Emslie) held that the pursuer had failed to establish that it was reasonably foreseeable as a probable result of his employer's failure to operate a double manning system that the pursuer, a field service engineer, would be criminally assaulted by a third party at the place where he was working; *French v Strathclyde Fire Board* [2013] CSOH 3 (reasonably foreseeable by a watch commander that firefighters under his control might suffer personal injuries if a gable collapsed while they were fighting the fire). See also *Khan v Meadows* [2021] UKSC 21 discussed at para 7.5 below.

2   1951 SC 542, 1951 SLT 357.

3   1951 SC 542 at 556.

4   See, eg, *Steel v Glasgow Iron and Steel Co Ltd* 1944 SC 237, 1945 SLT 70; *Videan v British Transport Commission* [1963] 2 QB 650, [1963] 3 WLR 374, CA.

3.14   It is not necessary reasonably to foresee the *extent* of the pursuer's injuries; it is enough that the injuries actually sustained by the pursuer are of a *kind* which would be foreseeable as a reasonable and probable consequence of the defender's careless conduct. Nor does every aspect of the accident have to be reasonably foreseeable. These points were settled by the House of Lords in the important decision, *Hughes v Lord Advocate*.[1] In order to work on underground cables, Post Office workers uncovered a manhole. They erected a canvas shelter over the manhole. At 5 pm, when it was dusk, they left the manhole unattended; they also left outside the shelter a ladder, a rope, and paraffin warning lamps. Two boys[2] saw the shelter and decided to explore. They carried the ladder, the rope and a paraffin lamp inside the tarpaulin. One boy tripped over the lamp which fell into the manhole. The paraffin spilled from the lamp, was vaporised by the heat and there was an explosion. There was a rush of flame and one of the lads fell into the manhole and suffered severe burns. It was agreed by expert witnesses that in the circumstances[3] an explosion was not reasonably foreseeable. But it was accepted that the workmen were careless in leaving the manhole unattended.

The House of Lords held that it was foreseeable as a reasonable and probable consequence of leaving the manhole unattended that a child might enter the tent with a lamp, that the paraffin might spill and the child suffer a burn, ie that a boy might be burned by the lamp. This was sufficient to establish a breach of the duty of care which the workmen undoubtedly owed to prevent physical harm to pedestrians by leaving the manhole unattended. The fact that there had been an unforeseeable explosion and that the child's burns were therefore much worse than could have been reasonably anticipated was irrelevant. As Lord Morris of Borth-y-Gest explained:[4]

> 'The circumstances that an explosion as such could not have been contemplated does not alter the fact that it could reasonably have been foreseen that a boy who played in and about the canvas shelter and played with the things that were thereabouts might get hurt and might in some way burn himself. That is just what happened. The pursuer did burn himself, though his burns were more grave than would have been expected. The fact that the features and developments of an accident may not reasonably have been foreseen does not mean that the accident itself was not foreseeable. The pursuer was, in my view, injured as a result of the type or kind of accident or occurrence that could reasonably have been foreseen.'

Hughes v Lord Advocate is therefore authority that the scope of a duty of care will extend to the kind or type of injury which is a reasonable and probable consequence of the defender's careless act or omission;[5] the fact that the injuries sustained are greater than could have been reasonably foreseen and/or that some of the causes of the accident were unforeseeable is irrelevant as long as the type of injury suffered by the pursuer and the fact that an accident could occur as a result of the defender's carelessness are reasonably foreseeable.[6]

1   1963 SC (HL) 31, 1963 SLT 150.
2   The pursuer, aged 8, and his 10-year-old *uncle*!
3   Cf if they had been working on a gas main.
4   *Hughes v Lord Advocate* 1963 SC (HL) 31 at 43–44.
5   One of the difficulties with *Page v Smith* [1996] AC 155, [1995] 2 All ER 736, HL is that foreseeable physical harm is a different type of injury from the unforeseeable psychiatric disorder which, in fact, occurred.
6   In *Galbraith's Curator ad Litem v Stewart (No 2)* 1998 SLT 1305, the Lord Ordinary (Nimmo Smith) held that it was enough that it was reasonably foreseeable that children would be attracted to pipes left unsecured overnight and that they might suffer personal injuries when playing with them: the precise nature of the accident which had occurred did not have to be reasonably foreseeable. In *Jolley v Sutton London Borough Council* [2000] 3 All ER 409, the House of Lords held that an accident to a child while attempting to repair an abandoned boat left near a block of council flats was reasonably foreseeable. The council had conceded that it was reasonably foreseeable that a child might be injured by falling through rotten planking when playing *on* the boat: but that it was not reasonably foreseeable that a child might be injured by the boat falling on the child who was *underneath* the boat attempting to repair it! Their Lordships held that it was sufficient that it was reasonably foreseeable that children might sustain physical harm by meddling with the boat. See also *Given v James Watt College* 2007 SLT 39 (employer liable to an employee who fell when she was frightened by a malfunctioning drinks dispensing machine even though this was the first time that the machine had emitted a flash).

(3) Omissions

3.15   It is a fundamental principle of the law of delict that A is not liable to B in delict simply because A did not confer a benefit on B. This includes the benefit of A preventing B from sustaining harm. As Stevens has said,[1] 'If in acting I fail to confer a benefit on you, which includes the failure to prevent harm, as I have made you no worse by my actions there is prima facie no liability'. Merely because it is reasonably foreseeable to A that harm will happen to B does not of itself generate a duty on A to act to prevent B suffering that harm. Consider the following example:

A, a professor of law, is standing in the quadrangle of the university. He sees B, another professor, who is very short-sighted, walking with a white stick across the quadrangle. There is a banana skin lying in B's path. Instead of warning B, A merely stands and watches. B slips on the banana skin. A walks away, giggling. Is A liable to B in delict for A's failure to warn B about the banana skin? The answer is no. Why? In spite of the fact that it is reasonably foreseeable by A that B may slip on the banana skin if A does not warn him, this does not generate a duty of care as A is not obliged to provide a benefit to B. As Lord Toulson has stated, 'The common law does not generally impose liability for pure omissions'.[2] As a matter of policy, the law does not compel us to be good Samaritans.[3]

But there may be additional factors present which create a closer degree of proximity between the parties so that the defender does owe the pursuer a duty of care and will be liable in delict for an omission to act to B's benefit. In *Robinson v Chief Constable of West Yorkshire* Lord Reed adopted a summary from academic literature listing four circumstances in which duties arise in respect of sources of danger not created by the defender.[4]

In particular, there may be a duty of care when the defender has assumed responsibility for the welfare of the pursuer. In *Barrett v Minister of Defence*[5] the Court of Appeal held that the Royal Navy did not owe a duty of care to prevent an adult naval airman from becoming drunk off-duty. However, after the deceased had collapsed and was no longer capable of looking after himself, the Royal Navy assumed responsibility for him and it was accepted that the Royal Navy had a duty to provide him with adequate medical care. But, unless there is some factor additional to foreseeability of harm, the law does not impose a duty of care on the defender to rescue the pursuer or to act in such a way that the pursuer will avoid an accident.

Duties of care may be imposed by status, thus parents are under a duty to rescue their child from danger. Duties may be imposed where the defender has a special level of control over the source of danger[6] or indeed where the defender has done something which prevents another from providing protection.

Returning to the example, it does not follow that B is without remedy. The university, as his employer, owes B a duty to take reasonable care for his safety at work;[7] moreover, as the occupier of the premises,[8] the university owes B a duty to take reasonable care that he is not harmed as a result of the state of the premises. If, of course, A deliberately dropped the banana skin in B's path, A would be liable for assault if A intended that B should slip. If A had carelessly dropped the banana skin, he could be liable since it is reasonably foreseeable that another person in the quadrangle could slip on the skin. But that duty of care is triggered by A's positive act in dropping the banana skin, ie A has created the risk of injury to B; it is no longer a case of a 'pure' omission.[9]

We must be careful to distinguish the cases of 'pure' omission where the law will not impose a duty to act from the situation where the defender has created the source of danger themselves. In the latter situation, where there is a pre-existing duty of care, the defender can be liable for careless omissions as well as careless acts. In the case of the driver of a vehicle and other road users or the manufacturer of a product and the ultimate consumer, for example, it is irrelevant for the purpose of the law of delict that the carelessness involves an omission to act as opposed to a positive action. Overtaking without first checking in the mirror is just as careless as driving too fast: failing to check whether a product is infested by a snail is just as careless as giving the wrong instructions on how a product is to be used.

1   *Torts and Rights* (Oxford, 2007) at p 9.
2   *Michael v Chief Constable of South Wales* [2015] UKSC 2 para 97.
3   Reasonable forseeability of physical injury is the standard criterion for determining the duty of care owed by people who undertake an activity which carries a risk of injury to others. But it is insufficient to justify the imposition of liability upon someone who simply does nothing: who neither creates the risk nor undertakes to do anything to avert it': *Gorringe v Calderdale MBC* [2004] UKHL15 at 17, per Lord Hoffmann. See also *Mitchell v Glasgow City Council* [2009] UKHL 11; 2009 SLT 247: 'A legal duty to take positive steps to prevent harm or injury to another requires the presence of some feature, additional to reasonable foreseeability that a failure to do so is likely to result in the person in question suffering harm or injury' per Lord Scott at para 39.
4   [2018] UKSC 8 para 34: Tofaris & Steel, 'Negligence Liability for Omissions and the Police', (2016) 75 CLJ 128. 1. 'A has assumed a responsibility to protect B from that danger, 2. A has done something which prevents another from protecting B from that danger 3. A has a special level of control over that source of danger or 4. A's status creates an obligation to protect B from that danger.'
5   [1995] 3 All ER 87.
6   *Dorset Yacht Co Ltd v Home Office* [1970] AC 1004; *Reeves v Metropolitan Commissioner of Police* [2000] 1 AC 360.
7   On employers' liability, see Chapter 12 below.
8   On occupiers' liability, see Chapter 10 below.
9   For an interesting discussion of pure omissions, see T B Smith, *A Short Commentary on the Law of Scotland* (W Green, 1962) p 672.

(4) Harm

3.16 It cannot be emphasised enough that even though there has been a breach of the duty of care, the delict is only completed and delictual liability is only incurred when *harm* is sustained by the pursuer.[1] There must be a concurrence of *damnum* (harm sustained) and *injuria* (breach of the duty of care) before delictual liability arises (*damnum injuria datum*).[2] If the pursuer does not suffer harm as a result of the defender's breach of a duty of care which he owes to the pursuer then there is no delictual liability.

Harm to the pursuer is a constituent of, as well as a consequence of, negligence.

This point was emphasised by the House of Lords in *Rothwell v Chemical and Insulating Co Ltd*.[3] The claimants had been negligently exposed to asbestos. Fibres had entered their lungs. They had developed pleural plaques. These are fibrous thickening of the pleural membrane which surrounds the lungs. Apart from exceptional cases – which did not arise in these claims – pleural plaques are asymptomatic, ie do not cause any symptoms, do not cause asbestosis, mesothelioma or lung cancer in the future: but the risk of contracting asbestos-related illnesses is significantly higher in persons with plaques than persons who have been exposed to asbestos but have not developed plaques. Because of the increased risk of future asbestos-related illness, persons diagnosed as having plaques become anxious about the possibility of the risk materialising. Because pleural plaques are benign and asymptomatic and do not cause any future asbestos-related disease, their Lordships held that the development of pleural plaques could not be characterised as harm or material damage. Accordingly, the claimants had no delictual cause of action and were not entitled to any compensation from the defendants. Two points should be noticed. The claimants could not simply sue for the anxiety caused by the increased risk of contracting asbestos-related illnesses because, in *Gregg v Scott*,[4] the House of Lords had held that the *risk* of contracting an illness in the future (and any related anxiety) does not, per se, constitute reparable harm. Second, the claimants could sue if and when they contracted an asbestos-related illness because the illness would constitute material harm and a delict would then have been committed.

While the reasoning in *Rothwell* is a paradigm of orthodoxy, the decision has been controversial. Before it, Scottish courts were prepared to make awards of provisional damages[5] if pursuers were diagnosed as having pleural plaques: this would provide compensation for their anxiety about their future health while enabling them to claim further compensation, should they develop an asbestos-related disease. Once pleural plaques were held not to constitute material harm, this was no longer possible as no delict had been committed. For this reason, the Scottish Parliament decided to reverse *Rothwell* and pass legislation under which pleural plaques are to constitute material harm for the purposes of the law of delict.[6] *Rothwell* was distinguished in the English case, *Dryden v Johnson Matthey Plc*.[7] The Supreme Court held that sensitisation to platinum salts to which the claimants

74   *The duty of care*

had negligently been exposed, constituted personal injury even though the condition was hidden and asymptomatic.

Pleural plaques apart, the law of delict does not provide compensation for the anxious healthy, ie hypochondriacs.

To summarise, unless the pursuer sustains the harm which the defender was under a duty of care to prevent, there is no liability, indeed there is no delict.

1   *Watson v Fram Reinforced Concrete Co (Scotland) Ltd and Winget Ltd* 1960 SC (HL) 92, 1960 SLT 321.
2   Thus, for example, the prescriptive period will only begin to run from the date that the pursuer suffers harm, not the date of the breach of duty: for example, when Mrs Donoghue became ill, not when Stevenson manufactured the ginger beer carelessly.
3   [2008] 1 AC 281.
4   [2005] AC 176.
5   On provisional damages see paras 16.18–16.19.
6   Damages (Asbestos-related Conditions) (Scotland) Act 2009. The validity of the 2009 Act was challenged on the basis that it was outside the legislative competence of the Scottish Parliament. The Supreme Court has held that the 2009 Act is valid: *Axa General Insurance Ltd v Lord Advocate* [2011] UKSC 46.
7   [2018] UKSC 18 [2019] AC 403.

F. SUMMARY

3.17 Negligent conduct does not, of itself give rise to liability. Liability will only arise where harm is caused in breach of a duty to avoid it. Duties of care are owed only to a person's neighbours in law and the harm that must be avoided is that which is reasonably likely to follow if care is not taken. Recognition of a duty of care requires first, that the pursuer is a person whom the defender ought to have had in their contemplation and second, that the harm complained of is of a type which ought to have been foreseeable to a reasonable person in the position of the defender. The two questions are inter-related and are addressed together in the concept of proximity. The duty will be owed in respect of harm that is foreseeable in the context of the relationship between the parties. This may be a relatively straightforward matter, eg in cases involving death or personal injury or property damage caused by negligent driving. The driver will owe a duty of care to all other road users and pedestrians in the vicinity to guard against these forms of loss. The duty here arises out of physical or spacial proximity. The act of driving itself creates the necessary relationship with others walking or driving down the same street. By contrast, employers owe employees various duties of care, eg to provide a safe system of work. If a company based in Glasgow has failed to provide safety instructions, it may find itself in breach of a duty of care owed to an employee working in China at the time of the injury. In this case there is no physical proximity; proximity is nevertheless provided by the employment relationship and the harm that is foreseeable within the context of that relationship.

Questions of duty also arise in circumstances where it is not clear that the defender ought to compensate the pursuer for their losses even if the defender can be shown to have been negligent. Should an auditor owe a duty to a person who has acted on the strength of a negligently conducted audit to their financial loss, for instance? Without factors pointing to proximity between the parties the most likely answer will be 'no'. Relevant factors might include: a contract between the parties; the defender's knowledge of the pursuer's identity, the defender's knowledge of the pursuer's reliance on the defender's conduct and so on, depending on the circumstances. Essentially, the relationship between the parties must be sufficiently close so that it can be said that the defender ought to have had loss to the pursuer in their contemplation when directing their mind to the conduct or activity that has caused the loss.

In circumstances where the court can infer an assumption of responsibility by the defender to guard the pursuer against the kind of harm that has arisen, then this itself serves to establish the necessary relationship and therefore proximity. An assumption of responsibility may act as a kind of trump card that will enable recognition of a duty of care in circumstances where there might otherwise be none. In novel circumstances, the courts will be circumspect before recognising a duty of care and will only do so in cases where this appears fair, just and reasonable. In this way the duty of care operates as a threshold device. The extent of liability for negligence is to advance incrementally, not by leaps and bounds. This provides scope for policy to influence the decision-making process, but it should be remembered that questions of fairness and justice are inherent at all stages in the recognition of duties of care.

CHAPTER 4

Duty of care as a threshold device

A. NOVEL CIRCUMSTANCES

4.1 The neighbourhood principle established in *Donoghue v Stevenson* provided a basis for the subsequent expansion of liability into areas where previously no duties would have arisen. The most significant developments occurred in 1963 in *Hedley Byrne v Heller and Partners*; 1970 in *Dorset Yacht Co v Home Office*; and 1982 in *McLoughlin v O'Brian*. In these cases, the House of Lords first recognised duties in respect of pure economic loss; the delictual conduct of third parties; and psychiatric harm suffered by secondary victims respectively.[1] This period of expansion reached its zenith in *Anns v Merton LBC* in 1985[2] and, from that time on, the general trend has been for caution, following the approach established in *Caparo Industries Plc v Dickman*.[3]

The incremental approach with the stricture that the recognition of a duty must be fair, just and reasonable, arose in the context of pure economic loss, but the fact that it is to be used in novel cases of physical harm as well as economic loss was put beyond doubt in *Mitchell v Glasgow City Council* where Lord Hope said:[4]

> 'But I see no good reason why, as a general guide to what is required, it should not be regarded as part of Scots law. It is really no more than an expression of the idea that lies at the heart of every judgment about legal policy. If liability is to attach, it should be in situations where this is readily understandable because, looking at both sides of the argument, it is fair and reasonable that there should be liability ...There is no principle of Scots law that contradicts it, and the fact that the law of liability for negligence has developed on common lines both north and south of the Border provides powerful support for the defender's argument that it should be applied in this case.'

1 See paras 3.7 above and 4.3 and 4.10 below.
2 See para 4.27 below.
3 See para 3.9 above.
4 [2009] UKHL 11, 2009 SLT 247. See also *Aitken v Scottish Ambulance Service* [2011] CSOH 49.

4.2   The role of policy in addressing the fair, just and reasonable question can be seen in many cases. *Marc Rich & Co AG v Bishop Rock Marine Co Ltd, The Nicholas H*[1] was a House of Lords' case concerning physical property damage. A surveyor (the defendant) advised the owner of a damaged vessel to continue on her voyage. The vessel sank and the cargo was lost. It was held that the surveyor did not owe a duty of care to the owner of the *cargo* (the plaintiff) to avoid damage to his property.

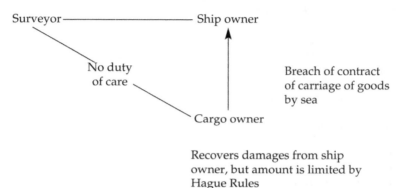

Surveyor ———————————— Ship owner

No duty of care

Breach of contract of carriage of goods by sea

Cargo owner

Recovers damages from ship owner, but amount is limited by Hague Rules

No duty of care arose since the relationship between the parties was not sufficiently proximate and it would have been unfair, unjust and unreasonable to hold otherwise. To have imposed a duty of care in this case would have disturbed 'the intricate blend' of internationally accepted rules of shipping law under which the owner of the cargo has a remedy against the owner of the ship in *contract* but the amount of compensation is limited.

In *Coleridge v Miller Construction Ltd*,[2] the defender cut an electric cable supplying power to the pursuer's factory. The absence of electricity caused damage to the pursuer's furnace and to the glass being manufactured. Although the pursuer had sustained physical damage to his property, the Lord Ordinary (MacLean) held that the defender did not owe the pursuer a duty of care. His reasoning was that although there was proximity between the parties, it was not fair, just and reasonable to impose a duty of care because this would upset the well-established liabilities of the parties' insurers. In *Santander v Keeper of the Registers of Scotland*,[3] the court held that it was not fair just or reasonable that the Keeper should owe a duty of care to the bank to prevent them sustaining economic loss when the Keeper registered a forged discharge of a standard security in the bank's favour. It has been held that it is not fair just or reasonable to impose a duty of care on a social worker to prevent him causing a client mental harm by having a consensual affair with her: *Shields v Crossroads (Orkney)*.[4] The social worker's behaviour was unprofessional; he was disqualified but was not liable to pay his 'victim' damages on the grounds of negligence. The role of policy is particularly clear in *D v East Berkshire Community Health NHS* Trust.[5] The House of Lords held that it was not fair, just or reasonable to impose a duty of care on a local authority towards the parents of a child whom they suspected of being a victim of abuse; but it was fair, just and reasonable that a duty was owed to the child. In denying a duty owed to the parents, the Court sought to avoid a conflict of interests in circumstances where the safety of the child outweighed any responsibility to the parents.

1   [1996] AC 211, [1995] 3 All ER 307, HL.
2   1997 SLT 485 OH. See also *British Telecommunications plc v James Thomson & Sons (Engineers) Ltd* 1999 SC (HL) 9. The House of Lords, reversing the Second Division of the Court of Session, held that a domestic sub-contractor did owe a duty of care to an employer whose insurance covered only nominated sub-contractors. Lord Mackay of Clashfern accepted that the *Caparo* test was appropriate: *1999 SC (HL) 9* at 12.
3   [2013] CSOH 24.
4   [2013] CSOH 144.
5   [2005] 2 AC 373.

B.   HARM CAUSED BY THIRD PARTIES

4.3   Ordinarily, a person is not liable for the acts of third parties, *culpa tenet suos auctores*.[1] Established exceptions include vicarious liability or where non-delegable duties are imposed.[2] Normally, where A breaches a duty owed to B, but the harm incurred by B is actually caused by C, C's act, if truly independent, will break the chain of causation between A's breach and B's loss.[3] There is, however, House of Lords' authority for the view that, in the right circumstances, a duty may be owed to guard the pursuer against the criminal acts of third parties.

In *Dorset Yacht Co Ltd v Home Office*,[4] borstal boys were working on the Isle of Wight under the custody and control of three borstal officers. The officers went to bed, leaving the boys to their own devices. Seven boys decided to escape. They went on board a yacht moored off the island, which collided and damaged the plaintiff's yacht. The House of Lords held that the borstal officers owed a duty of care to the plaintiff which they had broken in the circumstances. The officers were responsible for the boys and were under a duty to guard them and prevent them from absconding. It was foreseeable as a reasonable and probable consequence of leaving the boys alone that they would try to escape. Since the only means of escape was by sea, it was also reasonably foreseeable as a probable consequence that they would steal a yacht and, being inexperienced mariners, collide with another vessel.[5] If there had not been a special relationship between the officers and the third party who caused the damage, ie the boys, there would have been no liability.[6]

1   Fault attaches to its perpetrators.
2   See Ch 12 below.
3   See Ch 6 below.
4   [1970] AC 1004, [1970] 2 All ER 294, HL.
5   It is important to note that the duty was owed to the plaintiff only because it was reasonably foreseeable that damage might be caused to his yacht because the only method of effecting escape was by sea. If the boys had broken into a shop to steal food and drink, it is unlikely the court would have imposed a duty of care on the officers towards a member of the general public who suffered damage as a result of the acts of an absconding criminal.
6   See also, for example, *Reeves v Metropolitan Commissioner* [2000] 1 AC 360 (prison officers under a duty to prevent a prisoner from harming himself while in confinement).

4.4 In *Maloco v Littlewoods Organisation Ltd*,[1] the defender owned an empty cinema. Vandals broke in and started a fire which damaged neighbouring property. It was accepted by the court that the owner or occupier of property could owe a duty to proprietors of adjacent property to take reasonable care of his property so that it did not cause them physical harm or damage to their property. But there was no general duty to take reasonable care of property to prevent a *third party* from using the premises to cause physical injury or damage to neighbouring proprietors. Lord Mackay of Clashfern explained the decision in terms of reasonable foreseeability:[2]

> 'While no doubt in this case ... it was probable that children and young persons might attempt to break into the vacated cinema, this by no means establishes that it was a probable consequence of its being vacated with no steps being taken to maintain it lockfast that it would be set on fire with consequent risk of damage to neighbouring properties.'[3]

Lord Goff took the view that a duty could arise if the owner 'negligently causes or permits a source of danger to be created on his land, and can reasonably foresee that third parties may trespass on his land and, if interfering with the source of danger, may spark it off, thereby causing damage to the person or property'.[4] For example, a duty of care would arise if A kept explosives in his house, told persons that the explosives were there, but took no precautions to prevent trespassers from having access to the premises. Similarly, a duty of care would arise if the owner had allowed his property to become a fire hazard, knew persons had been trespassing on the premises and had already started fires, but did not take reasonable precautions to prevent access.[5] Both these examples involve sources of danger created by or at least within the control of owners and for which they might fairly be held responsible. No duty arose in the *Littlewoods* case since the defenders did not know that the derelict cinema had, in fact, become a fire hazard: derelict buildings are not, per se, fire hazards.

Following his earlier decision in *Perl (Exporters) Ltd v Camden LBC*,[6] Lord Goff treated *Maloco v Littlewoods* as a case of pure omission and doubted whether the owner or occupier of property ever owes a duty of care to adjacent proprietors to prevent a thief from gaining access to their premises:[7]

> ' ... I do not think that liability can be imposed on an occupier of property in negligence simply because it can be said that it is reasonably foreseeable, or even (having regard, for example, to some particular temptation to thieves in adjacent premises) that it is highly likely that, if he fails to keep his property lockfast, a thief may gain access to his property and thence to the adjacent premises. So to hold must presuppose that the occupier of property is under a general duty to prevent thieves from entering his property to gain access to neighbouring property, where there is a sufficient degree of foresight that this may occur. But there is no general duty to prevent third parties from causing damage to others, even though there is a high degree of foresight that they may do so. The practical effect is that everybody has to take such steps as he thinks fit to protect his own property, whether house or flat or shop, against thieves.'[8]

1   1987 SC (HL) 37, 1987 SCLR 489, 1987 SLT 425.
2   1987 SLT 425 at 431.
3   *Nolan v Iceland Frozen Foods* (3 December 1997, unreported), CC (Liverpool), where a supermarket was held liable for damage caused by children misusing abandoned trolleys – not an unusual occurrence.
4   1987 SLT 425 at 439. Lord Goff's approach was approved by the House of Lords in *Mitchell v Glasgow City Council* [2009] UKHL 11, 2009 SLT 247.
5   *Thomas Graham & Co Ltd v Church of Scotland General Trustees* 1982 SLT (Sh Ct) 26.
6   [1984] QB 342, [1983] 3 WLR 769.

7   *Maloco* was followed on this point in *Ferns v Scottish Homes* 2007 SLT (Sh Ct) 27.
8   *Maloco v Littlewoods Organisation Ltd* 1987 SLT 425 at 441.

4.5   In *Mitchell v Glasgow City* Council,[1] Mitchell, a tenant of the defender, had for several years been harassed and threatened by Drummond, his neighbour, who was also a tenant of the defender. After many complaints by Mitchell, eventually the defender had a meeting with Drummond in which he was told that he would be evicted. Drummond returned home and assaulted Mitchell who died from the attack. The House of Lords held that the defender did not owe Mitchell a duty of care to warn him about the meeting with Drummond. In accordance with the fundamental principle that there is no liability for pure omissions[2] their Lordships held that the defender did not owe a duty to prevent the risk of harm being caused to Mitchell by Drummond, a danger which the defender had not created and had not undertaken to avert. But Lord Hope maintained that a duty might arise if the Council had assumed responsibility for Mitchell's safety. Lord Hope said:[3]

> 'The situation would have been different if there had been a basis for saying that the defenders had assumed a responsibility to advise the deceased of the steps that they were taking, or in some other way had induced the deceased to rely on them to do so. It would then have been possible to say not only that there was a relationship of proximity but that a duty to warn was within the scope of that relationship … I would also hold, as a general rule, that a duty to warn another person that he is at risk of loss, injury or damage as the result of the criminal act of a third party will arise only where the person who is said to be under that duty has by his words or conduct assumed responsibility for the safety of the person at risk.'

In cases where a pursuer alleges a duty to prevent them suffering harm as a result of a third party's criminal activities, it is often impossible to establish a sufficient degree of proximity. In *Thomson v the Scottish Ministers*,[4] for example, the pursuer was the mother of a woman who was murdered by a prisoner who had been given short leave from jail. The Inner House held that the prison authorities did not owe the victim a duty of care to prevent her being harmed by the prisoner when he was released. There was no evidence that she was the subject of a special or distinct risk if the prisoner was released and therefore there was no proximity between her and the prison authorities.[5] By contrast, in *Kaizer v Scottish Ministers*,[6] prison authorities were held to owe a duty to a prisoner who was subjected to attempted murder. The pursuer founded on *Dorset Yacht Co v Home Office*. The racially motivated attack was carried out by another prisoner in fulfilment of a threat which the victim had reported to a prison officer who had neglected to pass this information on to his superiors.

But even where there is sufficient proximity because the pursuer knows that he is in danger from a particular person and has made his fears known to the relevant authority,[7] the House of Lords held in *Van Colle v Chief Constable of Hertfordshire*[8] that the core principle of public policy laid down in *Hill v Chief Constable of West Yorkshire*[9] *viz* that the police do not owe a common law duty of care to protect individuals against harm caused by criminals, should normally prevail. The imposition of such a duty of care would distort, by encouraging defensive action, the manner in which the police would otherwise deploy their limited resources and would cause those resources to be diverted from the performance of the public duties of the police. Accordingly, it is only when the police have voluntarily assumed responsibility for the pursuer's safety, for example to provide protection, that such a duty will be imposed. Accordingly, no duty was owed a woman who was stabbed 70 times by her ex-partner after she had made an emergency call to the police for protection. There was a mix-up between telephone operators and her call had been downgraded from one requiring an immediate response, so by the time the police finally attended, the murder had taken place. The majority held that there had been no assumption of responsibility on the part of the police.[10]

1 [2009] UKHL 11, 2009 SLT 247.
2 See above para 3.15
3 Ibid at para 29.
4 [2013] CSIH 63, 2013 SC 628.
5 See also *Hill v Chief Constable of West Yorkshire* 1989 AC 53 discussed at paras 11.5–11.6 below.
6 [2018] CSIH 36, 2018 SLT 918.
7 As happened in *Osman v UK* [1999] 1 FLR 193.
8 [2008] 3 WLR 593: see also *Brooks v Comr of Police of the Metropolis* [2005] 1WLR 1495.
9 [1989] AC 53, discussed above para 11.5.
10 *Michael v Chief Constable of South Wales* [2015] UKSC 2, [2015] SC 1732 Lady Hale and Lord Kerr dissenting.

4.6 By contrast, there is not the same difficulty in holding employers liable where employees suffer harm at the hands of criminals provided such harm is reasonably foreseeable within the context of the employment relationship. Employers were in breach of duty in requiring the pursuer to work on her own in an off-licence known to be susceptible to armed robbery.[1] Equally, it has been held that hotel proprietors owe a duty of care to guests to take reasonable care to protect them against injury by criminals[2] or theft of their belongings.[3]

The significance of *Dorset Yacht Co v Home Office* is probably restricted to the recognition that, in principle, the parameters of liability may extend to covering harm caused by the criminal acts of third parties. Liability having been extended in this way, subsequent case law demonstrates that such cases can generally be determined according to established principles on pure omissions, proximity and the presence or absence of an assumption of responsibility. There has been no development of a specialised body of precedent specific to harm caused by third parties as there has, say, in relation to psychiatric harm caused to secondary victims.[4]

1　Collins v First Quench Retailing Ltd 2003 SLT 1220. See further, E Russell, 'Lone Workers – The Employer's Duty in Respect of Double Manning and Security Screens', 2003 SLT (News) 241.
2　*Al-Najar v Cumberland Hotel* [2019] EWHC 1593 QB.
3　*Anande v Firoka (King's Cross) Ltd* [2018] EWHC 3679 QB.
4　See below paras 4.10–4.11.

C.　MENTAL HARM

4.7　The law has long recognised that A can owe a duty of care to B to prevent B suffering mental harm as a result of A's unintentional, but careless, conduct.[1] In order to succeed, the mental harm must amount to a recognised psychiatric disorder, not simply a fright. Initially at least, the duty of care arose only when the pursuer was in danger of suffering potential physical harm as a result of the defender's conduct. Put another way, where it was reasonably foreseeable by the defender that the pursuer could be physically injured as a result of the defender's conduct, it was also reasonably foreseeable that the pursuer might suffer mental harm if the defender's conduct did not actually cause physical injury to the pursuer but the pursuer had been terrified that it might do so. There was therefore a duty of care not to cause a psychiatric disorder to a person who was within the area of risk of physical harm as a result of the defender's careless conduct. In the leading case of *Page v Smith*,[2] the plaintiff was involved in a road accident caused by the defendant's careless driving. The accident was not serious and the plaintiff suffered no physical harm. However, the accident brought on a recurrence of the plaintiff's ME which had been in remission. The House of Lords held[3] that because the plaintiff was within the area of potential physical harm, he was to be regarded as a primary victim of the accident. In these circumstances, the defendant owed him a duty of care to prevent him suffering physical or psychiatric harm. It was irrelevant that he had not suffered physical harm or that a psychiatric disorder was not reasonably foreseeable because a person of ordinary fortitude would not have suffered mental harm in the circumstances. Thus a duty of care to prevent mental harm arises whenever the pursuer is a primary victim, ie when it is reasonably foreseeable that she might suffer physical injury. It does not matter that she did not sustain physical harm or that a psychiatric disorder was unforeseeable.[4]

1   See, eg, *Dulieu v White & Sons* [1901] 2 KB 669.
2   [1996] AC 155, [1995] 2 All ER 736, HL. In *Simmons v British Steel plc* 2004 SC (HL) 94 it was accepted by the House of Lords that *Page* was authoritative in Scotland. See also *Donachie v Chief Constable of Greater Manchester Police* [2004] EWCA Civ 405, [2004] All ER (D) 126 (Apr).
3   Lords Ackner, Browne-Wilkinson and Lloyd; Lords Keith and Jauncey dissented.
4   In *Rothwell v Chemical and Insulating Co Ltd* [2008] 1 AC 281, the House of Lords held that it was not reasonably foreseeable that an employee would suffer a mental disorder when he discovered that he had pleural plaques and therefore had an increased risk of contracting an asbestos-related illness in the future. The House rejected the argument that because the claimant was within the area of potential physical harm, the mental harm did not have to be reasonably foreseeable. *Page v Smith* was distinguished on the grounds that (i) in *Page* the foreseeable event – the collision – which might cause a physical or psychiatric injury had happened, while here the foreseeable event – contracting an asbestos-related illness – was still to occur, and (ii) in *Page* the psychiatric injury was caused by an event – the collision – which amounted to a breach of the duty, while here the psychiatric injury had been caused by the diagnosis that the claimant had pleural plaques and therefore learning that he had a greater risk of contracting an asbestos-related illness, and not by the employer's breach of duty in exposing him to asbestos in the first place. For further discussion of *Rothwell*, see above para 3.16.

4.8   It is therefore important to determine when a person is a primary victim. Since the decision of the House of Lords in *Frost v Chief Constable of the South Yorkshire Police*,[1] it might appear that the test is simply whether he has been exposed to physical danger:[2] in other words, whether or not the victim has been within the area of potential physical harm. Accordingly, persons who witnessed the death of fellow employees have been held not to constitute primary victims when they were not themselves in physical danger at the time of the accident.[3] Similarly, no duty of care is owed to prevent rescuers suffering mental harm unless they are also in potential physical danger.[4] But there can be exceptional cases where a pursuer will be treated as a primary victim even though he was not at risk of physical harm. These have included cases where the pursuer mistakenly thought that he had killed or injured a fellow employee;[5] parents who felt responsible for the sexual abuse of their children by a foster child introduced into their home by the defendant;[6] and parents whose dead children's organs were removed without permission.[7] On the other hand, a doctor or social worker does not owe a duty of care to a parent to prevent the parent from suffering mental harm if they mistakenly diagnose a child as having been abused by that parent.[8] An employee may recover damages for psychiatric disorder when his employer is in breach of his general duty to take reasonable care for the safety of his employees.[9]

1   [1999] 2 AC 455, [1999] 1 All ER 1, Lords Browne-Wilkinson, Steyn and Hoffmann; Lord Goff dissented and Lord Griffiths dissented in part.
2   Or had reasonable grounds to believe that he was in danger: see, for example, *Hunter v British Coal Corpn* [1999] QB 140, [1998] 2 All ER 97, CA.
3   *Robertson v Forth Road Bridge Joint Board* 1995 SC 364, 1996 SLT 263 (pursuer saw fellow employee blown off lorry on Forth Road Bridge); *McFarlane v EE Caledonia Ltd* [1994] 2 All ER 1 (plaintiff witnessed Piper Alpha explosion from a supply ship); *Campbell v North Lanarkshire Council* 2000 SLCR 373 (proof before answer allowed to determine whether pursuer was in personal danger).
4   *Frost v Chief Constable of the South Yorkshire Police* [1999] 1 All ER 1, [1999] 2 AC 455. Cf *Chadwick v British Transport Commission* [1967] 1 WLR 912, where the plaintiff was within the area of potential physical harm and *Cullin v London Fire and Civil Defence Authority* (31 March 1999, unreported), QB.
5   *Dooley v Cammell Laird & Co Ltd* [1951] 1 Lloyd's Rep 271; *Salter v U B Frozen & Chilled Foods Ltd* 2003 SLT 1011 (pursuer actively involved in the accident which caused the death of a fellow employee for which the pursuer was blameless).
6   *W v Essex CC* [2001] 2 AC 592. See also *McLoughlin v Jones* [2002] 2 WLR 1279 (plaintiff suffered a nervous breakdown having been wrongfully imprisoned as a consequence of his solicitor's negligence in preparing his defence. Plaintiff was treated as a primary victim in his claim against the solicitor for negligence).
7   *Stevens v Yorkhill NHS Trust* 2006 SLT 887; *AB v Leeds Teaching Hospital NHS Trust* [2004] EWHC 644 (QB), [2004] 2 FLR 365, [2004] 3 FCR 324, 77 BMLR 145.
8   *D v East Berkshire Community Health NHS Trust* [2005] AC 373. In *Fairlie v Perth and Kinross Healthcare NHS Trust* 2004 SLT 1200 the Lord Ordinary (Kingarth) considered that the parent in such a case might have a remedy in defamation or breach of his Article 8 right to respect for private life.
9   For employers' liability for psychiatric disorder as a consequence of stress at work, see discussion below at para 12.3.

4.9   Where a person sustains mental harm as a consequence of witnessing or learning of an accident to a third party (the primary victim), she is known as a secondary victim. For a long time, it was trite law that a defender did not owe a duty of care to a secondary victim to prevent her suffering a psychiatric disorder. The leading case in Scots law is *Bourhill v Young*.[1] Young was a motorcyclist. Driving too fast, he overtook a stationary tramcar on its near side. He then crashed into a car which was turning right into a side street some 50 feet from the tramcar. Young was killed. It was accepted that the accident was caused by Young's careless driving. At the time of the accident the pursuer, Mrs Bourhill, a fishwife, was on the far side of the tramcar, putting her creel on her back. She therefore did not see the collision but she heard the crash and, after Young's body was removed, saw the blood on the road. She maintained that as a result of the accident she suffered a 'nervous shock' which had caused her to miscarry. She sued Young's executor in delict. The complex factual situation can be shown as follows:

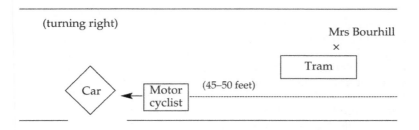

At the time of the accident Mrs Bourhill was 45–50 feet from the collision and on the far side of the tramcar. She was not within the area of risk of potential physical harm and – as we would say today – was therefore not a primary victim. In those circumstances, the House of Lords held that Young did not owe the pursuer a duty of care to prevent her suffering mental harm as a result of his careless driving. It was accepted that a driver owes a duty of care to other road users or persons in premises adjoining the highway, but only when they were 'so placed' that they could reasonably be expected to be physically harmed by the defender's failure to take care.[2] Lord Macmillan stated that:[3]

> 'The duty to take care is the duty to avoid doing or omitting to do anything the doing or omitting to do which may have as its reasonable and probable consequence injury to others, and the duty is owed to those to whom injury may reasonably and probably be anticipated if the duty is not observed.'

But while Young owed such a duty to the occupants of the motor car, he did not owe it to Mrs Bourhill because she was outwith the area of risk of potential physical harm. As Lord Wright observed,[4] she 'was completely outside the range of the collision. She merely heard a noise which upset her … She saw nothing of the actual accident, or indeed any marks of blood until later'. Lord Porter expressly articulated the policy considerations involved:[5]

'In the case of a civil action there is no such thing as negligence in the abstract. There must be neglect of the use of care towards a person towards whom the defendant owes the duty of observing care … The driver of a car or vehicle, even though careless, is entitled to assume that the ordinary frequenter of the streets has sufficient fortitude to endure such incidents as may from time to time be expected to occur in them, including the noise of a collision and the sight of injury to others, and is not to be considered negligent towards the one who does not possess the customary phlegm.'

Thus, as a general rule, there was no duty of care to prevent secondary victims from suffering mental harm; liability only extended to primary victims, ie persons who were placed in physical danger or reasonably in fear of such danger as a result of the defender's careless conduct. The application of this rule was demonstrated in *Weddle v Glasgow City Council*.[6] A pedestrian witnessed a bin lorry collide with another vehicle. She then encountered the victims of the incident including several dead bodies. Having failed to establish any reasonable belief that she was in danger of physical injury herself, her claim to be treated as a primary victim failed.

1   1942 SC (HL) 78, 1943 SLT 105. For a discussion of this case, see W W McBryde 'Bourhill v Young: the Case of the Pregnant Fishwife' in *Comparative and Historical Essays in Scots law* (Butterworths, 1992) pp 66 ff.
2   1942 SC (HL) 78 at 86 per Lord Russell of Killowen.
3   Ibid at 88.
4   Ibid at 93.
5   Ibid at 98.
6   2019 SLT (Sh Ct) 206, affirmed [2021] SAC (Civ) 17.

4.10   In *McLoughlin v O'Brian*[1] the House of Lords was persuaded to widen the scope of potential delictual liability for psychiatric disorder. In this case, the plaintiff's husband and three children were involved in a road accident at 4 pm. They were taken to hospital where it was discovered that one child was dead. The plaintiff was told of the accident at 6 pm and went to the hospital where she saw the victims. She later suffered a psychiatric disorder.

The Court of Appeal took the view that while it was reasonably foreseeable that a wife and mother might sustain mental harm in these circumstances, the defendant did not owe the plaintiff a duty of care because she was not present at the accident. In other words, she was not a primary but a secondary victim. The House of Lords rejected this argument and held that a duty of care existed in spite of the fact that the plaintiff had not been directly involved in the accident. While it was reasonably foreseeable that the spouse and mother of persons injured in an accident might suffer mental harm this in itself was not sufficient to create a duty of care. However, there were additional factors present in the case which provided the necessary degree of proximity between the parties from which a duty of care could be inferred. First, the plaintiff was with the victims shortly after the accident; accordingly, she had witnessed the aftermath of the accident. Second, she had personally *seen* the effects of the accident on her family and had not simply learned of the accident by letter or on television or from a third party.[2] It follows from *McLoughlin* that before a duty of care is owed to a secondary victim, not only must the risk of a psychiatric disorder to the pursuer be reasonably foreseeable but other factors must be present which show a sufficient degree of proximity between the parties. If these additional factors are *not* present, the court will not impose a duty of care.

These issues were further explored by the House of Lords in *Alcock v Chief Constable of South Yorkshire Police*.[3] Friends and relations of persons crushed to death at Hillsborough football ground brought claims for mental harm. The House of Lords held that before a duty of care arose, it had to be reasonably foreseeable that the plaintiffs would suffer a psychiatric disorder. The criterion could not be satisfied unless there was a close tie of love and affection between the plaintiff and the victim. This would be presumed if they were spouses or parent and child, but merely because they were related in some way would not per se be sufficient. Conversely, if they were not related, a plaintiff might still succeed if it could be shown that the requisite degree of love and affection *in fact* existed between the plaintiff and the victim.[4] Their Lordships then maintained that reasonable foreseeability was not sufficient and two *extra* factors for proximity had also to exist.The plaintiff had to witness the calamity or its aftermath (for example, by being at the stadium); identifying a dead relative or friend eight hours after the event was not enough. Secondly, the plaintiff must have seen or heard the accident: watching the event on television did not suffice since the defendant knew that it was the policy of the television company in such circumstances to ensure that no specific person who was injured could be identified.

1   [1983] 1 AC 410, [1982] 2 All ER 298, HL. For an earlier example of liability to a secondary victim, see *Hambrook v Stokes Bros* [1925] 1 KB 141, CA.

2   *McLoughlin v O'Brian* [1983] AC 410 at 421–423 per Lord Wilberforce. The use of the term 'proximity' here does not sit well with a modern understanding of the term. See para **3.12** above. While psychiatric harm to a close relative of the victim could be considered within the contemplation of a defender, the requirement for presence at the event and for direct perception seem more concerned with attribution or causation.

3   [1992] 1 AC 310, [1991] 4 All ER 707, HL.

4   In *Alcock,* the House suggested that in exceptionally horrific circumstances a duty of care might arise even though the secondary victim did not fulfil the 'love and affection' criterion. This is doubtful. In *Robertson v Forth Road Bridge Joint Board* 1994 SC 364, for example, the fact that the pursuer who had witnessed his fellow employee being blown off the Forth Road Bridge had been a friend of the deceased and had socialised with him for many years was held not to be sufficient to constitute the necessary degree of 'love and affection'. The same kind of reasoning was applied in *McFarlane v EE Caledonia Ltd* [1994] 2 All ER 1, where the plaintiff had witnessed the Piper Alpha explosion. So, in this respect, *Alcock* has never been followed – what could have been more horrific than the accidents in *Robertson* and *McFarlane*?

4.11   To summarise: a duty of care to prevent mental harm to a secondary victim will only arise if:

(1)   there is a tie of love and affection between the secondary victim and the primary victim;

(2)   the secondary victim was present at the accident or at its immediate aftermath; and

(3)   the psychiatric disorder was caused by direct perception of the accident or its immediate aftermath: it is not enough merely to have been informed of the accident.

The *Alcock* criteria for the imposition of a duty of care in relation to secondary victims were reaffirmed by the House of Lords in *Frost v Chief Constable South Yorkshire Police.*[1]

The law now appears to be settled, but its application can lead to arbitrary results. In *Vernon v Bosley (No 1),*[2] for example, two children were drowned when the car their nanny was driving drove into a river. Their father was called to the scene and saw the unsuccessful attempts to rescue his children trapped in the car. The father's claim for damages for a psychiatric disorder was successful. The defendant owed him a duty of care because:

(1)   he was the father of the primary victims; and

(2)   he witnessed the aftermath; and

(3)   his psychiatric illness arose from direct perception of the failed rescue attempt.

But if, for example, he had not been able to be present at the rescue but was simply informed of his daughters' deaths by telephone, no duty of care would have arisen because of the absence of reasons (2) and (3). Similarly, Mrs Bourhill would still fail in her claim since there was no tie of love and affection between her and Young's primary victims.[3]

There is authority that there is no breach of a duty to prevent mental harm unless it has been induced by a nervous shock, ie the 'sudden appreciation by sight or sound of a horrifying event, which violently agitates the mind'.[4] Claims have therefore been refused where a psychiatric disorder has been caused by a gradual process, for example nursing a dying child.[5] In *Young v McVean*,[6] a mother on her way to meet her son passed the scene of the accident in which he had been killed. Only later, when he did not turn up at the rendezvous, did it gradually dawn on her what had happened. Her claim failed.

1   [1999] 2 AC 455 where the police constables could not establish a sufficient tie of love and affection with the primary victims they were attempting to rescue: therefore the constables' claims as secondary victims failed. They were not within the area of potential physical harm and therefore could not be regarded as primary victims. See also *Keen v Tayside Contracts* 2003 SLT 500 (employee treated as secondary victim where he sustained mental harm by witnessing an accident and not being allowed to leave the scene by his supervisor: discussed beyond para 12.3).

2   [1997] 1 All ER 577. See also *Galli-Atkinson v Seghal* [2003] EWCA 697, [2003] All ER (D) 341 (Mar) where a mother visited a hospital mortuary to see her child whom she refused to believe was dead: this was regarded by the Court of Appeal as part of the aftermath of the accident. Cf *Taylor v A Novo* [2013] EWCA Civ 194 where a daughter whose mother died unexpectedly in hospital weeks after an accident at work could not establish sufficient proximity in an action against her mother's employer, as she had not witnessed the accident or its aftermath even though she had been present at her mother's death.

3   But could she have sued if she had been related to Young who was killed in the accident as a result of his own negligence? It is submitted that she could. Cf *Greatorex v Greatorex* [2000] 4 All ER 769 (father claimed damages for a psychiatric disorder sustained when he rescued his son from a car crash. The *Alcock* criteria were satisfied. However, the claim was refused on policy grounds as the son was solely responsible for his own injuries and the court could not countenance a parent suing his own child in such circumstances. *Sed quaere?*).

4   *Alcock v Chief Constable of South Yorkshire Police* [1992] 1 AC 310 per Lord Ackner at 401.

5   *Sion v Hampstead Health Authority* [1994] 5 Med LR 170, CA. Damages may
be awarded if there is a sudden realisation of the danger to the primary
victim within a continuing process: *Walters v North Glamorgan NHS Trust*
[2002] EWHC 321 (QB), [2003] PIQR P2, [2002] All ER (D) 65 (Mar).
6   [2014] CSOH 133, 2014 SLT 934.

4.12   We must distinguish these cases from the situation where
the defender has been in breach of his duty to take reasonable care
to prevent the pursuer suffering physical harm and the pursuer
suffers a mental disorder as well as physical harm. Whether
damages can be awarded for the mental as well as physical harm
is an issue of remoteness of losses.[1] In *Simmons v British Steel* plc,[2]
the House of Lords confirmed that because the defender must
take the pursuer as he finds him – the thin skull rule – where there
has been a breach of duty to prevent physical harm, damages
can be awarded for losses arising from an unforeseeable mental
disorder caused by the physical harm the victim has suffered.[3]
Where the defender is in breach of his duty to take reasonable care
to prevent damage to the pursuer's property, any mental harm
suffered by the owner from the loss or damage to his property
will be too remote unless in the circumstances mental harm to the
owner was reasonably foreseeable.[4] In *Yearworth v North Bristol
NHS* Trust,[5] the claimants were told that they might become sterile
as a result of chemotherapy. Before the treatment, they agreed that
the defendant could store samples of their semen for future use.
Owing to the negligence of the defendant, the semen thawed and
the sperms perished irretrievably. The Court held that the sperms
were the property of the men. Provided that the owner's mental
disorder was a reasonably foreseeable consequence of learning
that his sperms had been destroyed and could not be used for
fertilisation, the mental harm would not be too remote and
damages would be recoverable.[6]

The law in this area is considered to be unsatisfactory and the
Scottish Law Commission has made recommendations for reform.[7]

1   On remoteness of losses see beyond para **16.1** ff.
2   2004 SC (HL) 94.
3   *Page v Smith* [1996] AC 155 is not, of course, a remoteness case as the defender
did *not* cause the plaintiff any physical harm which led to a mental disorder.
4   *Attia v British Gas* [1988] 1 QB 304 (the owner of a house recovered damages
for mental harm suffered from witnessing her house burning down as a result
of the defendant's negligence. In the circumstances the owner's mental harm
was reasonably foreseeable and therefore not too remote).
5   [2009] EWCA Civ 37.
6   In this case the damages were likely to be small as happily the men had not
become permanently sterile as a consequence of the chemotherapy.
7   See Report on Damages for Psychiatric Injury (Scot Law Com No 196).

D. WRONGFUL LIFE, WRONGFUL BIRTH AND WRONGFUL CONCEPTION

(1) Wrongful life

4.13 It is generally accepted that a person owes a duty of care not to harm a foetus, ie a child *in utero*. Where a foetus is injured in its mother's womb, if the child is subsequently born alive, the *child* can sue the defender in delict in respect of its physical harm even though the injuries were sustained when the child was a foetus. In *McKay v Essex Area Health Authority*,[1] a mother contracted rubella (German measles) during her pregnancy. When the child was born, the baby was severely physically impaired because of the mother's illness. The mother alleged that owing to the hospital's carelessness, she had not been informed that her baby might be born with malformations. Since no tests had been carried out, the mother had been denied the opportunity of a lawful termination of her pregnancy. The Court of Appeal held that the hospital may have been in breach of a duty of care towards the *mother* which would entitle her to damages for having to bring up a physically impaired child. But the hospital did not owe a duty of care towards the *child* to allow the child's mother the opportunity to terminate the pregnancy. A foetus has no right to be born whole or not at all. This denial of the existence of a duty of care towards a foetus to terminate the pregnancy if the foetus is malformed is clearly based on principles of public policy.[2] Accordingly the law has refused to recognise wrongful life actions by denying the existence of a duty of care: again, we see the duty of care being used as a threshold device.

1   [1982] QB 1166, [1982] 2 All ER 771, CA.
2   Moreover, even if such a duty existed, the child's malformations were not caused by the careless conduct of the hospital but by the rubella; on the necessity for causation, see Chapter 6. Of course, if the hospital had caused the child's impairments, it *would* have been liable to the child, if born alive; see discussion beyond.

(2) Wrongful birth

4.14 While there will be no duty of care towards a foetus to terminate the pregnancy because it might be born with impairments, the Court of Appeal emphasised that the defendant could have been in breach of its duty towards the *mother* in not allowing her the opportunity of a termination. This is known as a wrongful birth action. In *McLelland v Greater Glasgow Health Board*,[1] an Extra Division accepted that wrongful birth actions can be pursued in Scots law. Thus, a hospital owes a duty of care to the parents of a child to provide the mother with an opportunity to terminate her pregnancy if her child is likely to be born physically or mentally disabled. While both parents can recover solatium for the distress of having a disabled child and the mother can recover solatium in respect of the pregnancy and birth, the basic economic cost of maintaining the child cannot be recovered: but any additional costs stemming from the special needs of a disabled child can be recovered.[2]

1   2002 SLT 446. See also cases discussed at 7.5 below.
2   For full discussion, see beyond para 16.6.

(3) Wrongful conception

4.15   In *McFarlane v Tayside Health Board*,[1] the pursuers sought damages for the birth of a healthy child who had been born as a result of a failed sterilisation on the father. The Lord Ordinary (Gill) admitted that the defenders owed a duty of care to the pursuers who were their patients but denied the pursuers' action of damages. Lord Gill argued that the parents had not sustained any reparable loss. He refused to classify pregnancy and labour as physical injury to the mother and he did not regard the cost of rearing the child as economic loss, since such loss was outweighed by the inestimable benefits of being the parents of a healthy child. This decision was reversed by the Second Division.[2] There it was held that the parents' right not to have a child had been infringed, ie that the unplanned conception constituted the harm (*damnum*). This was a reparable interest in modern Scots law.[3] Consequently in a wrongful conception action the mother could recover damages for pain and suffering caused by the pregnancy and birth; and both parents could recover compensation for the economic costs of bringing up the child whose birth had not been planned. Moreover, their damages would not be reduced because the mother had refused to terminate the pregnancy.

This decision was in turn appealed to the House of Lords. There it was accepted that a doctor does owe a duty of care to a man or a woman who undergoes sterilisation and if as a result of medical negligence an unplanned conception occurs then there is a breach of that duty of care. The House agreed that the mother could recover solatium for pain and suffering caused by the pregnancy and birth as well as any derivative economic loss of earnings during that period. But their Lordships held that it was contrary to contemporary values of distributive justice that the parents should be able to recover for the economic cost of maintaining a healthy and normal child.[4] The principle of non-recoverability for the cost of bringing up a normal and healthy child was reaffirmed by the House of Lords in *Rees v Darlington Memorial Hospital NHS Trust*.[5] However, a majority of their Lordships felt that an award of solatium did not adequately recognise the wrongful infringement of the mother's freedom to limit the size of her family and made her a conventional non-compensatory award of £15,000 to afford some measure of recognition of the wrongful conception of her child.

1   1997 SLT 211, OH, 2000 SC (HL) 1.
2   2000 SC (HL) 1.
3   In England, wrongful conception actions had been recognised for a long time. See, eg, *Thake v Maurice* [1986] QB 644, [1984] 2 All ER 513; *Gold v Haringey Health Authority* [1987] 2 All ER 888, CA. In *Goodwill v British Pregnancy Advisory Service* [1996] 2 All ER 161, CA, the Court of Appeal held that the duty of care did not extend to advising the future sexual partners of male patients that their vasectomy could undergo a spontaneous reversal. *Sed quaere?*
4   For further discussion on the damages issues, see para **16.6**. See also Joe Thomson 'Abandoning the Law of Delict' 2000 SLT (News) 43.
5   [2004] 1 AC 309, [2003] 4 All ER 987. *McFarlane* was followed even although the mother in *Rees* was blind.

E.   PURE ECONOMIC LOSS

(1)   The duty of care to avoid pure economic loss

4.16   Economic loss can be presented as taking one of three forms. Derivative economic losses caused in breach of a duty to guard against personal injury or property damage are recoverable, subject to rules on remoteness of losses. Secondary economic losses are those incurred as a result of negligently caused harm to somebody else's person or property. These are not recoverable.[1] Pure economic loss is the description used where the harm is purely financial and not connected to any other injury. As noted in Chapter 3, such losses were not recoverable when caused negligently before *Hedley Byrne v Heller & Partners Ltd*.[2] The reluctance to allow recovery in delict for pure economic loss is to protect the defender from potentially indeterminate liability.[3] The same consideration does not apply in the intentional delicts so economic losses caused intentionally, for example by fraud or wrongful occupation of property may be compensated.[4]

Hedley Byrne v Heller and Partners established the potential for a duty of care in the context of a careless misstatement made to and acted upon by the pursuer in reliance on the accuracy of the information. The duty could be established by an assumption of responsibility by the defender to avoid economic loss to the pursuer, this being one means of identifying a relationship, in Lord Devlin's words, 'equivalent to contract'. Hedley Byrne provided a basis for claims, for example where house purchasers had lost money having relied and acted upon negligently conducted surveys.[5]

1   See paras 4.29–4.32 below.
2   [1964] AC 465, [1963] 2 All ER 575, HL see para 3.7 above.
3   So, when a Scottish football team supporter claimed damages against FIFA and the SFA for economic loss incurred as a result of the delay to a World Cup match between Scotland and Estonia, it was held that the SFA and FIFA did not owe the pursuer a duty of care to ensure that the match took place as scheduled: *Macdonald v Fédération Internationale des Football Associations* 1999 SCLR 59, OH.
4   See, eg, *Saeed v Waheed* 1996 SLT (Ch Ct) 39, 1995 SCLR 504. The reasoning in Saeed is controversial because the Sheriff Principal (Nicholson) relied on English cases concerned with liability for pure economic loss arising from negligence. It is thought that the pursuer should have been awarded violent profits: see para 1.3 above.
5   See, eg *Martin v Bell-Ingram* 1986 SLT 575, *Smith v Eric S Bush* [1990] 1 AC 831

4.17   An attempt to rationalise the law on delictual liability for pure economic loss was made by the House of Lords in *Henderson v Merrett Syndicates Ltd*.[1] Actions for damages were brought by Lloyd's 'names' against Lloyd's members' agents and managing agents of syndicates. The 'names' alleged that they had suffered losses as a result of the negligence of the agents. Under contracts with their members' agents, the names gave the agents the exclusive right to undertake risks and reinsurance on their behalf. This was done directly through the members' agents or indirectly by the members' agents delegating the tasks to managing agents through a sub-agency contract. This can be illustrated as follows:

CONTRACT
Names ———————————————————————— Members' agents

sub-agency
agreements

Management agents

The obvious remedy was for the names to sue the members' agents for breach of contract. Unfortunately, this action was time-barred. So, an action against them and the management agents could lie only in tort/delict. The question before the House of Lords was whether the management agents and the members' agents owed a duty of care to the names. Their Lordships held that they did. Why?

Lord Goff of Chieveley was laying down a general duty of care. He maintained that a duty of care arises to prevent the plaintiff sustaining pure economic loss when the defendant has voluntarily assumed responsibility for the economic interests of the plaintiff with the knowledge that the plaintiff is relying on the defendant's expertise. This assumption of responsibility covers the provision of services as well as information; careless omissions as well as careless actions.[2]

In *Spring v Guardian Assurance plc*,[3] the House of Lords held that an employer owed a duty of care to a former employee when providing a reference for him. Because of the defendant's carelessness, the plaintiff had been unable to obtain a job. By agreeing to provide a reference, the employer had voluntarily assumed responsibility for Spring's financial interests, knowing that he would rely on the employer to prepare the reference carefully.[4] In *White v Jones*,[5] solicitors whose negligent failure to implement correctly the instructions of a testator were held to have assumed responsibility to potential beneficiaries who did not inherit as a consequence.

1   [1990] 2 AC 605, [1990] 1 All ER 568, HL.
2   The effect of Lord Goff's judgment is summarised at para **3.8** above.
3   [1995] 2 AC 296, [1994] 3 WLR 354.
4   See also *Donlon v Colonial Mutual Group (UK Holdings) Ltd* 1998 SC 244, 1997 SCLR 1088 (failure by employer to exercise reasonable care in ensuring that facts communicated to third parties were accurate). In *Durkin v DSG Retail Ltd* [2014] UKSC 21, the Supreme Court held that where Durkin asserted that his credit agreement with the defender had been rescinded, the defender was under a duty to investigate that assertion to reasonably satisfy itself that the

credit agreement remained enforceable before reporting to the credit reference
agencies that Durkin was in default: ibid per Lord Hodge at para 33.
5   [1995] 2 AC 207, [1995] 2 WLR 187 see paras 7.5–7.6 below.

4.18   Although the existence of a duty of care to prevent pure
economic loss to the plaintiff was recognised in *Hedley Byrne &
Co Ltd v Heller & Partners Ltd*,[1] in fact the plaintiff did not obtain
damages in that case. When they provided the information,
the defendants expressly stated that it was given 'without
responsibility on the part of the bank'. The House of Lords held
that this disclaimer was effective to protect the defendants from
liability. *Hedley Byrne v Heller* was an English case. The principle
has been accepted as part of Scots law.[2] In *Grant Estates Ltd v The
Royal Bank of Scotland*,[3] Lord Hodge considered[4] that the following
factors were relevant in determining whether there is a duty of
care to prevent financial loss when giving financial advice:[4]

(1)   It is not sufficient to set up a duty of care to assert the existence
       of an advisory relationship. There is a clear distinction
       between giving advice and assuming legal responsibility for
       that advice.

(2)   The absence of any written advisory agreement is a significant
       pointer against the existence of an advisory obligation.

(3)   The contractual terms the parties have agreed can define
       the parties' relationship in a way that no assumption of
       responsibility can be inferred.

(4)   The contractual delineation of responsibility and allocation
       of risk may preclude a party from founding on what has
       actually occurred if he has contracted to accept a particular
       state of affairs.

(5)   The approach in (4) extends to any retrospective agreement
       in relation to past events.

After their potential delictual liability towards purchasers of
property was established, surveyors started to insert a similar
disclaimer in their valuation reports or in the bank's contract
with the borrower/purchaser. Provided the disclaimer came
to the notice of the purchaser before the purchaser entered into
the contract of sale,[5] for a time these disclaimers were effective
to protect the surveyor from liability in delict.[6] However, where
the disclaimer is a term of the purchaser's contract with the
bank,[7] it cannot be relied on unless it satisfies the requirement
of reasonableness under the Unfair Contract Terms Act 1977

(UCTA 1977).[8] Moreover, the controls in UCTA 1977 also extend to disclaimers which are not contractual terms.[9] This includes any disclaimers in the surveyor's valuation report. Consequently, a surveyor cannot escape delictual liability by relying on a disclaimer unless it satisfies the requirement of reasonableness. In *Smith v Eric S Bush*[10] the House of Lords, applying the parallel English provisions of UCTA 1977, held that a disclaimer was not reasonable when the purchaser was of limited means and buying domestic property. If the purchaser was wealthy or the property bought was commercial, then a surveyor might be able to establish that the disclaimer was reasonable.[11] A similar view has been taken by the courts in Scotland.[12] In *Bank of Scotland v Fuller Peiser*,[13] for example, the defender provided the purchaser of a hotel with a valuation of the property. The valuation report stated that the defender accepted 'no responsibility' for anyone other than the purchaser. The pursuer relied on the report when they lent money to the purchaser. When the purchaser defaulted, the pursuer sought damages in delict from the defender. The Lord Ordinary (Eassie) held that the disclaimer satisfied the requirement of reasonableness under the UCTA 1977 because both parties were of equal bargaining power and could equally bear the loss. The disclaimer was therefore effective to prevent a duty of care from arising as the defender had *not* voluntarily assumed responsibility for the pursuer's economic interests.[14] Moreover, the defender must know that the pursuer does or will rely on his expertise. The necessity for 'concomitant reliance' by the pursuer, which is known to the defender, provides an element of mutuality between the parties which restricts the defender's potential delictual liability.[15]

Under the 'single survey' system introduced by the Housing (Scotland) Act 2006 surveyors will be liable to a purchaser incurring loss where the report is not based on an inspection of the house or has not been prepared with reasonable skill.[16]

1 [1964] AC 465, [1963] 3 WLR 101.
2 *John Kenway Ltd v Orcantic Ltd* 1979 SC 422, 1980 SLT 46, OH; *Eastern Marine Services (and Supplies) Ltd v Dickson Motors Ltd* 1981 SC 355, OH; *Twomax Ltd v Dickson, McFarlane and Robinson* 1982 SC 113, 1983 SLT 98, OH. The last decision must now be read in the light of the limitations laid down in *Caparo Industries plc v Dickman* [1990] 2 AC 605, [1990] 1 All ER 568, HL. See also *Cramaso LLP v Reidhaven Trs* [2011] CSIH 81.
3 [2012] CSOH 133.
4 Ibid at para 73.
5 If it did not come to the purchaser's notice before the contract of sale was agreed, the disclaimer was not effective: *Martin v Bell-Ingram* 1986 SC 208, 1986 SLT 575.

6 *Robbie v Graham and Sibbald* 1989 SCLR 578, 1989 SLT 870, OH.
7 *Melrose v Davidson and Robertson* 1993 SC 288, 1993 SLT 611.
8 Unfair Contract Terms Act 1977, ss 16 and 25(5). See *Melrose v Davidson and Robertson* 1993 SC 288, 1993 SLT 611. The UCTA now applies only in business-to-business contracts. Equivalent provisions applicable to consumer contracts are found in the Consumer Rights Act 2015 s 62.
9 Law Reform (Miscellaneous Provisions) (Scotland) Act 1990, s 68.
10 [1990] 1 AC 831, [1989] 2 All ER 514, HL.
11 As happened, for example, in *Omega Trust Co Ltd v Wright Son & Pepper (No 1)* [1997] 1 EGLR 120, CA.
12 *Bank of Scotland v Fuller Peiser* 2002 SLT 574. In *Smith v Eric S Bush; Harris v Wyre Forest District Council* [1990] 1 AC 831, [1989] 2 All ER 514, HL, the House of Lords also rejected the argument that the disclaimer prevented a duty of care arising in the first place. Instead, it held that the duty of care existed despite the disclaimer and that the disclaimer was therefore an exemption clause purporting to exclude liability. The matter is academic: by UCTA 1977, s 25(5) any clause which purports to prevent a duty of care from arising is also subject to the requirement of reasonableness before it can be effective. Where the disclaimer satisfies the requirement of reasonableness, no duty of care arises: *McCullagh v Lane Fox and Partners* [1996] 1 EGLR 35, (1995) *Times*, 22 December 1995, CA; *Bank of Scotland v Fuller Peiser* 2002 SLT 574.
13 2002 SLT 574. See J Thomson 'A General Duty to Prevent Pure Economic Loss' 2002 SLT (News) 225.
14 Cf *Smith v Eric S Bush; Harris v Wyre Forest District Council* [1990] 1 AC 831, [1989] 2 All ER 514, HL, discussed above.
15 It is enough that the defender knows that the pursuer will rely on his expertise; there is no need to show that the defender intended the pursuer to do so. See *Royal Bank of Scotland v Bannerman Johnstone Maclay* 2003 SC 125.
16 Housing (Scotland) Act (2006) (Consequential Provisions) Order (SI 2008/1889).

4.19 An assumption of responsibility is a sufficient, but not a necessary basis for a duty of care in respect of pure economic loss. *Caparo v Dickman*,[1] concerned an attempt by a party who was not the addressee to recover losses having relied on a misstatement made for purposes other than his own guidance or benefit. The claim failed for lack of proximity. It was left open, however, for duties to be established in circumstances where sufficient proximity existed.

Guidance on how proximity could be established in a careless misstatement case was provided in *Reeman v Department of Transport*.[2] It was held by the Court of Appeal that before a duty of care could arise by virtue of *Caparo,* the defendant's statement had to be plaintiff-specific, purpose-specific and transaction-specific.[3] Without knowledge of the party relying on a negligently given credit reference or the purpose or transaction in respect of which the reference was sought, there was no duty owed by a bank to a club which used an agent to seek credit references in order to protect client confidentiality. The club was in the position of an

undisclosed principal and the customer had defaulted on a debt
of around £800,000 for gaming chips.[4]

1   [1990] 2 AC 605 discussed at para 3.9 above.
2   [1997] 2 Lloyd's Rep 648, CA.
3   *Galoo Ltd (in liquidation) v Bright Grahame Murray* [1994] 1 WLR 1360,
     [1995] 1 All ER 16, CA; *Royal Bank of Scotland v Bannerman Johnstone Maclay*
     2003 SC 125.
4   *Playboy Club London Ltd v Banca Nazionale del Lavoro SpA* [2018] UKSC 43.

4.20   In *Customs and Excise Commissioners v Barclays Bank*,[1] after
reviewing the authorities, the House of Lords held that the
Henderson v Merrett test did not provide a 'single touchstone' for
the existence of a duty of care to prevent economic loss. While
it could be useful when there had in fact been an assumption of
responsibility, when this was not the case the court would have
to fall back on *Caparo* criteria and the 'fair, just and reasonable'
criterion. Lord Hoffmann took the view that where there had, in
fact, been an assumption of responsibility it would be fair, just
and reasonable to impose the duty *because of the relationship*: but it
could be fair, just and reasonable to impose a duty in the absence
of such an assumption. On the latter, Lord Hoffmann observed,[2]
'Questions of fairness and policy will enter into the decision and
it maybe more useful to try to identify these questions than simply
to bandy terms like "assumption of responsibility" and "fair, just
and reasonable"'. Lord Rodger was equally sceptical:[3]

> 'Part of the function of appeal courts is to try to assist judges and
> practitioners by boiling down a mass of case law and distilling
> some shorter statement of the applicable law. The temptation
> to try to identify some compact underlying rule which can
> then be applied to solve all future cases is obvious. [Counsel]
> submitted that in this area the House had identified such a rule
> in the need to find that the defendant had voluntarily assumed
> responsibility. But the unhappy experience with the rule so
> elegantly formulated by Lord Wilberforce in *Anns v Merton LBC*
> … suggests that appellate judges should follow the philosopher's
> advice to "Seek simplicity, and distrust it".'[4]

In the circumstances, the House held that the bank did not owe
Customs and Excise a duty to take reasonable care to ensure that
those of their customers who owed VAT did not remove funds from
their accounts. The irony is that the key factor why their Lordships
concluded that it would not be fair, just or reasonable to do so was
that the bank had not voluntarily assumed any responsibility for
the economic interests of the Commissioners! That said, there was
no relationship between the claimants and the bank that required

the bank to exercise care for the benefit of Customs and Excise. The bank had been served with a freezing injunction prohibiting the shifting of funds and while the claimants could expect the bank to conform to the order their reliance was not on the bank, but on the court to enforce the order.

1   [2007] 1 AC 181.
2   Ibid at para 36. His Lordship did concede that the *Henderson v Merrett* test had the merit of emphasising that a duty of care is usually generated by what the defender has decided to *do* and not by mere omissions: ibid at para 38.
3   Ibid at para 51.
4   On Lord Wilberforce's elegant formulation, see para 4.24. It is believed that the philosopher is Whitehead.

4.21 Where, however, bankers have reasonable grounds for believing that an order to transfer funds is an attempt at misappropriation, they are under a duty to the customer to refrain from executing the order.[1] In *Singularis Holdings Ltd (In Liquidation) v Daiwa Capital Markets Europe Ltd*,[2] bankers were found in breach of the duty owed to the company when its chairman and sole shareholder fraudulently misappropriated $204 million.

A solicitor who had sent three forms for the discharge of standard securities held on properties owned by her client, owed no duty to the lender who discharged the securities without further enquiry. The defender could not be said to have assumed responsibility in circumstances where it was unreasonable for the lender to have acted in reliance on her letter without having first taken steps to ensure that the secured loans had indeed been paid off.[3]

In *Seddon v DVLA*,[4] the purchaser of an AC Cobra motor car relied in part on its designation in the registration document as a historic vehicle from 1964. He paid £250,000. In fact, the car had been built to 1964 specification in 2008. DVLA had been aware that the car was advertised for sale and had marked it for investigation on the next change of keeper. When the new owner registered the car in his name, he was allocated a Q plate which reduced the value to £100,000. Unsurprisingly, the claim failed. There was no relationship between the owner and DVLA and therefore no proximity. There was, moreover, no negligence on the part of the DVLA who were acting properly in exercise of their statutory powers.

Where a party is induced to enter a contract by a misrepresentation by the seller, the contract may be avoided and, where the misrepresentation is made fraudulently or negligently, that is in breach of a duty to provide accurate information, the buyer may recover damages. Having misrepresented the number of grouse available to be shot on a grouse moor, the lessor was held to have assumed responsibility for the accuracy of his statement to the prospective lessee. Liability was not affected by the fact that the lease was taken by a company incorporated for that purpose by the pursuer whereas the misrepresentation had been made to him in his individual capacity. The Supreme Court held that the company could rely on the misrepresentation because it had a continuing effect from the time it was made until the conclusion of the lease.[5]

1   *Barclays Bank Plc v Quincecare Ltd* [1992] 4 All ER 363.
2   [2019] UKSC 50, [2020] AC 1189.
3   *Steel v NRAM Ltd* [2018] UKSC 13, 2018 SC (UKSC) 141. See G Dick, 'A Reappraisal of Solicitors' Liabilities to Opposing Parties and the (Further) Retreat from Caparo', 2019 23 *Edin LR* 247.
4   [2019] EWCA Civ 14, [2019] 1 WLR 4593.
5   *Cramasco LLP v Viscount Reidhaven's Trustees* [2014] UKSC 9, 2014 SC (UKSC) 121.

(2) Liability arising from defective performance of a contract

4.22   A enters a contract with B. In order to fulfil his contract with A, B enters into a contract with C. C's performance of his contract with B is carried out carelessly. As a result, A suffers pure economic loss. The facts can be represented as follows:

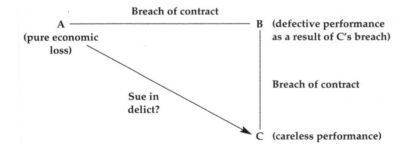

A's obvious remedy is to sue B for breach of contract. But if this is not possible (eg, if there is an exemption clause in A's contract with B) or not desirable (eg, if B is bankrupt) can A sue C in delict?

If C's careless performance of his contract with B had caused physical harm to A or physical damage to A's property, C would owe A a duty of care provided A's injury or the damage to A's property was reasonably foreseeable: ie, the *Donoghue v Stevenson* neighbourhood principle would apply.[1] Since A suffers only pure economic loss, reasonable foreseeability of such loss is not sufficient to give rise to a duty of care. But A, B and C are connected by a series of contracts. If C had broken his contract with B with the intention of harming A, A can sue C in *delict* for intentional infliction of harm by unlawful means and can recover for pure economic loss.[2] In this case, however, C has not broken his contract with B in order to harm A. Instead, C has by his *careless* conduct broken his contract with B with the result that B's performance of his contract with A is defective, causing A economic loss. In these circumstances, does C owe a duty of care to A not to perform his contract with B in a careless manner if it will cause A economic loss to do so?

In *Junior Books Ltd v Veitchi Co Ltd*,[3] the House of Lords held that such a duty of care could exist. The pursuers entered into a contract with Ogilvie (Builders) Ltd (the main contractor) for the construction of a factory. The pursuers' architects nominated Veitchi, a floor specialist, to lay a floor in the factory. In other words, Veitchi was a nominated sub-contractor. However, Veitchi's contract to lay the floor was with the main contractor, not Junior Books. The floor laid was seriously defective and had to be replaced by the pursuers. There was no averment that the floor laid was dangerous so as to be likely to cause physical harm to any persons in the factory or any damage to the pursuers' property. The pursuers sought damages from the defenders for the cost of replacing the floor. This complex factual situation can be illustrated as follows:

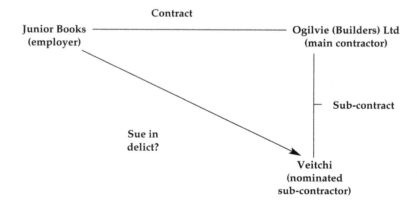

Although nominated by Junior Books' architect, Veitchi had no contractual relationship with Junior Books. Although Junior Books could have sued the main contractor for breach of contract, they chose not to do so. Their only remedy against Veitchi, therefore, lay in delict. Since there was no danger of any physical harm to persons in the factory or damage to the pursuer's property, the case fell outside the neighbourhood principle of reasonable foreseeability of harm laid down in *Donoghue v Stevenson*.[4] In other words, the case was concerned with the recovery of pure economic loss, ie the cost of replacing the defective floor. Nevertheless, the House of Lords held[5] that in the circumstances there was sufficient proximity between the parties for a duty of care to arise: the defenders were under a duty to prevent loss to the pursuers as a result of the defenders' careless performance of their contract with Ogilvie (Builders) Ltd.

Lord Roskill identified eight factors from which the requisite proximity for a duty of care could be inferred:[6]

'(1) The appellants [Veitchi] were nominated sub-contractors. (2) The appellants were specialists in flooring. (3) The appellants knew what products were required by the respondents [Junior Books] and their main contractors and specialised in the production of those products. (4) The appellants alone were responsible for the composition and construction of the flooring. (5) The respondents relied upon the appellants' skill and experience. (6) The appellants as nominated sub-contractors must have known that the respondents relied upon their skill and experience. (7) The relationship between the parties was as close as it could be, short of actual privity of contract. (8) The appellants must be taken to have known that if they did the work negligently (as it must be assumed that they did) the resulting defects would at some time require remedying by the respondents expending money upon the remedial measures as a consequence of which the respondents would suffer financial or economic loss.'

1   *Donoghue v Stevenson* 1932 SC (HL) 31, 1932 SLT 317.
2   On the delict, see paras 2.4– 2.5 above.
3   1982 SC (HL) 244, 1982 SLT 492.
4   Lord Keith of Kinkel took the view (1982 SC (HL) 244 at 267) that if such a danger was present, the neighbourhood principle in *Donoghue* was wide enough to cover the cost of averting such a danger. This is doubtful after the decision of the House of Lords in *Murphy v Brentwood District Council* [1991] 1 AC 398, [1990] 2 All ER 908, HL, discussed at para 4.27 below.
5   Lords Fraser of Tullybelton, Russell of Killowen, Keith of Kinkel and Roskill; Lord Brandon dissented.
6   *Junior Books Ltd v Veitchi Co Ltd* 1982 SC (HL) 244 at 277.

4.23   Several points should be noted. First, the defender and the pursuer are connected by a series of contracts which are subsisting at the time of the defenders' careless acts (ie the installation of the defective floor). Second, Veitchi had been nominated by the pursuers' architect. This is important because as a nominated sub-contractor, Veitchi must have known the identity of the employer, Junior Books, who was contracting with the main contractor, Ogilvie (Builders) Ltd. Third, because Veitchi knew that Junior Books required their services, knew that Junior Books relied upon their expertise, and knew that careless performance of their contract would require the floor to be repaired by Junior Books, Veitchi must have *known* that careless performance by them of their contract with Ogilvie (Builders) Ltd would cause *economic* loss to the pursuer.

Thus, for a *Junior Books* duty of care to arise, the pursuer A and defender C must be connected by a series of contracts: A–B–C.[1] In addition to reasonable foreseeability of loss as a result of his careless acts, C must know the identity of the pursuer A, know that A has a contract with B and know that A will suffer economic loss as a result of C's careless performance of his contract with B, since this will, in turn, render defective B's performance of his contract with A. In establishing this degree of knowledge, the fact that C is a nominated sub-contractor is important but not necessary.[2] A's reliance on C's expertise etc is important. It provides *evidence* that C knows that his careless performance will cause A economic loss. The crucial point is that C must know that the careless performance of his contract with B will cause A economic loss as a result of B's consequent defective performance of his contract with A.[3]

It is the present writer's submission that *Junior Books* liability could be seen as an extension of the economic delict of intentional infliction of harm by unlawful means. If in the above example, C broke his contract with B with the result that B renders defective performance of his contract with A, it is long settled that A can sue C in delict for pure economic loss if C broke his contract with B *with the intention* of harming A. *Junior Books* goes a step further by providing that A can sue C in delict where C carelessly performs his contract with B with the result that B renders defective performance of his contract with A, provided C *knew* that his careless performance of his contract with B would cause economic loss to A, ie C owes a duty of care to A not to perform his contract with B in a careless manner.

1   *Comex Houlder Diving Ltd v Colne Fishing Co Ltd (No 2)* 1992 SLT 89, OH; *Scott Lithgow Ltd v GEC Electrical Products Ltd* 1989 SC 412, 1992 SLT 244, OH; *Strathford East Kilbride Ltd v HLM Design Ltd* 1999 SLT 121.
2   In *Scott Lithgow Ltd v GEC Electrical Products Ltd* 1989 SC 412, 1992 SLT 244, OH, the Lord Ordinary (Clyde) thought at 250 ff that it would be enough if the defender had been approved by the pursuer.
3   On the other hand, if A's reliance on C's expertise is held to be necessary and given that C must know that A will suffer economic loss by C's careless performance of the contract, it could be argued that *Junior Books* liability is simply an example of the general *Henderson v Merrett* duty of care to prevent relational economic loss.

4.24   Read this way, the duty of care held to exist in *Junior Books* is kept within the narrowest of limits. First, it only applies where the parties are connected by contracts which are existing at the time of the defender's careless acts. In *D & F Estates Ltd v Church Commissioners for England*,[1] for example, the Church Commissioners owned a block of flats built by the main contractors. The main contractors sub-contracted the plaster work to sub-contractors. The plaster was defective but was not a source of danger. *After* the flats were built, a flat was leased to the plaintiffs. The plaintiffs sued *inter alios* the main contractors in delict for the cost of repairing the plaster work. The House of Lords held that the main contractors and the sub-contractors were not under a duty of care to prevent economic loss to the plaintiffs as a result of the defective plaster.[2] In the present writer's view, there was also no possibility of a *Junior Books* duty of care in this case because there was no contractual nexus between the plaintiffs and the main contractor or sub-contractor at the time of the careless act, as illustrated below.

Second, even if there is an existing contractual nexus, no *Junior Books* duty of care will arise unless the defender knows the identity of the pursuer; this will therefore prevent such a duty of care arising in most cases involving mass production. For example, if A manufactures components for B who uses them to produce products which he sells to C, a distributor, who sells them to X, Y and Z etc, A does not owe a *Junior Books* duty of care to X, Y or Z to prevent *economic loss*[3] due to A's careless performance of his contract with B in supplying B with defective components. This is because A will generally not know of the contracts between C and X, Y and Z:

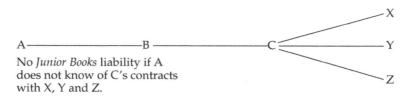

A————————————B ————————————C
No *Junior Books* liability if A
does not know of C's contracts
with X, Y and Z.

Third, even if there is an existing contractual nexus and the defender knows the identity of the pursuer, the terms of the contracts between the parties, for example exemption or indemnity clauses, may indicate that the parties intended to exclude potential liability in delict.[4] In those circumstances, the court is unlikely to find the existence of a *Junior Books* duty of care. Finally, the defender must anticipate loss to the particular pursuer as a result of the defender's defective performance.[5]

The limitations which are inherent in the *Junior Books* duty of care are therefore sufficient to keep potential liability for pure economic loss within relatively narrow parameters. Once again, we see the duty of care operating as a threshold device.

1   [1989] AC 177, [1988] 2 All ER 992, HL. See also *Strathford East Kilbride Ltd v HLM Design Ltd* 1999 SLT 121.

2   For discussion of the absence of a duty of care to prevent economic loss arising from a defective building, see para 4.27 ff below.

3   Of course, A may owe a *Donoghue v Stevenson* duty of care to X, Y and Z to prevent them suffering physical injury or damage to their property as a result of A's careless manufacture of the components.

4   Cf *British Telecommunications plc v James Thomson & Sons (Engineering) Ltd* 1999 SC (HL) 9 when the contractual relationships between the parties were taken into account to determine whether or not there was a duty of care on the defender to prevent the pursuer sustaining damage to his property.

5   *Simaan General Contracting Co v Pilkington Glass Ltd (No 2)* [1988] QB 758, [1988] 1 All ER 791, CA.

4.25   If it is accepted that the *Junior Books* duty of care is simply an extension of the wrong of intentional infliction of harm by unlawful means so as to trigger liability as a result of the defender's careless conduct as well as conduct intended to harm the pursuer, then it is thought that there is a future for *Junior Books* liability. Nevertheless, *Junior Books Ltd v Veitchi Co Ltd*[1] has been consistently distinguished in cases south of the border. In *D & F Estates Ltd v Church Commissioners for England*,[2] Lord Bridge opined[3] of *Junior Books*:

> 'The consensus of judicial opinion, with which I concur, seems to be that the decision of the majority is so far dependent on the unique, albeit non-contractual, relationship between the pursuer and the defender in that case and the unique scope of the duty of care owed by the defender to the pursuer arising from that relationship that the decision cannot be regarded as laying down any principle of general application in the law of tort or delict.'

The reason for this scepticism is that *Junior Books* has *not* been regarded as a case which is only concerned with defective performance of the pursuer's existing contracts (ie recovery of relational economic loss). Instead, it has been read as laying down potential liability for economic loss arising from the careless manufacture of a defective product which is not dangerous in the sense of causing physical harm to the pursuer or damage to her property (ie non-relational economic loss). If this were the case, then there would, indeed, be cause for concern. But if analysed as above, *Junior Books* liability does not have this potential. Within its relatively narrow sphere, *Junior Books* is both an important and principled decision. That said, in *Realstone v J & E Shepherd* the Lord Ordinary (Hodge) took the view that 'The risk of introducing uncertainty into complex commercial transactions justifies the retreat from *Junior Books*. That retreat having occurred, I consider that *Junior Books* does not provide a basis for the existence of an established duty of care.'[4]

1   1982 SC (HL) 244, 1982 SLT 492.
2   [1989] AC 177, [1988] 2 All ER 992, HL.
3   [1988] 2 All ER 992 at 1003.
4   [2008] CSOH 31 at para 22. *Junior Books* has, however, been approved by the Court of Appeal in Singapore! See *RSP Architects Planners and Engineers v Ocean Front Pte Ltd* (1998) 14 Const LJ 139, CA (Sing).

(3) Liability arising from defective products and buildings

4.26   A owes a duty of care to B when it is reasonably foreseeable that B will sustain physical harm or physical damage to his property as a result of A's careless conduct. In *Donoghue v Stevenson*[1] it was held that the manufacturer of a product owed a duty of care to the ultimate consumer to prevent the consumer suffering personal harm or physical damage to his property as a result of a defect in the product caused by the manufacturer's carelessness. The consumer is entitled to damages not only for pain and suffering but also for economic loss which *derives* from his personal injuries or the damage to his property, ie derivative economic loss.

There is an important limitation on the scope of *Donoghue v Stevenson* liability. The duty of care extends only to the pursuer's physical injuries or damage to his property which was caused by the defective product. The damage must be done to property other than the defective product itself. For example, if a defective vacuum cleaner explodes and burns the pursuer or burns the pursuer's carpet there is *Donoghue v Stevenson* liability. But if the defective vacuum simply does not work or it explodes and does not physically harm the pursuer or does not damage any other property of the pursuer there is no *Donoghue v Stevenson* liability. Why? In these circumstances, the pursuer has sustained only *pure* economic loss, ie the cost of repairing the vacuum cleaner or the difference in value between a defective and a non-defective cleaner. The courts have consistently refused to allow the pursuer to recover compensation in *delict* for such losses. Instead, the pursuer must resort to the law of contract to obtain compensation:

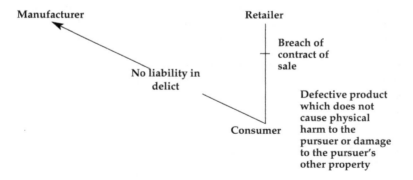

The consumer cannot sue the manufacturer in delict because the consumer has suffered only pure economic loss. The consumer must sue the retailer for *breach of contract* to recover any loss suffered as a result of the product being defective. If the ultimate consumer does not have a contract with the retailer, for example where the defective product was a gift from a third party, the consumer prima facie has no remedy. But the third party could assign the rights under *his* contract with the retailer to the consumer thus enabling the consumer to recover damages for breach of contract.

It should also be noticed that there will generally be no possibility of *Junior Books* liability in this situation. This is for two reasons: (1) no contractual chain or nexus exists between the manufacturer and the consumer at the time of the careless act since the consumer will only enter into a contract with the retailer *after* the product has been manufactured; and (2) the manufacturer will not know the identity of the consumer.[2] Similarly, there is no *Henderson v Merrett* duty of care[3] to prevent relational economic loss because the defender manufacturer does not voluntarily assume responsibility for the ultimate consumer's financial interests and there is no concomitant reliance on the consumer's part.

This principle of non-liability for economic loss also applies to the provision of services. In *D & F Estates Ltd v Church Commissioners for England*[4] the plaintiffs incurred expense in repairing defective plasterwork. The defective plasterwork was not a danger to the plaintiffs' person or property. The House of Lords held that the plaintiffs could not sue the defendants who were responsible for the defective plasterwork in *delict* because they had only suffered pure economic loss, ie the cost of repair. The plaintiffs' only remedy would be in contract.

1   1932 SC (HL) 31, 1932 SLT 317.
2   It might, of course, be different in both respects if the manufacturer were supplying a product specifically designed for the consumer.
3   *Henderson v Merrett Syndicates Ltd* [1995] 2 AC 145, [1994] 3 All ER 506, HL.
4   [1989] AC 177, [1988] 2 All ER 992, HL. There was no *Junior Books* liability in this case. See also *Strathford East Kilbride Ltd v HLM Design Ltd* 1999 SLT 121.

4.27   At one time there appeared to be an exception in respect of defective buildings. Local authorities are under a duty to ensure that buildings conform to building regulations and bye-laws: this is done by a local authority engineer approving the plans and the design of the proposed building. In *Anns v Merton London Borough Council*[1] the defendants approved the design of the foundations of a building. After it was built, the foundations were discovered to be defective. The House of Lords held that the local authority owed the owner[2] of the house a duty of care in this situation and that damages could include the cost of repair. It was also decided that the builder owed a similar duty of care to the owner of the property. The fact that the plaintiff had only suffered pure economic loss appeared to be irrelevant. The concept of the duty of care was clearly being used as a threshold device significantly to extend the parameters of delictual liability for pure economic loss. In a famous passage, Lord Wilberforce explained:[3]

> 'The position has now been reached that in order to establish that a duty of care arises in a particular situation, it is not necessary to bring the facts of that situation within those of previous situations in which a duty of care has been held to exist. Rather the question has to be approached in two stages. First one has to ask whether, as between the alleged wrongdoer and the person who has suffered damage there is a sufficient relationship of proximity or neighbourhood such that, in the reasonable contemplation of the former, carelessness on his part may be likely to cause damage to the latter, in which case a prima facie duty of care arises. Secondly, if the first question is answered affirmatively, it is necessary to consider whether there are any considerations which ought to negative, or to reduce or limit the scope of the duty or the class of person to whom it is owed or the damages to which a breach of it may give rise.'

Applying these principles, Lord Wilberforce held that a local authority owed a duty of care to the owner of a building which was subject to latent defects in construction when the plans had been inspected and approved by the local authority. The fact that the owner may suffer only pure economic loss was not sufficient to deny the existence of the duty on policy grounds since the class of potential plaintiffs was restricted to the owners or lessees of the property.

This was to prove to be the high-water mark of the extension of the parameters of delictual liability for defective buildings. The courts thereafter refused to use Lord Wilberforce's two-stage test further to extend the scope of liability. At length, *Anns* itself came to be doubted and was ultimately overruled in *Murphy v Brentwood District Council*.[4] In this case, a builder laid foundations of a house in accordance with designs approved by the local authority. The foundations proved to be defective. The owner could not afford the £45,000 required for repairs; instead, he sold the house for £35,000 less than its market value would have been if the foundations had been sound. The owner sued the local authority for the loss of the value of the house. The House of Lords held that *Anns* was wrongly decided. Neither a local authority nor a builder owes the owner of a house a duty of care in respect of pure economic loss arising from the defective construction of the property; and pure economic loss includes the cost of repairs or the loss of the property's value.

1 [1978] AC 728, [1977] 2 All ER 492, HL.
2 Technically, the plaintiff in this case was a lessee of the property.
3 [1978] AC 728 at 751–752.
4 [1991] 1 AC 398, [1990] 2 All ER 908, HL. The House of Lords doubted the value of Lord Wilberforce's two-stage test for the existence of a duty of care. Instead, a duty should only be imposed by analogy with earlier precedents, ie it is an incremental process. In this respect, *Murphy* has been followed in Scotland. '[I]n determining the existence and scope of a duty of care in a context in which a claim is made for economic loss, the court must have particular regard to the traditional categorisation of situations in which duties may or may not have been recognised in particular circumstances': *Nordic Oil Services Ltd v Berman* 1993 SLT 1164 at 1171 per the Lord Ordinary (Osborne). *Murphy* has not been followed in Australia or New Zealand: see *Bryan v Maloney* (1995) 11 Const LJ 274, HC (Aus); *Invercargill City Council v Hamlin* [1996] AC 624, [1996] 1 All ER 756, PC.

4.28 The House of Lords was also sceptical of what is known as the 'complex structure' doctrine. It can be argued that the foundations should be regarded as separate from the rest of the house. If they are defective and cause physical damage to another part of the house, for example by cracks in the walls, this is damage to 'other' property and falls within the *Donoghue v Stevenson* duty of care. The view was taken that this approach is unrealistic:[1]

> 'The reality is that the structural elements in any building form a single indivisible unit of which the different parts are essentially interdependent. To the extent that there is any defect in one part of the structure it must to a greater or lesser degree necessarily affect all other parts of the structure. Therefore any defect in the structure is a defect in the quality of the whole and it is quite artificial, in order to impose a legal liability which the law would not otherwise impose, to treat a defect in an integral structure, so far as it weakens the structure, as a dangerous defect liable to cause damage to "other property".'

But where a distinct item, such as a central heating boiler, is incorporated into the structure of a building there can be *Donoghue v Stevenson* liability if, as a result of a defect, it causes damage to the house. The owner in these circumstances could sue the manufacturer of the boiler for physical damage to his 'other' property, ie his house.

It is important to examine the implications of *Murphy* for purchasers of heritable property. Consider the following example. A, a company, enters into a contract with B to build a block of flats. After the flats are completed, A sells the flats to various purchasers including C. After a few years, cracks appear in C's flat. It is discovered that the foundations are unsound and that it will cost approximately £20,000 to have them repaired:

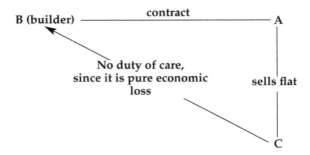

As a result of *Murphy*, C has no delictual remedy against B because C has suffered only pure economic loss, ie B does not owe C a duty of care in respect of the cost of repairs.[2] Although there is a contractual relationship between A and C, this will not help C because a seller of a flat (land) does not warrant the quality of the buildings sold. Moreover, B does not owe C a *Junior Books* duty of care because there is no contractual nexus between B and C at the time of the careless act since C only purchases the property *after* it is built.[3] Even if C had an option from A to purchase a flat while it was being built, a *Junior Books* duty of care will not arise unless B knows the identity of the purchaser, C. Similarly, there is no *Henderson v Merrett* duty of care to prevent relational economic loss because there is no voluntary assumption of responsibility and concomitant reliance.

Because of the absence of a delictual claim against B or a contractual claim against A, in order to protect his interests C should obtain an independent survey *before* purchasing the property. If, as a result of the surveyor's carelessness, the defects are not discovered, C can sue the surveyor for breach of contract. As we have seen,[4] even if C relied upon a survey carried out on behalf of C's bank for the purpose of obtaining a loan, C may be able to sue the surveyor in delict on the ground of careless misrepresentation where damages for pure economic loss are recoverable.

1   *Murphy v Brentwood District Council* [1990] 2 All ER 908 at 928 per Lord Bridge.
2   If C was physically injured or any property of C's other than the house was damaged, C can sue B in delict as B owes C a duty of care under the *Donoghue v Stevenson* neighbourhood principle.
3   *Strathford East Kilbride Ltd v HLM Design Ltd* 1999 SLT 121.
4   See para 4.18 above.

(4) Non-liability for secondary economic loss

4.29   We have been considering the situation where the defender has directly caused pure economic loss to the pursuer. However, there is a second situation where pure economic loss can arise. This is where the defender has caused physical harm to A or A's property and as a result B suffers pure economic loss. This will most often arise where B has a contract with A and as a consequence of the defender's wrongful conduct A can no longer perform the contract or the contract becomes less profitable. This is known as secondary economic loss.

In *Reavis v Clan Line Steamers Ltd*,[1] Mrs Reavis and her orchestra were involved in a collision at sea which was caused, *inter alia*, by the fault of the defender, the owner of the ship in which they were sailing. Some members of the orchestra drowned, while others were injured and the orchestra had to be disbanded. Mrs Reavis claimed that the services of the players had been secured by contracts of employment and she sought damages from the defender for the loss of profits she had sustained as a result of having to disband the orchestra. The court held that she was not entitled to recover. An employer is not entitled to sue in delict in respect of secondary economic loss sustained as a result of the death or personal injury of an employee caused by the negligence of a third party. In other words, the defender did not owe Mrs Reavis a duty of care to prevent her sustaining pure economic loss as a result of her employees being no longer able to perform their contracts of employment with her. If Mrs Reavis had been physically harmed, she could, of course, recover for derivative economic loss arising from her *own* injuries – but she could not sue in respect of the death or injury of her employees. (The injured employees and the families of the deceased employees, would, of course, have separate claims in delict against the defender.)

Accordingly, where a person is physically harmed or property is damaged, prima facie it is only the injured person or the owner of the property who has title to sue. Third parties who suffer economic loss as a result of the personal injuries or damage to the property are not entitled to sue for secondary economic loss because the defender does not owe them a duty of care. For example, in *Dynamco Ltd v Holland and Hannen and Cubitts (Scotland) Ltd*,[2] the defender's excavator damaged an underground electric supply cable owned by the South of Scotland Electricity Board. As a result, there was a power cut at the pursuer's factory which lasted for 15½ hours. The pursuer sued for the loss of profits while the factory was closed. The court held that although the defender owed a duty of care to the electricity board not to damage its property, ie the cable, the defender did not owe a duty to the pursuer in respect of secondary economic loss, even though such loss was reasonably foreseeable. In *Coleridge v Miller Construction Ltd*,[3] the power cut physically damaged the glass that the pursuer manufactured in his factory. The Lord Ordinary (MacLean) held that the test for the existence of a duty of care should be the same whether or not the pursuer suffered physical damage to his property or pure economic loss. In the absence of averments that the defender knew that the pursuer required a continuous supply of electricity, it was not reasonably foreseeable that the pursuer would suffer damage to his products if an electric cable were cut. Moreover, even if damage had been reasonably foreseeable it was not fair, just and reasonable to impose a duty of care in these circumstances because the pursuer should have insurance to cover any losses arising from power cuts howsoever caused. Thus, secondary physical damage is irrecoverable, as well as secondary economic loss.[4]

1   1925 SC 725, 1925 SLT 386, OH.
2   1971 SC 257, 1972 SLT 38.
3   1997 SLT 485, OH.
4   In *Skerries Salmon Ltd v The Braer Corpn* 1999 SLT 1196, the Lord Ordinary (Gill) held that the defender did not owe the pursuers a duty of care to prevent them from having to sell their salmon at low prices. The pursuers alleged that this was caused by a loss of public confidence in the quality of Shetland salmon after the *Braer* oil tanker had run aground. In the absence of any evidence that the pursuers' fish had been contaminated with oil, this was a case of secondary economic loss and no duty was owed. In *Landcatch Ltd v The Braer Corpn; Landcatch Ltd v International Oil Pollution Compensation Fund* 1999 SLT 1208 the pursuers were unable to supply fish farmers in Shetland with salmon smolt because salmon farming had been banned in designated areas contaminated by oil from the *Braer*. There were no contracts subsisting between the fish farmers and the pursuers at the time. This was held to be secondary economic loss and no duty of care arose.

4.30   In the important case of *Nacap Ltd v Moffat Plant Ltd*,[1] the pursuers entered into a contract with British Gas to lay a pipeline owned by British Gas in the North Sea. During the work, the defenders damaged the pipeline. As a result, Nacap were unable to complete the work in the time agreed in their contract with British Gas and consequently suffered economic loss. The Inner House held that the pursuers had no title to sue because they were not the owners of the pipeline. In other words, they could not sue in delict for the secondary economic loss they had sustained as a result of the damage to property owned by a third party, ie British Gas.

This approach has been followed in England. In *Candlewood Navigation Corpn Ltd v Mitsui OSK Lines Ltd, The Mineral Transporter*[2] the plaintiffs time-chartered a vessel from the owners of the ship. The vessel was damaged by the defendants. The Privy Council held that the plaintiffs could not recover damages for the hire charges they had to continue to pay and the loss of profits they had incurred while the ship underwent repairs. The defendants did not owe a duty of care to the plaintiffs in respect of the secondary economic loss they had suffered as a result of their contract with the owners becoming less profitable:

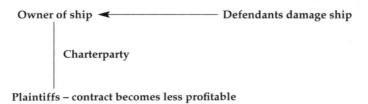

In this and the previous cases, a *Junior Books* duty of care does not arise because there is no contractual nexus between the parties. Even if in *Dynamco Ltd v Holland and Hannen and Cubitts (Scotland) Ltd*,[3] the defender had been engaged on a contract with the electricity board, who had, of course, a contract with its customer, Dynamco, *Junior Books* liability would still not have arisen because the defender would not have known the identity of the pursuer. Similarly, no *Henderson v Merrett* duty of care arises because in none of these cases did the defender voluntarily assume responsibility for the financial interests of the pursuers.

1 1987 SLT 221, reversing 1986 SLT 326.
2 [1986] AC 1, [1985] 2 All ER 935, PC.
3 1971 SC 257, 1972 SLT 38.

4.31 Nevertheless, in other circumstances it is thought that there could be sufficient proximity between the parties for a *Junior Books* or *Henderson v Merrett* duty to arise. In *Leigh and Sillavan Ltd v Aliakmon Shipping Co Ltd, The Aliakmon*,[1] the plaintiff (the buyers) entered into a cost and freight (c & f) contract for the purchase of steel coils. Under a c & f contract the seller arranges for the shipping of the goods and obtains a bill of lading from the shipper. The bill of lading is the contract of carriage of the goods. The buyer becomes the owner of the goods when the bill of lading is indorsed by the seller and delivered to the buyer against payment by the buyer of the price. On indorsement, the buyer 'steps into the shoes' of the seller in relation to the bill of lading issued by the shipper. Accordingly, if the goods are damaged in transit, the buyer can sue the shipper for breach of contract. This did not happen in this case because the c & f contract was varied by the parties with the effect that the seller remained owner even though the risk of damage to the goods passed to the buyers. The bill of lading was not indorsed, so that the buyers did not have title to sue the shippers for breach of contract. When they eventually became the owners of the goods, the plaintiff attempted to sue the shippers in delict. The complex facts can be shown thus:

Because the buyers assumed the risk under the contract of sale, they had no right to sue the seller for breach of contract when the goods were damaged. As a result of the variation, the buyers could not use the usual remedy in a c & f situation of suing the shipper for breach of contract. The House of Lords held that the buyers could not sue the shipper in delict because they were not the owners of the goods at the time the goods were damaged. *Junior Books Ltd v Veitchi & Co Ltd*[2] was distinguished on the ground that the pursuer in that case was the owner of the floor when it was carelessly laid.[3]

In the *Aliakmon* case,[4] an attempt was made to circumvent the principle of non-recovery in delict for secondary economic loss by invoking the doctrine of 'transferred loss'. In the Court of Appeal, Goff LJ as he then was formulated the doctrine thus:[5]

'Where A owes a duty of care in tort [delict] not to cause physical damage to B's property, and commits a breach of that duty in circumstances in which the loss of or physical damage to property will ordinarily fall on B but (as is reasonably foreseeable by A) such loss or damage, by reason of a contractual relationship falls on C, then C will be entitled, subject to the terms of any contract restricting A's liability to B, to bring an action in tort against A in respect of such loss or damage to the extent that it falls on him, C.'

This would have enabled the plaintiff to succeed in *Aliakmon* provided such loss was reasonably foreseeable by the defendant; it is submitted that it would have been reasonably foreseeable as in a normal c & f contract the buyer would have had an action to sue on the bill of lading if the goods were damaged in transit. Similarly, in *Nacap Ltd v Moffat Plant Ltd*[6] the pursuer could have relied on this doctrine, although it might have been more difficult to establish that the loss suffered as a result of the contract with British Gas was reasonably foreseeable.[7] However, the introduction of the principle of transferred loss into English law was vigorously rejected when the *Aliakmon* case was appealed to the House of Lords.[8] It is thought that, after *Nacap,* the principle would not fare any better north of the border.

1   [1986] AC 785, [1986] 2 All ER 145, HL, affirming [1985] 2 All ER 44, CA. The contractual position has now been overtaken by the Carriage of Goods by Sea Act 1992 which makes it easier for the buyer who undertakes the risk to sue the shipper for breach of contract.
2   1982 SC (HL) 244, 1982 SLT 492.
3   For similar reasons, it would be unlikely that the shipper had voluntarily assumed responsibility for the financial interests of the buyers. But if in *Reavis v Clan Line Steamers Ltd* 1925 SC 725, 1925 SLT 386, OH, Mrs Reavis had been killed or injured with the result that her employees suffered economic loss, it is submitted that there would now be a possibility of their recovering damages for economic loss under *Junior Books* if the defender, who had a contract of carriage with Mrs Reavis, had known the identity of her employees and the existence of the contracts of employment.
4   See *Leigh and Sillavan Ltd v Aliakmon Shipping Co Ltd, The Aliakmon* [1986] AC 785, [1986] 2 All ER 145, HL, affirming [1985] 2 All ER 44, CA.
5   [1985] 2 All ER 44 at 77.
6   1987 SLT 221, discussed at para 4.27 above.
7   Goff LJ expressly stated ([1985] 2 All ER 44 at 77) that the doctrine would not have helped the plaintiff in *Candlewood Navigation Corpn Ltd v Mitsui OSK Lines Ltd, The Mineral Transporter* [1986] AC 1, [1985] 2 All ER 935, PC; the present writer would have thought that loss to a time-charterer from a collision would be reasonably foreseeable by a shipowner: see para 4.30 above.
8   [1986] 2 All ER 145 at 157 per Lord Brandon.

4.32   It therefore appears that the courts have set their face against recovery in delict for secondary economic loss by restricting title to sue to the person who has been physically harmed or the owner of the damaged property. But where a person has a possessory title to the property, he may be able to sue. For example, if A pledges his watch worth £500 to B in return for a loan of £300, B, the pledgee, has a possessory title to the watch. If the watch is damaged by C, B can sue C in delict to the extent of his interest in the watch, ie up to £300.

Cases of possessory title apart, it is clear from *Nacap* that merely to have lawful possession of the property is not sufficient; the pursuers in that case had lawful possession of the pipeline which they were laying but title to sue in delict was denied. In *North Scottish Helicopters Ltd v United Technologies Corpn Inc (No 2)*,[1] however, the pursuers were allowed to sue in respect of economic loss sustained as a result of damage to a helicopter which they leased but did not own. Under the lease agreement with the owner, a finance company, the second pursuer had to maintain the helicopter, indemnify the finance company if the helicopter was damaged or destroyed and replace or repair the helicopter at the pursuer's expense. It was agreed with the finance company that the helicopter could be flown by the first pursuer, a subsidiary company of the second pursuer. The finance company had no obligation to provide a replacement if the helicopter was not operational. Owing to a fault in the manufacturing process, the helicopter went on fire and was destroyed. The pursuers sought damages for the economic loss sustained in indemnifying the finance company in terms of the lease and loss of profits sustained due to the absence of a helicopter. The complex facts can be shown thus:

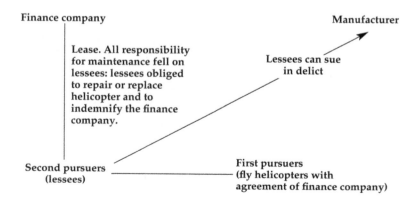

The Lord Ordinary (Davidson) held that because of the onerous terms of the lease and the fact that the finance company had agreed that the helicopter could be flown by the first pursuers, the second pursuers were 'owners' of the helicopter as a matter of substance even if, technically, the finance company was the owner as a matter of law. In other words, the pursuers had far more than lawful possession of the helicopter and this gave them title to sue despite not being the legal owner of the property. Thus, it appears that there can be exceptional circumstances when a non-owner has title to sue.

It was assumed in this case that the manufacturer owed a duty of care to the pursuer. It should be noticed, however, that the destruction of the helicopter was pure economic loss: the defective product did not cause physical harm to the pursuers or damage to any other property owned by the pursuers – it only destroyed itself! The manufacturer's duty of care could therefore not have arisen by virtue of the *Donoghue v Stevenson* neighbourhood principle. Nor could there be a *Junior Books* duty of care[2] owing to the absence of a contractual nexus between the pursuer and defender at the time of the fault in the manufacturing process. The action could therefore have been defended on the ground that the defender did not owe a duty of care to prevent pure economic loss arising to the pursuers and, indeed, the finance company, rather than the absence of the pursuers' title to sue for secondary economic loss.

In the cases we have been discussing, the only remedy available to a person who has sustained secondary economic loss is to obtain an assignation of the owner's rights against the defender. In Scots law, delictual rights as well as contractual rights can be assigned. For example, in *Nacap Ltd v Moffat Plant Ltd*,[3] British Gas could have assigned to the pursuer its rights as owner of the pipeline to sue the defender in delict. The difficulty here is that British Gas's loss arising from damage to its pipeline is not the same as the losses incurred by Nacap in being unable to perform their contract on time. But where, as in *Aliakmon*,[4] the owner has a contractual remedy against the defender, the assignation of the contractual rights to the pursuer will provide a just solution provided, of course, the owner is prepared to assign his rights.

1   1988 SLT 778n, OH.
2   *Junior Books Ltd v Veitchi Co Ltd* 1982 SC (HL) 244, 1982 SLT 492.
3   1987 SLT 221.
4   *Leigh and Sillavan Ltd v Aliakmon Shipping Co Ltd, The Aliakmon* [1986] AC 785, [1986] 2 All ER 145, HL.

(5) Conclusion

4.33   The law on delictual liability for pure economic loss has been an area of extensive judicial activity where the concept of the duty of care has been used to mark the boundaries of liability. These have shifted from time to time and the current position remains controversial as well as conceptually difficult and, indeed, uncertain. Why this is so has been summarised admirably by Mummery LJ in *The Rebecca Elaine*:[1]

> 'The judicial line has not been drawn arbitrarily; it is explicable by rational and pragmatic considerations, some more potent than others, some more often articulated than others: the disproportionate burden of imposing indeterminate liability of the kind envisaged by Judge Cardozo in the *Ultramares* case; the evidential difficulties in establishing causation and delimiting remoteness; the relative cost and practicability of obtaining insurance cover for risks of pure financial loss suffered to an unlimited degree by an amorphous class of claimants; the apprehension of a deluge, in an already overstretched legal system, of litigation by an indefinite number of claimants with multiple claims arising out of a single incident ... the dubious and lethal colonisation by the tort [delict] of negligence of the conceptual territory of contract; the perception that financial loss occupies a significantly lower place than physical injury to person and property in the scale of contemporary social and ethical values; and the inevitability (and acceptability) of widespread and uncompensatable financial loss in a free market economy, in which even intentional infliction of substantial financial loss (eg by one trade competitor on another) does not normally attract legal liability.'

1   *The Rebecca Elaine* [1999] 2 Lloyd's Rep 1 at 8.

CHAPTER 5

Breach of a duty of care

A. INTRODUCTION

5.1 A duty of care is a necessary pre-requisite for liability in negligence, but recognition or admission that a duty is owed, by no means guarantees that the pursuer's claim will succeed. There will be no liability unless it can be established that the defender breached the duty. The duty establishes the legal requirement for the defender to exercise care to avoid harm to the pursuer, but it cannot be said that the defender has been negligent until it is also established that they failed to exercise the degree of care incumbent on them. The question of how much care should have been taken or exactly what precautions should have been implemented, is addressed by reference to the standard of care. Where insufficient care has been exercised, that is where the defender's conduct has fallen short of the standard of care, then the duty has been breached and *culpa* in the form of negligence provides a basis for the obligation to make reparation. Provided, of course, that the breach caused the loss complained of.[1]

1   Causation is considered in Chapter 6 below.

5.2 Involuntary acts are not negligent. Before there is a breach of duty, the relevant act or omission must be voluntary on the part of the defender. In *Waugh v James K Allan Ltd*[1] a lorry driver, Gemmell, suffered symptoms consistent with a gastric attack. When he felt he had recovered, he drove the lorry. In fact the symptoms were the onset of thrombosis and he shortly thereafter died at the wheel. The lorry swerved and seriously injured a pedestrian. Although the lorry driver clearly owed the pursuer a duty of care, it was held that there was no breach of duty in this case. On the medical evidence, the driver had no reason to anticipate the onset of the thrombosis and had therefore acted reasonably in driving the lorry after he felt better. Accordingly, the driver's act which injured the pursuer, ie his death, was involuntary and there was therefore no breach of the duty of care. If, however, the driver should have realised that he was seriously ill, then the act of driving while unfit to do so would have been a voluntary act which could have amounted to a breach of duty. But, in the circumstances, Lord Reid observed:[2]

> 'I am therefore of opinion that the appellant [the pursuer] has failed to prove that Gemmell acted rashly or negligently in driving off so soon after his illness, and no other fault can be imputed to him. One must have great sympathy with the appellant who has suffered so severely through no fault of his own, but I find it impossible to blame Gemmell. Accordingly, I would dismiss this appeal.'

1   1964 SC (HL) 102, 1964 SLT 269. The pursuer was suing the driver's employer as vicariously liable for the employee's wrong: on vicarious liability, see paras 12.5 ff below.
2   1964 SC (HL) 102 at 106.

B.   THE STANDARD OF CARE – NEGLIGENCE

5.3   What the law requires is that the defender's conduct should not fall below the standard of the reasonable person in the position of the defender. The law does not expect the defender to go beyond this standard. The defender is only obliged to take reasonable care: he is not expected to ensure that his acts or omissions never harm the pursuer. This point was forcibly made in *Muir v Glasgow Corpn*,[1] where the House of Lords held that the duty of the manageress was only to take reasonable care and not to prevent any accident occurring on the premises.[2]

How then do we determine the standard of care of a reasonable person in any particular circumstance? Since the standard of care is that of the hypothetical reasonable person in the position of the defender, the issue is ultimately a question for the court. It falls to the pursuer to specify the care or precautions that a person, acting reasonably, would have taken in the circumstances. If the standard of care is inadequately specified, the claim will be challenged on relevancy. The defender is entitled to notice of the precise way in which they are alleged to have been at fault. The defender may, in any case contest the precautions specified by the pursuer and the court will determine the issue. If the defender did not take the steps deemed reasonable, then the defender has been negligent and has broken the duty of care owed to the pursuer. Of course, the actual conduct of the defender, what they did or did not do, is a question of fact. The facts may be determined at proof based on evidence. Equally the defender may admit the facts as averred by the pursuer but contest the standard of care contended for.

Establishing the standard of care involves a balancing process. The relevant factors to be considered include the probability of injury, the seriousness of the injury, the practicability of precautions, the cost of the precautions and the utility of the defender's activities. The practice of other persons in the same type of business or profession as the defender can also be important. The court then balances the costs of preventing harm to the pursuer against the risk of injury to the pursuer. By such a calculus of risk, there emerges the standard of the reasonable person in the position of the defender. If the defender's conduct has, *in fact*, not reached that standard, she has been negligent and therefore in breach of the duty of care owed to the pursuer.

Before considering these factors in detail there is a preliminary point. In determining the standard of care, the scientific knowledge available to the hypothetical reasonable person at that time can be crucial. In *Roe v Minister of Health*[3] a patient was given a spinal anaesthetic. As was ordinary practice at the time, the phials containing the anaesthetic were kept in a solution of phenol. Unknown to the hospital, the phials developed invisible cracks and the anaesthetic became impregnated with phenol. As a result of the phenol in the anaesthetic, the patient was paralysed. The court held that the defendant had not broken the duty of care owed to the plaintiff: given the state of scientific knowledge at the time, a reasonable medical practitioner could not have foreseen that paralysis of a patient was a reasonable and probable consequence of storing the phials in phenol.

1   1943 SC (HL) 3, 1944 SLT 60, discussed at paras 3.12–3.13 above
2   For more recent examples see *Harris v Perry* [2008] EWCA Civ 906, [2009] 1 WLR 19 CA; *Craig v Tullymurray Equestrian Centre* [2019] NIQB 94.
3   [1954] 2 QB 66, [1954] 2 All ER 131, CA.

(a) Probability of injury to the pursuer

5.4   Even if harm to the pursuer is foreseeable, a defender who causes such an injury is not negligent in failing to take precautions to avoid it if the risk of such an injury is so improbable that a reasonable person in the position of the defender would not have taken any precautions. Thus, for example, in *Bolton v Stone*[1] the plaintiff was injured by a cricket ball which had been hit out of a cricket ground. This had happened on six occasions in the previous 30 years and no one had been injured. The House of Lords held that the defendants had not been negligent in failing to take precautions since the risk of injury was so slight in the circumstances that a reasonable person in the position of the defendants would not have taken any precautions. Lord Reid explained:[2]

> 'In my judgment, the test to be applied here is whether the risk of damage to a person on the road was so small that a reasonable man in the position of the appellants [the defendants], considering the matter from the point of view of safety, would have thought it right to refrain from taking steps to prevent the damage. In considering the matter I think that it would be right to take into account, not only how remote is the chance that a person might be struck, but also how serious the consequences are likely to be if a person is struck, but I do not think that it would be right to take into account the difficulty of remedial measures. If cricket cannot be played on a ground without creating a substantial risk, then it should not be played there at all.'

In *Gillon v Chief Constable of Strathclyde Police*,[3] it was held that the risk of a police officer being injured by a player at a football match was so small that a reasonable employer – and the football club – were not required to take any precautions.

1   [1951] AC 850, [1951] 1 All ER 1078, HL.
2   [1951] 1 All ER 1078 at 1086. See in relation to golf balls 'driven' off course where the pursuer succeeded: *Whitefield v Barton* 1987 SCLR 259, Sh Ct. See also para 1.3 above, authorities cited in note 8.
3   1997 SLT 1218, (1996) *Times*, 22 November 1996, OH. This decision has been criticised on the basis that players run off the field of play all the time and such an accident was bound to happen. See D Brodie, *Reparation: Liability in Delict*, A12-005

(b) Seriousness of injury to potential pursuer

5.5 As Lord Reid indicated in the passage cited above, the seriousness of the consequences for a person if he is injured is a relevant factor. In *Paris v Stepney Borough Council*,[1] a mechanic who had the use of only one eye was not supplied with goggles. When he was removing a rusty bolt from a car with a hammer, a chip of metal flew into his good eye and as a result he became totally blind. The employer had known that the plaintiff had only one eye. It was accepted that it was not the practice in the industry to supply goggles to workers engaged on the plaintiff's tasks. The question, however, was whether the employer had been negligent in failing to provide goggles for an employee whom they knew was already partially sighted. In the Court of Appeal,[2] the plaintiff's claim failed. Asquith LJ took the view that while the greater risk of injury was a relevant factor, the risk of greater injury was not. The House of Lords[3] held, however, that the seriousness of the consequences of an injury for a particular plaintiff was a relevant consideration. Since the consequences of an eye injury for an already partially sighted person could be total blindness, the court held that the employer had been negligent in failing to provide him with goggles. It was irrelevant that the defendants might not have been negligent in failing to provide goggles to two-eyed workers. Lord Normand observed:[4]

> 'The court's task of deciding what precautions a reasonable and prudent man would take in the circumstances of a particular case may not be easy. Nevertheless, the judgment of the reasonable and prudent man should be allowed its common every day scope, and it should not be restrained from considering the foreseeable consequences of an accident and their seriousness for the person to whom the duty of care is owed ... the seriousness of the injury or damage risked and the likelihood of its being in fact caused may not be the only relevant factors. For example, Asquith LJ in *Daborn v Bath Tramways Motor Co Ltd and Smithey* [5] pointed out that it is sometimes necessary to take account of the consequences of not assuming a risk.'

1   [1951] AC 367, [1951] 1 All ER 42, HL.
2   [1949] 2 All ER 843, CA.
3   [1951] AC 367, [1951] 1 All ER 42, HL. See also *St George v Home Office* [2008] EWCA Civ 1068, [2009] 1 WLR 1670.
4   [1951] 1 All ER 42 at 49.
5   [1946] 2 All ER 333, CA.

(c) Utility of the activity

5.6   *Daborn v Bath Tramways Motor Co Ltd and Smithey*[1] concerned an ambulance with a left-hand drive which was used during World War II. The plaintiff had put a sign at the back of the vehicle which said, 'Caution – Left hand drive – No signals'. When she was turning to the right, having given a hand signal, she collided with a bus which she could not see was trying to overtake her. The plaintiff was injured. The defendant argued that the plaintiff, as well as the bus driver, had been negligent and that her damages should be reduced on the grounds of her contributory negligence.[2] The Court of Appeal held that the plaintiff had not been negligent. In the course of his judgment Asquith LJ said:[3]

> 'I think that the plaintiff did all that in the circumstances she could reasonably be required to do if you include in those circumstances, as I think you should: (i) the necessity in time of national emergency of employing all transport resources which

were available and (ii) the inherent limitations and incapacities of this particular form of transport. In considering whether reasonable care has been observed, one must balance the risk against the consequences of not assuming that risk, and in the present instance that calculation seems to me to work out in favour of the plaintiff.'

Thus, the social utility of the activities which it is foreseeable may cause injury must be taken into account. In *Watt v Hertfordshire County Council*[4] a woman was trapped under a vehicle. The fire service sent a lorry with a jack. During the attempt to rescue the woman, the jack slipped and a fireman was injured. He claimed that the defendants, his employers, were negligent in not using a specially adapted lorry. The court held that given the emergency the employers were justified in using the vehicle which was available, ie a reasonable employer would have used the vehicle. They had not therefore fallen below the standard of the reasonable person in their position and therefore had not broken the duty of care which they owed to their employee. In *French v Strathclyde Fire Board*[5] it was observed that when fighting a fire, it might be reasonable to take a risk to save a life which would not be reasonable to prevent damage to property.

There can also be a social value in not taking steps to prevent a foreseeable accident. In *Tomlinson v Congleton Borough Council*,[6] the House of Lords held that a local authority was not under an obligation to take steps to reduce or eliminate the dangers of swimming in a lake. It was enough that they had provided warning notices. To do more would hinder the general public from enjoying the amenities of the lakeside:

'The majority of people who went to the beaches to sunbathe, paddle and play with their children were enjoying themselves in a way which gave them pleasure and caused no risk to themselves or anyone else. This must be something to be taken into account in deciding whether it was reasonable to expect the council to destroy the beaches.'[7]

Conversely, if there is no social value in the defender's failure to take reasonable steps to eliminate or reduce a risk, the defender's omission to do so will be negligent.[8]

1   [1946] 2 All ER 333, CA.
2   On contributory negligence, see paras 6.12–6.13 below.
3   [1946] 2 All ER 333 at 336.
4   [1954] 2 All ER 368, [1954] 1 WLR 208, CA.
5   [2013] CSOH 3.
6   [2004] 1 AC 46.

7   [2004] 1 AC 46 per Lord Hoffmann at 84. His speech at 82–86 provides an excellent example of the calculus of risk. Lord Hoffmann also considered that. as a general rule. the owner or occupier of property did not owe a duty of care to prevent persons engaging in activities on their land such as swimming or mountaineering, which involved an inherent risk of personal harm: [2004] 1 AC 46 at 84.

8   *Jolley v Sutton Borough Council* [2000] 3 All ER 409 (no social value in failing to remove a rotting boat from a council estate!).

(d) Practicality of precautions

5.7   The hypothetical reasonable person in the position of the defender will – indeed, can – only take such precautions as are practicable to avoid the risk of harm. In *Quinn v Cameron and Roberton Ltd*,[1] for example, the pursuer developed pneumoconiosis as a result of prolonged exposure to silica dust where he was working. His case against his employers failed on the basis that since the danger to employees from silica dust in iron foundries was not appreciated during the period when the pursuer was working for the employer (nine years prior to 1951), the defenders were not in breach of their duty of care by not providing precautions. Another reason why they had not been negligent was that effective dust-extraction appliances were not available to the employers until 1950. The Lord President (Clyde) explained:[2]

> 'The Lord Ordinary has held it proved that the provision of dust extraction appliances at plough buffs was not general practice between 1946 and 1951, and the expert evidence is really unanimously in favour of this conclusion. Indeed any apparatus to cope with the dangerous dust only seems to have come into the market in 1950, and went into general practice thereafter.'

1   1956 SC 224, 1957 SLT 2. See also *Smith v P & O Bulk Shipping Ltd* [1998] 2 Lloyd's Rep 81, QBD (employer could not have known about danger from asbestos when plaintiff was employee).

2   1956 SC 224 at 233.

(e) Cost of precautions

5.8   The hypothetical reasonable person in the position of the defender will consider the cost of precautions and balance this against the probability of risk of harm and the seriousness of any injuries likely to be sustained. The defender's duty is not to be negligent; it is not to act to eliminate all risks of injury to the pursuer. Thus, for example, in *Latimer v AEC Ltd*[1] a factory floor became slippery because of a phenomenal rainstorm. In an attempt to avoid accidents, the employer spread three tons of sawdust on the floor. Nevertheless, an employee slipped and was injured on a part of the floor *not* covered by sawdust.[2] The plaintiff argued that the employer should have closed the factory while the floor was properly cleaned, thus eliminating the risk of employees slipping. This would, of course, have involved loss of production. The House of Lords held that the employer did all that a reasonable person would have done and was therefore not negligent. For Lord Tucker[3] the only question was:

> 'Has it been proved that the floor was so slippery that, remedial steps not being possible, a reasonably prudent employer would have closed down the factory rather than allow his employees to run the risks involved in continuing work? ... The absence of any evidence that anyone in the factory during the afternoon or night shift, other than the appellant, slipped, or experienced any difficulty, or that any complaint was made by or on behalf of the workers, all points to the conclusion that the danger was, in fact, not such as to impose on a reasonable employer the obligation [to close down the factory].'

In *Charlton v Forrest Printing Ink Co Ltd*[4] it was one of the tasks of a group of employees to collect the wages for the workforce from a bank and take them to the factory. The employer had warned them of the possibility of being robbed and advised them to vary the times – and the transport used – when they went to collect the wages. Nevertheless, there was a robbery and the plaintiff was blinded by acid which had been thrown in his face. The Court of Appeal held that the employer had taken reasonable precautions and had not been negligent in failing to use the services of Securicor to uplift the wages, which could have been done at a very modest cost. On the other hand, if a risk can be eliminated or reduced at little cost, then the defender's failure to do so will be negligent.[5] In *Napier v Scottish Ministers*,[6] on the other hand, it was held that the defenders were in breach of their duty to take reasonable care for the health and safety of the pursuer who was in prison and still had to slop out. The cost of the improvements necessary to eliminate the need for slopping out did not prevent liability arising.

1   [1953] AC 643, [1953] 2 All ER 449, HL.
2   In spite of using three tons, some areas were left uncovered!
3   [1953] 2 All ER 449 at 455.
4   [1980] IRLR 331, CA. The case was concerned with an employer's *contractual* duty to take reasonable care for the safety of employees; but the point is also applicable in respect of the employer's *delictual* duty of care towards his employees.

5   *Jolley v Sutton Borough Council* [2000] 3 All ER 409. It should be noted that in
     Tomlinson v Congleton Borough Council [2004] 1 AC 46, Lord Hoffmann at 83
     did not regard the cost of destroying the lakeside as an important factor as
     opposed to the loss of social utility which that would have involved.
6   2005 1 SC 229. There was also a breach of the pursuer's right under Article 3
     not to suffer torture or inhuman or degrading treatment or punishment.

(f) Practice of other persons in the same business, trade or profession as the defender

5.9   The standard to be reached is that of the hypothetical
reasonable person in the position of the defender. The practice
of other persons in the same business, trade or profession as the
defender will be at least an indication of the standard expected
by a reasonable person in that situation. This was recognised by
the Lord President (Dunedin) in *Morton v Wm Dixon Ltd*.[1] There
a miner sued his employer on the basis that the employer had
been negligent in failing to provide a 'shielding contrivance' to
prevent coal falling between a cage and the side of the mine shaft.
In determining whether the employer was negligent and in breach
of his duty of care, Lord Dunedin said:[2]

> 'I look upon this matter as one of great importance not merely
> for this particular case, but for cases of this sort generally. Where
> the negligence of an employer consists of what I may call a
> fault of omission, I think that it is absolutely necessary that the
> proof of fault of omission should be one of two kinds, either – to
> shew that the thing which he did not do was a thing which was
> commonly done by other persons in like circumstances, or – to
> shew that it was a thing which was so obviously wanted that it
> would be folly in anyone not to provide it.'

While the determination whether the defender has fallen below
the requisite standard is a question of fact, the standard of care
demanded is that of the hypothetical reasonable person and is
ultimately the standard which the court decides is appropriate
in a particular situation. If, for example, an employer does not
take certain precautions, the court may still take the view that
he did not reach the standard of care of the reasonable person
in that situation even though he was following the usual
practice in his trade or business in not taking the precautions. In
Cavanagh v Ulster Weaving Co Ltd[3] an employee who was wearing
rubber boots slipped off a roof ladder while carrying cement.
No handrail was provided on the ladder. There was evidence
that it was not the practice in the building trade to provide a

handrail in these circumstances. The House of Lords held that evidence of the practice, while important, was not conclusive in establishing the requisite standard of care: that remained the standard of the reasonable person in the defendant's position. Given the circumstances of this case, including the fact that the employee's boots were two sizes larger than they should have been, a reasonable employer would have supplied a handrail and therefore the defendant was negligent. Lord Dunedin's formula in *Morton v Wm Dixon Ltd*,[4] while important, was not 'intended to depart from or modify the fundamental principle that an employer is bound to take reasonable care for the safety of his workmen'.[5]

Conversely, where the defender has not followed the usual practice in his trade or profession, he may nevertheless have taken reasonable care. In *Brown v Rolls Royce Ltd*[6] it was common practice in the defenders' industry to supply workers in the position of the pursuer with a barrier cream. The defenders considered that barrier cream was ineffective and instead took other precautions advised by a medical officer. The pursuer contracted dermatitis. The House of Lords held that while the defenders' failure to follow the usual practice was prima facie evidence of negligence, it was not conclusive. Because the defenders had taken other precautions against the risk of their employees suffering dermatitis, the defenders had not failed to take reasonable care. In relation to Lord Dunedin's formula, Lord Keith of Avonholm observed:[7]

> 'As has been said before in this House, Lord Dunedin was laying down no proposition of law; nor did he say that, if a practice was averred and proved which might have avoided the accident, this was necessarily conclusive of negligence on the part of an employer who had not followed the practice. The ultimate test is lack of reasonable care for the safety of the workman in all the circumstances of the case.'

The standard of care required of professional men and women, such as members of the medical and legal professions, is discussed later in the book.[8]

1   1909 SC 807, 1909 1 SLT 346.
2   1909 SC 807 at 809. This *dictum* remains authoritative: see, eg, *Pratt v Scottish Ministers* 2013 SLT 590; *Shields v Crossroads (Orkney)* [2013] CSOH 144.
3   [1960] AC 145, [1959] 2 All ER 745, HL.
4   1909 SC 807 at 809.
5   *Cavanagh v Ulster Weaving Co Ltd* [1959] 2 All ER 745 at 751 per Lord Keith of Avonholm.
6   1960 SC (HL) 22, 1960 SLT 119.
7   1960 SC (HL) 22 at 26.
8   See Chapter 7.

C.   REMOTENESS OF INJURY

5.10   In some earlier Scottish cases, delictual liability has been rejected on the ground that the harm suffered by the pursuer was 'too remote'. In *Reavis v Clan Line Steamers Ltd*,[1] for example, the court denied Mrs Reavis compensation for the loss of her orchestra on the simple basis that this loss was 'too remote'. It is submitted that the better analysis is that the defender did not owe her a duty of care to prevent her suffering secondary economic loss. Similarly, in *Bourhill v Young*,[2] it was argued by some of the judges that the pursuer could not sue in delict because the mental harm she sustained was too remote. Again it is submitted that Mrs Bourhill's claim failed because Young did not owe her a duty of care in respect of inflicting mental harm because she was a secondary victim. Equally, she was outwith the geographical range over which a duty to avoid personal injury extended.

Readers familiar with previous editions of this text will have spotted that the treatment of *Muir v Glasgow Corporation*, as authority for the rule that the duty extends only to the reasonable and probable consequences of the defender's conduct, has been removed from the present chapter and considered in Chapter 3.[3] This follows from *Caparo* in which the scope of the duty is clearly linked to the relationship between the parties and is therefore an element of proximity.[4] In the modern law, the question of whether the harm suffered in a given case is reparable, may better be analysed in terms of whether it falls within the scope of the duty, rather than as a question of whether the duty has been breached. The point may be arguable[5] and the analytical shift from breach to duty is incomplete as the probability of the pursuer incurring a particular injury remains relevant in considering whether the defender has adhered to the standard of care of the reasonable person in that position.[6] Given that a particular injury or form of harm may be held to fall outside the scope of the duty or, alternatively that the probability of that injury was so low that the defender was not in breach having failed to guard against it, it may be questioned whether there is any continuing need for a concept of remoteness of injury.

Remoteness of injury must not be confused with remoteness of losses. Where there has been a breach of a duty of care and the pursuer has suffered harm, the pursuer may not be able to recover for all the losses suffered as a result of the defender's negligence. Some losses may be considered by the court to be too remote. For example, if A injures B as a result of negligent driving, B is entitled to damages for pain and suffering and derivative economic loss, such as loss of wages, loss of future earnings etc. But when as a result of the accident B was unable to post his football coupon, could he recover damages from A for the fortune he would have won if the coupon had been sent? In other words, is the loss of the winnings too remote to be compensated by A? This is a question of remoteness of losses and is discussed later in the book.[7]

1   1925 SC 725.
2   1942 SC (HL) 78, 1943 SLT 105.Discussed at para 4.9 above
3   See paras 3.12–3.13.
4   See paras 3.9–3.10 above.
5   But see, eg, *Khan v Meadows* [2021] UKSC 21 discussed at para 7.5 below.
6   See para 5.4 above.
7   See beyond para 16.1ff.

D.   CONCLUSION

5.11   In this chapter we have been discussing when a breach of a duty of care arises. The defender's act or omission must be voluntary; constituent harm to the pursuer must be foreseeable as a reasonable and probable consequence of the defender's act or omission; and, finally, the act or omission must amount to negligence, ie the defender must have failed to reach the standard of care of the hypothetical reasonable person in the position of the defender. Where those criteria are satisfied, there is a breach of the duty of care owed to the pursuer and a delict is committed when the pursuer sustains constituent harm as a result of the defender's breach of the duty of care.

CHAPTER 6

Causation and related issues

Before there is liability in delict, the pursuer must prove on the balance of probabilities that the defender's breach of her duty of care was the cause of the harm sustained by the pursuer. The concept of causation is a complex and difficult subject raising fundamental philosophical as well as legal issues. In a work of the present compass, only an outline of the relevant issues is given.[1]

1 For a superb account of the subject, see Hart and Honoré *Causation and the Law* (2nd edn, 1985). The book is an excellent example of the constructive use to which linguistic philosophy can be put in the context of law. See also B Pillans SULI *Delict* Chapter 7.

A. FACTUAL CAUSATION

6.1 The first essential is that the defender's acts or omissions are a cause of the harm suffered by the pursuer. This is a question of fact. If the defender's conduct is not a factual cause of the harm, there is no liability even if the defender has broken a duty of care which he owed to the pursuer. To use Latin terminology, the defender's breach of duty must be a *causa sine qua non* of the pursuer's material harm. In other words, 'but for' the defender's conduct, the pursuer would not have sustained the harm. If the pursuer would have suffered the same harm notwithstanding the defender's breach of duty, then the defender's conduct is not a factual cause of the harm, ie it is not a *causa sine qua non*. Accordingly, to determine whether the defender's breach of duty is a factual cause of the harm suffered by the pursuer, we must ask ourselves whether 'but for' the breach of duty, the harm would have occurred. If it would *not* have occurred, the defender's conduct is a factual cause of the pursuer's harm:[1] if it would still have occurred, the defender's conduct is *not* a factual cause of the pursuer's harm. The onus of satisfying the 'but for' test on the balance of probabilities rests on the pursuer:[2] it is not for the defender to provide an alternative explanation.[3]

In *Barnett v Chelsea and Kensington Hospital Management Committee*,[4] for example, the plaintiff's husband drank a cup of tea and became violently ill because the tea had been poisoned. The hospital doctor refused to treat the husband telling him to see his own doctor. The husband died. It was held that although the defendant may have been in breach of a duty of care, the hospital was not liable because the husband would still have died of the poison even if he had been treated by the hospital doctor, ie the husband did not die 'but for' the hospital's negligence. Accordingly, the breach of duty was not a *causa sine qua non* of the husband's death and the plaintiff's action failed.

In *Kay's Tutor v Ayrshire and Arran Health Board*,[5] a child was brought into hospital suffering from meningitis. He was given a massive overdose of penicillin.[6] The child thereupon suffered severe convulsions but, as a result of treatment, recovered. However, the child was left deaf. In an action against the hospital, the defenders admitted that they were in breach of their duty of care in administering the overdose of penicillin but denied that this breach of duty had caused the child's deafness. The House of Lords held that the onus lay on the pursuer (the child's father) to prove that 'but for' the overdose the child would not be deaf. In the absence of evidence to show that an overdose of penicillin caused deafness in a patient and given that deafness is common in patients who suffer meningitis, the pursuer failed to establish that 'but for' the breach of duty deafness would not have occurred. The breach was therefore not a *causa sine qua non* of the child's deafness and the pursuer's action failed.

1   It is enough if it can be shown that 'but for' the defender's act or omission it was probable that the injury would not have occurred: *Porter v Strathclyde Regional Council* 1991 SLT 446.

2   See, for example, *Dingley v Chief Constable of Strathclyde Police (No 1)* 1998 SC 548, OH (pursuer failed to establish on the balance of probabilities that a whiplash injury sustained in a road accident had triggered the onset of symptomatic multiple sclerosis); *Pickford v ICI plc* [1998] ICR 673, [1998] 3 All ER 462, HL (onus was on plaintiff to prove that her condition had an organic cause: the employer's failure to prove that the condition was psychogenic was no more than a relevant factor in determining whether or not the plaintiff had discharged the burden of proof. In the circumstances the plaintiff had failed to do so); *Thomson v Kvaerner Govan Ltd* 2004 *SLT* 24 (pursuer failed to establish that plank supplied by the defender was not of adequate strength and caused him to fall when he stepped on it); *McGinnes v Endeva Service Ltd* 2006 SLT 638 (pursuer could not establish that he would not have been assaulted by a third party if a second employee had accompanied him to the *locus* where he was working); *Clough v First Choice Holidays and Flights Ltd* [2006] EWCA Civ 15, [2006] PIQR P22 (the claimant could not establish that he would not have fallen off a wall into a swimming pool if the wall had

been painted with non-slip paint: 'The judge remained unpersuaded that the claimant's slip was caused, or materially contributed to, by the absence of non-slip paint on the surface of the wall. Non-slip paint would have made the surface less slippery, but not non-slippery, nor removed altogether *the risk* of a slip by someone walking on the top of the wall with wet feet' per President of the Queen's Bench Division (Sir Igor Judge) at para 47); *McGlinchey v General Motors UK Ltd* [2012] CSIH 91 (pursuer failed to establish that an accident in which she was crushed by her car was caused by its handbrake being defective).

3   *Thomson v Kvaerner Govan Ltd* 2004 SLT 24. In *Drake v Harbour* [2008] EWCA Civ 25, 121 Con LR 18, [2008] NPC 11, [2008] All ER (D) 283 (Jan), CA. Toulson LJ observed at para 28: ' ... where a claimant proves both that a defendant was negligent and that loss ensued which was of a kind likely to have resulted from such negligence, this will ordinarily be enough to enable a court to infer that it was probably so caused, even if the claimant is unable to prove positively the precise mechanism. That is not a principle of law, nor does it involve an alteration in the burden of proof; rather, it is a matter of common sense. The court must consider any alternative theories of causation advanced by the defendant before reaching its conclusion about where the probability lies. If it concludes that the only alternative suggestions put forward by the defendant are on balance improbable, that is likely to fortify the court's conclusion that it is legitimate to infer that the loss was caused by the proven negligence.'
4   [1969] 1 QB 428, [1968] 1 All ER 1068.
5   1987 SC (HL) 145, 1987 SLT 577, HL, affirming 1986 SLT 435.
6   30 times the prescribed amount.

6.2   This concept was taken a stage further by the House of Lords in *Bolitho v City and Hackney Health Authority*.[1] It was accepted that a doctor had been in breach of her duty of care by failing to attend her patient, a child. The child died. It was also accepted that the only way in which the child's life could have been saved was by intubation. However, evidence was led that a responsible body of medical opinion would not have intubated in the circumstances. In other words, if the doctor had attended her patient, she would not have been negligent if she had not attempted to save the child's life by intubating her. Consequently, the child would still have died even if the doctor had attended her. The logic appears strained, but it is nevertheless compelling. Since the patient would still have died even if she had received reasonable care, ie no intubation, the doctor's negligence in failing to attend her was not a factual cause of her death.[2]

Where the treatment of a patient would have had less than a 50 per cent chance of success, the failure to treat is not regarded as the cause of the pursuer's injuries or illness: in other words, the chances of success must be more than 50 per cent.[3] In *Gregg v Scott*[4] owing to the negligence of his GP, the treatment of the claimant's cancer was delayed by nine months. He argued that had he been referred to hospital when he first saw his GP there would have been a high likelihood of cure, whereas by the time treatment commenced his chances of recovery had fallen to below 50 per cent. Chances of recovery were defined as surviving for a period of ten years. At the trial it was established that even if he had been diagnosed and treated promptly, his chances of surviving for ten years would have been only 42 per cent: now they were only 25 per cent. Because his chances of surviving ten years were never 50 per cent or more, the trial judge held that on a balance of probability the complainant would not have survived for ten years even if treated promptly; therefore he had failed to establish that the negligent misdiagnosis would cause him to die prematurely. A majority of the House of Lords agreed. The claimant had to establish that the clinical negligence was the cause of the adverse consequences which had befallen him. Since the claimant would only have had a 42 per cent chance of surviving had he been treated immediately, he was unable to prove on the balance of probabilities that the failure to survive for ten years was the result of the negligent misdiagnosis rather than the cancer. The majority of their Lordships also held that the reduction in his chances of a cure – from 42 per cent to 25 per cent – was not a recoverable head of damage. Put another way, their Lordships refused to award damages for the increased risk of suffering harm in the future as opposed to the lost chance of avoiding a result which has in fact occurred.

Another striking example of the 'but for' test is *McWilliams v Sir William Arrol & Co and Lithgows Ltd*.[5] The pursuer's husband, a steel erector, was killed. It was held that the defenders were in breach of their duty of care towards McWilliams in failing to provide him with a safety belt. But it was also established that even if they had provided him with a safety belt, McWilliams would not have worn it. In these circumstances, the pursuer failed to prove that 'but for' the defenders' breach of duty the accident would not have occurred. The defenders' breach was not a *causa sine qua non* of McWilliams' death and the pursuer's action failed. In *McTear v Imperial Tobacco Co Ltd*,[6] the pursuer failed to establish that her husband would not have contracted lung cancer 'but for' smoking the defenders' brand of cigarettes. The Lord Ordinary (Nimmo-Smith) was persuaded by the defenders' argument that had their own brand been unavailable he would have smoked a different brand and developed lung cancer anyway.

In *Kaizer v Scottish Ministers*,[7] the defenders appealed against a decision finding them liable for an attack on a prisoner while on remand. A prison officer had neglected to inform his superiors of threats made against the prisoner. The court refused to accept the defenders' argument on causation to the effect that no effectual action would have been taken so the attack would have taken place notwithstanding the negligence of the prison officer. Given the extent of control exercisable by the prison authorities, the court was entitled to assume that the authorities would have taken action to minimise the risk.

Where the pursuer suffers harm which he would have suffered anyway, but as a result of the defender's breach of duty he suffers the harm at an earlier date, the Scottish courts have held that the 'but for' test is satisfied and an action will lie in delict.[8] Conversely, where a pursuer is injured as a result of the defender's breach of duty but later suffers an accident or disease unrelated to the defender's conduct, the fact that he would have been debilitated by the later accident or disease is taken into account in assessing the pursuer's loss.[9]

The 'but for' test also applies when the pursuer's claim is for pure economic loss. For example, D provides P with information about C which P uses to decide whether to enter into a transaction with C. P sustains economic loss as a consequence of the transaction with C. In an action to recover the loss from D, P must prove that he would not have entered into the transaction with C 'but for' D's misrepresentation in respect of C. If P would have entered into the transaction with C in the absence of D's advice, the action will fail for lack of factual causation.[10]

1   [1998] AC 232, [1997] 4 All ER 771, HL.
2   It would still be very difficult to explain to the child's parents why their action failed given the doctor's admitted negligence in not attending their child.
3   See *Kenyon v Bell* 1953 SC 125, 1952 SLT (Notes) 79, OH; *Hotson v East Berkshire Area Health Authority* [1987] 2 All ER 909, HL.
4   [2005] 2 AC 178.
5   1962 SC (HL) 70, 1962 SLT 121.
6   2005 2 SC 1, 2005 GWD 20-365.
7   [2018] CSIH 36. See para 4.5 above.
8   *Sutherland v North British Steel Group Ltd* 1986 SLT (Sh Ct) 29 (accelerated hernia operation).
9   See *Jobling v Associated Dairies Ltd* [1982] AC 794, [1981] 2 All ER 752, HL.
10 *Leeds & Holbeck Building Society v Alex Morison & Co (No 2)* 2001 SCLR 41.

6.3   Difficulties arise where there is more than one potential cause of the pursuer's injuries, ie the defender's breach of a duty of care and another source of danger which is not the responsibility of the defender. The starting point of the discussion is *Wardlaw v Bonnington Castings Ltd*.[1] A workman contracted pneumoconiosis from breathing dust in the atmosphere of his workplace. Some of the dust was caused by a hammer in relation to which there were no known or available precautions which could be taken to prevent the employee breathing contaminated air. Therefore, the defender was not in breach of the duty of care owed to the pursuer in respect of the dust caused by the hammer. However, there were other machines in the workshop which also produced dust for which adequate extraction plant was available and the employers were held responsible for not adequately maintaining the extracting plant.[2]

There were therefore two possible sources of the dust which had caused the pursuer's illness for only one of which the defender was delictually liable, ie the dust from the other machines. The House of Lords held that the onus lay on the pursuer to show that on the balance of probabilities the dust from the machines was a *causa sine qua non* of his illness. In the situation of two potential sources of danger, the pursuer would discharge the onus if he could show that the source for which the defender was responsible had materially contributed to his injury. Lord Reid observed:[3]

'It appears to me that the source of his [the pursuer's] disease was the dust from both sources, and the real question is whether the dust from the swing grinders [the other machines] materially contributed to the disease. What is a material contribution must be a question of degree. A contribution which comes within the exception *de minimis non curat lex* is not material but I think that any contribution which does not fall within that exception must be material.'

In this case, the dust from the machines did materially contribute to the pursuer's illness and the pursuer was successful. Thus, where there are two or more sources of harm to the pursuer which operate concurrently, the source for which the defender is responsible will be regarded as a *causa sine qua non* of the pursuer's injury if it materially contributed to the injury.

1 1956 SC (HL) 26, 1956 SLT 135.
2 This was a breach by the employer of their statutory duty under the Grinding of Metals (Miscellaneous Industries) Regulations 1925, SR & O 1925/904. On breach of statutory duty, see Chapter 11 below.
3 *Wardlaw v Bonnington Castings Ltd* 1956 SC (HL) 26 at 32.

6.4 The concept of factual causation was taken a considerable step further in *McGhee v National Coal Board*.[1] The pursuer worked all day in a hot and dusty kiln. He had to cycle home unwashed because the defender failed to provide on-site washing facilities.

After several days, the pursuer contracted dermatitis. It was admitted that the dermatitis was attributable to the work the pursuer did in the brick kiln, but the defender was not in breach of a duty of care in allowing the pursuer to work there. The breach of duty was the failure to provide on-site washing facilities. This omission only resulted in the pursuer cycling home unwashed: clearly, it did not relate to the hours he spent working in the kiln. Common sense would suggest that it was far more likely that the dermatitis was contracted when he was working in the kiln, for which the employer was not delictually liable, rather than during the short time he cycled home. But the expert evidence could not establish how dermatitis was contracted. *Wardlaw v Bonnington Castings Ltd*[2] could therefore not provide a solution since it could not be proven that the additional exposure to injury caused by cycling home unwashed had materially contributed to his injury. *Wardlaw v Bonnington Castings Ltd* is concerned with two sources of danger operating *concurrently*; but *McGhee v National Coal Board* is concerned with two sources of danger operating *consecutively* where the defender was responsible only for the later one. Therefore, it can be argued that the pursuer in *McGhee* would have to prove – which on the evidence he could not – that the later source of danger had caused, or at least materially contributed to, his dermatitis.

However, the House of Lords was prepared to take a broader view of causation. The medical evidence suggested that the fact that the pursuer had to cycle home caked with grime and sweat added materially to *the risk* that the disease might develop, although it could not explain why this was so. In the view of the House, materially to increase the risk of the pursuer's injuries was to be regarded as a material contribution to the injury. Lord Reid opined:[3]

> 'But it has often been said that the legal concept of causation is not based on logic or philosophy. It is based on the practical way in which the ordinary man's mind works in the every-day affairs of life. From a broad and practical viewpoint I can see no substantial difference between saying that what the defender did materially increased the risk of injury to the pursuer and saying that what the defender did made a material contribution to his injury.'

Lord Salmon observed:[4]

> 'In the circumstances of the present case,[5] the possibility of a distinction existing between (a) having materially increased the risk of contracting the disease and (b) having materially

contributed to causing the disease may no doubt be a fruitful source of interesting academic discussions between students of philosophy. Such a distinction is, however, far too unreal to be recognised by the common law!'

Thus, where there are two or more sources of danger for only one of which the defender is delictually liable, factual causation will be established if the pursuer can prove on the balance of probabilities *either* that the defender's breach of duty materially contributed to his injury *or* that the defender's breach of duty materially increased the risk of the pursuer sustaining injury. It does not matter if the sources of danger operate concurrently or consecutively.[6]

1   1973 SC (HL) 37, 1973 SLT 14; see Lord Hope of Craighead 'James McGhee – A Second Mrs Donoghue?' [2003] CLJ 587.
2   1956 SC (HL) 26, 1956 SLT 135.
3   *McGhee v National Coal Board* 1973 SC (HL) 37 at 53–54.
4   1973 SC (HL) 37 at 62.
5   Given the defender's admitted breach of a duty of care.
6   The implications of *McGhee* are remarkable. For example, suppose A has smoked cigarettes for 30 years. B, her employer, allows C and D, fellow employees, to smoke in a room occupied by A. A contracts lung cancer a week later. Since A's passive smoking of C and D's cigarette smoke materially increases the risk of A contracting lung cancer, C and D's smoking (and B's allowing them to smoke) could be treated as the cause of A contracting the disease. But common sense would suggest that A contracted the disease as a result of her own smoking habit. A would, of course, be contributorily negligent: see paras 6.12–6.13 below.

6.5   *McGhee v National Coal Board* was approved and extended by the House of Lords in *Fairchild v Glenhaven Funeral Services Ltd.*[1] F was employed by E1 and E2 at different times and for different periods. Both E1 and E2 were in breach of a duty of care to F by allowing him to breathe asbestos dust. F contracted cancer. The medical evidence established that the disease was contracted by breathing asbestos dust but, because of the limits of scientific knowledge, it could not be established that the cancer was the result of inhaling asbestos dust during his employment with E1 or E2 or both employers. But it was also proven that once the disease had been contracted, F's condition would not deteriorate because of further exposure to asbestos dust. Thus, causation could not be established based on a material contribution to F's illness. However, it was accepted that the *risk* of contracting the cancer increased in relation to the total exposure to asbestos dust. In these circumstances, their Lordships took the view that the normal 'but for' test should be suspended. Lord Nicholls considered that the plaintiff should succeed as 'any other outcome would be deeply offensive to instinctive notions of what justice requires and fairness demands'.[2] Since both E1 and E2 were in breach of the duty of care they owed to F and these breaches had materially increased the risk of F contracting cancer, *McGhee* was applicable and the causal requirement was satisfied.[3] It should be noted that in *McGhee,* the pursuer sustained harm as a consequence of the defender's breach of duty or the defender's non-delictual conduct, both of which materially increased the risk of his contracting dermatitis: even if the illness was not contracted as a result of the defender's breach of duty, it was nevertheless caused by the defender's conduct – albeit conduct that might not have been negligent. *Fairchild* goes further in that by increasing the risk of the pursuer sustaining harm as a result of the defender's breach of duty, the defender may be held to have caused the pursuer's illness when it was in fact caused by the negligence of another person.

In *Sienkiewicz v Grief (UK)* Ltd,[4] the defendant's negligent exposure of the plaintiff to asbestos over her working life at their premises increased her risk of contracting mesothelioma by only 18 per cent. Although this case only involved one defendant, the Supreme Court nevertheless held that the *Fairchild* exception applied and the plaintiff was entitled to succeed as the defendant had materially increased the risk of her contracting the disease. There was no need for her to prove that the defendant's negligence had doubled the risk of her contracting mesothelioma.[5]

There are, however, important limitations. First, as the Supreme Court re-emphasised in *Sienkiewicz,* the principle in *McGhee* and *Fairchild* only applies when it is impossible to establish scientifically the cause of the pursuer's injury. Second, while the *sources* of danger may be different, it must be established that each source could have in fact been the cause of the pursuer's injuries. In *Wardlaw, McGhee* and *Fairchild* it was clear that dust caused the pursuers' diseases: the only question was whether the defenders' breach of duty had materially contributed to, or increased the risk of, the pursuers' illnesses. By way of contrast, in *Kay's Tutor v Ayrshire and Arran Health Board,*[6] there was no evidence that the defender's breach of duty in giving the overdose of penicillin could in fact have caused the child's deafness. In these circumstances, *Wardlaw, McGhee* and *Fairchild* are irrelevant. As Lord Griffiths explained:[7]

> 'The principle in *McGhee* would only fall for consideration if it was first proved that it was an accepted medical fact that penicillin in some cases caused or aggravated deafness.

> The question would then arise whether when there are
> two competing causes of deafness, namely meningitis and
> penicillin, the law should presume in favour of the plaintiff
> [sic] that the tortious [sic] [delictual] cause was responsible for
> the damage.'

Moreover, the departure from the ordinary 'but for' rule only applies when there are two or more sources of the *same* noxious agent which caused the pursuer's illness or injuries: if there is more than one noxious agent which could have caused the pursuer's injuries or illness, the threshold 'but for' test of causal connection will not be relaxed. In *Wilsher v Essex Area Health Authority*,[8] a baby's medical condition could have been caused by a noxious agent (a) which arose because of the defendant's breach of duty: but there were another four different noxious agents – for which the defendant was not responsible – each of which could equally have harmed the child. The fact that the defendant's negligence materially increased the risk of the child from being harmed by noxious agent (a) was held not to be a sufficient causative link when the child's condition could have been caused by noxious agents (b), (c), (d) or (e).

In *Chester v Afshar*[9] the House of Lords was prepared to suspend the normal operation of the 'but for' test to ensure that a doctor's obligation to inform a patient of the risks inherent in a medical procedure would not be undermined. The purpose of the obligation was to enable a patient to make an informed decision on whether to agree to the procedure. This duty would be rendered almost obsolete if only those patients who would not have agreed to the procedure were able to sue when their doctor was in breach of this duty.

1 [2003] 1 AC 32, [2002] 3 All ER 305. See Joe Thomson 'The Raising of Lazarus: The Resurrection of *McGhee v National Coal Board*' (2003) 7 Edin LR 80.

2 [2002] 3 All ER 305 at 336. See also Lord Bingham at 312 and Lord Hoffmann at 341.

3 If *in fact* F had contracted cancer while in the employment of E1, it is difficult to see how the exposure to asbestos dust while in the employment of E2 materially increased the risk of F contracting cancer!

4 [2011] UKSC 10.

5 The pursuer will fail if the increase in the risk of contracting the disease as a result of the defender's negligence is minimal: *Garner v Salford City Council* [2013] EWHC 1573.

6 1987 SC (HL) 145, 1987 SLT 577. Discussed at para 6.1 above.

7 1987 SLT 577 at 581.

8 [1988] 1 All ER 871, HL, approved by the House of Lords in *Fairchild*.

9 [2005] 1 AC 134.

B. LEGAL CAUSATION

6.6 For the purpose of liability in delict, it is not enough that the defender's breach of duty is a factual cause or *causa sine qua non* of the pursuer's harm. While factual causation is a necessary condition of delictual liability, it is not sufficient. In addition, the defender's breach of duty must be the legal cause of the pursuer's harm. To use Latin terminology, it must be the *causa causans*. Various terms are used to describe legal causation: these include the direct, decisive, proximate, real, dominant, efficient, effective and substantial cause of the pursuer's loss or harm.

For example, A drops a brick on B's foot, breaking his toe. B is taken to hospital in an ambulance. The ambulance is driven carelessly and B is killed in a road accident. A's breach of duty is a *causa sine qua non* of B's death since 'but for' A's dropping the brick on his toe, B would not have been in the ambulance in which he died. But should A be delictually liable for B's death which was caused by the ambulance driver's careless driving? The answer is no. A's breach of duty, although a *causa sine qua non* of B's death, is not treated as the legal cause, ie it is not the *causa causans*. The *causa causans* is the ambulance driver's careless driving. We can say that the chain of causation between A's breach of duty and B's death has been broken because of the careless act of the ambulance driver, which prevents A's breach of duty from being the legal cause of B's death. To use legal terminology, the ambulance driver's conduct is a *novus actus interveniens* which breaks the chain of causation so that A is not delictually liable for B's death, although A remains liable for B's broken toe.

In this example, the *novus actus interveniens* was the conduct of a third party: the ambulance driver. But the conduct of the victim may also break the chain of causation. So, for example, if A drops a brick on B's foot, breaking his toe, whereupon B cuts his own throat to put himself out of pain, A will not be delictually liable for B's death. B's action has broken the chain of causation and, as a result, A's breach of duty is not regarded as the legal cause, the *causa causans*, of B's death.[1]

When, then, will an act of a third party or the act of the victim constitute *a novus actus interveniens,* breaking the chain of causation? Since we are concerned with determining legal causation, this is ultimately a question for the courts: the judges will *evaluate* whether in the circumstances it is fair to relieve the defender of his delictual liability. At one time, this was a crucial decision where the victim had contributed to his own injuries: for if the court decided that the pursuer's conduct was a *novus actus interveniens* so that the defender's breach of duty was not the *causa causans*, the pursuer was denied any compensation. However, as a result of the Law Reform (Contributory Negligence) Act 1945, the court now has the power to reduce the damages awarded to the pursuer in proportion to the pursuer's responsibility for her own injuries.[2] Although the 1945 Act has, in so far as the pursuer's conduct is concerned, reduced the importance of determining a single cause or *causa causans*, the court still retains the power of limiting a defender's delictual liability for breach of a duty of care. It does this by deciding that the breach is not the legal cause of the pursuer's injuries, for example because of the intervention of a third party. Therefore, the determination of legal causation remains important.

The decision as to whether a breach of duty constitutes the *causa causans* of the pursuer's injuries 'must be dealt with broadly and upon common sense principles as a jury would probably deal with it'.[3] Two factors are important, as we shall now see.

1   The victim's suicide will not break the chain of causation if the purpose of the defender's duty of care was to look after the victim (*Reeves v Metropolitan Commissioner* [2001]1 AC 360) or the defender's conduct caused the victim physical harm which led to depression which led to the victim's suicide (*Corr v IBC Vehicles* [2008] 1 AC 884).
2   On contributory negligence, see paras 6.12–6.13 below.
3   *Admiralty Comrs v SS Volute* [1922] AC 129, HL, at 144 per Birkenhead LC; *Galoo Ltd (in liquidation) v Bright Grahame Murray* [1995] 1 All ER 16, CA at 29 per Glidewell LJ, quoting an Australian decision: 'The answer in the end is "By the application of the court's common sense"'; *Simmons v British Steel plc* 2003 SLT 62 per the Lord Justice-Clerk (Gill) at 65: 'This is a case where the question of causation can be decided straightforwardly on a common sense view of the whole evidence.'

(1) Foreseeability

6.7   Where there has been a breach of duty by the defender, the act of a third party or the victim will not generally break the chain of causation if it was reasonably foreseeable that the subsequent act would take place. In *Sayers v Harlow Urban District Council*,[1] for example, the plaintiff entered a cubicle in a public lavatory maintained by the defendant. Owing to a fault in the lock, she could not reopen the door. She banged on the door and put her hand out of the window in unsuccessful attempts to attract attention. After 15 minutes, she tried to escape through the space between the top of the door and the roof. She put her left foot on the lavatory seat, her right foot on the toilet roll holder, one hand on the lavatory cistern and the other hand on the top of the door. When she found it impossible to squeeze through the space, she proceeded to come down but, because of her weight, the toilet roll holder rotated, she lost her balance and fell. The court held that it was reasonably foreseeable that a person in Mrs Sayers' position would try to escape and that this was not a hazardous enterprise. Accordingly, her attempted escape was not a *novus actus interveniens* and the defendant's breach of duty was the *causa causans* of the accident. However, when she found she could not escape, she was careless in putting so much weight on the toilet roll holder: although this did not break the chain of causation, it did constitute contributory negligence and her damages were reduced by 25 per cent.[2]

Even if the subsequent act of a third party or the pursuer is reasonably foreseeable, it may break the chain of causation if it was hazardous for the third party or the pursuer to act in such a way. In *McKew v Holland and Hannen and Cubitts (Scotland) Ltd*,[3] the pursuer injured his ankle as a result of the defender's breach of duty. Because of the fracture, his leg was liable to 'give way' from time to time. After the accident, the pursuer went to see a flat. The stairway leading to the fiat had no handrail. Although he knew that his leg was likely to give way at any time, after visiting the flat the pursuer went down the stairs in a normal manner ie he did not go down slowly so that he could sit on a step if his leg 'gave way'. His leg gave way and in panic the pursuer jumped down ten steps and was injured. The court held that the defender was not liable for the second injury. Although it was reasonably foreseeable that the pursuer might climb stairs which had no handrail, he had acted in a hazardous manner in walking down the stairs in the normal way without assistance. The defender's breach of duty which had caused the injury to the pursuer's ankle was not the *causa causans* of the pursuer's second injury. Instead, the pursuer's carelessness in walking down the stairs without assistance constituted hazardous conduct on the pursuer's part which broke the chain of causation between the defender's breach of duty and the pursuer's second injuries.

McKew was distinguished in *Spencer v Wincanton Holdings Ltd (Wincanton Logisitics Ltd)*.[4] Here the defendant admitted liability for the injuries the plaintiff had suffered from an accident at work which led to the amputation of his leg. Eight months after the amputation, he tripped and fell when he was filling his car at a garage without summoning help or steadying himself using his sticks or his prosthesis. As a result of this fall, he was confined to a wheelchair. The Court of Appeal held that the second accident was an unexpected but real consequence of the first accident. Whether an intervening event should be treated as breaking the chain of causation was ultimately a question of fairness, ie whether it was fair to relieve the defendant of liability for the subsequent event. The plaintiff's act of filling his car without any help fell far below the unreasonableness of the pursuer's behaviour in *McKew*. The defendant was therefore liable with a reduction of a third to reflect the plaintiff's contributory negligence. This case illustrates how legal causation is ultimately an evaluative judgment by the court on the extent of the defender's liability and whether it is fair that he should be liable for the full extent of the pursuer's injuries.[5]

In *Sabri-Tabrizi v Lothian Health Board*,[6] the pursuer became pregnant because of a failed sterilisation. She had a termination. Knowing that she was fertile, she had sexual intercourse with her husband on several occasions. She fell pregnant again. Although the defenders admitted liability for the first pregnancy, they denied liability for the second. The Lord Ordinary (Nimmo Smith) agreed:[7]

> 'The alleged negligence resulted in the pursuer's being still fertile, just as she would have been had the failed sterilisation operation never been carried out. The pursuer knew this, and consequently knew that there was a risk of her becoming pregnant if she had sexual intercourse with her husband ... She avers that she took precautions, but in so far as there remained a residual risk, in a question between her and the defenders I think that it is unreasonable of her to expose herself to that risk. Accordingly I regard her decision to have sexual intercourse in the knowledge that she was not sterile as constituting a *novus actus interveniens*, breaking the chain of causation, with the result that the defenders cannot be held liable for the second pregnancy and the consequences thereof.'

1   [1958] 2 All ER 342, [1958] 1 WLR 623, CA.
2   On contributory negligence, see paras 6.12–6.13 below.
3   1970 SC (HL) 20, 1970 SLT 68.
4   [2009] EWCA Civ 1404.
5   See also *Chubb Fire Ltd v Vicar of Spalding* [2010] EWCA Civ 981 (any liability of the defendant was broken as a result of the intervening acts of vandals).
6   1998 SC 373, 1998 SLT 607.
7   1998 SC 373, at 378.

(2) The order of events

6.8   The order of events may be important in determining whether the defender's breach of duty is the *causa causans* of the pursuer's injuries. In *Donaghy v National Coal Board*,[1] the defender broke the duty of care which was owed to the pursuer by leaving a detonator lying around the workplace. The pursuer took the detonator home and hit it with a hammer. As a result, he was injured. The court held that the pursuer's conduct amounted to a *novus actus interveniens*: it was unforeseeable, unreasonable, ie hazardous, and was the last act which had led to the accident. However, in *Davidson v City of Glasgow District Council*,[2] the second defender supplied the pursuer's employer, the first defender, with planks which were too short for a particular task. The employer rejected the planks but owing to the employer's alleged carelessness one of the short planks was not rejected. As a result of the plank being too short, there was an accident and the pursuer was injured. The pursuer sued the employer (first defender) and the supplier (the second defender). The second defender argued that the employer's failure to reject all the planks constituted a *novus actus interveniens*. The court held that merely because the employer's conduct was the 'last act' that led to the accident, this did not necessarily mean that it amounted to a *novus actus interveniens:*

> 'Even although there was in effect an intermediate inspection, and assuming in the alternative that the first defenders [the employer] failed to discover that one of the planks remained and was inadvertently used, it does not follow that that was negligence or that it broke the chain of causation and was the sole cause of the accident.'[3]

Thus, where an accident is caused to A as a result of a breach of duty by B *and* a breach of duty by C, the mere fact that B's breach of duty arose after C's breach of duty will not necessarily break the chain of causation to exonerate C from delictual liability. In *Grant v Sun Shipping Co Ltd*,[4] ship repairers working on a ship left hatches uncovered. By doing so, they were in breach of a duty of care owed to dock labourers on the ship. The ship owners also failed to ensure that the hatches were covered and did not provide an adequate system of lighting: this also constituted a breach of their duty of care to dock labourers on the ship. The pursuer, a dock labourer, fell through an unlit hatch. The House of Lords held that the shipowner's breach of duty did not constitute a *novus actus interveniens* breaking the chain of causation between the accident and the ship repairers' breach of duty of care towards the pursuer by leaving the hatches uncovered. Instead, both the ship owners and the ship repairers were jointly liable in delict.[5] Where there is joint liability, under s 3 of the Law Reform (Miscellaneous Provisions) (Scotland) Act 1940 the court has the power to apportion the damages between the defenders.[6]

1   1957 SLT (Notes) 35.
2   1993 SLT 479, OH.
3   1993 SLT 479 at 482 per Judge D B Robertson QC.
4   1948 SC (HL) 73, 1949 SLT 25.
5   See also *Davidson v City of Glasgow District Council* 1993 SLT 479, OH, discussed above.
6   On joint liability, see para 6.15 below.

(3) Conclusion

6.9   Where A's breach of a duty of care is a *causa sine qua non* of B's injuries, the courts appear unwilling to be persuaded that a subsequent act – even if careless – constitutes a *novus actus interveniens* unless it is so unusual or unexpected that it could not have been reasonably foreseeable, or so hazardous on the part of B, that it would be unreasonable to hold A liable. If the subsequent act is that of a third party, C, and constitutes a breach of duty owed by C to B, A and C will be held jointly liable in delict to B. If the subsequent act is that of B, A remains liable, ie B's act will not break the chain of causation but instead it will lead to a reduction of damages on the grounds of contributory negligence. Although this will be the usual result, there can, of course, still be exceptional cases where the chain of causation is broken and A's breach of duty is not treated as the *causa causans* of B's injuries. So, for example, if A injured B's foot and B suffered an infection in hospital, the chain of causation would not be broken as it is reasonably foreseeable that B might get an infection in hospital. But if the surgeon in the hospital is careless and amputates B's uninjured foot, the chain of causation is broken since the surgeon's conduct is so unusual and unexpected that it is not reasonably foreseeable and therefore it constitutes a *novus actus interveniens*. This exonerates A from delictual liability in respect of the amputation, but not, of course, in respect of the original injury to B's foot.

The chain of causation is not broken by an act of a third party where the defender's duty of care was to prevent the third party from causing injury or damage to the pursuer.[1] But as a general rule, A does not owe B a duty of care to prevent B from being injured as a result of the deliberate conduct of a third party, C.[2]

Here, of course, it is the absence of a duty of care which prevents A from being liable to B in delict.

1   *Dorset Yacht Co Ltd v Home Office* [1970] AC 1004, [1970] 2 All ER 294, HL; *Mitchell v Glasgow City Council* 2008 SLT 368, discussed above at para 5.9.

2   *Modbury Triangle Shopping Centre v Anzil* (2000) 205 CLR 254; *Chubb Fire Ltd v Vicar of Spalding* [2010] EWCA Civ 981. There are, of course, exceptions. See, for example, *Empress Car Co (Abertillery) Ltd v National Rivers Authority* [1998] 1 All ER 481, HL (a person causes a pollutant to enter controlled waters even if a necessary condition of the actual escape of the pollutant is the act of a third party, provided the third party's conduct is an act of normal life, eg vandalism, and not extraordinary).

C.   RELATED MATTERS

(1) Volenti non fit injuria

6.10   The chain of causation will be broken if the pursuer has voluntarily undertaken the risk of harm created by the defender's breach of duty. This is the doctrine of *volenti non fit injuria*. Because the chain of causation is broken and the defender's breach of duty is no longer the *causa causans* of the pursuer's injuries, the doctrine of *volenti* provides the defender with a complete defence to an action in delict. The theoretical basis of *volenti* is that by knowing acceptance of the risk, the pursuer has absolved the defender of the consequences of the defender's breach of the duty of care owed to the pursuer. In other words, the defender still owes the pursuer a duty of care, but the chain of causation is broken by the pursuer voluntarily undertaking the risk. When a sheriff determined that *volenti* applied and granted a decree of absolvitor without first accepting that defenders owed a duty and were in breach, the decision was overturned on appeal.[1]

Before the defender will succeed in the defence of *volenti non fit injuria* the defender must prove that before or at the same time as the negligent conduct,[2] the pursuer knowingly and willingly undertook the risk of the danger created by the defender's breach of duty. In *Titchener v British Railways Board*[3] the defender failed to maintain a fence made of sleepers which was positioned along a railway track. A 15-year-old girl climbed through the fence and went up the embankment to take a short cut across the railway line to a piece of waste ground where she intended to have a kiss and cuddle with her boyfriend. She was injured by a train when she was crossing the line. As we shall see,[4] the House of Lords held that in the circumstances the defender did not owe the pursuer a duty of care. But the House indicated that even if a duty of care had been owed and there had been a breach of duty, the defender would have had the defence of *volenti* since the pursuer knew and accepted the risk of being injured by a train when she crossed the line.

Because the pursuer must have knowledge of, and be *willing* to accept, the risk, the courts are unlikely to accept a plea of *volenti* in an action between employee and employer. Nevertheless, the defence succeeded in *ICI v Shatwell*.[5] Contrary to their employer's instructions the plaintiff and his brother, who were experienced shotfirers, agreed to test their detonators without first returning to a safety shelter. There was an explosion; the plaintiff was injured and his brother was killed. It was held that the employer had not been in breach of a duty of care towards the plaintiff.[6] However, the plaintiff sued the employer as vicariously liable for his brother's careless act in testing the detonator.[7] The House of Lords held that since the plaintiff had agreed with his brother to run the risk of injury by testing the detonators without first returning to a place of safety, the employer could successfully plead the defence of *volenti*.

1   *Raybould v T&N Gilmartin (Contractors) Ltd* [2018] SAC (civ) 31, 2019 SLT (Sh Ct) 1.
2   *Sabri-Tabrizi v Lothian Health Board* 1998 SC 373, 1998 SLT 607. A person who chooses to smoke cigarettes is not *volens* since the manufacturer is *not* negligent in manufacturing them: *McTear v Imperial Tobacco Ltd* 2005 SC 1 per the Lord Ordinary (Nimmo Smith) at paras 7.204 ff.
3   1984 SC (HL) 34, 1984 SLT 192. See also *Devlin v Strathclyde Regional Council* 1993 SLT 699, OH.
4   See para 16.11 below.
5   [1965] AC 656, [1964] 2 All ER 999.
6   Or in breach of any statutory duty.
7   On vicarious liability, see para 12.5 ff below.

6.11   The defence of *volenti* does not apply in the case of a rescuer. By virtue of s 149 of the Road Traffic Act 1988, the defence of *volenti* does not apply to a claim by a passenger against the driver of a vehicle which has compulsory third-party insurance. And so, where a passenger accepts a lift from a drunken driver and the car has compulsory third-party insurance, the driver cannot plead *volenti* if the passenger is injured as a result of the driver's breach of duty. The passenger's damages could be reduced on the ground of contributory negligence.

Where the duty of care is to *prevent* the defender from acting in a particular way, it would make nonsense of the existence of the duty if *volenti* could be used when the defender does the act the pursuer should have prevented. For example, the police owe a duty of care to prevent prisoners from harming themselves while on remand: if, in breach of their duty, a prisoner is able to injure or kill himself, the defence of *volenti* cannot be used.[1]

It is sometimes argued that the reason why a spectator at a dangerous sport, such as motor racing, cannot sue a participant who injures him by crashing into the crowd at high speed is that the spectator is *volens* of the risk of harm inherent in the sport. However, it is thought that the better way to analyse the situation is to argue that in the circumstances the participant does not owe the spectator a duty of care to avoid the possibility of such an accident. The organiser of the event may owe the spectator a duty of care, if, for example, the circuit was not suitable for racing or the safety precautions were inadequate; the spectator will not be *volens* of these risks simply by attending the event.[2] Where a participant in a dangerous sport is injured by another participant, again it is thought the reason an action in delict will not be successful is not that the pursuer was *volens,* but that the defender does not owe a duty of care to the pursuer to protect him from injuries the risk of which are inherent in the sport, for example being bruised when tackled at rugby football.[3] If the injury arises from conduct which is contrary to the rules of the game, the pursuer's remedy lies in assault rather than in a breach of a duty of care.

1   *Reeves v Metropolitan Commissioner* [2001] 1 AC 360.
2   See *Wooldridge v Sumner* [1963] 2 QB 43, [1962] 2 All ER 978, CA; *Lewis v Buckpool Golf Club* 1993 SLT (Sh Ct) 43.
3   *Cf Sharp v Highland and Islands Fire Board* 2005 SLT 855 which proceeded on the basis that players in a football match do owe each other a duty of care which will be breached if the injury was caused by an error going beyond what might reasonably be regarded as excusable. In the present writer's view where such an error occurs, the defender has been reckless and is liable for assault. However, a referee owes a duty of care to the players. When the referee has been negligent, an injured player is not *volens* merely by participating in the game: *Smoldon v Whitworth* [1997] PIQR P133, (1996) *Times,* 18 December 1996, CA.

(2) Contributory negligence

6.12   As we have seen, where the defender's breach of duty to the pursuer is a *causa sine qua non* of the pursuer's injuries, the courts are reluctant to accept that the pursuer's subsequentconduct is a *novus actus interveniens* or amounts to *volenti* so that the defender is exonerated from delictual liability. This is particularly the case where the pursuer has acted in the 'agony of the moment', ie reacts carelessly in a situation caused by the defender's breach of duty, for example jumps out of a window to escape a fire caused by the defender's negligence. Instead, the court will hold that the pursuer's conduct was a contributory cause of the injury. The effect of a finding of contributory negligence is to reduce the damages which would otherwise have been awarded to the pursuer, to reflect the pursuer's responsibility for the damage or injury sustained. Section 1(1) of the Law Reform (Contributory Negligence) Act 1945 provides:

> 'Where any person suffers *damage as the result partly of his own fault* and *partly due to the fault of any other person or persons*, a claim in respect of that damage shall not be defeated by reason of the fault of the person suffering the damage, but the *damages recoverable* in respect thereof *shall be reduced* to such an extent as the *court thinks just and equitable* having regard to the *claimant's share in the responsibility* for the damage.' [Emphasis added]

Before the 1945 Act applies, the pursuer must have suffered damage partly as a result of his own *fault*.[1] Fault covers the pursuer's deliberate as well as negligent actions.[2] In relation to the latter, the pursuer's act must fall below the standard of the reasonable person in the pursuer's position.[3] In *McGowan v W&JR Watson* Ltd,[4] it was observed that a momentary lapse caused by human fallibility would not fall below that standard when the pursuer had been injured because of a breach by his employer of an absolute statutory duty. The onus rests on the defender to prove that the pursuer was at fault. Although, for example, a passenger injured in a motor accident will usually be at fault if he or she fails to wear a seat belt, in *Mackay v Borthwick*,[5] the pursuer was held not to be contributorily negligent for failing to wear a seat belt since it was uncomfortable for her to wear it because she was suffering from a hiatus hernia. In *Pace v Culley*,[6] the pursuer, who was a taxi driver, failed to wear a seat belt because he had been advised by the police not to do so in the event that he might be attacked by his passengers. Although he accepted that failure to wear a seat belt could amount to contributory negligence, the Lord Ordinary (Weir) thought that the driver's conduct in this case was a misjudgement rather than a failure to take care for his own safety.[7] In *Blackhall v MacInnes*,[8] the pursuer was injured while she was changing the offside wheel of her motor car. She was held to be 20 per cent contributorily negligent because – contrary to the Highway Code – she had made no attempt to get the vehicle off the road although it was practicable to drive on the verge.

The defender must also prove that the pursuer's fault contributed to the harm sustained, ie 'but for' the pursuer's fault, the injuries or damage suffered would not have been as bad as actually occurred. In other words, the defender must establish that the pursuer's fault was a factual cause, a *causa sine qua non*, of the harm sustained. Thus, contributory negligence was established when the defender proved, on the balance of probabilities, that the pursuer would have suffered less severe neck injuries if she had worn a seat belt.[9]

1 'Fault' is defined in s 5(a) of the Law Reform (Contributory Negligence) Act 1945 as: 'wrongful act, breach of statutory duty or negligent act or omission which gives rise to liability in damages …'.
2 *Reeves v Metropolitan Commissioner* [2000] 1 AC 360 (prisoner killed himself: family's damages reduced by 50 per cent as a result of his suicide); *Corr v IBC Vehicles Ltd* [2008] 1 AC 884 (employee killed himself as a consequence of a mental disorder caused by a physical injury for which his employer was responsible: inappropriate to reduce for contributory negligence in absence of satisfactory material upon which to make a reduction).
3 See, eg, *Rickson v Bhakar* [2017] EWHC 264 QB; *McIntosh v Aviva Insurance Ltd* 2018 GWD 3-57.
4 2007 SLT 169.
5 1982 SLT 265, OH.
6 1992 SLT 1073, OH.
7 The contributory negligence, if any, would have been *de minimis* in respect of the total claim and could therefore be ignored.
8 1997 SLT 649, OH.
9 *Hanlon v Cuthbertson* 1981 SLT (Notes) 57, OH. Cf *Neil v Docherty and Akram* (23 May 1996, unreported), HC, where the plaintiff's injuries were sustained on initial impact, ie before she was ejected from the taxi because she was not wearing a seat belt.

6.13 But before a reduction can be made it must be established that the pursuer's conduct was a potent cause of the harm he has suffered.[1] In *St George v The Home Office*[2] the complainant was a prisoner. He was a drug addict and an alcoholic. In his cell, he was put in a top bunk. He suffered a withdrawal seizure and fell out of the bunk and sustained head injuries. While accepting that he might have been at fault in becoming addicted to drugs and alcohol, the Court of Appeal held that his addiction had no causal potency in relation to the defendant's negligent conduct which had led to his head injuries *viz* being put in a top bunk. In the same way, a patient who has suffered harm because of medical negligence is not contributorily negligent merely because her lifestyle choices, for example smoking or drinking, have led her to seek medical treatment. There is, of course, causal potency where the claimant's drug or alcohol induced state is closely connected in time and place to, or is mixed up with, the negligent conduct of the defender. This would arise where, for example, the pursuer was drunk as he was walking along a road when he was knocked down by the defender and the accident was attributable to a combination of their negligence.

When contributory negligence is established, the proportion to be deducted from the damages is a matter for the discretion of the judge, ie what the judge considers just and equitable having regard to the pursuer's share in the responsibility for the damage.[3] In *St George v The Home* Office, the Court of Appeal held that even if the prisoner's addiction had amounted to contributory negligence, in the circumstances it would not have been just and equitable to make any deduction. But in most cases if the pursuer is found contributorily negligent, some deduction will be made.

This can vary from as little as 5 per cent in 'agony of the moment' cases to as much as 80 per cent.[4] It is submitted that 100 per cent deduction is not possible under the Law Reform (Contributory Negligence) Act 1945 since in those circumstances the pursuer would be solely responsible and not 'share in the responsibility for the damage'.[5] A drunken pedestrian run down by a careless driver has had his damages reduced by 50 per cent as a result of contributory negligence.[6] The fact that a person is lying intoxicated in the middle of the road does not, however preclude an award of damages when run over by a negligent driver.[7] Similarly, a guest injured at a party had his damages reduced by 50 per cent because he had been drinking heavily.[8]

Damages for pure economic loss can be reduced on the grounds of the pursuer's contributory negligence.[9] However, in a case of fraudulent – as opposed to negligent – misrepresentation, the defender cannot seek to have the pursuer's damages reduced on the ground of the pursuer's contributory negligence.[10]

1 See, eg, *Fairley v Edinburgh Trams Ltd* [2019] CSOH 50, 2019 SLT 819.
2 [2008] EWCA Civ 1068. Appeal courts will not interfere with the apportionment at first instance unless, as Lord Hodge put it, the court had: 'manifestly and to a substantial degree gone wrong'. *Jackson v Murray* [2015] UKSC 5.
3 Appeal courts will not interfere with the apportionment at first instance unless, as Lord Hodge put it, the court had: "manifestly and to a substantial degree gone wrong". *Jackson v Murray* [2015] UKSC 5.
4 *Uddin v Associated Portland Cement Manufacturers Ltd* [1965] 2 QB 582, [1965] 2 All ER 213, CA.
5 If the pursuer is solely responsible, the defender will escape liability because either his breach of duty is not the *causa causans* or the pursuer is *volens*: see *ICI v Shatwell* [1965] AC 656. Cf *McEwan v Lothian Buses* 2006 SCLR 592 where the Lord Ordinary (Emslie) considered at para 32 that there was no logical reason why there could not be 100 per cent contributory negligence if the

degree of fault on the part of the defender was regarded as too small to warrant an apportionment.

6 *Malcolm v Fair* 1993 SLT 342, OH. See also *Kemp v Secretary of State for Scotland* 2000 SLT 471 (pursuer's damages reduced by one-third because he was drunk at the time of the accident). In *Gilfillan v Barbour* 2003 SC 1127 in cross actions arising from a collision, both parties had their damages reduced by 50 per cent as both had been careless. See also *Robb v Salamis (M and I) Ltd* 2007 SLT 158 (pursuer held to be 50 per cent contributorily negligent when he was injured when descending from a top bunk due to an unsuitable ladder: he knew that the ladders were often removed and not properly replaced: *sed quaere?*); *Wallace v Glasgow City Council* [2011] CSIH 57 (pursuer sustained foot injuries when opening a window in the staff toilet: damages reduced by 50 per cent as it was a deliberate act which she knew was dangerous); *Cowan v Hopetoun House Preservation Trust* [2013] CSOH 9 (pursuer who was attending a guided 'bat walk' at night at a stately home fell over a ha-ha on taking a short cut back to the car park: contributory negligence assessed as 75 per cent).

7 *Cameron v Swan [2021] CSIH 30, 2021 GWD 20-279.*

8 *Brannan v Airtours* (Times, 1 February 1999), CA. Although there is no duty to prevent an adult from becoming drunk, there may be a duty to look after the drunk person if she becomes incapable of looking after herself. When there is such a duty and it is broken, the plaintiff's damages can be reduced on the grounds that she got inebriated: *Barrett v Ministry of Defence* [1995] 3 All ER 87, CA (two-thirds contributorily negligent).

9 *Platform Home Loans Ltd v Oyston Shipways Ltd* [1999] 1 All ER 833, HL. For further discussion, see beyond para 16.9.

10 *Standard Chartered Bank v Pakistan National Shipping Corpn* [2003] 1 All ER 173, HL.

(3) Illegality

6.14   As a matter of public policy, if the pursuer is participating in a criminal activity at the time he is injured, he may be barred from obtaining reparation: for example if A and B steal a car and A is injured as a result of B's careless driving or a thief is shot by the owner of a house in the course of a burglary.[1] These are examples of the principle that a cause of action does not arise from a wrong committed by the pursuer: *ex turpi causa non oritur actio*. In *Gray v Thames Trains* Ltd,[2] the plaintiff suffered post-traumatic stress disorder after being injured in a train crash caused by the defendant's negligence. As a result of his psychological problems, he killed a man. He was convicted of manslaughter on the grounds of diminished responsibility and detained in a mental hospital. The House of Lords held that the plaintiff could not obtain compensation for loss of earnings for the time he was compulsorily detained as that loss had arisen from the plaintiff's criminal act, ie the manslaughter.[3] *Gray* was followed in *Henderson v Dorset Health Care University NHS Foundation Trust*[4] in which a patient who killed her mother during a severe psychotic episode was unable to recover damages against the health authority for their negligent failure to return her to hospital before the incident. Where the injuries have not been caused by the pursuer's criminal acts the defence will fail[5] unless the pursuer and defender were engaged in joint criminal activity.[6]

However, as the doctrine is a matter of public policy, the bar is not automatic and depends on the circumstances. In *Weir v Wyper*,[7] the pursuer was not barred when she was injured in a car crash even though she knew that the driver had only a provisional licence. When the action is not barred, the pursuer's damages could, of course, be reduced on the ground of contributory negligence.[8]

1   *Duncan v Ross Harper & Murphy* 1993 SLT 105n, OH.
2   [2009] UKHL 33.
3   See also *Stone & Rolls Ltd v Moore Stevens* [2009] UKHL 39 (where a 'one man-company' deliberately engaged in serious fraud, the *ex turpi causa* principle prevented the company suing its auditors in failing to detect the fraud).
4   [2020] UKSC 43, [2021] AC 562.
5   *McLaughlin v Morrison* [2014] CSOH 123, 2014 SLT 862. The pursuer was engaged in a criminal act, mounting an attack on licensed premises as part of a 'turf war', but this could not excuse the pursuer who knocked him down with her car intentionally causing life-changing injuries.
6   *Andersen v Hameed* [2010] CSOH 99 (a passenger in a car involved in an accident who had allowed himself to be driven while knowing the car had been taken without the owner's consent was participating in a joint criminal activity and was therefore not entitled to recover damages from the driver).
7   1992 SCLR 483, 1992 SLT 579, OH.
8   *Taylor v Leslie* 1998 SLT 1248, 1998 Rep LR 110, OH (defender drove car while unlicensed, uninsured and underage. Passenger killed. Conduct not regarded as reprehensible by the community of Shapinsay, a remote island. The deceased had encouraged the defender to speed. Damages reduced by 50 per cent).

(4) Joint fault

6.15   Joint fault arises where harm is caused to the pursuer as a result of the conduct of more than one defender. This is known as joint liability if the harm has been caused as a result of a breach by each defender of a duty of care owed to the pursuer; in the case of other delicts, it is known as joint wrongdoing. Before there can be joint liability, each breach of duty must have materially contributed to, or materially increased the risk of, the *same* delict to the pursuer. In *Anderson v St Andrew's Ambulance Association*[1] a passenger in a bus was injured in a collision between the bus and an ambulance. The bus driver had failed to observe a 'slow' sign; the ambulance driver had failed to observe a 'halt' sign. The court held that this was a case of joint liability, for both drivers were responsible for the same wrong suffered by the pursuer. Conversely, in *Fleming v McGillivray*[2] the court held that it was not a case of joint liability where an injured pursuer sued a van driver for careless driving and the owner of the van for failing to have compulsory third-party insurance: the driver was being sued for breach of his duty of care (delict 1), while the owner was being sued for breach of statutory duty in not having insurance (delict 2). Since they were not responsible for the same delict, this was not a case of joint liability or joint wrongdoing.

If A and B are jointly liable, the pursuer may sue A or B or both. If the pursuer sues only A and obtains a decree, if A pays the damages the pursuer cannot then sue B; but if A does not pay the damages, the pursuer can sue B. If the pursuer successfully sues both A and B, he will be awarded a joint and several decree. This entitles the pursuer to obtain *all* the damages from either A or B. In *Barker v Corus*,[3] the House of Lords held[4] that where the defendants' liability had only been established by relying on the *Fairchild* exception to 'but for' causation,[5] liability was not joint and several but should be apportioned between the defendants. This would mean that the complainant might not obtain all his damages if one or more of the defendants were insolvent and uninsured. *Barker* has now been reversed by retrospective legislation[6] but only in respect of cases, such as *Barker* itself, involving mesothelioma. The extent to which *Barker* will be followed in non-mesothelioma cases remains to be seen but it will only apply if resort has had to be made to the *Fairchild* exception. In *Stoddard v Wright*,[7] however, the Lord Ordinary (Uist) chose to follow the orthodox reasoning of Lord Rodger in *Barker* rejecting apportionment.

Where there is joint and several liability and A has paid all the damages, the court can apportion the damages between A and B; and if B was not sued in the original action, A can, nevertheless, recover from B the proportion of the damages which the court deems attributable to B's conduct.[8] Where the pursuer is contributorily negligent, the total damages to be paid by A or B will be reduced to reflect the pursuer's responsibility for the injury or harm suffered.

1   1943 SC 248, 1943 SLT 258.
2   1946 SC 1, 1945 SLT 301.
3   [2006] 2 AC 572.
4   Lord Rodger dissenting.
5   Discussed above at para 6.5.

6   Compensation Act 2006, s 3.
7   [2007] CSOH 138.
8   Law Reform (Miscellaneous Provisions) (Scotland) Act 1940, s 3. The proportions *inter se* the defenders are what the court, or jury, considers just in the circumstances: see, for example, *BOC v Groves* 1993 SLT 360, OH (75 per cent and 25 per cent); *Phee v Gordon* 2013 SLT 439. (Pursuer was injured by a stray golf ball. The golfer who hit the shot was 20 per cent liable and the golf club 80 per cent liable in view of the hazardous layout of the course.)

Part III

DELICTUAL LIABILITY IN SPECIFIC SOCIAL AND ECONOMIC CONTEXTS

INTRODUCTION

Having discussed the general principles of delictual liability, it is now proposed to examine the law of delict as it operates in certain specific social and economic contexts. As we shall see, the general principle of delictual liability for harm caused to the pursuer as a result of the defender's *culpa* is often supplemented by other common law principles, for example, nuisance and vicarious liability. More importantly, perhaps, in certain areas common law delictual liability has been supplemented or supplanted by statutory liability. It is thought that these developments are better understood if discussed in the context of the particular social and economic relationships in which they occur.

CHAPTER 7

Professional liability

7.1 The general principles of the law of delict apply where a person causes harm to another in the course of his trade, business or profession.[1] Often of course, the person harmed will be a client or a customer of the defender; if this is so, the pursuer's primary remedy will be to sue the defender in contract. Almost inevitably, the defender will have assumed responsibility for the interests of the client or customer and the customer or client will have relied on the defender's expertise. Accordingly, unless the terms of their contract expressly negative delictual liability, the defender will also owe the pursuer a *Henderson v Merrett*[2] duty of care to prevent economic loss arising from the defender's negligence.[3] Put another way, where the client and professional are directly linked by contract, concurrent liability in contract and delict can arise.[4] If there is no direct contractual relationship between the parties, liability can lie only in delict.

The question of duty, then, is approached in the same way as it is in other contexts in which negligence occurs. The specialty in professional negligence concerns the standard of care. In determining whether there has been a breach of a duty of care, the defender's conduct is judged by the standard of care expected in his or her profession.[5] Put another way, in order to establish that the defender was negligent, the pursuer must prove that the defender's conduct fell below that of the reasonable accountant, architect, lawyer, medical practitioner or surveyor etc. While ultimately a question of law,[6] the usual practice of persons in the same trade, business or profession as the defender will be a significant factor, but not necessarily decisive in determining whether the defender was negligent.

1   On professional negligence, see Kenneth Norrie, SULI *Delict* Chapter 19.
2   See *Henderson v Merrett Syndicates Ltd* [1995] 2 AC 145, [1994] 3 All ER 506, HL, discussed at para 4.16 ff above.
3   See Chapter 4 above, paras 4.16–4.21.
4   On concurrent liability see *Realstone Ltd v J&E Shepherd* [2008] CSOH 31, [2008] PNLR 21 per Lord Hodge at paras 10–25.

5   In *Andrews v Greater Glasgow Health Board* [2019] CSOH 31, 2019 SLT 727 it was held that a junior doctor owes the patient the same standard of care as a more experienced doctor.

6   *Bolitho v City and Hackney Health Authority* [1998] AC 232, [1997] 4 All ER 771, HL.

7.2   It can be particularly difficult to establish negligence where the defender's conduct involves an exercise of professional judgment. Often there will be several courses of action open to the defender. In these circumstances, the defender will *not* be negligent if she adopted a course of action which resulted in harm to the pursuer unless no reasonable professional person in her position would have chosen that option. Nor does it matter that the course of action chosen was *not* the normal practice in the profession. In the leading case of *Hunter v Hanley*[1] the pursuer alleged that the defender, a doctor, was negligent in using a needle which was unsuitable for treating the patient. In discussing the standard of care appropriate to a doctor, the Lord President (Clyde) observed:[2]

> '… in regard to deviation from ordinary professional practice … such deviation is not necessarily evidence of negligence. Indeed it would be disastrous if this were so, for all inducement to progress in medical science would then be destroyed. Even a substantial deviation from normal practice may be warranted by the particular circumstances. To establish liability by a doctor where deviation from normal practice is alleged, three facts require to be established. First of all it must be proved that there is a normal practice; secondly it must be proved that the defender has not adopted that practice; and thirdly (and this is of crucial importance) it must be established that the course which the doctor adopted is one which no professional man of ordinary skill would have taken if he had been acting with ordinary care'.

Thus, it is not enough that the defender's conduct deviated from normal practice: it must be demonstrated that no professional man of ordinary skill would have followed the course taken by the defender. However, a pursuer will not fail merely because she cannot establish that there was a normal practice which the defender did not follow: the crucial issue is the third *viz* that the course that the defender followed was one no professional man of ordinary skill would have taken if acting with ordinary care.[3] Even if the pursuer can establish that a responsible body of medical opinion regards the defender's decision or conduct as wrong, the defender will not be regarded as having been negligent if there is also a responsible body of medical opinion which regards the defender's decision or conduct as reasonable in the circumstances.[4]

1   1955 SC 200, 1955 SLT 213.
2   1955 SC 200 at 206. Lord Clyde's approach was approved by McNair J in the leading English case, *Bolam v Friern Hospital Management Committee* [1957] 2 All ER 118, [1957] 1 WLR 582.
3   *Gerrard v Royal Infirmary of Edinburgh NHS Trust* 2005 SC 192. In *Atwal Enterprises Ltd v Toner t/a Donal Toner Associates* 2006 SLT 537, the Lord Ordinary (Emslie) observed at 547 that it was well settled that liability for professional negligence could only arise where, on the evidence, no ordinarily competent and careful member of the profession could have been guilty of the particular failure alleged against the defender. This case concerned an architect.
4   *Maynard v West Midlands Regional Health Authority* [1985] 1 All ER 635, [1984] 1 WLR 634, HL. The number of specialist doctors who accept the defender's practices need not be substantial provided they are responsible: *Defreitas v O'Brien* [1995] 6 Med LR 108. If there is no recognised standard practice, the court must determine whether or not the defender took reasonable care in all the circumstances: *AB v Tameside and Glossop Health Authority* [1997] 8 Med LR 91, CA (defendant sent a secret letter to patients informing them that a health worker who had treated them was HIV positive: defendant not negligent simply because they sent a standard letter rather than organising face-to-face disclosure of the tiny risk of infection).

7.3   *Gordon v Wilson*[1] provides an illustration of the formidable difficulties facing a pursuer in an action of medical negligence, particularly where there are conflicting bodies of professional opinion. In that case, the pursuer argued that a doctor was negligent in delaying to refer a patient to a specialist.[2] Although the pursuer established that there was a responsible body of medical opinion which took the view that a reasonable doctor would have referred the patient to a specialist at an earlier stage, the court held that the defender was not negligent because the defender could show that there was also a responsible body of medical opinion to the effect that a reasonable doctor would not have referred the patient to a specialist until the defender had done so. Accordingly, the pursuer's action failed. Professional negligence cannot be established by preferring one body of professional opinion to another; instead, the pursuer must prove that no reasonable doctor exercising his ordinary clinical skills would have taken the defender's course of action in the circumstances of the case.[3]

The law was summarised by Lord Hodge in *Honisz v Lothian Health Board*:[4]

'First, as a general rule, where there are two opposing schools of thought among the relevant group of responsible medical practitioners as to the appropriateness of a particular practice, it is not the function of the court to prefer one school over the other … Secondly, however, the court does not defer to the opinion of the relevant professionals to the extent that, if a defender lead evidence that other responsible professionals among the relevant group of medical practitioners would have done what the impugned medical practitioner did, the judge must in all cases conclude that there has been no negligence. This is because, thirdly, in exceptional cases the court may conclude that a practice which responsible medical practitioners have perpetuated does not stand up to rational analysis ... Where the judge is satisfied that the body of professional opinion, on which the defender relies, is not reasonable or responsible he may find the medical practitioner guilty of negligence, despite that body of opinion sanctioning his conduct. This will rarely occur as the assessment and balancing of risks and benefits are matters of clinical judgment. Thus it will normally require compelling expert evidence to demonstrate that an opinion of another medical expert is one which that other expert could not have held if he had taken care to examine the basis of the practice. Where experts have applied their minds to the comparative risks and benefits of a course of action and have reached a defensible conclusion, the court will have no basis for rejecting their view and concluding that the pursuer has proved negligence in terms of the *Hunter v Hanley* test. As Lord Browne-Wilkinson said in *Bolitho* (at p 243D–E) "it is only where the judge can be satisfied that the body of expert opinion cannot logically be supported at all that such opinion will not provide the benchmark by which the defendant's conduct falls to be assessed".'

These cases were concerned with the medical profession. But as indicated above, the test for establishing the requisite standard of care is applicable in relation to other professions where an exercise of professional judgment is involved.[5]

1   1992 SLT 849 n, See also, for example, *Hannigan v Lanarkshire Acute Hospitals NHS Trust* [2012] CSOH 152; *JD v Lothian Health Board* 2018 SCLR 1.

2   It should also be remembered that in order to establish causation the pursuer must prove that 'but for' the doctor's omission the treatment would have had more than a 50 per cent chance of success: *Kenyon v Bell* 1953 SC 125; *Hotson v East Berkshire Area Health Authority* [1987] AC 750; *Gregg v Scott* [2005] 2 AC 176.

3   In *Bolitho v City and Hackney Health Authority* [1998] AC 232 it was stressed by the House of Lords that the body of medical opinion must be reasonable and responsible. In other words, there must be a logical basis for the opinion the experts support. Although this is ultimately a question of law, it would only be in rare cases that the court would reject the medical experts' views as unreasonable.

4   [2006] CSOH 24 at para 39. Lord Hodge's summary has been approved in many subsequent cases.

5   See, for example, *Campbell v Borders Health Board* [2012] CSIH 49; *Coyle v Lanarkshire Health Board* [2013] CSOH 167 (midwives); *Henderson v Merrett Syndicates Ltd (No 2)* [1997] LRLR 265, QBD (Comm Ct) (underwriting agents); *Sneesby v Goldings* [1995] 2 EGLR 102, CA (surveyors); *Scott v*

Lothian Regional Council 1999 Rep LR 15 (guidance teachers); *Leeds & Holbeck Building Society v Alex Morison & Co (No 2)* 2001 SCLR 41; *McCrindle v Maclay, Murray & Spens* [2013] CSOH 72 (lawyers); *Gilfillan v Barbour* 2003 SLT 1127 (police); *Atwal Enterprise Ltd v Toner t/a Donal Toner Associates* 2006 SLT 537 (architects); *WTL International Ltd Retirement Benefits Scheme Trustees v Edwards* [2010] CSOH 34 (actuaries).

7.4 While the standard of care established in *Hunter v Hanley*[1] applies generally across those whose practice can be considered 'professional',[2] it can be seen that some of the most difficult complications arise in the medical context.

In *Darnley v Croydon Health Services NHS Trust*,[3] the claimant who had been assaulted, attended an Accident and Emergency Unit with head injuries. Having been informed by the receptionist that he would face a four-to five-hour wait, he left after 19 minutes and went home. Unfortunately, he developed permanent brain damage which would not have occurred had he remained in the hospital. The receptionist had omitted to inform him that he would be triaged within 30 minutes of his arrival. The claim failed at first instance and in the Court of Appeal on the basis that there had been no assumption of responsibility and there was no duty on staff to provide accurate information about waiting times. The claimant was held responsible for his own injuries having chosen to leave against advice that he should wait. The decision was reversed in the Supreme Court. A hospital–patient relationship is established as soon as a patient presents for treatment. It is very well established that this relationship imposes on the hospital a duty of care. The duty of the receptionist was not to provide misleading information. The standard applied was that of an averagely competent and reasonably well-informed person performing the function of an A&E receptionist. The hospital, then, was in breach of duty; the claimant would not have gone home had the duty not to give misleading information been breached and would not have suffered the medical consequences. The hospital was liable.

The treatment of patients gives rise to issues of autonomy. Physical intervention without consent would, in most contexts, be considered an assault.[4] Medical treatment proceeds based on the patient's consent but, given the complexities of human health and the highly specialised nature of modern medicine, the consent of a patient to a given course of action may be more or less meaningless unless it is informed by discussion between doctor and patient regarding any risks inherent in the proposed procedure, alternative courses of action, the consequences of taking no action and so on depending on the circumstances. The duty to inform patients then, forms an important element of the duty of care owed by doctors to their patients. This is known as the doctrine of informed consent. Prior to the Supreme Court decision in *Montgomery v Lanarkshire Health Board*[5] the failure of a doctor to disclose risks with a very low probability of materialising would not normally be negligent.[6] During her ante-natal care, Mrs Montgomery's consultant had not informed her of a number of low probability risks associated with the vaginal delivery of a large baby from a small mother. Sadly, all these risks materialised, the child suffered hypoxia with consequent cerebral palsy affecting all four limbs. Mrs Mongomery's contention, that had she been informed of the risk of shoulder dystocia, she would have elected to have had the baby delivered by caesarean section, was accepted. It was held in the Supreme Court that the duty to disclose risks is not determined by the probability of the risk materialising, but by the significance which a reasonable person in the position of the patient would be likely to attach to the risk. Doctors, therefore, are under a duty to inform patients on risks which the patient would regard as significant.[7]

1   1955 SC 200, 1955 SLT 213.
2   For judicial discussion on the meaning of professional see *ICL Tech Ltd & Others v Johnston Oils Ltd* [2012] CSOH 62 per Lord Hodge at paras 14–23; *Dickson v Hygienic Institute* 1910 SC 352, 4 SLR 286 per Lord Dundas at 289.
3   [2018] UKSC 50.
4   See para 1.3 above.
5   [2015] UKSC 11, 2015 SLT 189.
6   *Sidaway v Board of Governors of the Bethlehem Royal Hospital and Maudsley Hospital* [1985] AC 571; followed in *Moyes v Lothian Health Board* 1990 SLT 444.
7   For discussion see E Reid, '*Montgomery v Lanarkshire Health Board* and the Rights of the Reasonable Patient' (2015) 19 ELR 360.

7.5   In *Khan v Meadows*,[1] the patient, Mrs Meadows, sought advice on whether she carried the gene for haemophilia. Her doctor arranged for her to be tested for haemophilia but neglected to inform her that she would require further genetic testing to affirm whether she carried the gene. She subsequently gave birth to a boy with both haemophilia and autism. Mrs Meadows established that she would have terminated her pregnancy had she known that she was indeed a carrier. In the High Court she was awarded damages based on the additional costs of raising a child with both conditions. The Court of Appeal reversed this decision so far as costs associated with autism were concerned. This was affirmed in the Supreme Court. Dr Khan was under a duty to provide the patient with sufficient information to enable her to make an informed decision on continuing or terminating her pregnancy based on the risk of haemophilia. That duty was breached. The child's autism was not connected in any way to the risk of haemophilia. The risk of autism, therefore, was not within the scope of the duty owed to the patient.[2]

A new duty of care was recognised, somewhat tentatively, in *ABC v St George's Healthcare* Trust.[3] The case concerned the disclosure of a father's confidential medical information to his daughter. The father suffered from Huntingdon's disease, but he did not want this information disclosed to his family. Huntingdon's disease is a hereditary condition with a 50 per cent chance of being passed to descendants. The daughter was eventually informed of the father's condition, but only after she had passed the 24-week stage of pregnancy by which time it was too late to terminate. Subsequently tests confirmed that she, too, had the condition. The question before the court was whether a duty was owed the daughter to inform her of her father's condition. Yip J found that in the circumstances there was a duty on the health care professionals involved to balance the interest of the daughter in being informed against the father's interest and the public interest in maintaining confidentiality. This duty had not been breached, because the defendants had done just that. Moreover, the claimant failed to establish her contention that she would have terminated the pregnancy had she been informed of her father's condition in time.[4]

Finally, in *Whittington Hospital NHS Trust v XX,*[5] a hospital had admitted negligence in failing to diagnose cervical cancer. The patient was rendered infertile by the treatment applied. It was held in the Supreme Court that she was able to recover damages which included the costs of surrogacy.

1   [2021] UKSC 21.
2   See further on the scope of the duty on professionals to give advice *Manchester Building Society v Grant Thornton UK LLP* [2021] UKSC 20, [2021] 3 WLR 81.
3   [2020] EWHC 455 (QB) This is an example of the recognition of a duty of care in novel circumstances involving the application of the fair, just and reasonable test. See para 4.1 above.
4   For discussion see C McMillan, 'ABC v St George's Healthcare Trust and Ors: A new duty of care?' (2020) 24 ELR 394.
5   [2020] UKSC 14.

7.6 The position of the legal professions requires further treatment. Where a solicitor takes instructions from her client, liability can arise in contract and delict.[1] The contract may stipulate a higher standard of care than that required by the law of negligence, ie strict liability rather than a failure to take reasonable care.[2] As a general rule, the solicitor owes a duty of care to her client: she does not owe a duty of care to a third party, for example a person who would benefit from an *inter vivos* transaction.[3] However, where a solicitor gives advice or information to a person who is not a client, ie who does not have a contractual relationship with the solicitor, the solicitor may be liable in delict provided the *Henderson v Merrett* criteria for a duty of care exist.[4] In other words, there must be voluntary assumption of responsibility by the solicitor and concomitant reliance on the third party's part or it must be fair, just and reasonable to impose the duty. Where such a duty exists, the pursuer will only succeed if it can be established that the solicitor was negligent in giving the advice, ie that a reasonable solicitor would not have given that advice in the circumstances.[5]

1   In *Stoffel & Co v Grondona* 2020 UKSC 47, [2021] AC 540 the fact that the transaction was funded by a fraudulent mortgage application did not prevent liability to the client when a law firm negligently failed to register the client's title to property.

2   *Mortgage Corporation Ltd v Mitchells Roberton* 1997 SLT 1305, OH.

3   *Tait v Brown & McRae* 1997 SLT (Sh Ct) 63.

4   *Newcastle Building Society v Paterson Robertson and Graham* 2001 SC 734 (pursuer lent money to borrower. It was a condition of the loan that the defenders, the borrower's solicitors, confirm certain matters in a report. The report was inaccurate. Held that the defenders owed a duty of care to the pursuer since the loan would not have gone ahead if the report had been accurate). No duty was owed to the lender In *Steel v NRAM* [2018] UKSC 13 discussed at para 4.21 above.

5   When the client is an experienced businessman and a transaction does not involve any hidden legal pitfalls, a solicitor is not obliged to investigate matters outwith his instructions or warn the client of the commercial risks in the transaction: *Pickergill v Riley* (2004), *Times* 2 March 2004. See also *Keith v Chalmers* 2004 SC 287.

7.7   What of the situation where a solicitor acts on the instructions of a client but as a result of the solicitor's carelessness does not give effect to the client's instructions with the result that a third party suffers loss? Normally, no duty of care is owed to the third party.[1] An important exception exists, however, when the third party is a 'disappointed legatee'. Consider the following problem.

A instructs a solicitor to draw up a will under which B is the principal beneficiary. As a result of the solicitor's carelessness, the will is invalid, and B does not obtain the legacy. There is no contractual relationship between B and the solicitor. Therefore, B's remedy, if any, lies in delict against the solicitor. B has suffered pure economic loss and before there is delictual liability the solicitor must owe B a duty of care to prevent B suffering such loss. Unlike the advice and information situations, B has not relied on the solicitor's expertise: B will probably *not* know the solicitor's identity. Even if the solicitor can be said to have assumed responsibility for B's interests, the *Henderson v Merrett* duty of care will not normally arise because of the absence of concomitant reliance on B's part. We have therefore a situation where the courts must be prepared on policy grounds to impose a duty of care before the solicitor can be liable in delict.[2]

For many years, the Scottish courts refused to recognise such a duty of care.[3] However, in England the issue was fully explored by the House of Lords in *White v Jones*.[4] After a family quarrel, a father struck his daughters out of his will. Later he relented. In spite of the family's attempts to encourage their father's solicitor to fulfil the old man's instructions, the father died before the will was altered in favour of the daughters. By a majority,[5] the House of Lords held that the solicitor owed a duty of care to the disappointed legatees. For Lord Goff and Lord Browne-Wilkinson it was enough that the solicitor had assumed responsibility for the potential beneficiaries: this was implicit when accepting their father's instructions. Concomitant reliance was not necessary to impose a duty of care in the case of disappointed legatees. Lord Nolan found actual reliance since the defender had acted as a solicitor for the family, not merely the father. Lord Mustill dissented owing to the absence of concomitant reliance which he felt was constitutive of a *Henderson v Merrett* duty of care.

1   There are very rare cases where a duty can arise because of exceptional degrees of proximity between the parties and the solicitor has assumed responsibility for the third party: *Mortgage Corporation Ltd v Mitchells Roberton* 1997 SLT 1305, OH.

2   Ie the duty of care is being used as a threshold device: see Chapter 4 above.

3   *Robertson v Fleming* (1861) 23 D (HL) 8, (1861) 4 Macq 167 per Lord Campbell LC at 177; *Weir v J M Hodge & Son* 1990 SLT 266 per the Lord Ordinary (Weir) at 270; *MacDougall v MacDougall's Executors* 1994 SLT 1178.

4   [1995] 2 AC 207, [1995] 1 All ER 691, HL.

5   Lord Goff of Chieveley, Lord Browne-Wilkinson and Lord Nolan; Lords Mustill and Keith of Kinkel dissented.

7.8   It is quite clear that the majority in *White v Jones* felt that a negligent solicitor *should* be liable in this situation. But, although we may be sympathetic to the policy, the reasoning is less than happy. In particular, the absence of the need for reliance makes it impossible to fit *White v Jones* within the *Henderson v Merrett* general duty of care to prevent economic loss. In spite of its difficulties, *White v Jones* has been transplanted into Scots law.[1]

Given that the potential pursuer falls into a restricted class, ie the 'legatee' named in the instructions and therefore known to the solicitor, it is thought that a duty of care can be justified in these circumstances.[2] For this reason, Scottish courts have not been prepared to extend *White v Jones* beyond disappointed legatees.[3] In *Fraser v McArthur* Stewart,[4] a solicitor advised his client that he could not divide the tenancy of a croft. Acting on that advice, the client nominated an individual as the tenant of the croft. After the client died, it was discovered that the advice was wrong and that the testator could have left the tenancy of the croft to be divided between his residuary legatees. The residuary legatees sued the solicitor in delict. The Lord Ordinary (Brailsford) held that while the solicitor had owed a duty of care to his client, he did not owe a duty of care to the residuary legatees. *White v Jones* should only apply where owing to the negligence of the solicitor the will did not represent the last stated intentions of the testator and the potential beneficiary was left disappointed. In *Matthews v Hunter & Robertson*[5] owing to the negligence of his solicitor, a man failed to evacuate a survivorship destination in favour of his former wife. As a result, when he died his estate was diminished by the value of the property which passed to his wife by virtue of the destination. The Lord Ordinary (Brodie) held that the deceased's executor could not recover damages in respect of the wrong advice given to the deceased because he did not sustain any loss while he was alive and there was therefore no actionable delictual claim which could transmit to the executor. Lord Brodie also considered that it would not be fair, just or reasonable to impose a duty of care on the solicitor vis-à-vis the executor, to take reasonable care to ensure that the estate was not diminished after the death of his client as a result of inaccurate advice that might have been given years before the executor had been nominated let alone confirmed. In *McLeod v Crawford*,[6] a solicitor advised a client to accept a full and final settlement rather than provisional damages. After the client died, his widow and children raised an action against the solicitor for professional negligence in respect of the advice he had given to the deceased. Lord Woolman held that the solicitor did not owe a duty of care to the widow or children. At the time the advice was given, there could have been a conflict of interests between the deceased and his family on the settlement he should choose. The solicitors had never assumed responsibility for the interests of the widow or the family. The necessary proximity was therefore absent and accordingly no duty of care arose. If there had been negligence the deceased's executor would have a remedy as the estate could sue.

1   *Robertson v Watt & Co* (4 July 1995, unreported), a decision of the Second Division; *Holmes v Bank of Scotland* 2002 SLT 544; *McLeod v Crawford* [2010] CSOH 101.
2   A better solution, perhaps, would be to allow the court to rectify the will so that it would correspond to the testator's final intentions, evidence of which would have to be very convincing!
3   *McLeod v Crawford* [2010] CSOH 101. In *McDonald v Sutherland* [2008] CSOH 150, the Lord Ordinary (Matthews) took the view (*obiter*) that *White v Jones* could apply to a disappointed liferenter if the liferent which he had purported to set up failed because of the solicitor's negligence.
4   2009 SLT 31.
5   [2007] CSOH 88.
6   [2010] CSOH 101.

7.9   Where there has been a breach of a duty of care by a solicitor, there may be difficulties in quantifying the pursuer's loss. In *Kyle v P & J Stormonth Darling WS*,[1] the defender failed to lodge the pursuer's appeal in time, with the result that the pursuer lost the opportunity to do so. In rejecting the defender's argument that the pursuer was entitled to damages only if it could be established on the balance of probabilities that the appeal would have been successful, the Lord Ordinary (Prosser) said:[2]

> 'where there has been deprivation of a legal right, that will in itself constitute a completed wrong, and one will be entitled, as a matter of valuation, to take into consideration all reasonable prospects of success, if they exceed nuisance value, even if they fall short of probability'.

In *Arthur J S Hall & Co v Simons*,[3] the House of Lords held that under English law barristers no longer have immunity from being sued for professional negligence in their conduct of civil or criminal cases. In his dissenting speech on the latter point, Lord Hope, a Scottish Lord of Appeal in Ordinary, considered that there should still be immunity in respect of the conduct of criminal proceedings. In *Wright v Paton Farrell*,[4] the First Division held that advocates and solicitors continued to have immunity under Scots law in respect of the conduct of criminal cases. The position in relation to the conduct of civil proceedings remains unclear,[5] however it is now established that claims may be brought against the Lord Advocate for malicious prosecution.[6] It has always been accepted that an advocate can be liable for giving negligent advice, for example an opinion on a point of law.[7]

1   1993 SC 57, 1994 SLT 191, affirming 1992 SLT 264, OH; *McCrindle Group Ltd v Maclay Murray & Spens*.[2013] CSOH 72. See also *Brits v Kilcoyne & Co* [2017] CSIH 47 (Ex Div) *Watkins v Hugh James Ford Simey* [2019] UKSC 54, [2019] 1 WLR 6549; and *Perry v Raleys Solicitors* [2019] UKSC 5.
2   1992 SLT 264 at 268.

3   [2002] 1 AC 615.
4   2006 SLT 269.
5   The difficulty is that the House of Lords in *Hall* did not overrule *Rondel v Worsley* [1969] 1 AC 191 which had given barristers immunity in respect of both civil and criminal proceedings. *Rondel* has been followed in Scotland. *Hall* is technically not binding on the Scottish courts.
6   *Whitehouse v Lord Advocate* 2020 SC 133 appealed on this point from *Whitehouse v Gormley* [2018] CSOH 93, see para 1.5 above.
7   *Saif Ali v Sydney Mitchell & Co* [1980] AC 198. In *Jones v Kaney* [2011] UKSC 13, the Supreme Court held that there was no longer any justification for continuing to hold expert witnesses immune from being sued for professional negligence in relation to evidence they gave in court or for the views they expressed in anticipation of court proceedings.

CHAPTER 8

Product liability

A. INTRODUCTION

8.1 The basis of product liability in Scots law[1] was, of course, laid down in *Donoghue v Stevenson*.[2] There it was held that the manufacturer of a product owes a duty of care to the ultimate consumer when a product is manufactured which is intended to reach the ultimate consumer in the form in which it left the manufacturer without the possibility of intermediate examination. If the product was manufactured carelessly with the result that the ultimate consumer suffered injury or harm to his property, the manufacturer is liable in delict. However, the onus lies on the pursuer to prove that there was a breach of duty by the manufacturer, ie that the manufacturer was negligent.[3] If negligence cannot be established, the action fails.

When a product is found to be faulty but has not yet caused damage to persons or other property, *Donoghue v Stevenson* liability is not engaged. Any loss, such as the cost of repair or the difference in value between a defective and non-defective product is purely economic and may be recoverable in contract.[4] Failure to discontinue use of a product found to be dangerous will be at the risk of the user and will normally prevent recovery of damages from the manufacturer.[5]

Apart from the difficulty of establishing negligence, other factors could operate to prevent the pursuer from succeeding. Where, for example, a manufacturer has provided an adequate warning that a product is potentially dangerous and this is ignored by the ultimate consumer, then there will be no liability because the pursuer's failure to heed the warning will constitute a *novus actus interveniens* which breaks the chain of causation.[6] Indeed, if it is well known that a product is dangerous, like alcohol or tobacco, if an adult of full age and capacity makes an informed decision to use it, there is no breach of the manufacturer's duty of care in merely making the product.[7]

1   On product liability and consumer protection, see Francis McManus, SULI *Delict* Chapter 16.
2   1932 SC (HL) 31, 1932 SLT 317. Discussed at para 3.2ff above.
3   If it is established that a product has failed because of a specified defect in the manufacturing process, it is open to a judge to hold that on the balance of probabilities this was due to the manufacturer's negligence: *Carroll v Fearon* [1998] PIQR P416, CA.
4   *D&F Estates v Church Commissioners for England* [1989] AC 187.
5   *Howmet v Economy Devices* [2016] EWCA Civ 847.
6   *Kubach v Hollands* [1937] 3 All ER 907, KB. On causation generally, see Chapter 6 above.
7   *McTear v Imperial Tobacco* 2005 2 SC 1. There could, of course, be a breach of duty if the alcohol or tobacco was contaminated by a different noxious substance.

B.   STATUTORY REGULATION

8.2   Because of these difficulties, but particularly the fact that the onus of proof of negligence lies on the ultimate consumer, the law has now imposed a statutory regime of strict liability in respect of product liability. What this means is that provided the case falls within the statutory provisions, the defender is liable in delict to compensate the pursuer without the pursuer having to prove that the defender was negligent. The strict liability regime for defective products is to be found in Part I of the Consumer Protection Act 1987. This statute implements EC Directive No 85/374/EEC and it is expressly enacted that it should be interpreted to comply with the Directive.[1] The general idea of the Act is simple: it is to place the primary responsibility for personal injury or damage to property caused by a defective product on the producer and to enable the consumer who has been injured by the defective product or whose property has been damaged by the defective product to obtain compensation from the producer without having to prove fault. However, as we shall see, the provisions of the statute are hideously complex. Before considering them, it should be noted that where the statutory regime is not applicable, common law liability remains[2] and pursuers may bring an action based on a breach of the *Donoghue v Stevenson* duty of care but will, of course, have to prove negligence if they are to be successful.

The Consumer Protection Act 1987 imposes strict liability on the producer of a product 'where any damage is caused wholly or partly by a defect in a product'.[3] Damage is defined as 'death or personal injury or any loss of or damage to property (including land)'.[4] Thus, if a person is killed or injured by a defective product, or his land or other property is damaged by a defective product, the producer of the product is liable to pay compensation without proof of fault. In other words, the producer is strictly liable.

1   Consumer Protection Act 1987, s 1(1). The Act came into force on 1 March 1988. References in this section are to CPA 1987 unless otherwise stated.
2   CPA 1987, s 2(6).
3   CPA 1987, s 2(1).
4   CPA 1987, s 5(1). 'Personal injury' includes any disease and any other impairment of a person's physical or mental condition: CPA 1987, s 45(1).

(1) Exceptions to strict liability

8.3   Damage to certain types of property is excluded from the statutory regime:

(a)   Loss or damage to the defective product itself.[1] The cost of repair or the difference in value between a defective and a non-defective product is not recoverable under the Consumer Protection Act 1987. Nor is it recoverable in delict at common law since it is pure economic loss. Where the product is a complex structure, loss or damage to the whole or part of the product caused by a defective component is also excluded. For example, if a motor car (complex product) is damaged as a result of a defective wheel (component), the damage to the car is excluded but not injury to the driver or damage to other property.

(b)   Property damaged or lost as a result of a defective product where the property *damaged or lost* is not for private use.[2] Property is not for private use if it is not of a description of property ordinarily intended for private use, occupation or consumption *and* it is not intended by the person suffering the loss or damage mainly for his own private use, occupation or consumption. What this means is that before the Act applies and there is strict liability, the property damaged must be 'consumer' property, ie of a kind ordinarily intended for private use which the person suffering the loss or damage intended to be used for private use. For example, if A produces a defective vacuum cleaner, the Act will apply if the cleaner damages the carpet in B's home but not if it damages the carpet in B's office or factory. It is important to note that it is the property which is damaged which must be 'consumer' as opposed to 'business' property.[3] If A produces a defective lorry which is used in B's business, the Act *will* apply if the defective lorry damages C's family motor car but the Act will not apply if the defective lorry damages C's van which he uses for his business. When the Act is excluded because the property damaged is not 'consumer' property, resort will have to be made to delictual liability at common law when negligence will have to be established.

(c)   Property damaged or lost as a result of a defective product, where the loss or damage does not exceed £275.[4] Where such loss or damage occurs, resort must again be made to delictual liability at common law when negligence will have to be established.[5] It should be noted that this exception only applies to damage to property. If, for example, A cuts his finger as a result of B's defective product, the Act still applies and B is strictly liable even if A's damages are less than £275.

1   CPA 1987, s 5(2).
2   CPA 1987, s 5(3).
3   See, eg, *Renfrew Gof Club v Motorcaddy Ltd* [2016] CSIH 57, 2016 SC 860.
4   CPA 1987, s 5(4). This includes interest.
5   Such an action would be brought under the small claims procedure.

(2) Definition of 'product'

8.4   Strict liability applies where damage is caused wholly or partly by a defect in a product. A 'product' is defined[1] as any goods or electricity. It includes – and this is important – components and raw materials which are parts of a complex product. So, if there is a complex product such as a motor car and a component of the car, for example a windscreen, is defective, that component, as well as the motor car, is regarded as a product for the purpose of the Consumer Protection Act 1987. 'Goods' also include 'substances, growing crops and things comprised in land by virtue of being attached to it and any ship, aircraft or vehicle'.[2] 'Substance' means any natural or artificial substance, whether in solid, liquid or gaseous form or in the form of vapour and includes substances which are comprised in or mixed with other goods, for example a cylinder of gas. Things comprised in land by virtue of being attached to it include, for example, the window frames of a house, a garden shed or a swing. 'Ship' includes any boat or vessel used for navigation; aircraft includes gliders, balloons and hovercraft; 'vehicle' is not defined. Game and agricultural produce constitute products for the purpose of the Act.[3] Blood used for transfusions has been held to be a product for the purposes of the Act.[4]

1   CPA 1987, s 1(2).
2   CPA 1987, s 45(1).
3   Initially game and agricultural produce were excluded from the regime: the exclusion was removed by the Consumer Protection Act 1987 (Product Liability) (Modification) (Scotland) Order 2001, SSI 2001/265 in response to the CJD crisis.
4   *A v National Blood Authority (No 1)* [2001] 3 All ER 289.

(3) Parties liable

8.5   As mentioned above, *prima facie* strict liability is imposed on the producer of the product. A 'producer' is defined as the person who manufactured the product[1] or who won or abstracted the substance.[2] Where a product is not manufactured, won or abstracted but its essential characteristics are attributable to an industrial or other process, the producer is the person who carried out the process: for example, where the product is pasteurised milk, the producer is the person who carried out the pasteurisation process.[3] A person who merely packages goods is not a producer. Any person who puts his own name on a product, or uses a trade mark on a product, is liable under the Consumer Protection Act 1987 if by so doing he holds himself out to be the producer.[4] This provision brings 'own branders' within the strict liability regime. Similarly, any person who imports products from abroad with a view to distributing them within the UK is liable under the Act.[5] This clearly is to protect ultimate consumers from having to sue a producer outwith the UK. The importer may, of course, have a remedy, for example in contract, against the producer. The producer of a component or of raw materials used in a complex product is *prima facie* jointly and severally liable with the producer of the complex product if it is defective.

Although strict liability falls on the producer, own brander or importer of a defective product, as a fall-back position a supplier of the product may also be liable. Thus, all parties in the distribution chain from the producer to the own brander or importer are potentially liable under the Act:

Producer ———— Wholesaler ———— Retailer ———— Purchaser

In this example, the wholesaler and retailer are suppliers within the meaning of the Act. However, a supplier will be liable only if the person who suffered the damage asked the supplier within a reasonable time of the damage being sustained to identify the producer or a supplier further up the chain of distribution and the supplier failed to provide the information within a reasonable time, provided it was not reasonably practicable for the person suffering the damage to identify the producer. In order to escape potential strict liability under the Act, a supplier must therefore keep records of his suppliers or producers.[6]

A supplier will not be strictly liable if the defective goods were not supplied in the course of business.[7] Accordingly, A will not be strictly liable if A sells his washing machine to his neighbour B in a private transaction or if A gives B the washing machine as a birthday present: but A will remain liable for breach of contract or in delict at common law if the washing machine is defective and injures B or damages B's property. Where we are dealing with a producer, own brander or importer, they will escape strict liability under the Act only if the goods were supplied otherwise than with a view to profit.[8] If, for example, A makes lemon curd which is *donated* to the local church sale of work, A is not liable, although he is a producer, because the goods were not supplied with a view to A's profit. But if A *sells* the lemon curd to the sale of work, A will remain liable under the Act. In both cases, the church will not be liable under the Act, since the only potential liability is as a supplier and the lemon curd was not sold in the course of a business. The church could, of course, be liable at common law.[9]

1　CPA 1987, s 2(2)(a).
2　CPA 1987, s 2(2)(b).
3　CPA 1987, s 2(2)(c).
4　CPA 1987, s 2(2)(b).
5　CPA1987, s 2(2)(c) as amended by Sch 3 of the Product Safety and Metrology etc (Amendment etc) (EU Exit) Regulations 2019 (SI 2019/696).
6　CPA 1987, s 2(3). If the producer has the power to determine when the supplier should put the product on to the market, the supplier may be treated as the producer for the purposes of the CPA 1987: *O'Bryne v Aventis Pasteur MSD Ltd* [2010] UKSC 23.
7　CPA 1987, s 4(1)(c)(i). Where a product was supplied and used for a specific medical service which was financed entirely from public funds, the ECJ held that it was nevertheless supplied for an economic or business purpose and the producer remained strictly liable: *Veedfald v Arhus Amtskommune* [2003] 1 CMLR 41.
8　CPA 1987, s 4(1)(c)(ii).
9　If A supplies a 'free gift' when selling another product, A will be strictly liable under the Act if the gift is given away in the course of A's business.

(4)　Meaning of 'defective product'

8.6　To attract strict liability, the damage must be caused 'wholly or partly' by a *defect* in the product.[1] What then is a defective product? A product is defective 'if the safety of the product is not such as persons generally are entitled to expect'.[2] For these purposes, 'safety shall include safety in the context of risks of damage to property as well as in the context of risks of death or personal injury'.[3] It will be noted that the test is what *consumers generally are* entitled to expect in terms of the safety of the product. The test is objective. If the product falls below the expectations of *consumers generally* then the product is defective.[4] This is in marked contrast to the concept of negligence at common law which is tested by the standards of the hypothetical reasonable person in the position of the manufacturer.[5] This reflects the focus of the CPA on the product itself rather than on the conduct of the manufacturer which is the concern of common law negligence. In *Abouzaid v Mothercare (UK) Ltd*,[6] for example, as he was seeking to assist with fastening an elasticated strap to a pushchair, the plaintiff lost the sight in one of his eyes when the strap recoiled. The Court of Appeal held that the test of defectiveness hinged upon the expectations of the public at large as to the safety of the product and the fact that the manufacturer had not appreciated that there was any risk of injury arising from the strap was irrelevant. In *A v National Blood Authority (No 1)*,[7] the producer knew that some of his blood products might be infected but at the time there were no practical precautions that could be taken. The court held that the blood product was defective because the public did not know of the risk and were entitled to expect that blood transfused to them would be free from infection.

On the other hand, when the public know there is a risk that a product might fail in its purpose, then the product will not be defective if the risk transpires.[8] Where the risk is obvious, for example that coffee served in a polystyrene cup will be hot to hold, the product is not defective.[9] In the medical context, where a product carries inherent risks as well as potential functional benefits the public generally would be expected to accept the risk of failure. In *Hastings v Finsbury Orthopaedics Ltd*,[10] the pursuer's failed prosthesis was held not to be defective as the risk with the product in question was no greater than it would have been with any of the available alternatives.

Although the Consumer Protection Act 1987 is concerned with products which are dangerous because badly manufactured or incompetently designed, it also applies to products which are superbly designed and excellently manufactured but which are inherently dangerous if not used carefully, for example drugs.[11] Such products will be defective if there are inadequate warnings or instructions as to use. Thus, tobacco or alcohol could be defective products if the warnings as to the dangers of use or abuse are not adequate.[12]

1   CPA 1987, s 2(1). The onus rests on the pursuer to prove that the product was defective: *Foster v Biosil* (2001) 59 BMLR 178; *McGlinchey v General Motors UK Ltd* [2012] CSIH 91.
2   CPA 1987, s 3(1).
3   CPA 1987, s 3(1).
4   See *Wilkes v DuPuy International Ltd* [2016] EWHC 3096 (QB).
5   For discussion, see para 5.10 ff above
6   [2001] TLR 136.
7   [2001] 3 All ER 289.
8   *Richardson v LRC Products* [2000] PIQR 164 (condom failed but public knew that no form of contraception is 100 per cent effective and the manufacturer never claimed that the product was).
9   *B (a child) v McDonald's Restaurants Ltd* [2002] EWHC 490 (QB).
10 [2021] CSIH 6. See also *Gee v DuPuy International Ltd* [2018] EWHC 1208 QB, [2018] Med LR 347.
11 *X v Schering Health Care Ltd* [2002] EWHC 1420 (QB) 70 BMLR 88 (third-generation combined oral contraceptives did not increase the level of risk of thrombosis and were not defective).
12 Cf *McTear v Imperial Tobacco* 2005 SC 1 for the position at common law.

8.7   In determining what consumers are entitled to expect, the court must consider all the circumstances of the case.[1] These include:

(a)   The purposes for which the product was marketed, its 'get up', any mark in relation to the product and any instructions or warnings.[2] Instructions or warnings are of particular importance where the product is inherently dangerous. If no warning is given, obviously the product will be defective. But if there is an adequate warning, for example in respect of drug dosage, will that satisfy the consumer's expectation of safety or must the container of the drug be, for example, child proof?

(b)   What might reasonably be expected to be done with or in relation to the product.[3] Theoretically, this should be what the *consumer* might *reasonably* expect to be done with the product rather than what the producer expects it to be used for. Ultimately, however, it will be the court's view of reasonable expectation which will prevail. The test is clearly objective. So for example, it is unlikely that a freezer which cannot be opened from within would be held to be defective even though a child climbed into the freezer and could not get out: freezers cannot reasonably be expected to be hiding places for toddlers!

(c)   The time when the product was supplied by its producer to another.[4] The relevant time for assessing the standard of safety of a product is the time at which it was supplied by the producer: the fact that products which are put on the market after that date have more safety features does not per se mean that the earlier product was defective at the time it was supplied.

Before there is strict liability under the Act, the pursuer has to show that the damage was '*caused* wholly or partly by a defect in a product'.[5] Therefore, as in the case of delictual liability at common law, the claim may fail unless there is a sufficient causative link between the damage and the defective product.[6] However, provided there are no causation problems, the pursuer who has suffered damage is entitled to compensation from the producer, own brander, importer or supplier without having to establish negligence. In other words, there is strict liability.

1   CPA 1987, s 3(2).
2   CPA 1987, s 3(2)(a). *Worsley v Tambrands Ltd* [2000] PIQR P95 (the manufacturer's warnings of the risk of toxic shock syndrome from the use of tampons were sufficient and the product was not defective).
3   CPA 1987, s 3(2)(b).
4   CPA 1987, s 3(2)(c).
5   CPA 1987, s 2(1) (emphasis added); *Foster v Biosil* (2001) 59 BMLR 178; *McGlinchey v General Motors UK Ltd* [2012] CSIH 91.
6   Although CPA 1987 applies when a defective product causes psychiatric illness, it will probably not apply to secondary victims since their illnesses are caused by their reactions to the injuries of primary victims rather than by the defective product which injured the primary victim concerned. So, for example, persons who suffer mental harm by witnessing a plane crash caused by a defect in the plane's engines cannot recover damages under the CPA 1967 from the manufacturer of the plane. On delictual liability for mental harm, see para 4.2 ff above.

(5) Defences to claim of strict liability

8.8 The Consumer Protection Act 1987 provides the defender with the following defences to a claim based on *strict* liability:

(a)   The defect in the product is attributable to the defender's compliance with statutory or any retained EU obligations.[1]

(b)   The defender did not at any time supply the product to another, for example the product was stolen.[2]

(c)   The defect did not exist in the product at the relevant times.[3] In the case of a producer, own brander or importer this will be the time he first supplied the product to another; in the case of a supplier, when the product was last supplied by a producer, an own brander or an importer into the UK . So, in the case of the producer etc, he will escape strict liability if the product was not defective when it entered circulation, but subsequently becomes defective.[4] There can, of course, still be delictual liability at common law. The supplier will escape strict liability if the product was not defective when it was last supplied by a producer etc even though the defect was subsequently caused by the supplier himself. For example, if a butcher keeps meat which was edible when he obtained it from the producer but sells it when it has gone off, the retailer will not be liable. This is, to say the least, an odd result but, of course, the retailer will be liable in contract to the purchaser and at common law in delict to the ultimate consumer when negligence will readily be inferred.

(d)   The state of scientific and technical knowledge at the relevant time[5] was not such that a producer of products of the same description as the product in question, might have been expected to have discovered the defect if it had existed in his products while they were under his control.[6] This is known as the 'state of the art' defence. It is controversial in that a producer can escape *strict* liability if the defect in his product would not have been known by manufacturers of a similar product, given the state of scientific and technical knowledge at the time. It is important to stress that the defence is not what the producer actually knew but what he would have known if he had consulted those who might be expected to know the state of research and all the available literature etc.[7] It has been held that the defence is not available if the producer knows that his product might have harmful consequences.[8]

This defence is similar to the common law principle that a defender cannot be liable in delict if, as a result of the scientific knowledge available to the hypothetical reasonable person at the time, injury to the pursuer was not a reasonable and probable consequence of the defender's conduct.[9] Moreover, the defence expressly refers to the awareness of producers of similar products. This is similar to the important role that the practice of persons in the same trade, business or profession of the defender plays in establishing a breach of a duty of care at common law.[10] It can therefore be argued that the 'state of the art' defence re-introduces negligence into the regime of strict liability laid down in the Consumer Protection Act 1987.

In many cases, the defence will not be available to the producer simply because, given the state of scientific and technical knowledge at the time, he[11] should have known the product was defective. Where the defence could be used is in the production of drugs whose side effects could not have been discovered given the state of scientific knowledge which existed at the time they were produced; it may take years before the side effects of certain drugs become apparent in patients. In these circumstances, the defence could be used by the defender. It is somewhat ironic that one of the reasons for the move towards a strict liability regime for defective products was to avoid the shortcomings of the law of negligence which became apparent in the thalidomide tragedy. The European Court of Justice has held that the scope of the Consumer Protection Act 1987, s 4(1)(e) is not in conflict with EU law.[12]

(e) If the defective product is a complex product, the producer of a component or of any raw materials contained in the complex product has a defence if the defect in the complex product is wholly attributable to the design of the complex product or to the fact that he complied with the instructions of the producer of the complex product;[13] otherwise both the producer of the complex product and the producer of the component or raw materials are jointly and severally liable.[14]

(f) Contributory negligence.[15] Liability under the Consumer Protection Act 1987 cannot be excluded by an exemption clause.[16]

This discussion of product liability is important because it illustrates how the common law of delictual liability based on the defender's *culpa* was thought to be inadequate to protect the interests of consumers who might be injured or whose property might be damaged by defective products. Accordingly, a regime of strict liability was introduced by statute so that the ultimate consumer would no longer have to prove fault before obtaining compensation. But the Consumer Protection Act 1987 is not comprehensive and on occasions it will still be necessary for a pursuer to resort to delictual liability at common law when negligence will have to be established.

1 CPA 1987, s 4(1)(a).

2 CPA 1987, s 4(1)(b). *Veedfald v Arhus Amtskommune* [2003] 1 CMLR 41 (kidney flushing fluid used to prepare a kidney for transplantation had been 'supplied' in terms of the directive).

3 CPA 1987, s 4(1)(d). See, eg, *Piper v JRI Manufacturing Ltd* [2006] EWCA Civ 1344, (2006) 92 BMLR 141.

4 *Richardson v LRC Products Ltd* [2000] PIQR 164 (condom became damaged by ozone after it left the factory!).

5 See discussion immediately above.

6 Consumer Protection Act 1987, s 4(1)(e).

7 *Richardson v LRC Products* [2000] PIQR 164. In *Abouzaid v Mothercare (UK) Ltd* [2001] TLR 136 the Court of Appeal doubted whether accident reports constituted 'technical knowledge'.

8 *A v National Blood Authority* [2001] 3 All ER 289. This case provides a very full discussion of when a product is defective and the nature of the 'state of the art' defence: see in particular pp 334–342.

9 *Roe v Minister of Health* [1954] 2 QB 66, [1954] 2 All ER 131, CA, discussed at para 5.6 above.

10 See paras 5.16 ff above.

11 Or, technically, producers of similar products.

12 *Commission of the European Communities v United Kingdom* (C300/95) [1997] All ER (EC) 481, ECJ (Fifth Chamber).

13 Consumer Protection Act 1987, s 2(4)(f).

14 See paras 6.12–6.13 above.

15 CPA 1987, s 6(4).

16 CPA 1987, s 7.

CHAPTER 9

Delictual liability for animals

A.   DELICTUAL LIABILITY AT COMMON LAW

9.1   Where the defender owes the pursuer a duty of care, the defender can be liable where the pursuer's injuries or damage to property is caused by an animal. In *Henderson v John Stuart (Farms) Ltd*,[1] an employee was killed by a bull when cleaning out its box. The employer was held to be negligent for failing to fit the box with baffles or escape gaps. In other words, the employer had broken the duty of care he owed to his employee by failing to provide a safe working environment.[2] While a farmer is not under an absolute obligation to prevent his animals from straying onto the highway, she could be liable for injury to a road user or damage to his property if such harm was reasonably foreseeable as a probable consequence of the animal being there. Unless the animal has strayed before, it is unlikely that harm to a road user would be reasonably foreseeable.[3] In *Sandison v* Coope,[4] a dog owner was found negligent when he called his unleashed dog back across a public road on a blind corner without first checking for hazards. The dog collided with a cyclist who suffered life-changing injuries.

In *Hill v Lovett*,[5] an employee of the defenders, who were veterinary surgeons, was bitten by one of their West Highland terriers when she went into the garden to clean the windows of the surgery. As a result, the unfortunate pursuer eventually had to have her leg amputated. The Lord Ordinary (Weir) held that the defenders had broken the duty of care they owed to the pursuer both as employers and occupiers of the garden,[6] in failing to take reasonable care to ensure that the pugnacious dogs were not in the garden when the pursuer was there. On the other hand, in *Welsh v* Grady,[7] the pursuer was knocked over by the defender's overfriendly black labrador. The Lord Ordinary (Malcolm) held that in the absence of some warning or reason to anticipate that a dog might cause harm it would not usually be negligent to let a large dog off the lead when walking in open fields; but it might be negligent to allow a black labrador to run around in a public place close to young children.[8] In the English case *Whippey v Jones*,[9] the Court of Appeal reversed a finding of negligence against the owner of Hector, a great dane, who had knocked over a jogger while off the lead. Applying *Donoghue v Stevenson* principles, the owner was not bound to have foreseen the event, there had to be a sufficient probability of injury to lead a reasonable person to anticipate it.

A very unusual case is *Cameron v Hamilton's Auction Marts Ltd.*[10] The defenders were driving cattle along the highway. A cow escaped, climbed the stairway of a property adjoining the road, turned on a tap and fell through the floor into the pursuer's shop, causing flooding and damage. Clearly the defender owed a *Donoghue v Stevenson* duty of care[11] to the pursuer as the owner of property adjacent to the highway. In these circumstances, the sheriff held that the defenders would be liable for breach of their duty of care if the cow had escaped because of their negligence.[12]

These cases, then, are examples of breach of an existing duty of care as a result of the defender's carelessness: the fact that the injuries and damage were caused by an animal is largely irrelevant. They are simply examples of common law delictual liability for negligence. However, at common law, certain animals were regarded as *ferae naturae,* ie as having vicious propensities. These included, for example, lions, tigers and elephants. If such an animal caused injury or damage to a person, the person in charge of the animal was strictly liable, ie there was no need to prove fault. Strict liability applied even though the animal had not shown any vicious propensities before.[13] On the other hand, certain animals were regarded as *domitae naturae,* ie as having no vicious propensities. These included, for example, dogs, cats and cattle, including bulls! If such an animal had *in fact* shown vicious propensities before the pursuer suffered injury or damage, then strict liability would attach to the defender. But as in *Henderson v John Stuart (Farms) Ltd,*[14] and *Hill v Lovett,*[15] even where the bull and the dog had not hitherto shown vicious tendencies so that strict liability could not be imposed, the defenders were nevertheless successfully sued in negligence for breach of their duty of care.[16]

1 1963 SC 245, 1963 SLT 22, OH. On delictual liability for animals, see generally Kenneth Norrie, SULI *Delict* Chapter 21.

2 On employers' liability, see Chapter 12 below.

3 *Davidson v McIrvine* 2007 SLT (Sh Ct) 71 (driver ran into a bull that had strayed onto the highway from the fields: damage to the motorist's car not reasonably foreseeable).

4 2016 Rep LR 70.
5 1992 SLT 994, OH.
6 On occupiers' liability, see paras 10.9 ff below.
7 2008 SLT 363.
8 'Walking dogs in the open fields around Wellbank, a village just north of Broughty Ferry, is a popular activity. It allows the human and the canine population fresh air, exercise, and opportunities for social interaction. Villagers meet, chat and walk together for a while, as their dogs play and run around. It would appear that the general practice is to keep dogs on their lead until the open and largely uncultivated fields are reached, when they are allowed to run free': ibid per Lord Malcolm at 364.
9 [2009] EWCA Civ 452, (2009) 159 NLJ 598.
10 1955 SLT (Sh Ct) 74, 71 Sh Ct Rep 285.
11 See *Donoghue v Stevenson* 1932 SC (HL) 31, 1932 SLT 317.
12 See also *Swan v Andrew Minto & Son* 1998 Rep LR 42; *Wormald v Walker* 2004 SCLR 733 (farmer could owe a duty of care to a motorist to prevent a road accident caused by a cow escaping from a field through a hole in a hedge).
13 See the English case of *Behrens v Bertram Mills Circus Ltd* [1957] 2 QB 1, [1957] 1 All ER 583, where the defendants were held strictly liable for the injuries caused to a midget by an elephant which had hitherto appeared docile.
14 1963 SC 245, 1963 SLT 22.
15 1992 SLT 994, OH.
16 Special rules applied to dogs under the Dogs Acts 1906–28; damage done by straying cattle was governed by the Winter Herding Act 1686.

B.   LIABILITY UNDER THE ANIMALS (SCOTLAND) ACT 1987

(1) Introduction

9.2   The common law on *strict liability* for injuries or damage caused by animals was regarded as unsatisfactory. For injury or damage caused by an animal after 10 June 1987, the common law on *strict* liability has been replaced by the provisions of the Animals (Scotland) Act 1987.[1] However, common law liability for injury or damage caused by an animal as a result of the defender's *negligence* has *not* been replaced by the provisions of the 1987 Act[2] and a pursuer is therefore able to sue on the general principles of *culpa* if his case does not fall within the strict liability regime imposed by the 1987 Act.[3]

Where the Animals (Scotland) Act 1987 applies, the defender's liability is strict, ie the defender is liable without the pursuer having to prove that the defender was negligent. The person who is liable is the *keeper* of the animal 'at the time of the injury or damage complained of'.[4] The keeper of an animal for the purposes of the Act is defined as follows:[5]

(a)   the owner of the animal: remains the owner, even if the animal has been abandoned or has escaped, until someone else becomes the owner;[6]

(b)   the person with possession of the animal:[7] remains in possession, even if the animal has been abandoned or has escaped, until someone else obtains possession.[8] However, a person is not a keeper of an animal by virtue of possession if he is detaining the animal to prevent it from causing injury or damage on his land[9] or is 'temporarily detaining it for the purpose of protecting it or any other person or other animal or restoring it as soon as is reasonably practicable to its owner or a possessor of it';[10]

(c)   a person with 'actual care and control of a child under the age of 16' who is the owner or has possession of the animal.[11] And so a parent of a child under the age of 16 is regarded as the keeper of any animal owned by the child provided the parent has actual care and control of the child.

Where an animal is owned by A but in the possession of B, A and B can be jointly and severally liable under the Act.

1   Animals (Scotland) Act 1987, s 1(8). References in this section are to the Animals (Scotland) Act 1987 unless otherwise stated.
2   See A(S)A 1987, s 1(8).
3   See for example *Welsh v Brady* 2008 SLT 363.
4   A(S)A 1987, s 1(1).
5   A(S)A 1987, s 5(1)(a).
6   A(S)A 1987, s 5(2)(b). The Crown does not become the owner if an animal is abandoned: A(S)A 1987, s 5(2)(c).
7   A(S)A 1987, s 5(1)(a).
8   A(S)A 1987, s 5(2)(b).
9   A(S)A 1987, s 3.
10   A(S)A 1987, s 5(2)(a).
11   A(S)A 1987, s 5(1)(b).

(2) Meaning of 'animal'

9.3   What animals fall within the Animals (Scotland) Act 1987? For strict liability to apply, s 1(1)(b) of the Animals (Scotland) Act 1987 provides that the animal must be of 'a species whose members generally are by virtue of their physical attributes or habits likely (unless controlled or restrained) to injure severely or kill persons or animals, or damage property to a material extent'. Read literally, this definition is potentially very wide indeed. Although bulls can clearly fall within the definition,[1] it could, for example, include a domestic cat, since a cat by virtue of its physical attributes or habits is likely to injure severely or kill animals like birds or mice! It will ultimately be for the court to decide whether a certain species falls within the statutory criteria.

For the purpose of s 1(1)(b), certain animals are deemed by s 1(3)(a) to be likely (unless controlled or restrained) to injure severely or kill persons or animals by biting or otherwise savaging, attacking or harrying. These are dogs and dangerous wild animals within the meaning of s 7(4) of the Dangerous Wild Animals Act 1976.[2] All types of dogs are regarded as animals for the purpose of the 1987 Act where the harm is caused by 'biting or otherwise savaging, attacking or harrying': in these circumstances strict liability is imposed on their keepers even if the dog concerned has never shown any vicious tendencies in the past. If the harm was not caused by 'biting, or otherwise savaging, attacking or harrying' there can be liability at common law if it can be established that the defender was negligent. Thus, there was no strict liability under the 1987 Act and no liability at common law when the victims had been knocked down by overly affectionate labradors.[3]

Where an animal is a dangerous wild animal within the meaning of the 1976 Act, by s 1(3)(a) it is also deemed to be a s 1(1)(b) animal. Dangerous wild animals include wild dogs, wolves, jackals, coyotes, foxes (but not the common red fox), cassowaries, Old World monkeys, crocodiles and alligators, emus, poisonous snakes, lions and tigers, cheetahs and panthers, Gila monsters and Mexican bearded lizards, gibbons, orangutans, gorillas and chimpanzees, ostriches and bears.[4] Again, strict liability only arises when the dangerous wild animal has caused the injuries or damage by 'biting or otherwise savaging, attacking or harrying'. In addition, by s 1(3)(b) cattle, horses, asses, mules, hinnies, sheep, pigs, goats and deer *in the course of foraging* are deemed to be likely (unless controlled or restrained) to damage to a material extent land or the produce of land for the purpose of s 1(1)(b) of the 1987 Act.[5]

1   *Foskett v McClymont* 1998 SC 96, 1998 SLT 892, OH. It is a question of fact whether the animal fulfils the statutory criteria.
2   A(S)A 1987, s 1(3)(a).
3   *Fairlie v Carruthers* 1996 SLT (Sh Ct) 56; *Welsh v Brady* 2008 SLT 363. (Upheld by the Inner House: 2009 SLT 747). In determining if the harm was caused by biting or otherwise savaging, attacking or harrying the court, of course, cannot look into a dog's mind to determine *mens rea*! The test is objective after considering what actually happened. Having found in these cases that the dogs could not be deemed to be s 1(1)(b) animals by virtue of s 1(3)(a), the courts held that there was also no liability for negligence since the defenders had no grounds to believe that their dogs would knock the pursuers over.

4   Dangerous Wild Animals Act 1976, s 7(4) and Sch 3.
5   Animals (Scotland) Act 1987, s 1(3)(b). In *Foskett v McClymont* 1998 SC 96,
     1998 SLT 892, OH, the bull was not automatically deemed to be an animal for
     the purpose of the Act since the damage did not occur during foraging and
     personal injury as opposed to property damage was involved.

9.4   As a result of these provisions a wide range of species are
deemed to be animals for the purpose of the Animals (Scotland)
Act 1987. But if an animal is not deemed by s 1(3) to fall within
the definition in s 1(1)(b), it is, of course, possible to argue that
it is nevertheless of a species which by virtue of the physical
attributes or habits of its members is likely to injure severely or
kill persons or other animals, or damage property to a material
extent. In assessing whether this is so, the age and sex of the
animal is relevant.[1] Thus a non-foraging cow is unlikely to fall
within the definition in s 1(1)(b), while a non-foraging bull could.[2]
In *Welsh v Brady*,[3] Lord Malcolm opined[4] that where a dog was
not deemed to be a s 1(1)(b) animal by virtue of s 1(3), 'the Act
does seem to leave the door open for the possibility, theoretical
or otherwise, that it might be proved that a particular type of dog
falls within s 1(1)(b) in situations which are outside the scope of
s 1(3). However, it is not easy to envisage to which breed or breeds
this might apply, and in any event, in my view it does not extend
to black labradors'.

The 1987 Act expressly *excludes* from the definition of 'animal'
viruses, bacteria, algae, fungi and protozoa.[5]

Where the animal falls within the definition in s 1(1)(b) or is
deemed to do so by virtue of s 1(3)(a) or (b), its keeper is strictly
liable, ie liable without establishing *culpa,* for any damage or injury
suffered by the pursuer which is directly referable to the animal's
dangerous attributes or habits.[6] In other words, the damage or
injury sustained must arise from the particular attributes or habits
of the species which bring the animal within the definition in
s 1(1)(b). So, for example, the keeper of a red setter dog is strictly
liable under the 1987 Act if the dog bites the pursuer since the
injury is directly referable to a dog's attribute or habit to bite.[7] But
if the pursuer's injury is sustained as a result of falling over the
red setter dog, the keeper is not strictly liable under the 1987 Act
although the keeper could be liable if he owed a duty of care to the
pursuer and negligence could be established.

Strict liability does not apply to injury or damage caused by the
mere fact that the animal in question was present on a road or in
any other place.[8] Thus, if a motorist was injured while trying to

avoid running over a dog, the keeper is not strictly liable under the Animals (Scotland) Act 1987 but may, of course, be liable at common law if a breach of a duty of care towards the pursuer can be established. The 1987 Act does not apply if the injury caused by the animal consists of a disease which was transmitted by means which were unlikely to cause severe injury other than disease.[9] So for example, if A is savaged by a rabid dog and contracts rabies, the keeper is strictly liable under the 1987 Act because the disease was transmitted by means which were likely to cause severe injury, ie the dog's bites. But if the animal had merely licked the pursuer thereby transmitting the disease, the keeper is not strictly liable under the 1987 Act, since the means, ie the licking, was unlikely to cause severe injury other than the disease. In the latter situation, the keeper could still be liable at common law provided there was a breach of a duty of care owed to the pursuer ie if negligence can be established.

1   A(S)A 1987, s 1(2)(a).
2   *Foskett v McClymont* 1998 SC 96, 1998 SLT 892, OH (insufficient averments to allow the pursuer to lead evidence that the bull in question fell within s 1(1) (b)).
3   2008 SLT 363.
4   Ibid at 368.
5   A(S)A 1987, s 7.
6   A(S)A 1987, s 1(1)(c).
7   So if a domestic cat was a dangerous animal, its keeper would only be liable if, for example, it killed the pursuer's pet bird. In other words, the injury must be referable to the attributes or habits of a domestic cat which bring the cat under the statutory definition.
8   Animals (Scotland) Act 1987, s 1(5). *Davidson v McIrvine* 2007 SLT (Sh Ct) 71 (car damaged when it ran into a bull which had strayed on to the road).
9   A(S)A 1987, s 1(4).

(3) Defences to liability under the Animals (Scotland) Act 1987

9.5 Even where the Animals (Scotland) Act 1987 applies and the keeper is *prima facie* strictly liable, there are several possible defences:

(a)   if the injury or damage was due wholly to the fault of the person sustaining it or, in the case of an injury sustained to another animal, the keeper of that animal.[1] This will cover the situation where, for example, the pursuer has goaded a docile animal which attacks the pursuer in defence;

(b)   if the person sustaining the injury or damage, or a keeper of the animal sustaining the injury, willingly accepted the risk of it as his.[2] The classic example is a person who willingly puts his head in a lion's mouth. This defence is a statutory form of *volens non fit injuria;*[3]

(c)   if the person who was injured or suffered damage was a trespasser, ie was not authorised to be on the keeper's property.[4] The effect of this provision is only to remove strict liability from the keeper. As we shall see,[5] the keeper of the animal as occupier of property owes a duty of care to any person who enters onto the property, including a trespasser. Consequently, although the keeper is not *strictly* liable under the 1987 Act to the trespasser who has been injured by an animal, the keeper may be liable as occupier of the property if negligence can be established. Strict liability in relation to a trespasser is not removed by s 2(1)(c) if the animal which caused the injury or damage was there for the purpose of protecting persons or property. But the keeper will get the benefit of s 2(1)(c) if it is shown that it was reasonable to keep such an animal there and that the use made of the animal was reasonable.[6] Consider the following example:

(i)   If A, a trespasser, is injured by B's goose,[7] *prima facie* s 2(1)(c) of the Animals (Scotland) Act 1987 applies and B is not strictly liable. But if the goose was on the land to protect B's warehouse, then s 2(1)(c) is disapplied and B is strictly liable. But if B can show that it is reasonable to have a goose as a 'guardbird', s 2(1)(c) is reapplied and B is not strictly liable. It is thought that B would succeed in this case since it is reasonable to have a goose as opposed to a tiger as a 'watch animal'.[8]

Where the animal concerned is a guard dog, the keeper remains strictly liable to a trespasser, ie s 2(1)(c) of the 1987 Act is disapplied unless the keeper can show that he has complied with the provisions of s 1 of the Guard Dogs Act 1975.[9] Under this section, *either* the dog's handler must be present and have the dog under his control, *or* the dog must be secured so that it is not at liberty to go freely about the premises. In addition, notices of the dog's presence must be displayed at every entrance to the property. Consider the following example:

(ii) If A, a trespasser, is injured by B's guard dog, *prima facie* s 2(1)(c) of the Animals (Scotland) Act 1987 does not apply and B remains strictly liable. But if B can show that he complied with the provisions of s 1 of the

Guard Dogs Act 1975, then s 2(1)(c) of the 1987 Act is reapplied and B is not strictly liable.

In both examples (i) and (ii), B would be liable to A if he was in breach of the duty of care he owes to A as occupier of the property. To be successful, A would have to prove that B did not take reasonable care to protect him from the danger arising from having the animal on the land,[10] ie that B was negligent.

Where the Animals (Scotland) Act 1987 applies, there is no defence on the ground of *damnum fatale* or, for example, of intervention by a third party which caused the animal to escape. This is because liability is strict. However, the pursuer's damages may be reduced on the grounds of contributory negligence.[11] In *Ferguson v Ferguson*,[12] the pursuer was found 85 per cent contributorily negligent when bitten by Dougie, a west highland terrier. Placing her face in front of the dog's, she had pulled its cheeks.

In this chapter we have seen how the general principles of delictual liability for negligence apply where harm has been caused by an animal. Even at common law it was thought to be in the interests of society that the owner of a dangerous animal should be liable without proof of fault. These rules were unclear and anachronistic and, in so far as strict liability is concerned, they have been replaced by the regime imposed by the 1987 Act. But where a case does not fall within the statutory regime of strict liability, the keeper may still be liable if he was in breach of a duty of care which he owed to the pursuer, but in these circumstances the onus rests on the pursuer to prove that the keeper was negligent.

1 A(S)A 1987, s 2(1)(a).
2 A(S)A 1987, s 2(1)(b).
3 For discussion of the *volens* doctrine, see paras 6.10–6.11 above.
4 Animals (Scotland) Act 1987, s 2(1)(c). In the case of injury to another animal if the keeper of that animal was not entitled to have the animal on the land.
5 On occupiers' liability, see paras 10.9 ff below.
6 A(S)A 1987, s 2(2).
7 Assuming, of course, that a goose is an animal for the purpose of A(S)A 1987, s 1(2)(b).
8 A(S)A 1987, s 2(2). In Scotland, geese were traditionally used to guard bonded warehouses!
9 A(S)A 1987, s 2(2).
10 On occupiers' liability, see para 10.9 ff below.
11 The keeper's statutory liability is treated as fault for the purposes of the Law Reform (Contributory Negligence) Act 1945: Animals (Scotland) Act 1987, s 1(6). On contributory negligence, see paras 6.12–6.13 above.
12 [2015] CSIH 63, 2015 SLT 561.

CHAPTER 10

Delictual liability arising from ownership or occupation of land

A. INTRODUCTON

10.1 Physical damage to land or buildings caused negligently is of course reparable according to general principles of negligence. Given that physical damage is most likely to originate with operations carried out in the immediate vicinity, there is not usually any great difficulty in establishing the existence of a duty of care provided the harm occasioned was foreseeable and thus within the scope of the duty. Delictual actions for damages or interdict may also be brought to protect property rights known as incidents of landownership. Incidents of landownership include the right to exclusive possession, protected principally by the laws of trespass and encroachment; the right to comfortable enjoyment of property free of serious disturbance or substantial inconvenience, protected by the law of nuisance and Article 8(1) ECHR;[1] and rights of support. Liability for subsidence to land caused by withdrawal of support from underneath is strict.[2] Liability for withdrawal of support within a building depends upon fault.[3] Actions for damages for withdrawal of support are sometimes grounded on nuisance, sometimes without reference to nuisance.[4]

The occupiers of property owe a statutory duty to those entering their land or premises to guard them against dangers due to the state of the premises or things done on the premises. This is known as occupiers' liability and a successful action depends on negligence. The duty does not extend beyond the occupiers' boundary so a person injured in the street, say by falling slates from a roof cannot rely on the statutory duty. In these circumstances it has been contended that the Roman quasi-delicts, the *actio de positis vel suspensis* (for things hung or suspended) and the *actio de effusis vel deiectis* (for things poured or thrown) which imposed strict liability on the occupiers of premises, have been accepted into Scots law. In *McColl v Hoo*,[5] the pursuer's car had been damaged by slates falling from a neighbour's roof. While the sheriff found the defender liable, this finding was reversed on appeal. *Campbell v Kennedy*,[6] in which it was established that no liability arises *ex dominio solo* (from ownership alone) was followed and it was held that the pursuer was required to prove *culpa*. In *McDyer v The Celtic Football and Athletic Club*,[7] a spectator was hit by a piece of wood which fell from the roof of one of the stands during the European Summer Special Olympic Games. In this case the incident happened within the defenders' premises and so it was held that the case fell under the Occupiers' Liability (Scotland) Act 1960. In *Gray v Dunlop*,[8] a young lad had a pot of urine emptied upon him in the street as he passed by a hostel. The sheriff was not prepared to find the occupier liable without proof of fault.

1   And potentially by the Protection from Harassment Act 1997 or the Antisocial Behaviour etc (Scotland) Act 2004. See, eg, *Moray Council v Debidin* 2012 GWD 32-643.
2   'The right of support is an incident of property … The owner, in virtue of his ownership, has the right to have his land left in its natural state and he enjoys that right *qua* owner. If the owner's right of support is breached, he becomes entitled to damages for surface damage without requiring to establish negligence' per LJC Thomson, *Angus v NCB* 1955 SC 175 at 181
3   *Thomson v St Cuthbert's Co-operative Association Ltd* 1958 SC 380, 1959 SLT 54; *Kennedy v Glenbelle Ltd* 1996 SC 95, 1996 SLT 1186.
4   See, eg, *GUS Property Management v Littlewoods Mail Order Stores* 1982 SC (HL) 157, 1982 SLT 533; *Stewart v Malik* [2009] CSIH 5, 2009 SC 265; and *K2 Restaurants v Glasgow City Council* [2013] CSIH 49, 2013 GWD 21-420.
5   1983 SLT (Sh Ct) 23.
6   (1864) 3 M 121.
7   2000 SLT 736.
8   1954 SLT (Sh Ct) 75.

B.   TRESPASS AND RELATED DELICTS

10.2   It is often wrongly assumed that Scots law does not recognise the wrong of trespass. Indeed, it has been judicially opined that the word 'trespasser' means nothing more in Scots law than 'a person who intrudes on the lands of another without that other's permission'.[1] However, as we shall see, a person who deliberately enters another's land may be interdicted from doing so again and is liable to pay damages if he has caused any harm to the property. Trespass is a *temporary* intrusion into property owned by another without the permission of the owner: for example, playing football in the owner's field or taking a short cut through his garden. Because heritable property is owned *a coelo usque ad centrum* (from the heavens to the centre of the earth) trespass protects an owner's air space as well as his land and the ground below his property. Thus, for example, the owner of a house successfully obtained an interdict preventing the respondent's crane from sweeping over his property when the respondent was building on adjacent land.[2] Because of this, statute provides that aircraft may fly over a person's land without liability for trespass.[3]

The primary remedy for trespass is interdict. No compensation is available unless there has been actual damage to the property because of the intrusion. There is therefore no liability for damages in Scots law merely for entering another's property. But the proprietor is entitled to use self-help to remove a trespasser provided it is reasonable in the circumstances; for example, the owner could ask a trespasser playing football in his field to leave but not threaten him with violence if the trespasser refuses to do so.[4] Interdict is an equitable remedy and is not granted automatically merely on proof of an unauthorised entry onto land. Before an interdict will be granted further intrusions must be likely and the intention of the trespasser is important. Any potential damage to the land because of the trespass will also be a relevant consideration. In *Winans v Macrae*,[5] for example, a shooting tenant of a lease of 200,000 acres was, perhaps understandably, refused an interdict to prevent a cottar's pet lamb from entering the property. It must be noted that extensive rights to cross property and to use property for recreational purposes are granted in the Land Reform (Scotland) Act 2003. The exercise of these rights will provide an effective defence to any action grounded in trespass.

In summary, apart from specific statutory offences, in Scots law trespass is not per se criminal, does not give rise to an action in damages unless actual damage has been done to the property and will only result in an interdict if likely to recur and any potential damage is not *de minimis*. However, the landowner is allowed a reasonable degree of self-help to remove the trespasser.

In this section, trespass has been defined as a *temporary* intrusion onto land. If a person enters onto another's property with the intention of occupying it for an indefinite period, for example a squatter, he does commit a criminal offence under the Trespass (Scotland) Act 1865. If the owner is not in possession at the time, the squatter is liable for the wrong of intrusion; if the owner is in possession and has been wrongfully removed by the squatter, the squatter is liable for the wrong of ejection. The rightful owner can seek summary ejection, violent profits[6] and compensation for actual losses incurred.

Trespass is concerned the temporary intrusion by a person onto the land of another. Sometimes property may intrude on a person's land without his consent, for example if a person builds beyond his boundaries and on his neighbour's land. This is an actionable wrong and is known as encroachment. The remedies are interdict, an order for removal or damages: self-help while sometimes unwise is nevertheless lawful.[7] Courts may refuse a removal order where the defender has acted in good faith, where there is no material detriment to the pursuer and where removal would cause a disproportionate loss to the defender compared to any benefit to be gained by the pursuer.[8]

1   *Dumbreck v Robert Addie & Sons (Colleries) Ltd* 1928 SC 547 at 554 per the Lord President (Clyde), 1928 SLT 341.On trespass see Gordon Cameron, SULI *Delict* paras 14.114 ff
2   *Brown v Lee Constructions Ltd* 1977 SLT (Notes) 61, OH.
3   Civil Aviation Act 1982, s 76.
4   If the self-help is excessive and results in physical harm to the trespasser, the owner can be liable for assault or negligence: *Revill v Newberry* [1996] QB 567, [1996] 1 All ER 291 (owner shot the trespasser!).
5   (1885) 12 R 1051.
6   Violent profits are the greatest profits the owner could have made if he was in actual possession of the land. It is thought that this should have been the remedy awarded in *Saeed v Waheed* 1996 SLT (Sh Ct) 39, 1995 SCLR 504, rather than damages for negligence.
7   For a discussion of encroachment, see Gretton and Steven *Property, Trusts and Succession* (Bloomsbury, 2017) paras 18.10ff.
8   *Anderson v Brattisanni's* 1978 SLT (Notes) 42.

C.   USE OF LAND IN *AEMULATIONEM VICINI*

10.3   When A owns land (X) which adjoins B's land (Y), A will be liable to B if he uses his land (X) in a way that is detrimental to B's enjoyment of his land (Y). Before A is liable for using his land *in aemulationem vicini*, A must use his land with the predominant motive of harming B and not to further A's legitimate interests.[1] If A's predominant motive is not to harm B, then A cannot be liable for this wrong, but A's conduct may amount to nuisance.[2] Liability then, depends on malice.

In *Campbell v Muir*[3] where the defender spitefully exercised his right to fish from a boat in a river in such a way that it prevented anglers on the opposite bank from being able to cast their rods, the Lord President (Dunedin) held that the pursuer would have been entitled to interdict because 'the defender was on the particular occasion acting *in aemulationem vicini* against his neighbour's right, and that that was a just ground for complaint'.[4] In *More v Boyle*[5] it was accepted by the sheriff that the doctrine of *in aemulationem vicini* is still part of Scots law.

Liability arises only if it can be shown that the defender acted with the predominant motive of harming the pursuer. It is, of course, difficult to establish malice, so an objective assessment must be made of the defender's conduct to infer malice. But unlike nuisance, which is usually concerned with a continuing wrong, liability for use of land *in aemulationem vicini* can arise from a single act of the defender provided the predominant motive of harm to the pursuer can be established. In the modern context, where the defender acts out of spite to harm or distress a neighbour, this may be actionable under the Protection from Harassment Act 1997 which avoids the difficult burden of proving malice.[6]

1   *Dewar v Fraser* (1767) Mor 12803
2   On nuisance, see paras 10.4–10.10 below.
3   [1895] AC 587, HL.
4   [1895] AC 587 at 597–598.
5   1908 SC 387, 15 SLT 737.
6   See para 1.7.

D. NUISANCE

10.4 While there are many apparent similarities between nuisance in Scots and English law, nuisance in England is structured very differently. It is divided into public and private nuisance with further sub-divisions within private nuisance. Nuisance in Scots law is said to be unitary, that is to say it is not divided into different categories.[1] Nuisance in Scots law, then, is not purely concerned with private interests but may be invoked for the protection of the neighbourhood more generally. This latter aspect of nuisance was perhaps of greater significance historically.[2] Offensive or noxious states of affairs affecting public health or the community can usually be dealt with by Local Authorities exercising powers under the Environmental Protection Act 1990 or other legislation.[3] Nevertheless, the unitary nature of Scots nuisance has other consequences. In England, private nuisance is understood as a 'tort to land' and title to sue is drawn very narrowly, a right of exclusive possession to the property affected is required.[4] There is relatively little case law on the point in Scotland, but it is not thought that title is circumscribed in the English fashion. Scots nuisance, while closely associated with property rights, isn't entirely a 'delict to land'; as already noted, it can be invoked to protect the neighbourhood and, as will be seen, it protects not only neighbouring property, but neighbours as well.[5] There are other jurisdictional differences, but the point of note is that care must be taken in applying English authorities North of the border.[6] English case law and legal reasoning do not necessarily map well onto the Scots doctrine. That said, there may yet be questions that arise where English authorities could prove useful. It should also be said that in both jurisdictions there are areas of legal uncertainty.[7]

1   Bell, *Principles*, para 974: 'Between public and private nuisance there is no useful distinction in the law of Scotland … The description of nuisance in Scotland is the same, whether the public or the individual be regarded … whatever is noxious or unsafe, or renders life uncomfortable to the public generally, or to the neighbourhood; whatever is intolerably offensive to individuals, in their dwelling houses, or inconsistent with the comfort of life … is a nuisance.'

2   '[A]ny member or members of the public may bring an action for the stopping of a public danger or nuisance.' DM Walker, *Delict*, 2nd edn (SULI/W Green (1981)) p 96. The most recent case where nuisance was invoked for the protection (from offensive fumes) of the neighbourhood generally appears to be *Farley & Ors v G Adam of Hillington* 1977 SLT (Sh Ct) 81.

3   EPA, s 79(1) lists statutory nuisances.

4   *Hunter v Canary Wharf Ltd* [1997] AC 655.

5   *Watt v Jamieson* 1954 SC 56, 1954 SLT 56; see para 10.5 below.

6   For a discussion of key differences see G Cameron, 'Cross-border Neighbour Law', 2014 JR 37. On the question of English influence on the origin of Scots nuisance, see G Cameron 'Scots and English Nuisance … Much the Same Thing?' (2005) 9 ELR 98.

7   Nuisance in Scots law has become considerably less obscure following the publication of Niall Whitty's analysis. See vol 14, *Stair Memorial Encyclopaedia*, 2001 reissue.

10.5   The definitive statement of nuisance in modern Scots law is a dictum of Lord President Cooper in *Watt v Jamieson*.[1]

'I deduce that the proper angle of approach to a case of alleged nuisance is rather from the standpoint of the victim of the loss or inconvenience than from the standpoint of the alleged offender; and that if any person so uses his property as to occasion serious disturbance or substantial inconvenience to his neighbour or material damage to his neighbour's property, it is in the general case irrelevant to plead merely that he was making a normal and familiar use of his own property. The balance in all such cases has to be held between the freedom of a proprietor to use his property as he pleases and the duty on a proprietor not to inflict material loss or inconvenience on adjoining proprietors and adjoining property; and in every case the answer depends on considerations of fact and degree … The critical question is whether what he was exposed to was *plus quam tolerabile* when due weight has been given to all the surrounding circumstances of the offensive conduct and its effects.'

Establishing nuisance does not turn on the reasonableness or otherwise of the defender's conduct though that may be taken into account in the balancing process, but whether the disturbance to the pursuer is more than a person ought reasonably to tolerate in the circumstances. Nuisance is seen from the standpoint of the victim.

For ease of presentation, it may be helpful to differentiate between serious disturbance and substantial inconvenience on the one hand and material damage on the other. The former will be considered first. Non-tangible interferences with a neighbour's ability to enjoy and use his or her land, disturbances and inconveniences in short, may be termed amenity nuisance. This is nuisance in its classic form. Petitions to interdict nuisances in the forms of noise, pollution of air (smoke and smells), pollution of water, unnatural heat and vibration, were most frequent during the nineteenth century and driven by continuing processes of urbanisation and industrialisation.[2] The subsequent decline in litigation can be explained by various factors. Things or activities that threatened health became subjected to increasingly effective administrative regulation and with the advent of statutory planning regimes from 1909,[3] residential and industrial land uses became increasingly separated. It is probably also fair to say that the people with the wherewithal to fund litigation were the same as those who were able to take advantage of new public transport systems to move their residences away from the smoky inner cities where they worked, to the leafy suburbs where they would be less likely to encounter brick works, lime kilns, foundries, dye works, glue works, abattoirs, tanneries and so on.

1   1954 SC 56 at 58.
2   The right to clean air and water fit for primary purposes, principally washing and watering animals, are incidents of landownership that were very important at the early stages of the development of Scots nuisance.
3   Housing and Town Planning Act 1909. For the development of administrative regulation of nuisance see G Cameron, Neighbourhood Liability in Scotland 1850-2000, in J Gordley (ed), *The Development of Liability Between Neighbours*, vol 2, (2010) CUP pp 161–170.

10.6   Where the complaint concerns amenity nuisance, the object of the exercise is usually to put a stop to it, that is to abate the nuisance. The primary remedy is interdict although this is often accompanied by a plea for declarator.[1] An interdict need not necessarily put an end to the activity or operation, the terms of the interdict should be drafted no more widely that is required to put an end to its deleterious effects, in short, the activity can be allowed to continue provided the nuisance is abated. Interdict can also be awarded to prevent a nuisance from occurring. It must of course be clear that the activity will indeed cause more than reasonably tolerable disturbance.[2]

Assuming general requirements for the grant of interdict are met, interdict will be granted where nuisance is established,[3] that is where the disturbance is determined to be *plus quam tolerabile*, more than reasonably tolerable in the circumstances. When interdict is sought there is no requirement to establish fault on the part of the defender. To amount to nuisance the disturbance must be material so its nature, extent and severity must be established in every case. These are matters of fact or degree; measurements of time, volume and so on will be necessary to establish a *prima facie* case.[4] Beyond that, the relevant circumstances to be weighed in the balance will vary. The possibility of remedial measures by either party will be taken into account. The nature of the locality may be relevant. Residents in a city may reasonably be expected to tolerate degrees of disturbance that would be intolerable, say in the Outer Isles. The Archbishop of Glasgow failed to interdict the use of drop hammers in a forge in a part of Glasgow with much heavy industry.[5] It will aid the defender if it can be established that the pursuer is more than usually sensitive to the disturbance complained of.[6] In *MacBean v Scottish Water*,[7] the Lord Ordinary (Woolman) found that the pursuer's residence was affected by smells from a nearby water treatment plant, but remedial measures having been put in place, on the evidence the remaining level of disturbance was not more than reasonably tolerable.

1   Other remedies that may be sought include orders *ad factum praestandum* to enforce remedial action. *Hugh Blackwood (Farms) Ltd v Motherwell DC* 1988 GWD 30-1290 shows a pursuer going for a full house. He concluded for declarator, interdict, a decree ordaining drainage works to be carried out and damages.

2   See, eg the firing of a pit being close to residences, *Fleming v Hislop* (1886) 13 R (HL) 43, or a concert, *Cumnock and Doon Valley DC v Dance Energy Associates* 1992 GWD 24-1441.

3   Interdict will be refused in the absence of reasonable apprehension that the activity or state of affairs objected to will continue or be repeated *Hay's Trustees v Young* (1877) 4 R 398.

4   In *MacBean v Scottish Water* [2021] CSIH 36 findings relied in part on the evidence of 'smell assessors'. In *King v Advocate General for Scotland* [2005] CSOH 169 the pursuer's action at common law failed, evidence of low-flying aircraft over her property was sketchy and insufficient. In *Canmore Housing v Bairnsfather* interim interdict under s 47 of the Court of Session Act 1988 was refused. The complaint concerned derelict cars parked against the pursuer's premises, but the pursuer failed to establish that the alleged fire risk was material.

5 *Maguire v Charles McNeil Ltd* 1922 SC 174, 1922 SLT 193.
6 See, eg, *Simpson v Miller* (1863) 2 M 255 in which a woman complained of vibrations from a baker's dough mixing machine which did not appear to affect the other residents in the tenement.
7 [2020] CSOH 55, affirmed [2021] CSIH 55.

10.7 The public interest in the continuation of an activity or operation is not a basis for refusing interdict though of course, public interest will be taken into account in the balance. If the nuisance is relatively trivial then it may not pass the *plus quam tolerabile* test in any case. Public right does not trump private right. Having first determined that nuisance exists, where the public interest in continuation of the activity is overwhelming, the court may suspend the operation of interdict in order to allow remedial measures to be put in place.[1] Equally, the parties may agree that the defender should be given the opportunity to abate the nuisance.[2] In *Ben Nevis Distillery v The North British Aluminium Co Ltd*,[3] interdict was suspended to allow the defender to implement remedial measures to reduce the air pollution of which the pursuer complained. The public interest in the defender's operation was substantial, the company was a major employer in the area and contributed 72 per cent of the total aluminium production for the UK.[4]

1 This contrasts with the position in England where the court may grant damages in lieu of injunction. The Scottish courts do not have an equivalent power.
2 As happened in *MacBean v Scottish Water* [2021] CSIH 55.
3 1948 SC 592, 1948 SLT 450.
4 See also *Webster v Lord Advocate* 1985 SC 173, 1985 SLT 361.

10.8 Where the loss suffered is tangible physical harm to property,[1] unless the harm is continuing or a repeat is anticipated, interdict is no longer a useful remedy and an action for damages will be raised. Most damages actions grounded on nuisance arise from withdrawal of support within a tenement or from damage caused by flooding although that by no means exhausts the possibilities.[2] While there had been controversy over whether *culpa* required to be proved to recover damages in nuisance that matter was resolved by the House of Lords in *RHM Bakeries Ltd v Strathclyde Regional Council*.[3] The need to establish *culpa* was affirmed. Lord Fraser was concerned not to place too great a burden on pursuers who were not to be required to 'aver the precise nature of the fault committed'. He continued:[4]

'As a general rule it would, in my opinion, be relevant for a pursuer to make averments to the effect that his property has been damaged by a flood caused by an event on the defender's land, such as the collapse of sewer which it was the defender's duty to maintain, that properly maintained sewers do not collapse, and that the collapse is evidence that the defender had failed in his duty to maintain the sewer. The onus will then be on the defender to explain the event in some way consistent with absence of fault on his part.'

A formulation along these lines was pled unsuccessfully by the pursuers in *Argyll & Clyde Health Board v Strathclyde Regional Council*.[5] In that case a water main in the control of the defenders had burst flooding the pursuers' premises. The pursuers pleadings were based on a failure on the part of the defender to maintain the pipe, but they had not specified the maintenance regime that ought to have been operated. Their contention then, was that the defenders had been negligent, but without specification of the standard of care they had failed to give the defenders due notice of the case against them. The action was held irrelevant and lacking in specification.

This gave rise to the argument advanced by the defenders in *Kennedy v Glenbelle Ltd*,[6] that liability in damages for nuisance required proof of negligence. It is true that *culpa* was used as a synonym for negligence in older cases and texts, but its generic nature was affirmed in *Kennedy* by Lord President Hope who listed five ways in which *culpa* could be established: (1) malice, in which harm to the victim is intended; (2) intention, evidenced by a deliberate act done in the knowledge that harm will be the likely consequence; (3) recklessness, where the defender acts regardless of the likely consequences or is indifferent to them; (4) and conduct causing a special risk of abnormal damage which, Lord Hope conceded, might just be another form of recklessness. Finally, (5) *culpa* may be constituted by negligence. Lord Hope also stated that where *culpa* is established by demonstrating negligence 'the ordinary principles of negligence' will provide an equivalent remedy'.[7] *Kennedy* involved damage to an upper property caused by the removal of support from below. Pleadings of *culpa* in terms of a deliberate act done in the knowledge that harm would result were deemed sufficient to allow the case to go to proof.

1   which may include moveable property, see, eg, *Ireland v Smith* (1895) 33 SLR 156, 3 SLT 180.

2   See, eg, withdrawal of support within tenement, *Hamilton v Wahla* 1999 GWD 25-1217; flooding: *GA Estates Ltd v Caviapen Trustees Ltd No 1* 1993 SLT 1037; *Viewpoint Housing Association v Edinburgh City Council* [2007] CSOH 114, 2007 SLT 772; *Sabet v Fife Council* [2019] CSOH 26; exposure of gable ends to the elements: *Powrie Castle Properties Ltd v Dundee City Council*

2001 SCLR 146; *Morris Amusements Ltd v Glasgow City Council* [2009] CSOH 84, 2009 SLT 697; water pollution: *Black Loch Angling Club v Tarmac Ltd* 2012 SCLR 501; *Devon Angling Association v Scottish Water* [2018] SAC Civ 9; fire in house: *Cunningham v Cameron* [2013] CSOH 193; fungal growth on house: *Chalmers v Diageo Scotland Ltd* [2017] CSOH 36.]

3   1985 SC (HL) 17, 1985 SLT 214.
4   1985 SLT 214 at 219.
5   1988 SLT 381.
6   1996 SC 95, 1996 SLT 1186.
7   1996 SLT 1186 at 1189.

10.9 *RHM Bakeries v Strathclyde Regional Council*[1] and *Kennedy v Glenbelle*,[2] remain the leading authorities on damages claims in nuisance. Where *culpa* is averred in terms of intention, the pursuer must establish that the act was undertaken deliberately, but how far does the pursuer have to go in establishing the defender's knowledge of the likely consequences? In *Anderson v White*,[3] the Lord Ordinary (Philip) found that the defenders had actual or constructive knowledge of the damage to the pursuers' land caused by water backing up behind a dam in defenders' control, because of the complaints that had been made to them. In *Sabet v Fife* Council,[4] the common law case against the second defender, an upstream proprietor, was based on his failure to remove debris which had blocked a weir for four months before overflowing in heavy weather causing flooding to the pursuers' home. The Lord Ordinary (Ericht) held that the pursuers' averments, that the weir was prone to blockage, that it had been blocked for four months and that the defender ought to have known about the history of flooding at the weir and of the danger this posed to their property, were matters for the pursuer to establish at proof before answer.

Of course, *Sabet* did not involve a deliberate act, but a negligent omission. The pursuers contended that the defender was under a positive duty to protect them against an abnormal risk of flooding by removing debris from the weir, thus avoiding the pleading pitfall encountered in *Argyll & Clyde Health Board*.[5] The approach taken should hold good for intentional harm cases also. Knowledge which the defenders had or ought to have had must be established and if *culpa* is framed in terms of negligence there must be at least some specification of what it was the defender ought to have done that they did not, Lord Fraser's stipulation on not overburdening pursuers with precise averments of *culpa* notwithstanding. Indeed, taken together, Lord Fraser's approach to pleading (should we call this *culpa* lite?) and Lord Hope's ruling that negligence is only one form of culpable conduct with apparent acceptance that nuisance may be occasioned negligently, seem to serve the needs of litigation well.

Lord Fraser's relaxed approach was applied in *Black Loch Angling Club v Tarmac Ltd*,[6] in which sheriff Sinclair said: 'Given the circumstances of such cases, the pursuer was not expected to give much notice to the defender of what was alleged to be the nature of the fault. He merely had to show that something had happened which should not have happened had the defender taken proper care.'[7] The circumstances were that the water quality of the pursuers' loch was adversely affected by waste water which had drained from the defenders' quarry. This meant that fishing was not viable as the fish could not see the flies. The club lost revenue. The sheriff found that, in failing to inspect a leaking bund and in failing to take note of and respond to the presence of weathered rock on site, the defender's fault was more probably than not the source of contamination to the loch.

A similar approach to pleading *culpa* was taken in *McKenna v O'Hare*.[8] The foundations of the pursuers' property had been contaminated by kerosene which had seeped from the next-door garden, necessitating the demolition and rebuilding of the property. Following proof, it was not possible to determine whether the cause of the contamination had been a spill by the neighbour while moving an oil tank, which would have been negligence, or a deliberate act in emptying kerosene onto the ground, which would have been reckless at least. The point is that Lord Fraser's approach serves well where the pursuer cannot be expected to know the precise form of fault and suggests that nuisance and negligence cannot be entirely separated. This suggestion gains further strength from *Cunningham v Cameron*.[9] The case involved joint wrongdoers responsible for a house fire. The first defender, the upstairs neighbour, was at fault in having blocked the outlet to the pursuer's central heating flue by placing wood against it, a deliberate act with the obvious potential to case danger. The second defender, a gas engineer who had serviced the system, had, negligently and in breach of contract, failed to spot a fault in the installation. In apportionment, the Lord Ordinary (Tyre) did not make a decision on causative potency but held the first defender's conduct more blameworthy and so he was held to bear the greater part of liability.

1 1985 SC (HL) 17, 1985 SLT 214.
2 1996 SC 95, 1996 SLT 1186.
3 2000 SLT 37. The case was allowed to go to proof before answer.

4   [2019] CSOH 26. See also *Edwards v Fife Council* [2019] CSOH 27 These
     cases are reminiscent of the English case *Sedleigh-Denfield v O'Callaghan*
     [1940] AC 880, one of the authorities upon which LP Cooper formulated his
     view on nuisance, see para 10.5 above.
5   Discussed in para 10.8 above.
6   2012 SCLR 501.
7   Ibid.
8   [2017] SAC Civ 16.
9   2013 CSOH 193.

10.10   It should be appreciated that the distinction drawn in the
text between amenity nuisance and material damage was drawn
only for ease of presentation. There is no such division in the law.
Damages will be available for amenity nuisance though where the
harm is restricted to disturbance or inconvenience they may be
difficult to quantify and fault must, of course, be proved. In *Shanlin
v Collins*, damages were awarded in respect of illness caused by
the barking of a neighbour's dogs.[1] In *The Globe (Aberdeen) Ltd
v NSWA*,[2] the pursuers were allowed proof before answer when
they sought to recover business losses consequent on road works
outside the pub which continued for nine months rather than the
six weeks for which they were originally scheduled. The pursuers
alleged that the mess created by the operation, particularly mud
on the pavements, made the pub unattractive to customers.

Where the harm takes the form of amenity nuisance, the niche
occupied by this delict is clear. It is not possible to interdict harm
caused negligently, because of course there is no wrong until the
harm has taken place. One question that arises with physical
harm to property is whether it should be necessary to satisfy the
plus quam tolerabile requirement. It doesn't seem to make much
sense to question how much flooding of one's home, or how
much subsidence a person ought reasonably to bear. That said,
physical harm is not always obviously material. In *Chalmers v
Diageo Scotland Ltd*,[3] the pursuers sought damages for the growth
of black fungus on the exterior of their house. This was a known
effect of ethanol emitted from the defenders' bonded warehouses.
Relying on *Kennedy v Glenbelle*,[4] the Lord Ordinary (Ericht)
explained: 'In my view, the issue of whether something exceeds
what is reasonably tolerable is by its very nature dependent on
the facts and circumstances and should be decided after enquiry.'[5]
In *Chalmers*, proof before answer was allowed. The *plus quam
tolerabile* requirement then, is a test of materiality which must be
established at proof in any action grounded on nuisance.

1   1973 Sh Ct 21. See also *Chalmers v Dixon* (1876) 3 R 461. This is consistent with
     the protection afforded neighbours as well as neigbouring property noted

above at 10.4 and contrasts with the English position where it has been held that damages for personal injury cannot be recovered in private nuisance: *Transco Plc v Stockport MBC* [2003] UKHL 61, [2004] 2 AC 1. The position is different in public nuisance, see *Corby Group Litigation Claimants v Corby BC* [2008] EWCA Civ 463, [2009] QB 335.

2   2000 SC 392, 2000 SLT 674; see also *Hand v NSWA* 2002 SLT 798, 2002 SCLR 493.

3   [2017] CSOH 36.

4   Dictum of Lord President Hope, 1996 SC 95 at p 99 B–C: 'A claim for damages in nuisance is a delictual claim … It arises where there is an invasion of the pursuer's interest in land to an extent which exceeds what is reasonably tolerable. The plus *quam* tolerabile test is peculiar to the liability in damages for nuisance. Where that test is satisfied and *culpa* is established, the requirements for the delictual liability are fulfilled.' Cited in *Chalmers v Diageo Scotland Ltd* 2017 CSOH 36 at para 13.

5   Ibid, para 14.

E. OCCUPIERS' LIABILITY

10.11 Scots common law was strongly influenced by English law. As a result of the decision of the House of Lords in *Dumbreck v Robert Addie & Sons*,[1] the duty of care towards a person entering onto property depended on the status of the person who was injured, ie whether he was a licensee, for example a lodger or member of the occupier's family; an invitee, for example a guest; or a trespasser. In the case of a trespasser, liability was restricted to intentional, as opposed to negligently caused, harm. However, as a matter of law, these classifications were swept away by the Occupiers' Liability (Scotland) Act 1960.[2]

The general thrust of the Act is that occupiers of property owe a duty to take such care in respect of persons entering their land or premises as is reasonable in all the circumstances of the case. The statutory duty rests on the person 'occupying or having control of land or other premises' who is referred to in the Act as the 'occupier of premises'.[3] Where the owner of the property is also the occupier of the premises, the statutory duty lies with them. If the owner is not the occupier, they will not be liable under the 1960 Act but may incur liability at common law if they are in breach of a duty of care. A person occupies the land or other premises if they are in possession of the property, for example as a tenant. But a person will also be treated as the occupier if they have control of the land or other premises. A person has 'control' if they are entitled to take the steps in relation to the land or property which the statute requires to fulfil the duty of taking reasonable care of the premises. So, for example, the owner of derelict property who is not *in fact* in possession is nevertheless the occupier because he has control of the premises. Similarly, an owner who moves out during building works, but who returns to her home each day has not relinquished control.[4] The determination whether a defender has sufficient possession or control to be an occupier is one of fact and degree in the light of the circumstances of the particular case.[5]

While 'land' is self-explanatory, 'premises' are not defined in the 1960 Act. They would include houses, flats, sheds, garages, shops etc; land would include gardens. Moreover, the statutory duty to take such care as is reasonable in all the circumstances expressly applies to occupiers of 'any fixed or moveable structure, including any vessel, vehicle or aircraft'.[6] Thus the 1960 Act applies to a wide range of property: eg ships, barges, oil rigs, buses, caravans, cars, tractors, helicopters, planes and hovercraft. It is *not* therefore restricted to heritable property.

1   1929 SC (HL) 51, 1929 SLT 242. See T B Smith 'Full Circle: The Law of Occupiers' Liability in Scotland' in *Studies Critical and Comparative* (1962, W Green) p 154. On occupiers' liability, see Angus McAllister, SULI *Delict* Chapter 17.

2   In this section, references are to the Occupiers' Liability (Scotland) Act 1960 unless otherwise stated.

3   OL(S)A 1960, s 1(1). The common law rules for determining whether a person is an occupier for these purposes is expressly reserved in the Act: s 1(2).

4   *Dawson v Page* [2012] CSOH 33, affirmed [2012 CSIH 24, 2013 SC 482.

5   *Feely v Co-operative Wholesale Society* 1990 SCLR 356, 1990 SLT 547, OH. On the difficulties of determining who is the relevant occupier when the property is in multi-occupation, see *Gallacher v Kleinwort Benson (Trustee) Ltd* 2003 SCLR 384.

6   OL(S)A 1960, s 1(3)(a).

10.12   Section 2(1) of the Occupiers' Liability (Scotland) Act 1960 lays down the nature and extent of the statutory duty:

'The care which an occupier of premises is required, by reason of his occupation or control of the premises, to show towards a person entering thereon in respect of dangers which are due to the state of the premises or to anything done or omitted to be done on them and for which the occupier is in law responsible shall ... be such care as in all the circumstances of the case is reasonable to see that that person will not suffer injury or damage by reason of any such danger.'

It will be noted that the 1960 Act imposes a positive duty on the occupier to take such care as is reasonable in all the circumstances to ensure that a person entering the premises will not suffer injury or damage by reason of any danger on the premises. Nevertheless, the onus lies on the pursuer to show that the occupier did not take the care that was reasonable in the circumstances: it is not enough simply to aver that there was a danger and that the pursuer suffered injury or damage as a result.[1] In *McGuffie v Forth Valley Health Board*,[2] for example, the pursuer slipped on snow on the defender's premises which had not been removed by the defender. The pursuer's action failed because she had not specified the period in which it would have been reasonable for the defender to have removed the snow or instructed its employees to do so. However, in *Porter v Strathclyde Regional Council*,[3] the pursuer slipped on food which had been spilled on the floor of a nursery under the control of the defender. She was able to establish that the defender did not have a system of working whereby an employee would mop up the mess soon after it was spilled. The failure to have such a system was held to be a breach of the occupier's statutory duty to take reasonable care to prevent the pursuer from slipping on the floor as it was probable that the accident would not have occurred if such a system had been in operation.[4]

The Occupiers' Liability (Scotland) Act 1960 applies where the injury or damage arose from dangers 'which are due to the state of the premises *or* to anything done or omitted to be done on them'.[5] Dangers 'due to the state of the premises' clearly covers dangers such as dry rot arising from dilapidated buildings. It would also include uneven roads,[6] a sunken gulley beside a cycle path,[7] a ha-ha[8] slippery floors and unsafe furniture or plenishings.[9] In *Taylor v Glasgow Corpn*,[10] where a child died as a result of eating poisonous berries which were growing in the Glasgow Botanic Gardens, the poisonous berries constituted a danger due to the state of the premises. But the statutory duty also applies to dangers which are due to anything done or omitted to be done on the premises. Thus the 1960 Act would apply to dangers caused by the occupier's failure to provide adequate lighting or to secure a fence, as well as by his positively creating a hazard. As we have seen, the failure to ensure that a pursuer would not enter a garden to clean windows while pugnacious West Highland terriers were also there has been held to be a breach of the 1960 Act.[11] But it is submitted that in the usual case there will be no breach of the 1960 Act where the pursuer sustains physical harm as a consequence of the criminal acts of a third party carried out on the defender's property.[12] In *Honeybourne v Burgess*[13] it was held that hiring a bouncer who violently ejected a patron did not constitute a danger due to anything done or omitted to be done on the premises.

1   *Wallace v City of Glasgow District Council* 1985 SLT 23; *Leonard v Loch Lomond and the Trossachs National Park Authority* [2014] CSOH 38. However, the pursuer

may be able to rely on the *res ipsa loquitur* principle: *McDyer v Celtic Football and Athletic Co Ltd* 2000 SLT 736.

2 1991 SLT 231.

3 1991 SLT 446.

4 However, the pursuer's damages were reduced by 50 per cent as a result of her contributory negligence.

5 Occupiers' Liability (Scotland) Act 1960, s 2(1) (italics added).

6 *Beggs v Motherwell Bridge Fabricators Ltd* 1998 SLT 1215, 1997 SCLR 1019, OH.

7 *Anderson v Scottish Ministers* [2009] CSOH 92.

8 *Cowan v Hopetoun House Preservation Trust* [2013] CSOH 9.

9 *Kerr v East Ayrshire Council* 2005 SLT (Sh Ct) 67 (glass pane in front door held to be a danger); *Bell v North Ayrshire Council* [2007] CSOH 144 (window that stuck held not to be a danger).

10 1922 SC (HL) 1, 1921 2 SLT 254. This was, of course, a case before the 1960 Act.

11 *Hill v Lovett* 1992 SLT 994, OH, discussed in the context of liability for animals, para 9.1 above.

12 See *Modbury Triangle v Anzil* (2000) 205 CLR 254 (no breach of duty where plaintiff assaulted by a third party in an unlit car park owned by the defendant).

13 2006 SLT 585.

10.13 It is important to appreciate that the occupier's statutory obligation is only to take such care as is reasonable in all the circumstances to prevent injury or damage from such dangers: it is not to eliminate the risk that an accident might happen. Accordingly, in determining whether the occupier has taken reasonable care, the calculus of risk is relevant. The court will consider such factors as the nature of the danger, the occupier's knowledge of the danger,[1] the extent of the injury or harm, the probability of the injury or harm arising, the age of the person injured, whether the pursuer was permitted onto the premises and the cost of eliminating the danger. Thus, in *McGlone v British Railways Board*,[2] the defender was held to have taken reasonable care in respect of the danger of a 12-year-old child being burnt by a transformer. The defender had put up warnings and surrounded the transformer with a barbed wire fence which had proved not to be impenetrable. Nevertheless, the House of Lords held that to provide an impenetrable and unclimbable fence went beyond what was reasonable in the circumstances, given that a 12-year-old child should have realised the danger he would incur if he climbed through the barbed wire. In the circumstances, the defender had discharged its duty of reasonable care by erecting an obstacle which a 12-year-old would take some trouble to overcome before he would be in danger. If the fence could have been penetrated by a three-year-old, then there might well have been a breach of the duty to take reasonable care in respect of a child of that age. The fact that the pursuer was a trespasser was also held to be a relevant factor in assessing whether reasonable care had been taken.[3]

A similar approach can be discerned in *Titchener v British Railways Board*.[4] A young man was killed by a train and his 15-year-old girlfriend was seriously injured. The couple had taken a short cut over the line to have a 'kiss and a cuddle' in a derelict brickworks. The defender had provided a fence made of sleepers but there were gaps in the fence through which it was possible for persons to reach the railway line. It was argued that the Board had been in breach of its duty of reasonable care in failing to maintain the fence and thus ensure that there were no gaps providing access to the railway. The House of Lords held that the statutory duty was owed to the particular pursuer, ie a 15-year-old girl who knew the danger involved in crossing a railway line. Accordingly, in determining whether the defender had taken reasonable care, the pursuer's age and knowledge were relevant factors. In these circumstances, the fence – even with gaps – gave adequate warning to a girl of 15 who knew the danger of crossing the line. Indeed, Lord Fraser thought[5] that the defender would have taken reasonable care in respect of the pursuer if there had been no fence at all! It would therefore appear that the more obvious and greater the danger, the *less* by way of warning is required for the average person; conversely, *more* is required if the pursuer is, for example, a young child.

1   It would appear that the defender must know of the danger: *Keane v Walker Contracts (Scotland) Ltd* 1999 GWD 9-410. *Sed quaere?* It is surely enough that the defender ought reasonably to have known of the danger. In *Duff v East Dunbartonshire Council* 2002 Rep LR 98, the First Division held that the owner of land will be presumed to know any physical features which might constitute a danger and should be fenced (drop of six feet from embankment to rocks by river bed: need for fence or at least warning notices). In *Kirkham v Link Housing Group* [2012] CSIH 58, the court observed at para 33: 'the Occupiers' Liability (Scotland) Act 1960 does not impose a duty of insurance on the defenders. The defenders must have knowledge, actual or deemed of any danger before they can be found liable in terms of the Act.'

2   1966 SC (HL) 1, 1966 SLT 2.

3   See also *McLeod v British Railways Board* 2001 SLT 238. In *Platt v Liverpool City Council* CCRTF 97/0072/C, CA the court described as 'absurd' the contention that the defendant had not taken reasonable care to prevent children from entering dangerous premises, when it had put an eight-foot-high corrugated metal fence around the property.

4   1984 SC (HL) 34, 1984 SLT 192. See also *Devlin v Strathclyde Regional Council* 1993 SLT 699, OH (no breach of duty in respect of injuries to a 14-year-old child deliberately jumping on a skylight cover on a roof: the child was also a trespasser).

5   1984 SLT 192 at 195.

10.14 It has been held that any duty on occupiers to fence off dangers does not apply to dangers inherent in the ordinary and familiar features of the landscape whether natural or man-made, for example a loch or reservoir.[1] This was recognised a century ago:

> 'in a town, as well as in the country, there are physical features which may be productive of injury to careless persons or to young children against which it is impossible to guard by protective measures. The situation of a town on the banks of a river is a familiar feature; and whether the stream be sluggish like the Clyde at Glasgow, or swift and variable like the Ness at Inverness, or the Tay at Perth, there is always danger to the individual who may be so unfortunate as to fall into the stream. But in none of these places has it been found necessary to fence the river to prevent children or careless persons from falling into the water'.[2]

In *Tomlinson v Congleton BC*,[3] the House of Lords reaffirmed the principle 'that it is contrary to common sense, and therefore not sound law, to expect [the occupier] to provide protection against an obvious danger on his land arising from a natural feature such as a lake or a cliff and to impose a duty on him to do so'.[4] Moreover, it was thought that it would be extremely rare for an occupier to be under a duty to prevent people taking risks inherent in the activities they chose to undertake on the occupier's land, for example swimming or mountaineering.[5] It was not the policy of the law 'to require the protection of the foolhardy or reckless few to deprive, or interfere with, the enjoyment by the remainder of society of the liberties and amenities to which they are rightly entitled'.[6] In other words, an individual should be allowed to engage in dangerous but otherwise harmless pastimes at her own risk, enabling the rest of society fully to enjoy the pleasures of the countryside and saving the occupier considerable expense.

The defence of *volenti non fit injuria* can be used by the defender.[7] Thus, if there had been a breach of duty in *Titchener*, the House of Lords indicated that *volenti* would have been a defence.[8] Damages may be reduced on the ground of contributory negligence. The parties are free to vary the statutory duty by *agreement*.[9] This enables the occupier to undertake a more onerous or less onerous obligation. Where the premises are used for business, any exemption clause excluding or limiting the occupier's liability for death or personal injuries is void and any clause restricting liability for other kinds of damage is unenforceable unless it satisfies the requirement of reasonableness.[10]

By s 3 of the Occupiers' Liability (Scotland) Act 1960, a landlord who is responsible for the maintenance or repair of premises which have been let owes a similar obligation to persons who enter the premises in respect of dangers arising from the landlord's failure to maintain or repair the property. The statutory obligation extends to anyone lawfully on the premises, such as the tenant's child.[11] The landlord is not obliged to *improve* the premises.[12]

1 *Graham v East of Scotland Water Authority* 2002 SCLR 340; *Fegan v Highland Council* 2007 SC 723. However, in *Cowan v Hopetoun House Preservation Trust* [2013] CSOH 9 the Lord Ordinary (Bracadale) held at para 36 that a 'ha-ha falls to be distinguished from natural features such as riverbanks and cliffs and from man-made features such as canals, railway embankments and jetties. It is an unusual feature of a concealed nature, particularly in the dark. While the ha-ha was a permanent feature of the landscape at Hopetoun House, it is an unusual feature about which someone crossing the lawn in the dark would be likely to be unaware'.
2 *Stevenson v Corpn of Glasgow* 1908 SC 1034 per Lord McLaren at 1039.
3 [2004] 1 AC 46 (young man broke his neck when diving in a lake where swimming was prohibited).
4 Ibid per Lord Hutton at 89.
5 Ibid per Lord Hoffmann at 84.
6 Ibid per Lord Hobhouse at 96.
7 Occupiers' Liability (Scotland) Act 1960, s 2(1).
8 *Volenti* would also have been a defence in *Devlin v Strathclyde Regional Council* 1993 SLT 699, OH.
9 OL(S)A 1960, s 2(1). A non-contractual notice is therefore ineffective.
10 Unfair Contract Terms Act 1977, s 16; Consumer Rights Act 2015 s 65(1) (4). Note the exception in s 66(4).
11 *Guy v Strathkelvin District Council* 1997 SCLR 405, OH.
12 *Scott v Glasgow City Council* 1997 Hous LR 107, Sh Ct.

CHAPTER 11

Breach of statutory duty and liability of public authorities

A. BREACH OF STATUTORY DUTY

11.1 The common law principles of delictual liability may be supplemented or supplanted by delictual liability for breach of a statutory duty.[1] Provided the pursuer can establish that he was harmed or suffered damage to his property as a result of the defender's breach of statutory duty, the pursuer will obtain reparation: it is not necessary for the pursuer to establish delictual liability at common law. The statutory duty may be similar to the common law standard of reasonable care as, for example, in the case of the Occupiers' Liability (Scotland) Act 1960.[2] More often, however, the statute may impose a standard which is higher than that expected of the reasonable person at common law, ie the statute imposes strict liability on the defender. We have seen examples of this in Part I of the Consumer Protection Act 1987[3] and in the Animals (Scotland) Act 1987.[4] These statutes expressly stipulate that breach of the statutory duty gives rise to a civil remedy in delict for reparation. Conversely, some statutes expressly stipulate that a breach of statutory duty does not give rise to a civil remedy for reparation even if a person sustains harm as a result.[5]

But there are many statutes which are silent on whether a person is entitled to seek reparation in a civil action if he or she suffers personal injury or damage due to a breach of statutory duty. Yet, it has long been recognised, that even where a statute is silent on the matter, a person who has suffered loss may still be able to seek reparation in a delictual action for breach of statutory duty. Thus, for example, where an employee was injured at work and the injury arose as a result of a breach of the employer's statutory duty to maintain machinery, the court held that the employer was liable to compensate the employee for breach of statutory duty even though the statute provided criminal sanctions for breach.[6]

218   *Breach of statutory duty and liability of public authorities*

What criteria are used by the courts to determine whether a breach of statutory duty gives rise to a civil action in delict where the statute is silent on the matter? The answer appears to be that it is a question of construction of the particular statute to discover whether Parliament intended to confer on the pursuer the right to obtain reparation for breach of statutory duty. This gives the courts considerable discretion albeit within the confines of the language of the statute. And, like the use of the duty of care as a threshold device,[7] the decision whether or not to allow the pursuer an action for breach of statutory duty will ultimately turn on policy considerations, ie whether or not such an action makes social or economic sense. That said, there are certain presumptions which are used by the courts when construing a statute in order to determine whether a civil remedy lies for breach of statutory duty and these will now be briefly considered.

1   On breach of statutory duty see Eleanor Russell, SULI *Delict* chapter 6.
2   Discussed in Chapter 10 above.
3   Discussed in Chapter 8 above.
4   Discussed in Chapter 9 above.
5   For example the Health and Safety at Work etc Act 1974, s 47.
6   *Groves v Lord Wimborne* [1898] 2 QB 402, CA.
7   For further discussion, see Chapter 4 above.

11.2   As a general principle, where a statute provides a specific mode of enforcement of the statutory duties, the presumption is that Parliament did not intend that a civil action for damages in delict was necessary as an *additional* sanction if the statutory obligation is breached. For example, in *Morrison Sports Ltd v Scottish Power*,[1] after construing the legislation on the supply of electricity to the public, Lord Rodger observed (at para 37):

'Looked at as a whole, therefore, the scheme of the legislation with its carefully worked out provisions for various forms of enforcement on behalf of the public, points against individuals having a private right of action for damages for contravention of regulations made under it.'

Conversely, if the statute does not provide a specific mode of enforcement of the statutory duties, then there is a presumption that Parliament did intend that a civil action for damages would lie. So, for example, in *Dawson v Bingley Urban District Council*,[2] the defendant's breach of statutory duty in failing to provide a notice indicating the position of a fire plug, with the result that there was a delay in putting out a fire at the plaintiff's premises, was held to be actionable by the plaintiff in a civil action. The statute did not provide a penalty or other remedy for breach of the statutory obligations.

Where the pursuer already has a private law remedy against the defender if the statute was broken, for example for breach of contract, it is presumed that Parliament did not intend that the pursuer should have the additional remedy of suing in delict for breach of statutory duty. Although the position is not clear, it is submitted that the existence of a right to seek judicial review should not be presumed to exclude the possibility of a civil remedy for breach of statutory duty: judicial review is simply a procedure and damages are available only if the pursuer has a private law remedy. Accordingly, the right to seek judicial review, while a factor to be taken into consideration by the courts, should not be conclusive in deciding whether Parliament intended that the pursuer should also have the private law remedy of suing in delict for breach of statutory duty.[3]

1   [2010] UKSC 37.
2   [1911] 2 KB 149, 80 LJKB 842, 104 LT 659, 75 JP 289, CA.
3   *Hague v Deputy Governor of Parkhurst Prison* [1992] 1 AC 58, [1991] 3 All ER 733, HL, at 752 per Lord Jauncey.

11.3   Where a statute provides a penalty for breach of statutory duty, the general presumption is that Parliament did not intend that there should be the additional sanction of delictual liability for breach of statutory duty.[1] There are two exceptions to this rule.[2]

First, if it is apparent that the statutory obligations were passed for the protection of a particular class of individuals, then a delictual action for breach of statutory duty may lie if the pursuer belongs to that class and has suffered injury or loss. This explains how employees were able to sue for breach, for example, of the Factories Acts, even though this legislation imposed criminal penalties on employers who were in breach.[3] Similarly, performers whose work was recorded by record companies without their permission, in breach of the Dramatic and Musical Performers' Protection Act 1958, were held to have been intended by Parliament to be able to pursue private law remedies for breach of statutory duty in spite of the fact that the statute also provided criminal sanctions.[4] But it must be clear that the pursuer falls within the class. So, for example, in *RCA Corpn v Pollard*[5] it was held that companies who had exclusive recording contracts with performers could not sue for breach of statutory duty under the 1958 Act.

If the statute is not designed to protect a particular class and provides penalties for breach, no action for breach of statutory duty will lie.[6] But it may be difficult to determine whether the legislation was designed to protect a particular class. In *Cutler v Wandsworth Stadium Ltd (in liquidation)*,[7] for example, the appellant brought proceedings against a licensed dog track to compel it to allow him space at the track to carry on his profession as a bookmaker. Statute provided that the occupier of a licensed track 'shall take such steps as are necessary to secure that … there is available for the bookmaker's space on the track where they can conveniently carry on bookmaking in connection with dog races run on the track'. The House of Lords held that the purpose of the legislation was to protect those members of the public who wished to place bets by ensuring that there was a choice of bookmakers at the track: it was not to give bookmakers the right of a place at the track. Accordingly, the appellant was not entitled to a remedy for breach of statutory duty. But it could equally be argued that it was Parliament's intention to protect the rights of bookmakers to earn their living. The decision in *Cutler* was ultimately a matter of policy. It is interesting to note that the courts are more prepared to construe statutes as giving a delictual remedy for breach of statutory duty where the pursuer has been physically injured[8] than, as in *Cutler*, where the pursuer has suffered only pure economic loss because of the breach of the statutory obligations.

Nevertheless, in the leading Scottish case of *Pullar v Window Clean Ltd*,[9] the Inner House of the Court of Session refused to accept that planning legislation which, *inter alia*, provided that window sashes should be so constructed to enable the window to be cleaned from the inside, was intended to protect window cleaners. There was therefore no breach of statutory duty when a window cleaner fell from the outside sill because the sashes had not been constructed in accordance with the legislation: 'The solution in each case must depend upon what the intention of Parliament was in enacting the obligation in question, and what persons consequently have a right to enforce it or to found upon it as a basis for a claim in damages.'[10]

1 See, eg, *Morrison Sports Ltd v Scottish Power* [2010] UKSC 37.
2 *Lonrho Ltd v Shell Petroleum Co Ltd (No 2)* [1981] 2 All ER 456 at 461 per Lord Diplock.
3 See also *Littlejohn v Wood & Davidson Ltd* 1997 SLT 1353, OH (Merchant Shipping Act 1988, s 31(1) intended to protect a particular class of persons, ie persons on board ships: civil claims for damages allowed in spite of existence of criminal sanctions).
4 *Ex parte Island Records Ltd* [1978] Ch 122, [1978] 3 All ER 824, CA.
5 [1983] Ch 135, [1982] 3 All ER 771, CA.
6 *Morrison Sports Ltd v Scottish Power* [2010] UKSC 37.
7 [1949] AC 398, [1949] 1 All ER 544, HL.

8 As in the case of the Factories Acts.
9 1956 SC 13, 1956 SLT 17.
10 1956 SC 13 at 20 per the Lord President (Clyde).

11.4   Even when the legislation is designed to protect a particular class, there may be other factors which deny an action for breach of statutory duty, albeit that the statute does *not* provide criminal sanctions for its breach. In X *(minors) v Bedfordshire County Council,*[1] children sued a local authority (i) for personal injuries sustained by being removed from their parents in care proceedings; and (ii) for personal injuries sustained by not being removed from their parents in care proceedings. Although the children were clearly within the class of persons the care legislation was designed to protect, the House of Lords held that Parliament did not intend that the children should have a private law right to sue for breach of the statute. This was because the legislation involved an administrative system designed to promote the social welfare of the community and the local authority's duties were expressed in broad language. Moreover, Parliament could not possibly have intended that a local authority should be liable *without proof of fault* merely because a court subsequently decided that children should not have been taken into care and vice versa.[2] In short, given the discretion inevitably involved in childcare legislation, bona fide mistakes would arise and such mistakes were not to be compensated in the absence of fault.[3]

In *Lonrho Ltd v Shell Petroleum Co Ltd (No 2),*[4] Lord Diplock maintained that there was a second exception where a private law remedy could arise for breach of statutory duty even though the statute provided criminal penalties for its breach:

> 'The second exception is where the statute creates a public right (ie a right to be enjoyed by all those of Her Majesty's subjects who wish to avail themselves of it) and a particular member of the public suffers ... "particular, direct and substantial" damage other and different from that which was common to all the rest of the public.'[5]

The extent of this exception has not been developed and need not be discussed further.

Once it has been decided as a matter of construction that Parliament intended that a delictual action should lie for breach of statutory duty, a person who has suffered harm must show that the statute was intended to protect a person in his position, ie that the pursuer falls within the class to be protected and that the damage sustained is of the kind that the statute was designed to prevent. In *Gorris v Scott*,[6] for example, statutory regulations required that sheep or cattle being shipped from a foreign country to the UK had to be put in pens. The defendant failed to provide the pens and as a result the plaintiff's sheep were washed overboard in a storm. The plaintiff's action for breach of statutory duty failed because the court held that the purpose of the pens was to prevent animals from being infected by contagious diseases, not to prevent them from being swept overboard. If the sheep had died as a result of a contagious disease, a delictual claim for breach of statutory duty would have been successful.

The defender must, of course, have broken the statutory duty which was incumbent upon him. Whether or not the defender's conduct constitutes a breach will depend on the interpretation of the particular provision. Statutes may impose absolute liability, strict liability, or reasonable practicability. If a breach of the statutory duty is established, ie the defender has broken the duty,[7] there is no need for the pursuer to prove fault. But the pursuer must establish that the breach of statutory duty caused the harm.[8] Unless, as in the case of the Occupiers' Liability (Scotland) Act 1960,[9] the defence is expressly stated to be available, *volenti non fit injuria* cannot be pleaded.[10] This is because a person cannot agree to take a risk of harm which Parliament has legislated to prevent arising. However, the pursuer's damages may be substantially reduced as a result of contributory negligence.

1   [1995] 2 AC 633, [1995] 3 All ER 353, HL.
2   On potential liability at common law for negligence see beyond para 11.5 ff. In *Thames Trains Ltd v Health and Safety Executive* [2003] EWCA Civ 720, the Court of Appeal held that the HSE did not owe a statutory duty giving rise to a private action by passengers who had sustained personal injuries in a train crash caused by faulty signals: but its failure to exercise its powers carefully could give rise to a claim in negligence (cf strict liability for breach of statutory duty).
3   See also, for example, *O'Rourke v Camden London Borough Council* [1998] AC 188, [1997] 3 All ER 23, HL.
4   [1982] AC 173, [1981] 2 All ER 456, HL.
5   [1981] 2 All ER 456 at 461.
6   (1874) LR 9 Exch 125.
7   For examples see discussion of Part I of the Consumer Protection Act 1987, the Animals (Scotland) Act 1987 and the Occupiers' Liability (Scotland) Act 1960, above.
8   On causation generally, see Chapter 6 above.
9   Occupiers' Liability (Scotland) Act 1960, s 2(3).
10 See, for example, *Wheeler v New Merton Board Mills Ltd* [1933] 2 KB 669, CA.

B. LIABILITY OF PUBLIC AUTHORITIES

11.5 Ministers of the Crown, local authorities and other governmental agencies are often given statutory powers to implement policy. This will often involve the exercise of discretion. Consider the following examples:

(1) A minister is given the power to send some criminals to an open prison: if such a criminal should escape, steal and damage a person's motor car, is the minister liable in delict?[1]

(2) A local authority is given the power to inspect and approve the plans of buildings: if the local authority approves the plans for the foundations of a house, is the local authority liable to the owner of the house if the foundations were unsuitable and have to be repaired?

(3) A minister is empowered to give information to the public on the risks of HIV infection: is the minister liable to a person who contracts HIV through injecting heroin if the information only disclosed the risk of infection from sexual contact and omitted the danger of infection from drug abuse?

In *X (minors) v Bedfordshire County Council*,[2] the House of Lords recognised that if a state agency exercised its statutory powers carelessly, there could be liability at common law in negligence. But before there can be liability in negligence, the careless exercise of the statutory powers must amount to a breach of a pre-existing duty of care owed by the agency to the pursuer. Traditionally, the courts have been reluctant to impose on a state agency a duty of care to exercise its powers carefully unless three hurdles were overcome.

(1) If the agency's statutory discretion involves broad issues of policy, the issue is non-justiciable. The paradigm is when an authority must allocate scarce resources. If, for example, a local authority chose to spend resources on library provision rather than on increasing the number of fire engines, a person who suffered burns in a fire which could not be contained because of the absence of the fire brigade would be unable to sue because the issue of whether more resources should have been spent on fire engines as opposed to books is non-justiciable. In *Kent v Griffiths*[3] Lord Woolf MR recognised that the allocation of resources in respect of the provision of sufficient ambulances and enough staff to man them were matters which were probably not justiciable. In *Ryder*

v Highland Council,[4] the Lord Ordinary (Tyre) thought that the authority's decision not to operate a 24-hour treatment service to remove snow and ice from the A9 was not a justiciable issue.

(2)   Where the statutory discretion operates at an operational as opposed to a broad policy level, for a long time it was argued that a duty of care could not be imposed unless the purported exercise of the power was beyond the ambit of the statutory discretion. In determining this issue, the courts adopted quasi-administrative law principles. In particular, it was considered that this hurdle could only be overcome if the exercise of the discretion was such that no reasonable state agency would have acted in this way. In other words, where the mistake, albeit careless, was one which a reasonable state agency or local authority could have made in the bona fide exercise of its powers, a duty of care could not be imposed and accordingly liability at common law for negligence could not arise. So, for example, if a fire authority prioritised calls, provided the prioritisation was not unreasonable, the decision would fall within the ambit of the statutory discretion and no liability would arise even if, with hindsight, the prioritisation was mistaken. However, because of developments discussed in (3) below, it is submitted that this 'public law' hurdle is no longer a precondition for the imposition of a duty of care although it remains crucial if the pursuer is seeking judicial review rather than damages for negligence.

(3)   The reason why the 'public law' hurdle is now of little, if any, significance is because before the court will impose a duty of care there must be proximity between the parties and the *Caparo* criteria that it is fair, just and reasonable to impose the duty must be satisfied.[5] This enables the courts to decline to impose a duty of care either because of the absence of proximity or on the broader 'fair, just and reasonable' criteria. In *Hill v Chief Constable of West Yorkshire*,[6] for example, the House of Lords held that the chief constable did not owe a duty of care to the mother of the last victim of the Yorkshire Ripper. Not only was there no proximity,[7] but Lord Templeman also considered that it would not be fair, just and reasonable to impose a duty of care on the chief constable in relation to his function of investigating crime.[8] Similarly, in *X (minors) v Bedfordshire County Council*[8] it was not thought fair, just and reasonable to impose a duty of care

on a local authority or its social workers when exercising their discretion whether or not to take potentially abused children into care. In so doing, the courts were in effect granting to state agencies blanket immunity from liability in negligence when exercising their discretionary powers.[9]

1 Of course, the criminal will be liable in delict.
2 [1995] 2 AC 633, [1995] 3 All ER 353, HL. This case and other 'older' authorities must now be viewed in the light of more recent authorities. See *GN v Poole BC* [2019] UKSC 25 per Lord Reed at paras 36–58.
3 [2001] QB 36 at 53.
4 [2013] CSOH 95.
5 See *Caparo Industries plc v Dickman* [1990] 2 AC 605, [1990] 1 All ER 568, HL.
6 [1989] AC 53, [1988], 2 All ER 238, HL.
7 See also *Thomson v Scottish Ministers* [2013] CSIH 63 discussed at para 4.5 above
8 [1995] 2 AC 633, [1995] 3 All ER 353, HL.
9 See also *Forbes v City of Dundee District Council* 1997 SLT 1330, 1997 SCLR 682, OH (not fair, just and reasonable to impose a duty of care on a local authority to ensure that steps were built in accordance with building regulations: the pursuer could, of course, sue the owner/occupier of the building); *Onifade v Secretary of State for Social Security* 1999 GWD 17-819 (no duty of care to prevent pursuer from suffering economic loss as a consequence of an erroneous decision by an adjudication officer refusing the pursuer income support); *Santander v Keeper of the Registers of Scotland* [2013] CSOH 24 (not fair, just and reasonable to impose a duty of care on the Keeper to prevent the bank suffering economic loss when the Keeper registered a forged discharge of a standard security in favour of the bank. The bank and the Keeper were both victims of the forger's crime, but the bank had given the forger the original loan and had sufficient assets to take the risk that she might default and forge a discharge).

11.6 However, the courts can no longer grant blanket immunity as a matter of course. First, in *Osman v United Kingdom*[1] the European Court of Human Rights held that to strike out a claim on the ground that the police enjoyed blanket immunity was a breach of the claimant's right under Article 6 of the European Convention on Human Rights which provides that 'In the determination of his civil rights and obligations ... everyone is entitled to a fair and public hearing'. After a period of consternation on the scope of *Osman*,[2] the European Court of Human Rights then took the view that there was no breach of Article 6 merely because an action was dismissed due to the absence of a duty of care, provided that the claimant had had the opportunity to argue that in the circumstances of her case it was fair, just and reasonable to impose a duty and that it would be disproportionate to the harm sustained not to do so.[3] Second, the European Court of Human Rights considered[4] that where a local authority failed to take steps to protect a child who was the subject of abuse, there could be a breach of the *child's* right under Article 3 of the Convention which provides that 'No one shall be subjected to torture or to inhuman or degrading treatment or punishment'. Similarly, failure to have and follow fair procedures when taking a child into care was held by the Court to constitute a breach of the *parent's* right under Article 8 of the Convention 'to respect for his private and family life'.[5] In these cases the claimants obtained substantial damages for breach of their Convention rights in circumstances where damages were not available in delict because of the judges' refusal to impose a duty of care.

As a result of these developments, the courts are now more ready to impose a duty of care on a local authority. In *Barrett v Enfield London Borough Council*,[6] the House of Lords distinguished *X (minors) v Bedfordshire Council* and held that once a child had been taken into care, a local authority could owe the child a common law duty to prevent him suffering mental harm caused by the authority's failure to provide suitable support: it was irrelevant that the local authority's decisions involved the exercise of discretion on the part of professional social workers. In *D v East Berkshire Community NHS Trust*[7] it was accepted that a local authority owed a duty of care to *a child* in relation to the investigation of suspected abuse and the initiation and pursuit of care proceedings.[8] But the House of Lords held that a local authority did not owe the child's *parents* a duty of care to prevent them suffering mental harm if they were wrongly suspected by doctors or social workers of abusing their child: where there was a potential conflict of interests between the parent and child in care proceedings, the child's welfare was the paramount consideration. It was therefore neither fair, just or reasonable to impose such a duty. In *Trent Strategic Health Authority v Jain*[9] the plaintiffs were the proprietors of a nursing home. The authority took proceedings under the Registered Homes Act 1984 to cancel the plaintiffs' registration. They did so under an emergency procedure where the plaintiffs had no right to be heard. On appeal the owners of the home were fully exonerated. However, by then the home had been shut for four months and their business was ruined. Nevertheless, the House of Lords held that the authority did not owe them a duty of care when the authority applied to have their registration revoked. The purpose of the authority's statutory powers was to protect the residents of care and nursing homes: in an emergency it could be necessary to have the proprietor's registration cancelled immediately. There was therefore a potential conflict of interest between the owners and the residents in the homes. Therefore, the authority did not owe the proprietors a duty of care when exercising their statutory powers[10]

1 [1999] 1 FLR 193.
2 See, for example, *Barrett v Enfield Borough Council* [2001] 2 AC 550 per Lord Browne-Wilkinson at 559–560; *Kent v Griffiths* [2001] QB 36 per Lord Woolf MR at 50.
3 *Z v United Kingdom* [2001] 2 FLR 612.
4 *Z v United Kingdom* [2001] 2 FLR 612 ('appeal' from *X (minors) v Bedfordshire County Council* [1995] 2 AC 633); *E v United Kingdom* (2003) 36 EHRR 31 (action against Scottish local authority for failure to protect children from sex abuse by their stepfather).
5 *TP and KM v United Kingdom* [2001] 2 FLR 549. Claimants failed to establish a breach of Article 8 in *Williams v Hackney LBC* [2018] UKSC 37, [2019] AC 421.
6 [2001] 2 AC 550. See also *S v Gloucester County Council* [2000] 3 All ER 346 (local authority owed a duty of care to a child not to be sexually abused by a foster parent).
7 [2005] AC 373.
8 To that extent, *X (minors) v Bedfordshire County Council* was not followed as being inconsistent with the child's rights under the European Convention on Human Rights. The authority of *D v Berkshire CC* has been limited. See *GN v Poole BC* [2019] UKSC 25 per Lord Reed at para 42. For discussion see J Ford, *Poole Borough Council v GN*, and the Piecemeal Dismantling of Local Authorities' Immunity, (2020) 24 ELR 256.
9 [2009] UK HL 4.
10 This case arose before the Human Rights Act 1998. The court thought that had it been in force the plaintiff would have obtained compensation for breaches of Article 6 and Article 1 of the First Protocol: 'Every natural or legal person is entitled to the peaceful enjoyment of his possessions. No one shall be deprived of his possessions except in the public interest and subject to the conditions provided for by law.'

11.7 On the other hand, the courts have become more ready to accept that an employee of a state agency may owe a direct duty of care to the claimant for which the local authority is vicariously liable if the employee is negligent. In *Phelps v Hillingdon London Borough Council*,[1] the House of Lords held that while, in the performance of their duties under the Education Acts, education authorities owed no relevant duty of care to school children, nevertheless individual employees of the authorities might owe a common law duty of care if they had assumed responsibility for the child: if this duty was breached then the local authority would be vicariously liable. Consequently, the local authority in this case could be vicariously liable for an educational psychologist's failure to assess and provide appropriate assistance for a pupil with special needs.[2]

The law has been much clarified in recent decisions. In *GN v Poole Borough Council*,[3] the claimants sought damages from the local authority alleging breach of s 17 of the the Children's Act

1989 which required the authority to safeguard and promote the welfare of children. A mother and two children had been housed next to 'neighbours from hell' and had suffered physical and psychiatric harm. They contended the authority was in breach in failing to re-house them. The provisions of the Act did not provide a basis for imposition of a duty of care at common law and in the absence of an assumption of responsibility, their case failed, no duty was owed. In addressing the liability of public authorities in the exercise or lack of exercise of their statutory functions, Lord Reed summed up the current law as follows:[4]

'(1) [P]ublic authorities may owe a duty of care in circumstances where the principles applicable to private individuals would impose such a duty. Unless such a duty would be inconsistent with, and is therefore excluded by, the legislation from which their powers or duties are derived; (2) that public authorities do not owe a duty of care at common law merely because they have statutory powers or duties, even if, by exercising their statutory functions, they could prevent a person from suffering harm; and (3) that public authorities can come under a common law duty to protect from harm in circumstances where the principles applicable to private individuals would impose such a duty, as for example where the authority has created the source of danger or has assumed a responsibility to protect the claimant from harm, unless the imposition of such a duty would be inconsistent with the relevant legislation.'

1   [2001] 2 AC 619.
2   See also *A v Essex County Council* [2003] 1 FLR 615 (local authority vicariously liable for social workers' failure to inform potential adoptive parents that the child to be adopted was seriously disturbed).
3   [2019] UKSC 25, [2020] AC 780.
4   Ibid at para 65.

11.8   We have been considering potential liability in negligence for the careless exercise of statutory powers. A similar approach has been taken when a local authority or state agency has failed to use a statutory power which it was not obliged to exercise under the legislation. In *Stovin v Wise and Norfolk County Council*,[1] a local authority had a statutory power to direct a landowner to remove a wall which was a danger to users of the highway. Before the plaintiff was injured in a road accident, the local authority had known the wall was a hazard but had not exercised the power to have the danger removed. The House of Lords held that while the local authority had a public law duty to consider whether to exercise the power, this did not automatically confer a common law right on an individual to obtain damages if injured as a consequence of the authority's decision not to exercise its powers. A common law duty of care would only arise from such an omission if (i) the local authority's failure to exercise the power was irrational (the 'public law' hurdle), and (ii) the legislation did not exclude the right of a person to seek damages if harm was sustained because the power was not exercised. However, in *Gorringe v Calderdale MBC*,[2] Lord Hoffman held that it was 'difficult to imagine a case in which a common law duty can be founded simply upon the failure (however irrational) to provide some benefit which a public authority has power (or a public duty) to provide'. Here the local authority had not provided a warning on a stretch of road of the danger of driving too fast. This omission could not in itself generate a common law duty of care when the authority's failure to exercise its powers under s 39 of the Road Traffic Act 1988 to promote road safety did not give rise to a private law remedy for breach of statutory duty. Accordingly, the possibility raised in *Stovin v Wise* of deriving a common law duty of care merely from a failure to exercise a statutory power would appear to be closed.

The view from *Stovin* and *Gorringe*, that statutory powers do not give rise to a duty to confer a benefit on members of the public, is an important element in the development of the modern law.[3] However, these cases left open the possibility of a duty of care where one would arise under the general principles of common law negligence. So, a duty will arise where the authority has itself created the source of the danger or where it has assumed responsibility towards the pursuer.[4]

In *Capital and Counties plc v Hampshire County Council*,[5] the Court of Appeal held that a fire brigade did not owe a duty of care to a member of the public to answer calls for help because there was no proximity at that stage. Once the brigade had turned up and begun fighting the fire, a duty of care arose not to increase the risk of injury or damage caused by the original fire because of carelessness in carrying out the operations.

Capital and Counties has also proved influential and has been applied to disapprove several Scots decisions. First, however, it should be noted that while other emergency services do not incur duties of care on being called out,[6] the position of the ambulance service differs. In *Kent v Griffiths*,[7] the claimant suffered brain damage because an ambulance which she had summoned failed to arrive within a reasonable time of her call. No explanation was given for the delay: indeed, the crew had falsified the time records. The Court of Appeal held that, since there was an ambulance available and there had been no alternative demands on the crew, they owed the plaintiff a duty of care to arrive within a reasonable time of her call; by accepting the call they had assumed responsibility for the patient.[8]

1   [1996] UKHL15, [1996] AC 923, [1996] 3 All ER 801.
2   [2004] UKHL15.
3   See, eg, *Robinson v Chief Constable of South Yorkshire* [2018] UKSC 8 per Lord Reed paras 31, 35–36,39, 41, 54 and 69.
4   *Gorringe v Calderdale MBC* [2004] UKHL15 per Lord Hoffman at para 38.
5   [1997] QB 1004, [1997] 2 All ER 865, CA.
6   In *OLL v Secretary of State for the Home Dept* [1997] 3 All ER 897, following *Capital and Counties* plc, Moy J held that the coastguard service was under no enforceable private law duty to respond to an emergency call: if it did, it was only liable in negligence for positive acts which directly caused greater injury than would have occurred if it had not intervened at all.
7   [2001] QB 36.
8   See also *Aitken v Scottish Ambulance Service* [2011] CSOH 49. A child died in hospital after arriving by ambulance. There had been a delay of 21 minutes between the emergency call being answered and the ambulance dispatched. Proof before answer allowed to establish whether there had been breach of a duty of care which arose when the ambulance service assumed responsibility for the welfare of the child.

11.9   In *Gibson v Orr*,[1] a bridge carrying a public road collapsed. The police coned off the north side and positioned a police vehicle as a warning to drivers on the south side. After an hour, they left without having received confirmation that any barrier or warning was in place on the south side. The pursuer was injured when the car in which he was a passenger was driven onto the bridge from the south side and fell into the river, the Lord Ordinary (Hamilton) held that the police owed the pursuer a duty of care. By purporting to take control of the hazard, the police constables entered into proximate relationships with those road users likely to be immediately and directly affected by that hazard and there were no policy reasons why it would not be fair, just and reasonable to impose the duty. The difficulty is that the accident would have happened in the same way even if the service had not been provided at all.

In *Duff v Highland and Islands Fire Board*,[2] it was held that a fire brigade owed a duty of care not to be careless when engaged in firefighting. The defender had attended to a fire in the pursuer's chimney which restarted after the brigade had left, causing the destruction of the pursuer's house! This decision was followed in similar circumstances in *Burnett v Grampian Fire and Rescue Service*.[3]

Gibson, Duff and *Burnett* were all disapproved in *AJ Allan (Blairnyle) Ltd v Strathclyde Fire Services*.[4] This was a further case in which a building burnt down after the fire service had left having attended and apparently extinguished an earlier fire. *Capital and Counties* was applied and it was held that there was no assumption of responsibility and the duty on the fire service, which had not been breached, was restricted to not making matters worse.[5]

In *MacDonald v Aberdeenshire*,[6] the Inner House accepted that Scots Law differed from English law in that 'road authorities are liable in negligence, but only in respect of hazards, in the sense of defects that are unlikely to be noticed by road users who exercise reasonable care and skill'. Since the duty is restricted to the removal of hazards that would *not* be noticed by a reasonably skilful driver, the scope of the duty is narrow. Applying the Scottish test would give the same result as in *Stovin* as the hazard there was obvious. Similarly, there would be no liability if the authority failed to clear snow as the reasonable driver would easily recognise the hazard.[7]

1   1999 SC 420.
2   1995 SLT 1362.
3   2007 SCLR 192.
4   [2016] CSIH 5 per Lady Paton paras 33 & 36 and Lady Dorrian para 39.
5   For discussion see R MacLeod, 'Has Fire Service Liability Been Extinguished in Scotland?' 2016 JR 201; G Gordon, 'A Song of Fire and Ice' (2017) 21 *ELR* 122.
6   2013 CSIH 83.
7   See also *Dewar v Scottish Borders Council* [2017] CSOH 68; *Bowes v Highland Council* [2018] CSIH 38. For discussion see E Russell, 'The Liability of Roads Authorities Revisited', 2018 *JR* 283.

11.10   Returning to the question of police immunity from liability in the course of investigating crime[1] the position has now been determined by the *Supreme Court in Robinson v Chief Constable of West Yorkshire*[2] in line with other developments on liability arising from the exercise of statutory functions.[3] The general duty of the police to enforce the law does not bring with it any duty to confer a benefit on members of the public in the absence of special circumstances such as an assumption of responsibility. There is, however, no general rule that the police are not under any duty of care when discharging their functions of preventing and investigating crime.[4] The police can incur duties of care in the same way as private individuals or bodies, for instance where they themselves have created the source of the danger. The claimant in *Robinson* was an elderly pedestrian who found herself at the bottom of a ruck involving two burly police officers and a suspected drug dealer. A duty was owed to her by the officers as a person within the immediate vicinity whose physical injury was a foreseeable consequence of the officers attempting an arrest in the street.

A failure to conduct an effective investigation into crimes of serious violence on the other hand, may breach Article 3 of ECHR.[5] Article 2 of the European Convention provides that: 'Everyone's right to life shall be protected by law. No one shall be deprived of his life intentionally.' A State Agency can therefore be liable for a breach of Article 2 if it has failed to take sufficient measures to protect a person's life: this could include the person being killed by a third party. But before there is a breach of Article 2 it must be shown that the public authority had or ought to have known at the time of a real and immediate risk to the life of an identified individual from the criminal acts of a third party[6] and that it failed to take reasonable measures to avoid that risk. This is a very high test. In *Van Colle v Chief Constable of* Herefordshire,[7] the state had called Van Colle as a witness in a trial. Since there was no evidence to suggest that the accused was violent, it could not have been reasonably anticipated that the accused would kill him: consequently, there was no breach of Article 2. For the same reason there was no breach of Article 2 in *Mitchell v Glasgow City Council*[8] or *Thomson v Scottish Ministers.*[9]

There is little doubt that this has been one of the most difficult areas of the law of delict. However, '[t]he shifting sands which have bedevilled this area of the law over many years have been converted into firm terrain'.[10]

1   See *Hill v Chief Constable of South Yorkshire* [1989] AC 53, [1988] 2 All ER 238 see para 11.5 above.
2   [2019] UKSC 8.
3   The decision, that no duty was owed by the police in *Michael v Chief Constable of South Wales* [2015] UKSC 2, [2016] AC 1732 discussed at para 4.5 above, was not made on police immunity, but on the absence of an assumption of responsibility to protect the claimant against the criminal act of a third party.
4   *Robinson v Chief Constable of West Yorkshire* [2018] UKSC 8 per Lord Reed, paras 34–37, 50, 55 and 70.
5   *Commissioner of Police of the Metropolis v DSD* [2018] UKSC 11, [2019] AC 196.
6   There could also be a breach of Article 2 if a state agency fails to prevent a person killing herself when there was a real and immediate risk that she might do so, for example if she was in a mental hospital suffering from depression: *Savage v South Essex Partnership Trust* [2008] UKHL 74; *Rabone v Pennine Care NHS Trust* [2012] UKSC 2 In *Smith v Ministry of Defence* [2013] UKSC 41 the Supreme Court held that the court's jurisdiction to protect persons from a breach of Article 2 extended to members of the armed forces serving abroad.
7   [2008] 3 WLR 593.
8   [2009] UKHL 11, 2009 SLT 265, discussed above at para 4.5.
9   [2013] CSIH 63.
10   *HMA v Adiukwu* [2020] CSIH 47, 2021 SC 38 per Lady Dorrian at para 7.

CHAPTER 12

Employers' liability and vicarious liability

A. EMPLOYERS' LIABILITY

12.1 It is an implied term of the contract of employment that an employer will take reasonable care for the safety of his employees. If an employer does not take reasonable care, he will be in material breach of contract. In these circumstances, an employee may withdraw his labour and sue for damages. An employer may be in breach of his contractual obligations even if the employee has not suffered any harm. In addition to his contractual obligations, an employer owes a *Donoghue v Stevenson* duty of care[1] to his employees to prevent them from suffering physical or psychiatric harm as a result of the employer's negligent conduct. Accordingly, an employee who is injured may sue his employer in delict as well as for breach of contract; but the employee cannot be compensated twice for the same loss. If the employee does not suffer any harm, there can be no liability in delict though there might still be a remedy for breach of contract.[2]

The obligation to take reasonable care for the safety of his employees is personal to the employer, ie it cannot be delegated by the employer to senior employees or a third party.[3] However, in a modern industrial context, in order to *fulfil* the obligation of reasonable care, an employer may have to appoint a safety officer and/or safety committee. The scope of the duty incumbent on an employer includes taking reasonable care to supply the employee with proper plant and equipment, to select competent fellow workers and to provide a safe system of working; but it is a *general* duty to take reasonable care. For example, an employer can be liable for failure to *devise* a safe system of working.[4] Where an employer fails to instruct an employee to use protective devices or clothes, or fails to provide adequate training, a breach of the duty to take reasonable care can arise: *Pickford v ICI plc*.[5] An employer may also have to train employees to protect themselves from violent third parties they may meet in the course of their employment, for example school children![6]

Moreover, it cannot be overemphasised that at common law the employer is only expected to maintain the standards of the reasonable person in his position, ie it is only to take reasonable care. An employer is not expected to ensure that an employee is never harmed. In assessing whether a particular employer has taken reasonable care, the calculus of risk will be relevant.[7] The court will therefore consider such factors as the nature of the danger, the employer's knowledge of the danger, the extent of the harm, the probability of the harm arising and the cost of eliminating the risk.[8]

1   See *Donoghue v Stevenson* 1932 SC (HL) 31, 1932 SLT 317, and Chapter 3 above. The existence of a contract between the employer and employee is an important factor in establishing the 'foreseeability of harm' criterion.

2   *Rothwell v Chemical and Insulating Co* [2008] 1 AC 281 (pleural plaques do not constitute harm and therefore no delictual liability) discussed above at para 5.2. Dismissal of an employee who refuses to work in an unsafe system will be unfair. Employment Rights Act 1996 s 100 (1).

3   *Hislop v Durham* (1842) 4 D 1168; *Wilsons and Clyde Coal Co Ltd v English* 1937 SC (HL) 46. In *MacIver v J & A Gardner Ltd* 2001 SLT 585, it was held that an employer owed a duty of care to a ship's master who was the safety officer in charge of the ship. On non-delegable duties, see below at para 12.20

4   *McGregor v AAH Pharmaceuticals Ltd* 1996 SLT 1161, OH.

5   *Pickford v ICI plc* [1996] ICR 566, [1996] IRLR 622, CA; *Kennedy v Cordia (Services) LLP (Scotland)* [2016] UKSC 6.

6   *McLeod v Aberdeen City Council* 1999 GWD 23-1115.

7   *Brisco v Secretary of State for Scotland* 1997 SC 14; *McErlean v J & B Scotland Ltd* 1997 SLT 1326; *Mcginnes v Endeva Service Ltd.* 2006 SLT 638. On the calculus of risk generally, see para 5.10 ff above.

8   *Latimer v AEC Ltd* [1953] AC 643, [1953] 2 All ER 449, HL; *Hatton v Sutherland* [2002] 2 All ER 1; *Barber v Somerset County Council* [2004] UKHL 13; *Baker v Quantum Group Clothing Ltd* [2011] UKSC 17.

12.2   In *Davie v New Merton Board Mills Ltd*,[1] for example, an employee was injured when a piece of a chisel he was using broke off and a splinter went into his eye. The defect in the chisel was latent and arose because the metal used for the chisel had not been tempered properly by the manufacturer. The employer had bought the chisel from a reputable retailer who had in turn bought it from a reputable wholesaler who had purchased it from the manufacturer. In these circumstances, the House of Lords held that the employer had taken reasonable care and the employee's action against the *employer* failed. The employee could, of course, have sued the manufacturer in delict for breach of the manufacturer's *Donoghue v Stevenson* duty of care which he owed to the ultimate consumer of the product.[2] However, the view was taken that this was placing too heavy an onus on an employee. Accordingly, under the Employers' Liability (Defective Equipment) Act 1969,[3] if an employee suffers physical harm as a result of a defect in equipment[4] provided by the employer and the defect is attributable wholly or partly to the fault of a third party,[5] for example the manufacturer, then the defect is deemed to be also attributable to negligence on the part of the employer. In other words, the employee can sue the employer without the need to prove that the employer was negligent. The *employer* will then seek redress against the third party either in contract or, theoretically at least, in delict.

The employer must take reasonable care in selecting competent workers who will not cause harm to the other employees. If the employer fails to do so and an employee is injured as a result, the employee can sue the employee for breach of the duty of care.[6] Again it must be emphasised that the employer is only expected to take reasonable care. Before the employer can be negligent, he must know that the employee he has appointed could be a danger to fellow workers.[7] The contract of employment is not a contract *uberrimae fidei*; the employer must therefore make reasonable enquiries to determine whether an aspirant employee would be a source of danger to fellow employees if he were to be engaged. For example, the employer should ask whether an applicant for a job as a van driver has a clean driving licence and whether he has been convicted of careless or reckless driving.[8]

Many injuries in the workplace are attributable to failures to provide safe systems of work. For example, the lack of a system to ensure that stepladders were available where they were needed placed employers in breach when an employee lost her footing climbing shelves to retrieve a box from the topmost one.[9] A delivery man who injured his back carrying a 48kg television should have been provided with a sack barrow.[10] A harbour operator failed to provide a safe system for loading lorries onto a ferry. The bosun, who was struck by a reversing trailer, suffered a serious injury to his arm.[11] The duty to provide a safe system of working is owed to the individual employee. So, if an employer knows that an employee is an epileptic or has only one eye, the standards required to constitute reasonable care may be greater in respect of that employee than the other workers. Accordingly, the employer may be negligent vis-à-vis that employee even if his conduct would not amount to negligence if the employee were not epileptic or had two eyes.[12]

1 [1959] AC 604.
2 See *Donoghue v Stevenson* 1932 SC (HL) 31, 1932 SLT 317. On product liability generally, see Chapter 8 above.
3 Employers' Liability (Defective Equipment) Act 1969, s 1(1).
4 The courts have taken a wide view of the meaning of 'equipment' to protect employees: see, for example, *Knowles v Liverpool City Council* [1993] 4 All ER 321, [1993] 1 WLR 1428, HL (council employee injured by a defective flagstone: flagstone held to constitute equipment).
5 The pursuer is not obliged to identify the third party who was at fault: *Edwards v Butlins Ltd* 1998 SLT 500, 1997 GWD 21-1052.
6 The duty extends to providing adequate supervision of employees whose behaviour at work might injure a fellow worker: *Gibson v British Rail Maintenance* 1995 SC 7, 1995 SLT 953 (pursuer injured by a ball which was being used in a game played by two other employees: employer liable because foreman was absent when the game was being played); *Ward v Scotrail Railways Ltd* 1999 SC 255 (pursuer suffered a psychiatric disorder as a result of a fellow employee's sexual molestation: employer would be in breach of the duty if he failed to stop the harassment); *Waters v Commissioner of Police of the Metropolis* [2000] 4 All ER 934 (plaintiff claimed to have been raped and buggered by a fellow officer in her police residential accommodation: defendant did not investigate her complaint and she suffered victimisation and harassment from the other officers for bringing a complaint. The House of Lords held that the defendant was in breach of duty in their failure to prevent her fellow officers from taking retaliatory steps against the plaintiff).
7 See, eg, *Hudson v Ridge Manufacturing Co Ltd* [1957] 2 QB 348, [1957] 2 All ER 348.
8 Subject to the offences being spent under the Rehabilitation of Offenders Act 1974.
9 *McGregor v AAA Pharmaceuticals Ltd* 1998 SLT 1161.
10 *Lindsay v TNT Express (UK) Ltd* 1996 GWD 38-2231.
11 *Lee v Ardrossan Harbour Co Ltd* 1992 SLT 340.
12 *Paris v Stepney Borough Council* [1951] AC 367, [1951] 1 All ER 42, HL.

12.3   The employer's general duty includes taking reasonable steps to prevent the employee suffering *psychiatric*[1] as well as physical harm.[2] In *Hatton v Sutherland*,[3] the Court of Appeal held that where an employee has sustained psychiatric harm there are no special control mechanisms and the ordinary principles of employers' liability apply. Accordingly, the employee must show that the employer was in breach of the duty of care. As we have seen,[4] there will be no breach unless it can be shown that the harm sustained by the pursuer was a reasonably foreseeable consequence of the employer's conduct. But by its nature psychiatric harm is less foreseeable than physical harm. Moreover, in *Hatton* the court took the view that an employer is usually entitled to assume that an employee can withstand the normal pressures of work unless the employer knows that the employee is particularly vulnerable.[5] This could arise, for example, where the employer was aware that the employee had had a nervous breakdown before[6] or the employee's doctor had informed him that the working conditions were causing the employee to suffer depression[7] or there have been unexplained and uncharacteristic absences from work. There can be liability if the psychiatric injury was caused by an excessive workload, ie where the employee was required to perform duties far beyond those agreed in her contract.[8]

An employer does not have a general duty to monitor employees to see whether they are at risk of suffering psychiatric harm and taking steps to prevent them doing so.[9] But even if psychiatric harm was reasonably foreseeable, there is no liability unless the employee can show that there were reasonable steps which the employer should have taken to prevent him suffering mental harm.[10] The economic costs to the business of reducing the risk and fairness to other employees will be important factors in determining whether or not the employer had taken reasonable care. If the only way to prevent the employee suffering mental harm was to dismiss him from the job, an employer is not in breach if the employee chooses to continue working.[11] In short, while an employer's general duty of care to protect his employees includes psychiatric as well as physical harm, it will be very difficult to establish a breach of duty in respect of psychiatric harm caused by stressful work unless the employer knew that the employee was particularly vulnerable and there were reasonable – as opposed to difficult or expensive – steps to reduce the pressure on the employee.

Where an employee suffers psychiatric harm from witnessing the physical – or mental – injuries of a third person, for example a fellow employee,[12] the employer does not owe a duty of care unless the employee was within the area of risk of potential physical harm[13] or the *Alcock* criteria for liability in respect to psychiatric injury to secondary victims are satisfied.[14] In *Keen v Tayside Contracts*,[15] for example, a worker was instructed by his employer to assist the emergency services at the scene of a road accident where he saw the crushed and burned bodies of the victims. The pursuer's supervisor refused him permission to leave the scene of the accident even though he asked to do so. The pursuer claimed that the employer was negligent in (a) failing to instruct supervisors to let employees leave the scene of an accident where there were dead and mutilated bodies and (b) failing to provide post-incident support for employees who had been disturbed by seeing the victims. The Lord Ordinary (Paton) dismissed the action. Although acting in the course of his employment, the pursuer was a secondary victim since the psychiatric harm was caused by witnessing the victims of the road accident: the *Alcock* criteria could not be satisfied as there was no relationship of love and affection between the victims and the pursuer.[16]

1 Stress, in itself, does not per se constitute psychiatric harm though it may lead to a psychiatric disorder such as acute stress reaction, PTSD or depression if allowed to continue unabated.

2 *Fraser v State Hospitals Board for Scotland* 2001 SLT 1051; *Cross v Highland and Islands Enterprise* 2001 SLT 1060; *Green v Argyll & Bute Council* 2002 GWD 9-295. In *McCarthy v Highland Council* [2011] CSIH 51 the defender was found liable for the psychiatric injury suffered by a teacher as a result of their failure to provide her with a dedicated male support worker after she had been assaulted on several occasions by a pupil who required special educational needs.

3 [2002] 2 All ER 1 approved by the House of Lords in *Barber v Somerset County Council* [2004] UKHL 13.

4 See para 5.3 ff above.

5 See, eg, *K v Chief Constable, Police Scotland* [2020] CSIH 18.

6 *Walker v Northumberland CC* [1995] 1 All ER 737.

7 *Stevenson v East Dunbartonshire Council* 2003 SLT 97; *Barber v Somerset County Council* [2004] UKHL 13.

8 *Flood v University of Glasgow* 2010 SLT 167. The excessive workload enabled the Inner House to distinguish the case from *Hatton*.

9 *Chapman v The Lord Advocate* 2006 SCLR 186; *Donaldson v The Scottish Ministers* 2009 SLT 240 (prison officer had been suffering from stress but employer was told that he was fit to return to work: employer could not reasonably foresee that he would suffer a psychiatric disorder).

10 If the employer has taken reasonable steps there will be no breach of duty: see, eg, *Pratt v Scottish Ministers* 2013 SLT 590.

11 *Walker v Northumberland CC* [1995] 1 All ER 737.

12 See, eg, *Robertson v Forth Road Bridge Joint Board* 1995 SC 364; *Hunter v British Coal Corporation* [1999] QB 140.

13 In which case the employee is a primary victim and is protected by the employer's general duty to take reasonable care of his employees. It can be difficult to determine whether an employee has sufficient proximity to the accident which caused the harm to the third party to be regarded as a participant and therefore a primary victim. See *Robertson v Forth Road Bridge Joint Board* 1995 SC 364; *Campbell v North Lanarkshire Council* 2000 SCLR 245; *Young v Charles Church (Southern) Ltd* 2000 SCLR 373; *Salter v UB Frozen & Chilled Foods Ltd* 2003 SLT 1011.

14 Namely that there was a relationship of love and affection between the employee and the person who was injured, proximity to the accident or its immediate aftermath and direct visual observation of the accident or its aftermath.

15 2003 SLT 500.

16 This is consistent with the decision of the House of Lords in *Frost v Chief Constable of South Yorkshire Police* [1999] AC 455 where the injuries to the third parties witnessed by the plaintiffs were also caused by their employer. For discussion, see para 4.5 above. In *Donaldson v the Scottish Ministers* 2009 SLT 240 the pursuer suffered a psychiatric illness from watching one prisoner assaulting another prisoner. The Lord Ordinary (Woolman) held that the pursuer had not demonstrated what the employee should have done to avoid the incident.

12.4 The employer must provide a safe environment in which employees work.[1] Where an employee works at a place which is not under the control of his employer, the employer can still be liable for failing to inspect the premises to ensure that the employee is not exposed to unnecessary risks.[2] It has been held that there can be a breach of the duty if the employer has not taken reasonable steps to protect an employee from the risk of illness arising from passive smoking.[3]

At common law the onus lay on the employee to prove that the harm sustained was a breach of the employer's duty of care, ie that the employer was negligent. Since the nineteenth century, safety at work has been the subject of statutory regulations. These provide detailed safety requirements for machinery, particular processes and operations. Although earlier statutes provided criminal sanctions in cases of breach, the courts allowed an employee who was injured as a result to sue the employer in delict for breach of statutory duty. Moreover, as the statutes often imposed strict liability, an employee who sued for breach of statutory duty did not have to establish negligence. But, of course, the employee had to show that the employer was in breach of the statutory obligations.[4]

The Health and Safety at Work etc Act 1974 lays down the minimum standards required of employers for safety at the workplace. However, it is a criminal statute and it is expressly enacted that its breach does not give rise to a private law remedy for breach of statutory duty. Confusingly, the morass of safety legislation, in particular the Factories Act 1961, continued in force for a while and breach of these provisions did give rise to an action for breach of statutory duty. But now much of this legislation has been repealed and replaced by statutory regulations implementing EU directives.[5] Breach of these detailed regulations no longer gives rise to delictual liability.[6] Nevertheless, where an employee is injured in circumstances that amount to a breach of these regulations, it is important to remember that they may still be able to plead the employer's negligence where there is an equivalent duty at common law.

An employer may owe the employee a duty of care under the Occupiers' Liability (Scotland) Act 1960, as well as the general duty of care owed to employees at common law.[7]

---

1   For example, that the level of noise in the workplace will not cause deafness. The pursuer must establish the level of the noise: *Robinson v Midlothian Council* [2009] CSOH 109.

2   *Crombie v McDermott Scotland Ltd* 1996 SLT 1238, 1996 Rep LR 122, OH; *Muir v North Ayrshire Council* 2005 SLT 963 (pursuer was a home help who was injured in the house of a client: employer could be liable as they knew the environment in which she was working).

3   *Rae v Strathclyde Joint Police Board* 1999 GWD 12-571.

4   See, for example, *Thomson v Kvaerner Govan Ltd* 2004 SLT 24, HL.

5   See, for example, the Provision and Use of Work Equipment Regulations 1998, and the Manual Handling Operations Regulations 1992. On the Provision and Use of Work Equipment Regulations 1998, see *Smith v Northamptonshire CC* [2009] UKHL 27, where the Supreme Court stated that courts should be careful not to impose upon employers responsibilities that went far beyond those at which the Directive and Regulations were aimed; on the Manual Handling Operations Regulations 1992, see for example, *MacDonald v Wood Group Engineering (North Sea) Ltd* [2010] CSOH 165. On the Workplace (Health, Safety and Welfare) Regulations 1992, see for example, *Munro v Aberdeen City Council* [2009] CSOH 129; *Gillie v Scottish Borders Council* [2013] CSOH 76. On the Noise at Work Regulations 1989, see *Robinson v Midlothian Council* [2009] CSOH 109.

6   Health and Safety at Work Act 1974 s 47(1) and (2). as amended by the Enterprise and Regulatory Reform Act 2013 s.69. See also *Gilchrist v Asda Stores Ltd* [2015] CSOH 77 per Lady Stacey at para 14.

7   *Hill v Lovett* 1992 SLT 994, OH.

B.   VICARIOUS LIABILITY

(1) Introduction

12.5   In certain circumstances a person may be liable for the delicts committed by another. This is known as vicarious liability. Although the doctrine arises out of several relationships, the most common by far is that of employer and employee. An employer is vicariously liable for the wrongs committed by the employee in the course of their employment. This arises when the employee concerned harms a third party or another employee provided the delict was closely connected with their employment. Although the employer and employee are jointly and severally liable, in practice the pursuer will sue the employer who is more likely to have funds or be insured. Where it is an employee who has been injured, the employer is obliged by statute to have insurance so that funds are available if vicariously liability is found.[1] Where an employee has been negligent, if the employer is found vicariously liable, the employer can, in theory at least, recover the damages he has paid from the employee, since the employee's wrongful conduct constitutes a breach by the employee of the contract of employment.[2] In practice, an employer – or his insurers – do not exercise this right to sue the employee for breach of contract.

1   Employers' Liability (Compulsory Insurance) Act 1969. In Scotland, it has been held that failure to insure can result in the directors of a company being personally liable in a claim for damages for breach of statutory duty: *Quinn v McGinty* 1999 SLT (Sh Ct) 27. In England, it has been held by the Court of Appeal that no civil liability lies for breach of the Employers' Liability (Compulsory Insurance) Act 1969: see *Richardson v Pitt-Stanley* [1995] QB 123, [1995] 1 All ER 460, CA.

2   *Lister v Romford Ice and Cold Storage Co Ltd* [1957] AC 555, [1957] 1 All ER 125, HL.

(2) Relationship between wrongdoer and employer

12.6   The first issue is to determine whether the relationship between wrongdoer and person alleged to be vicariously liable is one that gives rise to vicarious liability. Traditionally this has involved an inquiry whether the person who committed the wrong is working under a contract of employment (*locatio operarum*) or is an independent contractor working under a contract for services (*locatio operis faciendi*). The rule, that a person is not vicariously liable for delicts committed by independent contractors stands, but vicarious liability may also arise from relationships 'akin to employment'.[1] The traditional test for distinguishing between a contract of employment and a contract for services is that of 'control':[2] an employer has the power to control not only what the employee should do but also *how* he should do it. If A has a cleaner who regularly cleans A's house, there is a contract of employment since A can tell the cleaner not only what to do but the manner in which the work is to be done. On the other hand, if A wishes to have a suit dry cleaned, while he may tell the cleaners what to do, A does not have the power to tell them how to carry out the dry-cleaning process: here A is simply entering into a contract for the services of the dry cleaner and not a contract of employment.

The 'control' test has been a useful criterion where the work involved is relatively unskilled. But it is of less value where the alleged employer is a company or large organisation and the work involved is specialist and sophisticated. The courts have therefore had to develop other criteria. Where a person works as an integral part of an organisation, he is likely to be working under a contract of employment, particularly if there is some element of control.[3] Although the parties' expressed intention in their contract is an important factor, the 'label' they have used to describe their relationship is not decisive. As Lord Denning MR observed in *Massey v Crown Life Insurance Co*:[4]

'If the true relationship of the parties is that of master and servant under a contract of service [a contract of employment], the parties cannot alter the truth of that relationship by putting a different label upon it.'

However, if the relationship between the parties is ambiguous, the 'label' in the contract may be a crucial factor in determining the true relationship between them.[4] Other important factors include the payment of National Insurance contributions, the pension position, the payment of Schedule D or Schedule E taxation, whether the worker is paid a fee or a sum on a regular basis and the arrangements for termination of the contract.

1   See paras 12.7–12.8 below.
2   *Yewans v Nokes* (1880) 6 QBD 530. On vicarious liability, see Aidan O'Donnell, SULI *Delict* Chapter 4.
3   *Stevenson, Jordan and Harrison Ltd v MacDonald and Evans* (1952) 69 RPC 10, [1952] 1 TLR 101, CA.
4   [1978] ICR 590 at 594, [1978] 2 All ER 576 at 579, CA.

12.7   In the vast majority of cases, it will be clear whether the contract between the parties is one of employment or for services. In ambiguous cases, the courts consider a range of factors. This has long been recognised as the proper approach in Scots law.[1] Significant developments have taken place in recent years. In *Various Claimants v Catholic Child Welfare Society*[2] (The *Christian Brothers* case) Lord Phillips listed five factors which would justify a finding of vicarious liability. In reviewing these factors in *Cox v Ministry of* Justice,[3] Lord Reed considered that the first, that the defender was more likely than the wrongdoer to be insured, should not normally be considered and the fifth, control, was unlikely to be of independent significance in most cases. The key factors, then, are: that the delict should have been committed as a result of activity carried out by the wrongdoer on behalf of the defender; that the wrongdoer's activity is likely to be part of the business activity of the defender; and that the defender, by employing the wrongdoer to carry on activity will have created the risk of the delict committed by the wrongdoer. These factors are not strict tests to be given equal weight, their consideration and weighting will depend on the circumstances of the case. Business activity is broadly construed, the activity need not be commercial.

1   See, eg, *Short v J & W Henderson Ltd* 1946 SC (HL) 24, 1946 SLT 230; *United Wholesale Grocers Ltd v Sher* 1993 SLT 284, OH.
2   [2012] UKSC 56.
3   [2016] UKSC 10 at paras 20–21.

12.8 Under this approach the requirement for a contract of employment has been relaxed and courts have held persons vicariously liable for delicts committed by those who were not, strictly speaking, employees. For example, in the *Christian Brothers* case,[1] the Supreme Court found trustees vicariously liable for child sexual abuse carried out by monks who, while not employees, were nevertheless in a relationship akin to employment. In *Cox v Minister for Justice*, the prison service was vicariously liable when a prisoner performing kitchen duties dropped a sack of flour injuring his supervisor. Lord Reed summarised the modern approach:[2]

> 'A relationship other than employment is in principle capable of giving rise to vicarious liability where harm is wrongfully done by an individual who carries on activities as an integral part of the business activities carried on by a defendant and for its benefit (rather than his activities being entirely attributable to the conduct of a recognisably independent business of his own or of a third party), and where the commission of the wrongful act is a risk created by the defendant by assigning those activities to the individual in question.'

Cox was followed in the sheriff court case, *Grubb v Shannon*.[3] The pursuer suffered an allergic reaction to eyebrow tinting negligently applied by a self-employed beautician working in the defender's beauty parlour. The relationship between the beautician and defender was held to be akin to employment and vicarious liability was established. In *Various Claimants v Barclays Bank*,[4] the Supreme Court made it clear that the position of independent contractors has not changed. A doctor had subjected bank employees to intrusive and unnecessary procedures while conducting medicals on behalf of the bank. Since he was clearly in practice on his own account with his own list of patients and clients, which included the bank, he was an independent contractor for whose acts the bank could not be vicariously liable. In *Shannon* the sheriff ruled explicitly that the beautician was not an independent contractor.

1   [2012] UKSC 56.
2   *Cox v Ministry of Justice* [2016] UKSC 10 at para 23.
3   [2018] SC GLA 13; 2018 GWD 10-126.
4   [2020] UKSC 13.

(3) Wrongs of an employee

12.9 Turning to the question of conduct for which the defender should be vicariously liable, for many years the position was that the employer would be vicariously liable for the wrongs committed by the employee 'in the course of the employment'. In other words, before an employer is vicariously liable, the employee's acts or omissions which constitute the delict must fall within the scope of his employment. The traditional exposition of the doctrine in Scots law is to be found in the judgment of the Lord President (Clyde) in *Kirby v National Coal Board*:[1]

> 'But, in the decisions, four different types of situation have been envisaged as guides to the solution of this problem. In the first place, if the master actually authorised the particular act, he is clearly [vicariously] liable for it. Secondly, where the workman does some work which he is appointed to do, but does it in a way which his master has not authorised and would not have authorised had he known of it, the master is nevertheless still responsible, for the servant's act is still within the scope of his employment. On the other hand, in the third place, if the servant is employed only to do a particular work or a particular class of work, and he does something outside the scope of that work, the master is not responsible for any mischief the servant may do to a third party. Lastly, if the servant uses his master's time or his master's tools for his own purposes, the master is not responsible.'

The first of these four situations is relatively straightforward. Authority for conduct need not be express, it may be implied. In *Neville v C & A Modes Ltd*,[1] the pursuer was suspected of shoplifting by employees of the defender. She was forcibly taken from the street back into the shop and there accused of theft. The pursuer argued that the defender was vicariously liable for defamation of character. The Inner House held that the defender's employees had a duty under their contracts of employment to protect the defender's property and take action to prevent theft. The employees' action had therefore been authorised by the defender, ie was within the scope of their employment, albeit that it may have been defamatory in the circumstances of this case.[1] Obviously the terms of the contract are important, but the courts are not prepared to accept that, for the purpose of vicarious liability, the scope of employment is limited to the employee's express contractual duties. Lord Clyde's second situation extends the meaning of 'scope of employment' to cover unauthorised modes of conducting authorised work. For example, in *Century Insurance Co Ltd v Northern Ireland Road Transport Board*,[4] an explosion took place when an employee lit a cigarette while transferring petrol. The House of Lords held that this was an unauthorised mode of doing his job which was to transfer petrol and that the employer therefore remained vicariously liable. In *Taylor v Glasgow District Council*,[5] a building control officer had been given actual authority to issue building warrants and completion certificates. He issued false documents as part of a fraudulent scheme with a development company. The company sold the property to Taylor who sustained economic loss. It was held that the defender could be vicariously liable for the fraudulent conduct of its employee because he had been given actual authority to issue the documents. The fact that the defender did not benefit from the fraud was irrelevant: the only question was whether the employee's conduct was an improper mode of doing what he was authorised to do.

1   1958 SC 514 at 532–533, 1959 SLT 7.
2   1945 SC 175, 1945 SLT 189
3   On defamation see Chapter 15 below.
4   [1942] AC 509, [1942] 1 All ER 491, HL.
5   1997 SC 183, 1997 SLT 537.

12.10   Vicarious liability may also arise where an employee acts in disregard of instructions. In *Rose v Plenty*,[1] a milkman was expressly instructed by his employer not to use boys to help him deliver milk or to give boys lifts in his milk float. In breach of this order, he continued to use a 13-year-old boy to help him. The lad was injured because of the milkman's negligent driving of the float. The employers argued that they were not vicariously liable because the employee was acting outside the scope of his employment. In other words, his work was delivering milk without the help of young boys, therefore he was acting outside the scope of his employment when he delivered milk with the boy's assistance. However, the Court of Appeal held[2] that the express prohibition did not change the scope of the milkman's employment. As Lord Denning MR explained:[3]

> 'In considering whether a prohibited act was within the course of the employment it depends very much on the purpose for which it is done. If it is done for his employer's business, it is usually done in the course of his employment, even though it is a prohibited act ... But if it is done for some purpose other than his master's business, as, for instance, giving a lift to a hitchhiker, such an act, if prohibited, may not be in the course of his employment ... In the present case it seems to me that the course of Mr Plenty's [the milkman's] employment was to distribute the milk, collect the money and to bring back the bottles to the van. He got, or allowed this young boy, Leslie Rose, to do part of that business which was the employer's business. It seems to me that although prohibited, it was conduct which was

within the course of employment ... I agree it is a nice point in these cases on which side of the line the case falls.'

Where the wrongdoer was acting for the employer's purposes this points to the conduct being within the scope of employment, In *Williams v Hemphill (A & W) Ltd*,[4] members of the Boys' Brigade were at a camp at Benderloch. A company of Girl Guides was also at the camp. The girls were to return to Dollar by train. A lorry driver was instructed by his employer to take the boys back to Glasgow. He was persuaded by some of the boys to return to Glasgow via Connell, Stirling and Dollar railway stations so the boys could catch a glimpse of the girls. The shortest route back to Glasgow was via Loch Lomond. There was an accident and one of the boys, who had not instigated the change of route, was injured. The employers would not have authorised the route the driver had taken. The question was whether, by deviating from the authorised route, the driver was no longer acting within the scope of his employment with the result that the employer would not have been vicariously liable. The House of Lords held that it was ultimately a question of degree whether, as a result of the deviation, the employee was no longer engaged on the employer's business. In this case, the dominant purpose of the journey was to transport the boys to Glasgow and the driver was still engaged in that task when the accident occurred, despite not having taken the most direct route. As Lord Pearce explained:[5]

'In weighing up, therefore, the question of degree whether the admittedly substantial deviation of the vehicle with its passengers and baggage was such as to make the lorry's progress a frolic of the servant unconnected with or in substitution for the master's business, the presence of the passengers is a decisive factor against regarding it as a mere frolic of the servant. In the present case the defenders remained liable, in spite of the deviation, for their driver's negligence.'[6]

In both *Rose v Plenty* and *Williams v Hemphill* the Court found in favour of vicarious liability because the wrongdoers could both be said to have been engaged on their employers' business and therefore were within the scope of their employment. The alternative, in both cases would have been a finding that the employee was off 'on a frolic of his own', that is, acting for his own purposes and therefore outside the scope of his employment. In this context, 'frolic' does not connote triviality. Instead, the court must consider whether the employee's conduct amounts to 'an unrelated and independent venture of his own: a personal matter, rather than a matter connected to his authorised duties'.[7] For example, in *Kirby v National Coal Board*,[8] a miner, during a temporary break, went to a prohibited place to smoke. When he struck a match, there was an explosion and the pursuer was injured. The Court held that by going to the prohibited area to smoke, he was no longer acting within the scope of his employment – mining – and consequently the defender was not vicariously liable.

1   [1975] ICR 430, [1976] 1 All ER 97, CA.
2   Lord Denning MR and Scarman LJ; Lawton LJ dissented.
3   *Rose v Plenty* [1976] 1 All ER 97 at 100–101.
4   1966 SC (HL) 31, 1996 SLT 33.
5   1966 SC (HL) 31 at 46.
6   Lord Pearce did indicate, however, that there must be limits set by common sense: eg, if the deviation involved going to Glasgow via Inverness!
7   *Ward v Scotrail Railways* 1999 SC 255 per Lord Reed at 264.
8   1958 SC 514, 1959 SLT 7.

12.11   The law on vicarious liability has been in a state of flux. The modern approach is to seek a close connection between the wrongful conduct and the wrongdoer's employment. In *Trotman v North Yorkshire County Council*,[1] the Court of Appeal held that sexual misconduct on the part of a teacher was not an unauthorised mode of carrying out his teaching duties; consequently, the local authority was not vicariously liable for the assault. In *Lister v Hesley Hall*,[2] the warden of a school boarding house sexually abused boys who were in his care. Over-ruling Trotman, the House of Lords held that an employee's unauthorised actions could still be within the scope of his employment if the wrongful behaviour was so closely connected with his employment that it would be fair and just to hold the employer vicariously liable. In Lister, the warden had been employed to look after the children and this would involve physical proximity between them if he was to fulfil his responsibilities. There was therefore a very close connection between the nature of the warden's employment and the sexual assault, the risks of which were inherent in that position.

The close connection test was affirmed by the House of Lords in *Dubai Aluminium Co Ltd v Salaam*[3] and *Majrowski v Guys and St Thomas's NHS Trust*.[4] In *Sharp v Highland and Islands Fire Board*,[5] the Lord Ordinary (Macphail) simply accepted that *Lister* was the leading authority on vicarious liability in both English and Scots law. The test is by now well established.

The general principle is stated in a dictum of Lord Nicholls in *Dubai Aluminium*:[6]

'[T]he wrongful conduct must be so closely connected with acts the partner or employee was authorised to do that, for the purpose of the liability of the firm or the employer to third parties, the wrongful conduct *may fairly and properly be regarded* as done by the partner while acting in the ordinary course of the firm's business or the employee's employment.'

It is the connection between wrongdoer and employment that makes it fair and proper to impose vicarious liability. If a sufficient connection can be established then questions of fairness and justice do not form additional considerations.[7] The issues of relationship and conduct are not totally discrete matters; vicarious liability will be imposed where it is fair and just that, in the context of their relationship, the employer should answer for the delicts of the wrongdoer.[8]

1   [1999] LGR 584, CA.
2   [2001] UKHL 22, [2002] 1 AC 215, [2001] 2 All ER 769, [2001] 1 WLR 1311, HL.
3   [2002] UKHL 48, [2003] 1 All ER 97.
4   [2007] 1 AC 224.
5   2005 SLT 855.
6   [2002] UKHL 48 at para 23.
7   See *Wm Morrison (Supermarkets) Plc v Various Claimants* [2020] UKSC 12 per Lord Reed at para 24.
8   See *Cox v Ministry of Justice* [2016] UKSC 10, [2016] AC 660 per Lord Reed at para 2.

12.12   In *Mohamud v Wm Morrison (Supermarkets) Plc*,[1] Khan, an employee in a petrol station verbally abused a customer who had come in with an enquiry and ordered him never to return to the premises before assaulting him. Lord Toulson applied a two-stage approach:[2]

'[T]he court has to consider two matters. The first question is what functions or "field of activities" have been entrusted by the employer to the employee, or, in everyday language, what was the nature of his job … this question must be addressed broadly … Secondly, the court must decide whether there was sufficient connection between the position in which he was employed and his wrongful conduct to make it right for the employer to be held liable.'

Having determined that Khan was employed to attend to customers and answer their queries, he was held to be acting within the field of activities entrusted to him when he responded to the customer's enquiry. The process having started within the scope of Khan's duties there was no significant break in the chain of events that would have allowed the Court to view the assault as a separate incident. Moreover, in warning the victim off his employer's premises, Khan was purporting to go about his employer's business. The assault was therefore connected to Khan's employment. Having entrusted Khan with serving customers it was held fair that the employers should be liable when Khan abused that trust.

In the later case of *Wm Morrison Supermarkets Plc v Various Claimants*,[3] an employee, Skelton, had been given the job of collating payroll data and transferring it to the accountants, KPMG. Being somewhat disaffected with his employers, Skelton also posted a copy of the data on the internet, thus placing Morrisons in breach of confidence, breach of privacy and breach of data protection legislation. The employees affected sued Morrisons. Leaving aside the elements of personal liability, the question of whether Morrisons should be vicariously liable to the claimants for Skelton's conduct was addressed in the Supreme Court. Lord Reed held that the field of activities entrusted to Skelton did not extend to posting the data on the internet and so, given his motives were purely personal, his conduct was not sufficiently connected to his employment for his employers to incur vicarious liability.

1   [2016] UKSC 11, [2016] SC 677.
2   *Mohamud v Wm Morrison (Supermarkets) Plc* [2016] UKSC 11 at para 44.
3   [2020] UKSC 12.

12.13   The introduction of the close connection test gave rise to concerns that this would create elements of uncertainty in the law. It was argued that the test should be restricted to cases of intentional wrongdoing and indeed much of the subsequent case law arises from such conduct.[1] It appears clear, however, that the test is of general application and with the continuing generation of case law it becomes easier to comment further on the way in which the law is developing.

The close connection test may be better seen as a refinement of rather than a replacement for the traditional approach. The older considerations continue to be relevant. As Lord Carloway observed in the Inner House:[2]

> 'Ultimately, in a case of the present type, there is much to be said for asking, within the context of establishing the close connection test and thus that the employee was acting within the scope of his employment, the question of whether, on the contrary, the employee was engaged in a frolic of his own ...'

The Supreme Court cases also can be described in traditional terms. In *Mohamud*, Khan was performing an authorised task in an unauthorised fashion. In *Morrison*, by contrast, Skelton's conduct was outside the scope of the task assigned to him. In the modern approach however, neither observation is sufficient to explain the decision in these cases, decisions will turn on whether a close connection can be established.

The difference between the traditional and modern approaches is that while it remains important to determine the employee's authorised functions, the term 'scope of employment' is no longer required to bear such a wide range of meaning.[3] This can be seen in Lord Toulson's two-stage approach.[4] In determining the function or field of activities assigned to the wrongdoer the only question addressed at the first stage is what, broadly were the employee's duties, what was the employee entrusted to do? Whatever the finding is on this point, this does not, of itself, determine the issue of vicarious liability. Only after the employee's function or field of activities is ascertained are other questions addressed, such as whether the employer's business purposes were being served or whether the employment relationship created the risk of the wrongful conduct. These and other relevant questions assist in the process of establishing or negating a close connection between the wrong done and the employment relationship. In short, the close connection test absorbs some of the issues that once contributed to determining whether the conduct was within the scope or course of employment. The remaining difficulty is that the factors to be taken into account in determining or negating a close connection will differ depending on the factual context.

1   M Loubser and E Reid 'Vicarious Liability for Intentional Wrongdoing' 2003 *JR* 143.
2   *Wilson v Exel UK Ltd* [2010] CSIH 35, 2010 SLT 671 at para 30.
3   See dictum of Denning MR, para 12.10 above.
4   See para 12.12 above.

12.14   This element of uncertainty is inherent in the close connection test. In *Dubai Aluminium* Lord Nicolls observed:[1]

'This "close connection" test focuses attention in the right direction. But it affords no guidance on the type or degree of connection which will normally be regarded as sufficiently close to prompt the legal conclusion that the risk of the wrongful act occurring, and any loss flowing from the wrongful act, should fall on the firm or employer rather than the third party who was wronged. It provides no clear assistance on when ... an incident is to be regarded as sufficiently work-related, as distinct from personal ...This lack of precision is inevitable, given the infinite range of circumstances where the issue arises. The crucial feature or features, either producing or negativing vicarious liability, vary widely from one case or type of case to the next. Essentially the court makes an evaluative judgment in each case, having regard to all the circumstances and, importantly, having regard also to the assistance provided by previous court decisions. In this field the latter form of assistance is particularly valuable.'

Since vicarious liability is context dependent, a factor that is decisive in one case may have little or no bearing on another. The field of activities or particular tasks assigned to the employee must always be determined, but the way in which the conduct is connected to the employment relationship will vary. The mere fact that employment provided the opportunity for the conduct will not provide a sufficiently close connection without further connecting factors. In *Wilson v EXEL UK Ltd*, [2] an employer was not vicariously liable when one employee assaulted another by pulling her pigtail. The assault had no connection with the employee's tasks. In *Vaickuviene v Sainsbury*,[3] an employee whose job was to stack shelves murdered a fellow employee on the employer's premises during working hours. The employer was held not to be vicariously liable. The employment simply provided the murderer with the opportunity to carry out his own personal campaign of harassment of his victim with tragic consequences. In such circumstances, employers may be in breach of their common law duty of care to provide the victim with competent and non-dangerous fellow employees.[4]

1   [2002] UKHL 48 at paras 25–26.
2   [2010] CSIH 35.
3   [2013] CSIH 67.
4   See para 12.2 above.

12.15   In the *Christian Brothers* case,[1] the Supreme Court accepted that a relevant factor in determining whether an employer should be vicariously liable is the risk to others which an employer creates when he entrusts duties, tasks and functions to an employee. This is known as enterprise risk. It is certainly a satisfactory rationale of the sexual abuse cases. However, it has been used in other contexts. In *Brink's Global Services v Igrox*,[2] for example, an employee was instructed to fumigate a container. Because he was employed by the firm, he gained access to the container. He delayed the fumigating process, opened the container and stole silver bars. The Court of Appeal held that theft by an employee from the very container he had been instructed to fumigate was a risk reasonably incidental to the purpose for which he was employed. There was, therefore, a sufficiently close connection between the theft and his employment that it was fair and just that the employer should be vicariously liable.

The fair allocation of risk provides a policy rationale for vicarious liability as Lord Nicholls explained:[3]

> 'The underlying legal policy is based on the recognition that carrying on a business enterprise necessarily involves risks to others. It involves the risk that others will be hurt by the agents through whom the business is carried on. When those risks ripen into loss, it is just that the business should be responsible for compensating the person who has been wronged.'

Nevertheless, in *Morrison*, Lord Reed rejected enterprise risk as a relevant factor in a question of conduct as opposed to relationship.[4] This should not eliminate enterprise risk as a connecting factor generally, but it does make clear that risk will not be relevant in all cases. The problem with enterprise risk is that it can be stated so broadly that it cannot always serve to make any meaningful connection let alone a close one. As Lord Reed noted in *Cox*:[5]

> '[T]he risk of an individual behaving negligently, or indeed committing an intentional wrong, is a fact of life, anyone who employs others to carry out activities is likely to create the risk of their behaving tortiously within the field of activities assigned to them." This view is reinforced by Lord Toulson in *Mohamud*: in which he described the risk of an employee abusing his position as "one of life's unavoidable facts.'[6]

The role of risk as a connecting factor should therefore be restricted to contexts in which it is a predictable or at least identifiable incident of the employee's role, something much more likely to occur than a mere possibility. In *Lister*, Lord Millett observed:[7]

> 'The fact that his employment gave the employee the opportunity to commit the wrong is not enough to make the employer liable. He is liable only if the risk is one which experience shows is inherent in the nature of the business.'

The obvious example of an inherent risk in employment is any job that involves driving a vehicle. A road accident is an inherent risk, but the use of a delivery vehicle to commit a burglary is only a possibility. Enterprise risk was a connecting factor in the sexual abuse cases and in *Brink's Global Services*, but it was of no relevance in *Morrison* since the risk that Shelton would post the personal data entrusted to him on the internet to spite his employers could not be seen as inherent in the task allocated to him. Skelton's action was no more than a possibility.

The furtherance of the employer's business interests provides a strong connecting factor. *Rose v Plenty* and *Williams v Hemphill* remain good authorities, but of course this connection was also present in the sexual abuse cases. In *NA v Nottinghamshire CC*,[8] a local authority was vicariously liable to a child for the abusive conduct of foster parents whose function in fostering was carried out for the benefit of the authority.

1   [2012] UKSC 56
2   [2010] EWCA Civ 207, [2011] IRLR 343.
3   *Dubai Aluminium Co Ltd v Salaam* [2002] UKHL 48 at para 21.
4   *Wm Morrison Supermarkets Plc v Various Claimants* [2020] UKSC 12 at para 31.
5   *Cox v Ministry of Justice* [2016] UKSC 10 at para 23.
6   *Mohamud v Wm Morrison Supermarkets Plc* [2016] UKSC 11 at para 40.
7   *Lister v Hesley Hall* [2001] UKHL 22 at para 65.
8   [2017] UKSC 60.

12.16   The surest approach to establishing vicarious liability lies where it can be shown that the conduct fell within the field of activities entrusted to the employee or, in the narrow sense, within the scope of employment. While this does not absolutely determine the issue of vicarious liability, the suggestion from *Mohamud* is that the further requirement to establish a close connection will be less onerous than in cases where conduct within the scope of employment is doubtful. As Lord Carloway observed:[1]

> 'It will almost always (if not always) be presumed to be fair and just to impose liability if the employee's actings are within the scope of, or in the course of his employment.'

Where conduct within the scope of employment is doubtful, the burden of establishing a close connection will be greater; the factors most likely to effect a close connection are furthering the employer's business interests or, in appropriate cases, creation of the risk by the employer but this does not exhaust the possibilities. Where the conduct is intentional, this opens up the possibility of arguing against a connection if it can be established that the employee was off on a frolic of their own. It has been suggested that the essential difference between the traditional approach and the close connection test is that 'the apparent subversion of what the employee was actually authorised to do no longer displaces liability for his or her wrongdoing'.[2] This contention was made with reference to the over-ruling of *Trotman* in *Lister* and before *Morrison*, nevertheless it remains true in the right circumstances. The important point is that in cases such as *Lister* and the *Christian Brothers* case there were other, strong connecting factors in place. In the absence of such factors, it will be possible to negate vicarious liability where the employee's motive for the conduct is purely personal.

So, like enterprise risk, the motive of the employee will be relevant in some contexts and not others. Lord Toulson considered it irrelevant in *Mohamud*, in which the conduct was viewed as within the scope of the employee's duties, but where the conduct was outside the scope of the employee's duties in *Morrison*, the fact that Skelton was pursuing a personal vendetta effectively determined the case against vicarious liability.

1   *Vaickuviene v J Sainsbury Plc* [2013] CSIH 67 at para 25.
2   E Reid, 'Loose Connections: Matters of the Heart and Delictual Liability' 2014 *Edin LR 97* at 103.

12.17   Even where the conduct is within the field of activities assigned to the employee it remains open in the right circumstances to deny vicarious liability. In *Morrison*, Lord Reed approved the following dictum of Lord Wilberforce in *Kooragong Investments Pty Ltd v Richardson & Wrench Ltd*:[1]

> 'The underlying principle remains that a servant, even when performing acts of the class which he was authorised or employed to do, may so clearly depart from the scope of his employment that his master will not be liable for his acts.'

So, if A employs B as a welder in A's workshop and B, on his own account, contracts with C to do some welding on C's car using A's welding gear, then A will not be vicariously liable to C when B negligently sets fire to C's car. B's conduct is clearly within the field of activities assigned to him, welding, but his act is not sufficiently connected to his employment with A for it to be fair to hold A vicariously liable. B's employment with A has provided the opportunity, but A's business purposes are not being served if B is 'doing a homer' and while the risk of fire is inherent in welding, the risk in this instance was not created by A. B's motive in doing the job is purely personal. This is an example of the fourth situation in Lord Clyde's dictum, an employee using the employer's tools for their own purposes.[2]

Where employees have been engaged on personal vendettas or frolics of their own it is difficult to establish vicarious liability. In *Smith v Crossley Bros Ltd*,[3] an apprentice was injured by fellow employees during initiation rites.[4] The defendant was not vicariously liable because the actings constituted a frolic and were outside the scope of the workers' employment, nor was the defendant personally liable for breach of duty to provide competent fellow workers.[5] On the other hand, in *Harrison v Michelin Tyre Co Ltd*,[6] an employee injured his back as the result of a fall caused by a prank. By means of a hand trolley, a fellow employee had raised and then dropped a duckboard on which the plaintiff was standing. Because the prankster had been pushing the trolley as part of his job, the act was held to be within the course of his employment and the employer was vicariously liable.

Both these cases pre-date *Lister*. The application of the close connection test in the context of personal vendettas can be seen by comparing two Privy Council cases brought by the victims of shooting. When Kelvin Laurent, a probationer police officer, abandoned his post and his duties to travel to a bar where his ex-partner worked, he found her associating with another man. Intending to shoot the man he wounded a British tourist instead. Laurent's wrongful use of the gun was not so closely connected with acts which he was authorised to do that it could be regarded as done in the course of his employment. The claim based on vicarious liability failed, but the employer was held personally liable in negligently entrusting Laurent with the gun.[7]

By contrast, when off-duty constable Morgan announced 'police!' and demanded immediate use of a public telephone from Bernard who was using it, the employer was vicariously liable when Bernard refused to surrender the phone and Morgan shot him, wounding him in the head. When Bernard recovered consciousness, he was in hospital and surrounded by officers. Constable Morgan promptly placed Bernard under arrest and handcuffed him to the bed. The connection between the wrongful act and employment was made because Morgan was purporting to be acting on police business and clearly took the view that Bernard had interfered with the execution of his duties as a police officer.[8] It may be suggested that in circumstances where the victim reasonably understands the wrongdoer to be representing the employer this will support an argument for a close connection.[9]

1   [1982] AC 462 at p 473, approved in [2020] UKSC at para 35.
2   See para 12.9 above.
3   (1971) 95 So Jo 655, CA.
4   The unfortunate lad had a compressed-air pipe placed in close proximity to his rectum.
5   See para 12.2 above.
6   [1985] 1 All ER 918, [1985] ICR 696.
7   *Attorney General of British Virgin Islands v Hartwell* [2004] UKPC 12.
8   *Bernard v Attorney General of Jamaica* [2004] UKPC 47

9 See also *Mohamud v Wm Morrison Supermarkets Plc* [2016] UKSC 11. An owner of a night club has been held to be vicariously liable for assaults carried out by 'bouncers' on a customer who had kicked in the door of the premises: the bouncers were not on a frolic of their own but had been attempting to preserve the integrity of the club, albeit in a *very* unauthorised way! See *Vasey v Surrey Free Inns plc* [1996] PIQR P373 CA. Post-*Lister*, it has been accepted that such assaults are sufficiently closely connected with the risk of physical harm inherent in the nature of a bouncer's job for vicarious liability to be imposed: *Mattis v Pollock (t/a Flamingo's Nightclub)* [2003] 1 WLR 2158, CA. See also *Ashmore v Rock Steady Security Ltd* 2006 SLT 207; *Honeybourne v Burgess* 2006 SLT 585.

12.18

(3) Pro hac vice employment

In certain situations, an employee may be hired out to work under the instructions of another employer. For example, A, a general contractor, may hire equipment from B to be operated by an employee of B but under A's instruction. If the 'borrowed' employee is negligent and injures one of A's employees or a third party, who is vicariously liable, A or B? The general rule is that the employer with whom the borrowed employee has a contract of employment remains vicariously liable even though the employee works under the general instructions of another. And so, in our example, B remains vicariously liable. B will only escape vicarious liability if he has delegated to A not only the power to control what B's employee does but also *how* the employee should do the job. The onus rests on B to establish that the full plethora of control has passed from B to A. This will be almost impossible to establish where B's employee operates sophisticated equipment.

This principle was settled by the House of Lords in the leading case of *Mersey Docks and Harbour Board v Coggins and Griffith (Liverpool) Ltd*.[1] The plaintiff hired a mobile crane to the defendant which was to be operated by an employee of the plaintiff. It was agreed in the contract of hire that the operator of the crane was to be treated as an employee of Coggins. The craneman injured a worker while operating the crane negligently. The question arose whether the plaintiff or the defendant should be vicariously liable. The House of Lords held that *in a question with the injured third party,* vicarious liability could not be determined by the contractual arrangements made between the plaintiff and defendant to which the injured person had not been a party. *Prima facie* the plaintiff was the employer and was vicariously liable unless it could be established that full control of the craneman had passed to Coggins. While Coggins could tell the craneman *what* to do, since he was a highly skilled worker they could *not* tell him *how* to do his job. Accordingly, Mersey Docks had failed to discharge the onus which lay upon them to prove that their employee had been transferred *pro hac vice* to Coggins. Therefore, as far as the injured person was concerned, he could sue Mersey Docks as vicariously liable for the negligence of their employee, the craneman. But because of the terms of their contract of hire with Coggins, Mersey Docks could recover the damages from Coggins since they had agreed to treat the crane man as their employee.[2]

An exception has been made to the general principle that an employee may not serve two masters. In *Viasystems (Tyneside) Ltd v Thermal Transfer (Northern) Ltd,*[3] the Court of Appeal held both the original employer and a subcontractor vicariously liable for the negligence of a fitter's mate. He was, at the relevant time, under the supervision and control of both a fellow employee, a fitter and another fitter who was contracted to the subcontractor. This is known as dual vicarious liability. Dual vicarious liability has been accepted and applied in the English Courts,[4] but its use should be regarded as exceptional.[5] It has not been considered in the Scottish courts, so has been neither rejected nor accepted.

1   [1947] AC 1, [1946] 2 All ER 345, HL.
2   This principle has been accepted as part of Scots law: see *Park v Tractor Shovels Ltd* 1980 SLT 94, OH; *Royal Bank of Scotland v Bannerman Johnstone Maclay* 2005 SC 437 (proof allowed on whether an employee had been transferred *pro hac vice* to act as financial controller for customer of the defenders).
3   [2005] EWCA Civ 1155, [2006] QB 510.
4   *Catholic Child Welfare Society v Various Claimants* [2012] UKSC 56.
5   See *Kalma v African Minerals* [2018] EWHC 3506 QB.

(4) Principal and agent

12.19   A principal can be vicariously liable for the wrongs of his agent. This will arise if: (i) the acts of the agent were expressly authorised by the principal; (ii) the principal ratified the agent's acts after they were done; or (iii) the delict is within the actual or ostensible authority of the agent. For vicarious liability to arise it is not enough that X permits Y to do a particular act, for example drive X's car: instead, X must have delegated a task or duty to Y.[1] The principle is important in the context of employment where an employer prima facie escapes vicarious liability because the employee is working outside the scope of his employment: the employer may still be vicariously liable as principal if in the circumstances the employee is acting within his actual or ostensible authority as the employer's agent at the time of the wrongful act.[2] A partnership can be vicariously liable for the delicts of its agents, the partners, provided the wrongful conduct can fairly and properly be regarded as done by the partner while acting in the ordinary course of the firm's business: such conduct can include fraud.[3]

The committee of a club or other unincorporated association are not vicariously liable for the wrongs of the other members of association.[4]

1   *Morgans v Launchbury* [1973] AC 127, [1972] 2 All ER 606, HL.
2   *Taylor v Glasgow District Council* 1997 SC 183, 1997 SLT 537.
3   See, generally, *Dubai Aluminium Co Ltd v Salaam* [2003] 2 AC 366, [2003] 1 All ER 97.
4   *Harrison v West of Scotland Kart Club* 2004 SC 615.

C.   NON-DELEGABLE DUTIES

12.20   It has been noted that the duty of care owed by an employer to employees is personal and cannot be delegated to a third party.[1] This is the most common example of a non-delegable duty, but such duties arise in other contexts so, for example, a hospital will owe a non-delegable duty to patients in its care.[2] The Home Office was found to owe a non-delegable duty to a woman who had received negligent medical treatment while detained in an immigration centre.[3]

Lord Sumption reviewed the authorities on non-delegable duties in *Woodland v Essex County Council*.[4] In that case an education authority was held to owe a non-delegable duty to a child who suffered brain injury during a swimming lesson. The lesson was part of the school curriculum which had been delegated to a contractor. Lord Sumption identified two contexts in which non-delegable duties arise. The first is where the parties are in a relationship that imposes positive duties on the defender to care for the claimant. In such circumstances, care functions may be delegated but the defender must ensure that the care given is to the requisite standard and will be answerable for any breach. The second is in the context of extra-hazardous activities. This category, Lord Sumption said, is 'ripe for re-examination'.[5]

The law on non-delegable duties for extra-hazardous activities does indeed lack clarity, not least because of the difficulty in defining an activity as extra-hazardous as opposed to merely hazardous.[6] Scots cases that may be cited in support of non-delegable duties, have tended to involve nuisance or withdrawal of support.[7] It was held in *Esso Petroleum v Scottish Ministers*[8] that a right of support is not a pre-requisite for a non-delegable duty. Non-delegable duties may serve a purpose in circumstances where a contractor instructs operations that will inevitably cause harm whether or not care is taken. In such circumstances the contractor ought not to be able to shelter behind the rules of vicarious liability when some hapless sub- contractor undertakes the operation. The issue would benefit from further exploration in the Inner House.

1   On an employer's duty to take reasonable care, see para 12.1 ff above.
2   *X (Minors) v Bedfordshire CC* [1995] 2 AC 537 per Lord Browne-Wilkinson at 740. *Bell v Alliance Medical Ltd* [2015] CSOH 54.
3   *GB v Home Office* [2015] EWHC 819. Non-delegable duties also arise in dental treatment, *Ramdhean v Agedo* [2020] 1 WLUK 406.
4   [2013] UKSC 66, [2014] AC 537.
5   *Woodland v Essex County Council* [2013] UKSC 66 at para 25.
6   In England, liability based on non-delegable duty for damage caused by independent contractors is to be kept within narrow bounds. *Biffa Waste Services Ltd v Maschinenfabrik Ernst Hese GmbH* [2008] EWCA Civ 1257.
7   *Stewart v Malik* [2009] CSIH 5, 2009 SC 265. See also *Morris Amusements Ltd v Glasgow City Council* [2009] CSOH 84, 2009 SLT 697
8   [2016] CSOH 15, 2016 SCLR 539 per Lord Tyre at para 19.

CHAPTER 13

Delict and the family

It is now proposed to consider delictual liability in the context of family relationships. We will be concerned with delictual liability *between* members of the family and the rights of members of the family to seek reparation if a relative is injured or killed.

A. TITLE TO SUE

13.1 At common law, spouses could not sue each other in delict. If a woman was injured as a result of her husband's negligent driving, she could not obtain reparation. This rule was clearly anachronistic, especially as the loss would ultimately fall on her husband's insurance company. The position was changed by s 2 of the Law Reform (Husband and Wife) Act 1962, which provided that each of the spouses had 'the like rights' to bring proceedings against the other in respect of a delict 'as if they were not married'. The 1962 Act has been repealed,[1] but of course the common law does not revive.

A spouse is not liable for the wrongs of the other spouse unless liability is established on a basis other than marriage itself. So, for example, a wife could be vicariously liable for a delict committed by her husband, if she were his employer and the delict arose in the course of his employment.

As a general rule, a child or young person under the age of 16 has no active legal capacity.[2] However, a child under 16 can instruct a solicitor in connection with any civil matter provided she has a general understanding of what it means to do so. A child of 12 or more is presumed to be of sufficient age and maturity to have such understanding, although a child under 12 may instruct a solicitor if she, in fact, has such an understanding.[3] If the child has the capacity to instruct a solicitor, she has capacity to pursue or defend a civil action.[4] Accordingly a child with sufficient capacity can pursue an action in delict. If the child does not have such capacity, the action must be brought by the child's legal representative who will usually be the child's parents.[5]

The Age of Legal Capacity (Scotland) Act 1991 does not affect the delictual responsibility of children and young persons under the age of 16.[6] Thus a child under the age of 16 can, theoretically at least, be sued if the child has committed a delict. Parents are not vicariously liable for the wrongs committed by their children. But where a child causes harm as a result of a parent's negligence, the parent may be liable for a breach of a duty of care which the parent owed to the pursuer. For example, if a child runs in front of a car and the driver is injured trying to avoid the child, the mother may be liable in delict if she has not taken reasonable care to ensure that the child was not on the road.[7] Because the 1991 Act does not affect the age of delictual responsibility, a child who has been injured may have any damages awarded reduced on the ground of contributory negligence.[8] In *McKinnell v White*,[9] for example, a child of five was held to be 50 per cent contributorily negligent because he ran in front of a speeding motorist. The Lord Ordinary (Fraser) took the view that by the age of five a child brought up in an urban environment should have been aware of the danger of road traffic. It has always been competent for a child to sue his or her parent in delict.[10]

Where a foetus sustains injury *in utero,* the unborn baby has no right to sue in delict unless and until it has been born alive. Only on birth does a child obtain legal personality. However, provided the defender owed a duty of care towards the foetus, if the baby is born alive, an action in delict can be brought on the child's behalf in respect of the harm sustained *in utero.* This is sometimes said to be a consequence of the civil law principle *nasciturus pro iam nato habetur quotiens de eius agitur,* namely that in a matter affecting its interests, an unborn child *in utero* should be deemed to be born (the *nasciturus* doctrine).[11] It is submitted that there is no need to rely on the *nasciturus* doctrine to achieve this result. Given that the defender owes a *Donoghue v Stevenson* duty of care[12] to the foetus, based on reasonable foreseeability of injury *in utero,* then if there is a breach of the duty which causes harm to the foetus, a wrong will be committed when the baby is born. It is at that stage, ie when the baby is born alive, that the wrong is completed because, while the breach of duty took place during the pregnancy, harm for the purpose of delictual liability is not sustained by the child until the child is born.[13] It is only then that *constituent harm* arises as a result of the breach of the duty of care: *damnum injuria datum.*

Because it is competent for a child to sue a parent, a mother who injures her foetus during the pregnancy could be sued by her child in delict, provided the child is born alive. A mother clearly owes a duty of care to the foetus. If during her pregnancy she fails to take reasonable care, for example if she abuses drugs or falls down the stair when drunk, then she can be liable if her breach of duty of care results in harm to the child when born alive. It would therefore appear that a mother carries a potential litigant in her womb for nine months! Similarly, a father who injures his wife's foetus through, for example, negligent driving may be liable in delict if the child is born alive suffering from harm as a result of the injuries sustained *in utero*.

In practice, it is likely that where a foetus is injured *in utero* the mother will also have sustained physical or psychiatric harm. If the defender owed her a duty of care which has been broken, the mother may sue for the harm she has suffered. Where the mother miscarries as a result of the defender's breach of duty, she may obtain damages for the loss of her baby. Of course, in these circumstances, the unborn child has no title to sue because the child has not been born alive.

1 By Schedule 3 to the Family Law (Scotland) Act 2006.
2 Age of Legal Capacity (Scotland) Act 1991, s 1(1)(a).
3 ALC(S)A 1991, s 2(4A).
4 ALC(S)A 1991, s 2(5A).
5 Children (Scotland) Act 1995, s 1(1)(d). If the parent is the defender, for example if the child was injured as a result of her mother's careless driving, a *curator ad litem* will be appointed to represent the child.
6 ALC(S)A 1991, s 1(3)(c).
7 *Hardie v Sneddon* 1917 SC 1, 1916 2 SLT 197.
8 On contributory negligence, see paras 6.12–6.13 above.
9 1971 SLT (Notes) 61, OH. See also *McCluskey v Wallace* 1998 SC 711 (four-year-old child, 20 per cent contributory negligence). There is no general rule to determine the degree of a child's contributory negligence. The danger to which the child is exposed and the child's capacity to appreciate that risk are important: *Galbraith's Curator ad Litem v Stewart (No 2)* 1998 SLT 1305, OH (eight-year-old child, no contributory negligence).
10 *Young v Rankin* 1934 SC 499, 1934 SLT 445.
11 *Cohen v Shaw* 1992 SCLR 182n, 1992 SLT 1022, OH.
12 See Chapter 3 above.
13 *Hamilton v Fife Health Board* 1993 SC 369, 1993 SLT 624.

B.   PERSONAL INJURIES TO A RELATIVE

13.2   In *Robertson v Turnbull*,[1] it was held that where a person was injured, the defender did not owe a threshold duty of care to the victim's spouse or relatives who had suffered economic loss as a result of the injuries sustained. So, for example, members of the injured person's family could not sue in delict for loss of support.[2] The victim can, of course, sue for loss of future earnings as derivative economic loss.[3] Moreover, at common law, a pursuer who was injured could not recover damages for the economic loss suffered by a relative as a result of the pursuer's injuries, for example where a spouse had given up work in order to nurse her injured husband.[4]

The common law on this point has now been superseded by s 8 of the Administration of Justice Act 1982. This provides that where a person has sustained personal injuries, the injured person can recover damages which amount to reasonable remuneration for necessary services rendered to the pursuer by a relative.[5] The services rendered by the relative must be physical services, such as nursing.[6] Thus it has been held that s 8 of the 1982 Act did not apply when a relative had donated bone marrow to the pursuer who would otherwise have died.[7] The quantification of damages by reference to the number of hours of providing services and a modest notional hourly rate is well established.[8] But the courts often take a broad view when reaching an appropriate figure.[9] The damages can be reduced to take into account the injured person's contributory negligence.[10]

The pursuer, ie the injured person, then accounts to the relative for any damages recovered under this provision.[11] Originally, damages could only be awarded in respect of services rendered up to the date of the action;[12] but now damages can be awarded for services likely to be rendered by a relative to the injured person in the future.[13] Damages are not available under s 8 of the 1982 Act if the relative expressly agreed that no payment should be made in respect of the services rendered or to be rendered.[14] Where the injured person has died before the action is concluded, the deceased's executor may recover damages for necessary services rendered by a relative before the victim died.[15]

Where a person who was not in employment was injured, at common law he had no right to sue for loss of earnings since *ex hypothesi* he was not earning. This was particularly unfair to wives who had given up their jobs to look after the home or children. Section 9(1) of the Administration of Justice Act 1982 gives an injured person who has been providing unpaid personal services to a relative[16] the right to sue for damages if the pursuer is unable to continue to do so as a result of the injuries sustained. The personal services must be services which (a) were or might have been expected to have been rendered by the pursuer before the injuries; (b) were of a kind which when rendered by a person other than a relative would ordinarily have been obtainable on payment; and (c) the injured person but for the injuries in question might have been expected to render gratuitously to a relative.[17]

In *Ingham v John G Russell (Transport) Ltd*[18] the Inner House refused to restrict the concept of personal services to services which were rendered to the person of the relative, such as nursing, as opposed to the relative's property, such as cleaning the relative's house. It was enough that the services had been rendered *in person* by the injured person and therefore included maintenance or DIY services rendered by the injured person to his spouse. It is therefore clear that an injured woman, for example, can recover damages if she is unable to provide unpaid housekeeping and child-rearing services for her spouse, cohabitant or children. Because the personal services must have been rendered gratuitously before s 9 applies, the Administration of Justice Act 1982 recognises the fact that work in the home is still *prima facie* unpaid but that its economic value is such that justice demands that the injured person should receive compensation for the inability to continue to provide it, even though technically the pursuer has not suffered any patrimonial loss, ie loss of earnings.

Where the injured person's expectation of life has been diminished as a result of her injuries, in assessing the amount of damages under s 9(1), the court is to assume that the pursuer would have lived until the notional date of death.[19] In other words the pursuer can obtain damages for the inability to provide gratuitous personal services to a relative during the lost years.

Where the injured person has died, a relative may claim as a head of loss a reasonable sum in respect of the loss of gratuitous personal services rendered to the relative by the deceased.[20] Before he can do so, the pursuer must be a relative who has the right to claim damages for loss of support by the deceased under the Damages (Scotland) Act 2011. Accordingly, it is to the provisions of the 2011 Act that we shall now turn.

1 1982 SC (HL) 1, 1982 SLT 96. This case removed the doubts raised by *dicta* in *Dick v Burgh of Falkirk* 1976 SC (HL) 1 that a defender could owe a duty of care to the victim's relatives. *Turnbull* is consistent with the settled policy of the law not to grant remedies to third parties in respect of injuries to other people: for discussion see *D v East Berkshire Community Health NHS Trust* [2005] AC 373 per Lord Rodger at paras 100ff.
2 This is an example of non-recoverability of secondary economic loss. Similarly, a child cannot sue for economic loss incurred as a result of serious injuries

suffered by his mother (she was in a persistent vegetative state): *Buckley v Farrow* [1997] PIQR Q78, CA.

3 On loss of future earnings, see para 16.15 ff below.

4 *Edgar v Lord Advocate* 1965 SC 67, 1965 SLT 158.

5 'Personal injuries' means (a) any disease and (b) any impairment of a person's physical or mental condition: s 13(1) of the 1982 Act. 'Relative' includes the injured person's spouse or divorced spouse, civil partner or former civil partner, opposite sex and same sex cohabitants, any ascendant or descendant, any brother, sister, uncle or aunt or their issue and any person accepted by the injured party as a child of the family: any relationship by affinity is treated as a relationship by consanguinity and the half blood is treated as a relationship of the whole blood; a stepchild is treated as a child and illegitimacy is irrelevant: s 13 (1) of the 1982 Act.

6 BNA nursing and home help rates can be useful but are by no means conclusive of what reasonable remuneration should be in a particular case. See, for example, *Kennedy v Lees of Scotland* 1997 SLT 510 (use of agency rates rejected as unsuitable where victim had not received substantial nursing, but only short visits from relatives).

7 *Duffy v Lanarkshire Health Board* 1998 SCLR 1142, 1998 Rep LR 119, OH. In *Sturgeon v Gallacher* 2003 SLT 67, the pursuer ran a farm in partnership with his wife. After he had been injured in an accident, his son laboured on the farm for £50 a week. The Lord Ordinary (Emslie) held that the son's work did not constitute necessary services for the purpose of Administration of Justice Act 1982, s 8 as they were rendered to the partnership, not the pursuer. The pursuer could, however, include the extra outlay (the son's wages) in his claim for loss of earnings.

8 *Wallace v Glasgow* City Council [2010] CSOH 88, per Lord Tyre at para 30. Reversed on another point in *Wallace v Glasgow City Council* [2011] CSIH 57.

9 *Kerr v Stiell Facilities* [2009] CSOH 67 following *Clark v Chief Constable of Lothian and Borders* 1993 SC 320.

10 *Yale v Forbes* 2004 SLT (Sh Ct) 13.

11 Administration of Justice Act 1982, s 8(2). But where the relative is the defender, it has been held that a claim under s 8 is incompetent: *Kozikowska v Kozikowski* 1996 SLT 386. It was thought contrary to public policy that the pursuer should remunerate the person she blamed for her injuries – *sed quaere*?

12 *Forsyth's Curator Bonis v Govan Shipbuilders* 1989 SCLR 78, 1989 SLT 91.

13 Administration of Justice Act 1982, s 8(3).

14 Administration of Justice Act 1982, s 8(1) and (3). See *Denheen v British Railways Board* 1988 SLT 320n, 1986 SLT 249, OH.

15 See, for example, *McManus' Executrix v Babcock Energy Ltd* 1999 SC 569; *Murray's Executrix v Greenock Dockyard Co Ltd* 2004 SLT 346.

16 For the definition of 'relative', see the Administration of Justice Act 1982, s 13, discussed at note 5 above.

17 Administration of Justice Act 1982, s 9(3).

18 1991 SC 201, 1991 SLT 739.

90 Administration of Justice Act 1982, s 9(1A). Damages for loss of expectation of life are discussed at paras 13.4 and 16.12 beyond.

20 Administration of Justice Act 1982, s 9(2); *Ingham v John G Russell (Transport) Ltd* 1991 SC 201, 1991 SLT 379. It can be difficult to quantify the value of such services, particularly when the deceased was simply 'a normal, average married man living in family who did the correspondingly normal, average things which a father and husband does around the house, the garden and the family car': *Beggs v Motherwell Bridge Fabricators Ltd* 1997 SCLR 1019,

1998 SLT 1215 at 1223 per the Lord Ordinary (Eassie). See also *Farrelly v Yarrow Shipbuilders Ltd* 1994 SCLR 407, 1994 SLT 1349n, OH; *McManus' Executrix v Babcock Energy Ltd* 1999 SC 569. *Murray's Executrix v Greenock Dockyard Co Ltd* 2004 SLT 346 (£2,100 awarded as deceased only occasionally helped out).

C. DEATH OF A RELATIVE

13.3   If a person dies as a result of another's wrong, two potential claims arise. First, the deceased's own claim which can transmit to the deceased's executor who can pursue the action for the benefit of the deceased's estate. Second, a dependent claim by the deceased's relatives.

(1) The deceased's claim

13.4   Where a person is killed outright as a result of the defender's wrong, the deceased's executor cannot raise an action in delict in respect of the death.[1] In these circumstances, the only claims are those of the deceased's relatives. However, if a person is injured and subsequently dies as a result of the injuries, the deceased's right to sue in delict in respect of personal injuries transmits to the executor who can sue on behalf of the deceased's estate. This complex area of the law is now regulated by the Damages (Scotland) Act 2011.[2]

Where a person dies the rights which vested in the deceased immediately before his death to sue for damages in respect of personal injuries transmit to the executor.[3] As a result, the executor can raise an action or, if an action has been raised by the deceased before he died, continue the action on behalf of the deceased's estate.[4] The executor may sue in respect of patrimonial loss, for example loss of earnings sustained by the deceased, but only up to the date of death.[5] In other words, patrimonial loss attributable to any period after the deceased's death, for example loss of future earnings, is non-transmissible to the executor. This is necessary to prevent double compensation given that the defender may have to meet claims for loss of support brought by the deceased's relatives.

The deceased's right to damages for non-patrimonial loss by way of solatium is also transmissible to the executor,[6] but again in assessing damages for solatium the court is to have regard only to the period ending immediately before the deceased's death.[7]

Solatium is damages for pain and suffering arising from the personal injuries. In assessing damages for solatium, the court is entitled to have regard to the extent to which the deceased suffered because he was aware that his expectation of life had been reduced as a result of the injuries.[8]

The effect of these provisions can be illustrated by the following example. A is seriously injured as a result of the negligent driving of B. A dies two years after the accident.[9] If A had begun an action against B, A's executor can continue the action provided it has not been concluded.[10] If A had not begun proceedings, A's executor can bring an action against B.[11] However, the executor's claims for patrimonial loss and solatium are restricted to losses incurred by the deceased at the date of death: any patrimonial loss referable to a period after the date of death cannot be recovered by the executor. If the action is successful,[12] the damages awarded become part of the deceased's estate. This means that they will be distributed to the deceased's legatees if there is a will or to a surviving spouse or civil partner and the deceased's heirs according to the rules of intestate succession where the deceased died without a will. If A has relatives, they may have a claim against B if A's death *was* as a result of the personal injuries A has sustained. It is to the relative's dependent claim that we now turn.

1 Where death is caused by a fatal accident, the deceased's executor can obtain damages for the deceased's fear of impending death. However, it has been questioned whether Parliament intended the court to carry out 'the difficult – and often distasteful – task of trying to assess the feelings of pain and apprehensions of mortality of someone so abruptly and severely injured as so be in the imminent and real danger of death within a period of minutes': *Beggs v Motherwell Bridge Fabricators Ltd* 1998 SLT 1215 at 1223–1224 per the Lord Ordinary (Eassie). The sum awarded was £250! The deceased's immediate family may also have such a claim: see para 13.6 below. In England no damages are awarded under this head; *Hicks v Chief Constable of South Yorkshire Police* [1992] 2 All ER 65, HL.

2 References in this chapter are to the Damages (Scotland) Act 2011 unless otherwise stated.

3 Damages (Scotland) Act 2011, s 2(1)(a).

4 D(S)A 2011, s 10. Where the action was brought by the deceased it is not concluded while an appeal is competent or before any appeal taken has been disposed of, s 10(2).

5 D(S)A 2011, s 2(2).

6 Damages (Scotland) Act 2011, s 2(1). See, eg, *McManus' Executrix v Babcock Energy Ltd* 1999 SC 569. This case was distinguished in *Murray's Executrix v Greenock Dockyard Co Ltd* 2004 SLT 346 on the ground that the deceased while dying of an insidious disease had suffered less than McManus.

7 D(S)A 2011, s 2(2).

8 D(S)A 2011, s 1(1) and (2). Otherwise, no damages by way of solatium are recoverable in respect of loss of expectation of life: s 1(3). In an action in respect

of personal injuries, damages can also be awarded in respect of patrimonial loss arising from the fact that the injured person's expectation of life has been reduced: s 1(1) and (2): discussed at para 16.16 beyond. Where the action is brought by the executor, however, only patrimonial loss arising before the date of death can be recovered: s 2(2). Where the injured person has no dependent relatives who could sue for loss of support should the victim die, the rule that patrimonial loss can only be claimed by an executor up until the date of death may tempt the defender to delay settling the claim until the victim dies.

9 It is irrelevant whether the death was a result of A's injuries.
10 Damages (Scotland) Act 2011, s 10(1)(b). An action is not concluded while any appeal is competent or before any appeal taken has been disposed of: s 10(2).
11 D(S)A 2011, s 10(1)(a).
12 Any defences, eg *volens*, which B could use in an action by A are good against an action brought by A's executor. Similarly, damages can be reduced as a result of A's contributory negligence.

(2) The dependent claims

13.5 Where a person dies in consequence of personal injuries sustained by him as a result of the defender's conduct, then if the defender would have been liable to pay damages to the deceased if he had lived, she is also liable to pay damages to a certain class of the deceased's relatives.[1] It will be seen that a relative's right to sue is *dependent* on the defender being liable to pay damages if an action had been brought by the deceased in respect of the personal injuries sustained. Accordingly, the relative's claim can be defeated if the deceased would not have succeeded against the defender, for example if the defender did not owe a duty of care to the deceased or had not broken the duty or the deceased was *volens*. The relative's damages can also be reduced on the grounds of the deceased's contributory negligence.[2]

By s 4(2) of the 2011 Act it is expressly enacted that the relative's claim cannot be brought if the defender had discharged his liability to the deceased before he died. In other words, if the deceased had settled his claim before he died, this automatically excludes the deceased's relative's dependent claim. But because of the amount of damages which can be awarded to the deceased's relatives for non-patrimonial loss, the dependent claims are often more valuable than the deceased's claim. This led to a cruel dilemma where the victim was diagnosed with mesothelioma and knew that he would die within a very short time: should he accept a settlement which would exclude his family's right to sue after he had died or refuse and lose the financial support which could make his last months more bearable? To ease this dilemma, the 2011 Act provides that where the personal injury is mesothelioma, a settlement does not exclude the deceased's relatives' rights to claim damages for non-patrimonial loss.[3]

The nature of the dependent claim turns on whether the pursuer is a member of the deceased's immediate family or a wider class of relatives specified in the Damages (Scotland) Act 2011.

1   D(S)A 2011, ss 3 and 4. Personal Injuries means any disease and any impairment of a person's physical or mental condition: s 14(1). Where a child who has been born alive dies from injuries sustained *in utero* the parents have title to sue as the child could have sued the defender when the child was born alive: *Hamilton v Fife Health Board* 1993 SC 369. There would be no claim under the 2011 Act if the child was not born alive.
2   See, eg, *Beggs v Motherwell Bridge Fabricators Ltd* 1998 SLT 1215, 1997 SCLR 1019, OH (deceased 20 per cent contributorily negligent).
3   D(S)A 2011, s 5.

(a) The immediate family

13.6   The deceased's immediate family consists of the following relatives:[1]

(1)   the deceased's spouse or civil partner;

(2)   the deceased's cohabitant, ie any person not being the spouse or civil partner of the deceased who immediately before the death was living with the deceased as husband and wife or in a relationship which has the characteristics of the relationship between civil partners;

(3)   the deceased's children: this includes children who have been accepted by the deceased as children of the family. A posthumous child is included;[2]

(4)   the deceased's parents: this includes any person who accepted the deceased as a child of his or her family;

(5)   the deceased's brothers and sisters: this includes any person brought up in the same household as the deceased and who was accepted as a child of the family in which the deceased was a child; and

(6)   the deceased's grandparent or the deceased's grandchild.

It will be clear that relatives now include members of the deceased's de facto family, thus reflecting contemporary family structures.

Any relationship by affinity is treated as a relationship by consanguinity;[3] any relationship of the half blood is treated as a relationship of the whole blood; and the stepchild of any person is treated as his child.[4]But in a claim for damages for non-patrimonial loss persons who would qualify only by affinity, for example the deceased's mother-in-law or father-in-law or son-in-law or daughter-in-law are excluded and step-parents and step-children are excluded unless they qualify because they had accepted the deceased as a child of their family or the deceased had accepted them as a child of the deceased's family.[5]

Members of the deceased's immediate family may claim damages for the following:

(1)   Damages for patrimonial loss

   (a)   Loss of support

A relative can claim damages to compensate the relative for any loss of support which the relative has sustained or is likely to sustain as a result of the deceased, A's, death. This covers both loss of support up until the date of proof and loss of support in the future. The loss of support constitutes the multiplicand and an appropriate multiplier is found by reference to the Ogden tables.[6] These claims can be substantial.

The 2011 Act introduces a set of rules by which a relative's loss of support – and consequently the multiplicand – is to be calculated. The total amount available to support the deceased, A's, relatives is an amount equivalent to 75 per cent of A's net income.[7] Where the relatives are A's surviving spouse, civil partner or cohabitant and/or a dependent child, the total 75 per cent constitutes the family's loss of support.[8] A dependent child is a child who, at the date of A's death, had not attained the age of 18 and to whom A owed an obligation of aliment, ie A's child or a child whom A had accepted as a child of A's family.[9] In the case of other members of A's immediate family, including A's child or accepted child who is 18 or over, the loss of support is the actual amount of that loss, ie what support the relative in fact received from A.[10] Where the pursuers are A's surviving spouse, civil partner or cohabitant and/or a dependent child and another immediate relative, the sum awarded to the last is deducted from the 75 per cent of A's income and the balance is the loss of support for the former. For example:

A's net income is £40K. The total available for loss of support is £30K. If A's only relative is A's wife, she will have the full £30K as loss of support. If A is survived by A's wife and a dependent child, the loss of support for A's wife and child is £30K. If A is survived by his wife, a dependent child and A's mother whom he has supported by giving her £5K a year, then A's mother's loss of support is £5K and the wife and child's loss is £25K.

While the 2011 Act does not expressly do so, it is submitted that in applying this formula as a general rule the income of the surviving immediate relative should be ignored. However, by s 7(2) of the 2011 Act, the court may apply a different percentage 'if satisfied that it is necessary to do so for the purpose of avoiding a manifestly and materially unfair result'. This discretion should be used only in exceptional circumstances: otherwise the courts could run a coach and four through the utility of the 75 per cent rule. But it might be used if A's surviving spouse or civil partner was very wealthy and A had not contributed much to the family expenses. Conversely, it could be used when A had many dependent children and could not have spent anything like 25 per cent of his net income on himself.

No account is taken of any patrimonial gains which accrue to the relative by way of succession or settlement as a result of A's death. Similarly no account is taken of insurance monies, pensions etc which the relative may receive.[11] If the deceased had obtained a provisional award of damages before his death, in assessing the relative's loss of support the court takes into account such part of the provisional award as was intended to compensate the deceased for any period beyond the date when he died.[12]

Unless a claim falls under the provisions of the 2011 Act, no person can obtain damages by reason of relationship to the deceased.[13] For the purpose of the legislation, loss of support has been narrowly construed. In *Mackintosh v Morrice's Executors*,[14] H and W were killed in a car crash. Before they died, they had transferred large sums to their daughters who were the pursuers in the action. This had been done to avoid the incidence of inheritance tax when the couple died. H and W were in good health and it was probable that they would have survived for seven years from the date of transfer so that no inheritance tax would have been payable. The accident took place within the seven years. The daughters claimed sums representing the inheritance tax which they had paid but which would not have been due if their parents had not died prematurely in the car crash. Their claims failed because such claims are restricted to any loss of support sustained by them as a result of their parents' deaths. A sum representing a diminution in the value of their parents' estates which the pursuers inherited as residuary legatees could not be regarded as support given to them by their parents while they were alive. Their claim as their parents' executrices also failed because executors can only recover patrimonial losses sustained by deceased persons during their lifetimes:[15] and since there was no liability to pay inheritance tax until they died, the loss to the parents' estates was sustained after they had died and therefore did not transmit to their executrices.

(b) Funeral expenses

The relative can recover any reasonable expenses incurred by the relative in relation to A's funeral.[16]

(c) Loss of A's personal services

The relative is entitled to include as a head of damages a reasonable sum in respect of the loss of gratuitous personal services rendered to the relative by A.[17] 'Personal services' has the same meaning as in s 9(1) of the Administration of Justice Act 1982.[18]

(2) Damages for non-patrimonial loss

By s 4(3)(b) of the 2011 Act a member of the deceased's immediate family can claim such sum of damages as the court thinks just by way of compensation for all or any of the following:

(a) distress and anxiety endured by the relative in contemplation of the suffering of A before A's death;

(b) the grief and sorrow of the relative caused by A's death;[19]

(c)   the loss of such non-patrimonial benefit as the relative might be expected to derive from A's society and guidance if A had not died.

In making such an award, the court is not obliged to ascribe any of the award to any of these heads of loss.

The amount of damages to be awarded for non-patrimonial loss is entirely a matter for the discretion of the court. There is no official tariff. Juries have tended to make more generous awards than judges sitting without a jury. In order to reduce the disparity between judicial and jury awards in *Hamilton v Ferguson Transport (Spean Bridge) Ltd*[20] the Inner House directed judges to consider the awards made by juries as well as judges in similar cases. In addition, the Inner House took the view that in jury trials the judge should suggest a spectrum of the level of damages for non-patrimonial loss which would be appropriate; this spectrum is for the assistance of the jury and is not binding on them.[21] It will be interesting to see whether as a consequence the level of damages for non-patrimonial loss awarded by judges and juries will converge.

What is clear is that in contemporary Scotland life is considered to be more precious than it may have been thought to be by earlier generations. Consequently the loss of a life of a close relative seems a greater loss than before. This change has resulted in higher awards of damages for loss than used to be the case. In *Ryder v First Aberdeen Ltd*,[22] for example, an award of £40K was thought to be appropriate for a son's loss of his mother.[23]

1   Damages (Scotland) Act 2011, ss 4(5)(a) and 14(1).

2   *Cohen v Shaw* 1992 SLT 1022.

3   See *Monteith v Cape Insulation Ltd* 1998 SC 903.

4   D(S)A 2011, s 14(2).

5   D(S)A 2011, s 4(5)(a) and (b).

6   *McManus' Executrix v Babcock Energy Ltd* 1999 SC 569. The multiplicand only applies to the calculation of future loss of support: D(S)A 2011, s 7(1)(d). On multiplicands and multipliers see para 16.15 ff beyond.

7   D(S)A 2011, s 7(1)(a).

8   D(S)A 2011, s 7(c)(i).

9   D(S)A 2011, s 7(3).

10   D(S)A 2011, s 7(1)(b).

11   D(S)A 2011, s 8(1).

12   D(S)A 2011, s 8(3).

13   D(S)A 2011, s 8(5).

14   2007 SC 6.

15 See also *Milligan's Executors v Hewats* [2013] CSOH 60 (executors could not sue the deceased's solicitors since the deceased had not sustained any loss before he died).

16 D(S)A 2011, s 4(3)(a).

17 D(S)A 2011, s 6(1).

18 D(S)A 2001, s 6(2). For discussion of s 9(1) of the 1982 Act see para 13(1) above. See, eg, *McGee v RJK Building Services Ltd* [2013] CSOH 10.

19 The pursuer is entitled to establish the gravity of her grief and sorrow by bringing evidence that she sustained a psychiatric disorder as a consequence of the death: *Gillies v Lynch* 2003 SCLR 467. However, damages for psychiatric disorder will only arise if the defender owed an independent duty of care to the pursuer to prevent her sustaining psychiatric harm: for discussion, see above para 4.2 ff In *Cruickshank v Fairfield Rowan Ltd* 2005 SLT 462, the Lord Ordinary (Brodie) confessed at 466 'to some difficulty with the notion that it is possible to discern in the circumstances of one family, bonds of affection that are stronger or a degree of emotional investment in the future of a child that is more profound, than in the circumstances of another family, and so in the circumstances in the one case to be very special and in the other case not'.

20 [2012] CSIH 52. See also *Young v McVean* [2014] CSOH 13, 2014 SLT 934 and *Currie v Esure Services Ltd* [2014] CSIH 112, 2015 SC 351.

21 See, eg, *Kelly v Upper Clyde Shipbuilders* 2 July 2012, OH.

22 [2013] CSOH 95.

23 See also *McGee v RJK Building Services Ltd* [2013] CSOH 10. In *Currie v Esure Services* [2014] CSOH 34 parents were awarded £42K each in respect of the loss of their son: the deceased's brother was awarded £22.5K.

(b) Specified relatives

13.7 The specified relatives include the deceased's ascendants and descendants (other than a parent or grandparent or a child or a grandchild), former spouse or civil partner, but not a former cohabitant, uncles and aunts, nephews and nieces and cousins. Such relatives include the appropriate 'in-laws', and half blood is to be treated as full blood. A step-child who has not been accepted as a child of the deceased's family is to be treated as a child.[1]

Specified relatives can claim damages for patrimonial loss arising from A's death. In relation to loss of support, the relative must establish the actual value of the support he received from A. The relative cannot take advantage of the 75 per cent rule. Relatives can also claim for reasonable funeral expenses and loss of A's gratuitous personal services. A specified relative is not entitled to damages for non-patrimonial loss. The fact that the deceased had no legal obligation to support the specified relative is irrelevant: reparation is made for the loss of *de facto* financial support both before the date of death and in the future.

1   D(S)A 2011, ss 14(1)(e)–(g) and (2).

(c) Transmission

13.8   The right of a relative of A to a dependent claim under the
Damages (Scotland) Act 2011 can transmit to the executor of the
relative if the relative dies before an award of damages is made.[1] For
example, if A dies leaving his wife, B, B's right to sue as a member
of A's immediate family transmits to her executor if she dies before
an award of damages has been made to her. In determining the
amount of damages payable to the relative's executor, the court
can only have regard to the period ending immediately before
the relative's death.[2] This proviso, while obviously important in
respect of the relative's claim for loss of support, could also affect
a claim for non-patrimonial loss under s 4(3) of the 2011 Act if the
relative died shortly after the deceased person.

1   D(S)A 2011, s 9(2).
2   D(S)A 2011, s 9(2).

CHAPTER 14

Delict and road traffic

A. INTRODUCTION

14.1 In modern society, motor vehicles that are driven carelessly are a major cause of accidents. Accidents involving vehicles are probably the area of the law of delict with which ordinary people are most likely to be involved. Where a person suffers personal injuries or damage to property because of a road accident, the general principles of delictual liability apply. Indeed, the paradigm of a duty of care based on reasonable foreseeability of harm[1] is the duty of care which a driver owes to other road users. The pursuer must establish a breach of duty on the part of the defender, causation and harm, as in any other action for reparation.[2] However, because of the frequency of such accidents, the common law has been supplemented by statutory provisions designed to ensure that victims of road accidents receive compensation. Moreover, the practices of insurance companies are of particular importance in this area. The 'peculiarities' of delictual liability for careless driving are discussed in this section.

1 On duty of care generally, see Chapter 3 above.
2 See Chapters 5 and 6 above.

B. THE STANDARD OF CARE

14.2 As stated above, before a driver is liable in delict the pursuer must establish that he was in breach of duty; in other words, that the defender did not reach the standard of care of the reasonable driver in his situation and was therefore negligent. In road traffic cases, considerable assistance in establishing that the defender did not exercise reasonable care is provided by the Highway Code, an HMSO publication. The Road Traffic Act 1988 provides:[1]

'A failure on the part of a person to observe the provisions of the Highway Code shall not in itself render that person liable to criminal proceedings of any kind but any such failure may in any proceedings (whether civil or criminal …) be relied upon by any party to the proceedings as tending to establish or negative any liability which is in question in those proceedings.'

Although a breach of the terms of the Highway Code will not per se establish negligence,[2] if the conduct averred is, in fact, in breach of the Code then this will be highly persuasive in establishing that the defender did not take reasonable care.[3]

Under the Road Traffic Act 1988, it is a criminal offence to cause death by dangerous driving;[4] to cause serious injury by dangerous driving;[5] to drive dangerously;[6] to drive without due care and attention;[7] to cause death while driving without due care and attention when unfit to drive through drink or drugs;[8] and to cause death by driving without due attention or reasonable consideration.[9] Moreover, statutory regulations designed to protect road users provide offences where vehicles are (1) constructed in such a manner as to create a hazard;[10] and (2) used in such a way as causes danger to other road users.[11] Although breach of these statutory provisions and regulations does not give rise to delictual liability for breach of statutory duty,[12] a conviction will be important evidence in establishing negligence on the part of the defender.[13]

1 Road Traffic Act 1988, s 38(7).
2 For example, merely because the defender was driving above the speed limit does not in itself establish that he was not taking reasonable care: speed is not per se the cause of an accident. See *Colborne v Wallace* 1993 GWD 17-1121 per the Sheriff Principal (Nicholson).
3 See, eg, *Robertson v J Sidney Smith* 1999 GWD 4-214. Although the Highway Code is within judicial knowledge, its provisions cannot be used in place of evidence: *Cavin v Kinnaird* 1993 SCLR 618, 1994 SLT 111.
4 Road Traffic Act 1988, s 1. For these purposes, dangerous driving means driving which falls below what would be expected of a competent and careful driver when it would be obvious to a competent and careful driver that driving in that way would be dangerous. The 1988 Act was amended by the Road Traffic Act 1991.
5 RTA 1988, s 1A.
6 RTA 1988, s 2.
7 RTA 1988, s 3.
8 RTA 1988, s 3A. It is enough to be above the prescribed limits for alcohol.
9 RTA 1988, s 2B.
10 For example, it is an offence to drive a vehicle which exceeds the maximum length stipulated in the Road Vehicles (Construction and Use) Regulations 1986 (SI 1986/1078).
11 For example, it is an offence to carry an object on a vehicle which overhangs that vehicle in excess of a distance prescribed in the regulations, without the leading edge being suitably marked.
12 On breach of statutory duty, see Chapter 11 above.
13 See, eg, *Cameron v Swan* [2021] CSIH 30, 2021 GWD 20-279.

C. THE NATURE OF THE LOSSES

14.3   Where there has been a road accident, any damages for death or personal injury will be assessed according to the ordinary principles of delict.[1]

Where a motor car is damaged in an accident, the owner is entitled to the value of the car if it is 'a write off' or the cost of repair. In addition, the owner is entitled to loss of use of the damaged car while it is being repaired or replaced. This is calculated as being the reasonable cost of hiring a car while the damaged vehicle is off the road. Car hire companies usually require the motorist to produce an acceptable debit or credit card 'up front' so that they will be paid for the rental which the motorist will eventually recover from the defender's insurer. However, there are accident hire companies or credit hire companies which do not require a debit or credit card 'up front'. Instead, when the motorist seeks a replacement car while his own is off the road, the company assesses the merits of his case. If satisfied that the claim is unanswerable, the company provides a car and then pursues the motorist's claim against the defender's insurer. For these services, the accident or credit hire company charges an additional fee beyond the 'spot rate' for simple car hire.

In *Dimond v Lovell*,[2] the House of Lords held that compensation for loss of use of a damaged car was restricted to the spot rate for hiring a car from a company other than an accident or credit hire company, ie the additional fee element charged by an accident or credit hire company was not recoverable. Given the number of claims involved, this was a very important decision for insurance companies who would have to meet only the reasonable cost of hire of the car and not the additional fees charged by an accident or credit hire company. In *Lagden v O'Connor*,[3] however, the motorist was unable to afford the cost of hiring a replacement car from a car hire company: unless he was able to use the services of an accident or credit hire company, he would have been unable to have a replacement car at all. In these circumstances the House held that the motorist's loss could be calculated based on the accident or credit hire company's charges including the additional fee. In reaching this conclusion, the majority of their Lordships held that the impecuniosity of the plaintiff should be taken into account: Lord Wright's opinion in *The Liesboch*[4] that a claimant's lack of means should *not* be taken into account when assessing his loss was no longer to be followed. The court realised that there could be difficulties in determining when a motorist was so impecunious that he was entitled to use the services of an accident or credit hire company but thought that the fear this would lead to an increase in litigation and delay in reaching settlements was exaggerated.[5] This remains to be seen.

1   On death, see Chapter 13 above; on personal injury, see beyond Chapter 16.
2   [2002] 1 AC 384.
3   [2004] 1 All ER 277.
4   [1933] AC 449.
5   For example, there are persons who are quite well off but do not have credit or debit cards and persons who are unable to hire a car without using an agreed overdraft facility. Why should the latter not recover the cost of borrowing to hire the replacement car?

D.   OBTAINING COMPENSATION

14.4   It is obvious that cars and other motor vehicles create considerable hazards to road users, whether they be pedestrians, cyclists or other drivers. To ensure that there is a fund available to provide compensation in the event of delictual liability as a result of a road accident, the owner of a vehicle is obliged to take out insurance. A motor vehicle must be insured in respect of 'third-party liability', ie it must be insured in respect of delictual liability for a person other than the owner himself. This compulsory third-party insurance covers liability for causing death or personal injuries or property damage to the victim. It is a criminal offence to drive a vehicle which does not have a valid third-party liability policy of insurance or to allow a vehicle to be driven without such insurance.[1]

Although it is only third-party liability insurance which is compulsory, many drivers purchase additional insurance to cover their own losses which are incurred in an accident for which they are wholly or partly responsible. These losses include, for example, the cost of repair of the insured's own vehicle and the cost of hiring an alternative vehicle for a limited period while the insured's vehicle is being repaired. These are known as insured losses. Where a driver purchases additional insurance as well as third-party liability insurance, this is known as a comprehensive policy of insurance. Comprehensive insurance does not usually cover death or personal injuries sustained by the driver as a result of his own negligence. It is common practice for the insurer to require the holder of a comprehensive policy to meet the first part of a claim made under that policy. This is typically between the first £50 and £300 of the claim. This sum of money is known as uninsured loss. Any loss not covered by the comprehensive policy, such as a claim in respect of death or personal injury of the driver, is an uninsured loss.

To summarise the position. If, as a result of negligent driving, A causes physical harm or property damage to B, B can sue A in delict and his compensation will be covered by A's compulsory third-party insurance. If B has a comprehensive insurance policy, he may elect to claim for his insured losses under the policy, but he is not obliged to do so; he must, of course, sue A for any uninsured losses. If the accident was not the result of A's negligence, B cannot sue A; but if B has a comprehensive policy of insurance, he can claim under the policy for insured losses even if the accident was the result of B's negligence.

Where a person suffers property damage as a result of another driver's negligence, if he elects to claim for insured losses under his comprehensive policy of insurance then the principles of subrogation apply. This means that the insurer 'steps into the shoes' of the insured and is entitled to sue the negligent driver to recover the monies paid out under the comprehensive policy of insurance. In these circumstances, the action is raised in the name of the insured rather than in the name of the insurance company. The defender is cited personally but, again under principles of subrogation, the defender's compulsory third-party insurance company will in effect take over the defence if the action has been intimated to them.

In practice, insurers may have inter-office agreements whereby actions do not have to be raised even if delictual liability is disputed. In order to reduce their overall expenses, the insurers accept that they will meet their own outlays under the appropriate insurance policies without attempting to recover these from each other in defended civil proceedings. However, such agreements, often known as 'knock for knock' agreements, are becoming less common because insurers are battling to minimise losses. Insurers who previously would have 'confirmed' a 'knock for knock' agreement with the third-party insurers are resorting to litigation to recover their outlays under their comprehensive insurance policy in full.

It should be emphasised that even if a comprehensive insurer confirms a 'knock for knock' agreement with a negligent driver's third-party insurer, this does not affect the insured driver's right to sue the negligent driver personally in delict to recover his uninsured losses. If he is successful, he is entitled to look to the defender's compulsory third-party insurer for any sums not recovered from the defender which are due under the decree provided appropriate intimation of the action has been made to the insurance company.

An insurance company may be entitled under general principles of contract to refuse to indemnify the insured losses. This could arise, for example, if the insured was in material breach of the terms of the policy of insurance by not paying the premiums or if the policy could be rescinded by the insurance company on the ground of misrepresentation. However, where a pursuer successfully obtains decree against a negligent driver and seeks to recover his compensation from the defender's compulsory third-party insurer, under the Road Traffic Act 1988 the insurance company cannot refuse payment on the ground that under general principles of contract it is not bound to indemnify the insured defender unless the insurance company takes steps to obtain a declarator from the court that it is entitled to avoid the policy. Where a policy was taken out under a fictitious name, the insurer was not liable to a woman injured by an unknown driver. [2]

Similarly, should a driver cancel a compulsory third-party liability policy of insurance, the insurer remains liable for any losses suffered by a third party in a subsequent accident caused by the negligence of the driver provided the contract has not been rescinded. The insurance company can then recover its outlays from the 'former' insured driver. In these circumstances, the insurer is known as a 'Road Traffic Act insurer'. The Road Traffic Act insurer will escape liability if the company does not retain an insurable interest in the vehicle. This would occur, for example, if the 'former' insured driver sold the car with the actual policy document in the glove compartment!

1   Road Traffic Act 1988, s 143(a).
2   *Cameron v Liverpool Victoria Insurance Co Ltd* [2019] UKSC 6.

(1) Motor Insurers' Bureau

14.5   The legislation requiring owners of vehicles to have third-party liability insurance was clearly designed to protect third parties. Such protection is not afforded where an individual flouts the law and drives a vehicle without appropriate insurance cover, although, of course, it is possible in these circumstances that the defender will have sufficient assets to meet a successful action for reparation.

In order to protect third parties in this situation, a body called the Motor Insurers' Bureau (MIB) entered into an agreement with the Ministry of Transport on 17 June 1946 to provide from 1 July 1946 compensation for victims of road accidents where the injured parties were unable to obtain compensation due to the defender's lack of appropriate third-party insurance. There have been various revised agreements since then, but the present text covering accidents on or after 31 December 1988 provides compensation for victims of those accidents in respect of death, personal injury and property damage. The December 1988 Agreement followed an EEC Directive[1] on motor insurance requiring member states to extend third-party insurance to include property damage.

Clause 2 of the agreement provides that the MIB will 'pay or satisfy or cause to be satisfied to or to the satisfaction of the person or persons in whose favour the judgment was given' any sum due under the decree or judgment which remains unsatisfied for a period of seven days from the time at which the decree or judgment should have been in force. The MIB's liability includes any element of interest or expenses included in the decree.

This obligation is subject to certain conditions, the most important being that notification of the commencement of the proceedings must be given to the MIB before, or within seven days after, the commencement of the proceedings. The claimant must take all reasonable steps to obtain judgment or decree against all those liable for the death, personal injury or property damage, and against any principal where such a person is a servant or agent. Additionally, the MIB will have no liability where the claim is in respect of damage to a motor vehicle where the claimant knew or ought reasonably to have known that at the time of the use of the vehicle it was not properly insured in terms of the Road Traffic Act 1988.

Similarly, where the claim is in respect of personal injury, the MIB has no liability where the claimant was a passenger in or on a vehicle which he knew or should reasonably have known was not insured in terms of the Road Traffic Act 1988, although this exception applies only where the decree the MIB is being asked to satisfy is obtained against the owner or person using the vehicle in which the claimant was a passenger. The MIB has no liability if the accident does not take place on a road or highway to which the public has access.[2]

The MIB is not liable where the vehicle in which a person was injured was being used in the course or furtherance of a crime.

Thus, a car passenger could not claim when he was injured in a car accident when in possession of cannabis with intent to supply.[3]

The MIB's liability in respect of property claims is limited by the fact that there is currently a £175 excess payable, ie the first £175 is not paid. The Bureau's maximum liability is £250,000. The MIB is only required to compensate for damage which is required to be insured against by law, ie under compulsory third-party insurance.

Where an offending driver cannot be traced, this agreement is of no effect. However, a sister agreement, referred to as 'the MIB untraced drivers' agreement' then comes into play. There have been several revised agreements. For accidents on or after 14 February 2003, the relevant agreement is that of 7 February 2003. It covers property damage as well as personal injury. Application must be made within three years of the injury being sustained or within nine months if there is a claim for property damage.

Owing to the expenses involved in pursuing a claim against an uninsured driver, the MIB has now arranged free legal expenses cover for which the pursuer can apply when a claim is being brought against such a driver. The scheme, MIBLES, is available in respect of claims made on or after 13 November 2003.

1   Second Council Directive 84/5, OJ L8 11.1.84 p 17. This Directive has been held not to be directly effective: *Evans v Motor Insurers' Bureau* [1999] Lloyd's Rep JR 30.
2   *Clarke v Kato* [1998] 4 All ER 417, [1998] 1 WLR 1647, HL (MIB not liable where accident took place in car park).
3   *Delaney v Pickett* [2011] EWCA Civ 1532.

CHAPTER 15

Defamation and malicious publication

A. INTRODUCTION

15.1 The law has long recognised a person's interest in her honour and reputation. Accordingly, where A makes a false statement about B with the intention of harming B's honour or reputation then B has a delictual action against A. In Roman law, there was a specific remedy, the *actio injuriarum*, which provided compensation (solatium) for insult *(contumelia)*. In order to succeed, it had to be established that a false statement was made with the intention of insulting the victim. It followed, therefore, that the action lay even if the statement had only been made to the victim herself, ie where the statement had not been made to a third party. If the statement had been published to a third party and, as a result, the victim suffered economic (patrimonial) loss, in the later Roman Empire such loss could, in theory at least, be recovered under general principles of *culpa*: *damnum injuria datum*. Accordingly, where intention to insult could not be established, but the statement was made carelessly to a third party, the only damages that could be obtained were for patrimonial loss: but, if intention to insult could be established, solatium would also be available under the *actio injuriarum*. Given the influence of Roman law, Scots law could have developed a simple set of principles:

(1)　if A makes an untrue statement about B to B, with the intention of insulting B, then B can sue A for solatium even if the statement is not published to a third party, provided intention to insult can be proved; and

(2)　if A makes an untrue statement about B to C, then B could recover damages for patrimonial loss on the basis of *culpa* but only obtain solatium if intention to insult could also be established.

But since *culpa* covers both intentional and unintentional, but careless, conduct, the fact that the remedies were originally based on two separate, if related, principles, ie *culpa* and the *actio injuriarum*, was overlooked.[1] Moreover, the law in this area was influenced by the English law of libel and slander with its emphasis on the defendant's malice. As a result, the Scots law of defamation and verbal injury became complex and contentious.

1   For discussion of the confusion, see T B Smith *A Short Commentary on the Law of Scotland* (W Green, 1962) pp 724–732. For comprehensive discussion of the law prior to the DMPS see K Norrie, *Defamation and Related Actions in Scots Law*, (1995), Butterworths; for historical coverage see J Blackie, Defamation, Chapter 10 in Reid and Zimmermann (eds) *A History of Private Law in Scotland Vol 2*, (2000) Oxford University Press.

15.2   Much of the law law has now been put on a statutory footing with the enactment of the Defamation and Malicious Publication (Scotland) Act 2021.[1] The Act is to some extent a codifying statute, that is it brings into one place much of the disparate common law and statutory elements that made up the body of the law prior to enactment and any proceedings brought will be governed by the statute. Some elements of the common law have been specifically abolished, principally the major defences[2] and the law concerning verbal injury.[3] There are important points however, on which it remains necessary to turn to the common law. Decisions of the English courts on the Defamation Act 2013,[4] moreover, are very likely to be employed as persuasive authority on the points on which the Acts coincide.

The Act addresses the problem of 'libel tourism', that is raising actions in a jurisdiction perceived as favourable to pursuers, by providing that courts do not have jurisdiction to hear cases brought against persons not domiciled in the UK, unless the court is satisfied that Scotland is the most appropriate place to bring proceedings.[5] Another important feature of the Act is that it also takes into account the fact that much modern communication is conducted online.

1   Hereinafter DMPS. The Act received Royal Assent on 21 April 2021. At the time of writing, ss 36–40 have come into force.
2   DMPS, s 8.
3   DMPS, s 27.
4   Those few provisions which applied in Scotland are now repealed inasmuch as they affect Scots law.
5   DMPS, s 19(2). This would usually be case where the statement is published and circulated within Scotland. It is thought that 'libel tourism' was encountered far more frequently in England. On a related point, the presumption in favour of jury trial has been removed, DMPS, s 20. Juries are perceived as awarding greater sums in damages than judges. Again, this was more of an issue in England.

B. DEFAMATION

(1) Defamatory meaning

15.3   The prevalent common law definition of a defamatory statement is one which 'tends to lower [the pursuer] in the estimation of right thinking members of society generally'.[1] This definition is maintained in the Act albeit the slightly troubling concept of 'right thinking people' has been updated so: 'A statement about a person is defamatory if it causes harm to the person's reputation (that is, if it tends to lower the person's reputation in the estimation of ordinary persons).'[2] The Act then, is focused on the protection of harm to reputation and not on affront or insult. It remains the case that the question of whether a statement is defamatory is one of law, to be decided by the court.[3] The Act maintains the objectivity of the test, ie whether the reasonable person would decide that this type of statement was defamatory.

A statement or action may appear to be harmless, yet when taken in the context of the facts and circumstances in which it was made, a defamatory meaning may be inferred. For example, to announce the birth of twins to a married couple in a newspaper appears innocuous until it is appreciated that they married only a month before, thus implying pre-marital sexual intercourse.[4] In this situation, Scots law allows a pursuer to plead the facts and circumstances from which the defamatory meaning of the statement or act can be drawn. This is known as 'the doctrine of innuendo'.

The onus rests on the pursuer to state the meaning of the acts or statement in the light of the relevant facts and circumstances. In *Cuthbert v Linklater*,[5] for example, the pursuer argued that the defender, an author, had defamed her when a female character in his novel took a Union Jack from Edinburgh Castle and placed it in a men's public urinal. An ardent Scottish nationalist, the pursuer had in fact taken a Union Jack from Stirling Castle and had tossed it at a guard. Consequently, by innuendo, a reasonable reader would assume that the character in the novel was meant to be her and that she was capable of acting indelicately. The court accepted the argument.[6]

The test on whether an innuendo can be inferred is that of the ordinary reasonable person,[7] ie whether a reasonable person would regard the words as offensive if placed in the same position as the pursuer. The question whether the statement or act plus the innuendo placed upon them by the reasonable person amounts to defamation is a matter of law to be decided by the court. It is a question of fact whether the statement or act was taken as having a defamatory meaning by those to whom it was actually communicated.

Defamatory statements were never restricted to the spoken or written word.[8] 'Statement' is defined in the Act to mean: 'words, pictures, visual images, gestures or any other method of signifying meaning.'[9]

1   *Sim v Stretch*, [1936] 2 All ER 1237, HL at 1240 per Lord Atkin
2   DMPS, s 1(4)(a).
3   Accordingly, the defence can make a plea to the relevancy of the issue.
4   *Morrison v Ritchie & Co* (1902) 4 F 645.
5   1935 SLT 94.
6   See also *Wragg v D C Thomson & Co Ltd* 1909 2 SLT 315, where a newspaper published an article that a certain George Reeves had shot his wife twice and then killed himself. The paper omitted to mention that the incident took place in the USA. At the time it was published, George Reeves, a famous music hall artiste, was appearing in Glasgow. The court held that there was an innuendo that the incident referred to him.
7   *Duncan v Associated Scottish Newspapers Ltd* 1929 SC 14 at 21 per Lord Anderson; *Lord Robertson of Port Ellen v Newsquest (Sunday Herald) Ltd* 2006 SCLR 792.
8   See, eg, *Monson v Tussauds Ltd* [1894] 1 QB 61 in which the placing of a waxwork of a man acquitted of murder alongside others of those found guilty was held to be defamatory.
9   DMPS, s 36(b).

15.4   Before looking more closely at the Act it may be useful to provide some examples of statements that have been held to be defamatory in the past.

It has been held defamatory to undermine a person's moral character. Thus it is defamatory to call a woman a prostitute or an adulteress or even to suggest that she lacks 'proper womanly delicacy'.[1] At one time it was clearly defamatory to state that a person was homosexual.[2] But with changing values, it has been observed judicially that an allegation of homosexuality should no longer be regarded as defamatory per se.[3] In *Cowan v Bennett*,[4] the sheriff stated that an imputation of homosexuality is not defamatory. Nevertheless, allegations that a nun was dishonest, unchaste and a lesbian have been held to be capable of amounting to defamation.[5]

It is defamatory to call a person a hypocrite.[6] It appears no longer to be defamatory merely to call a person a liar or a 'stranger to the truth':[7] but to call a person a thief and a liar has been held to be defamatory.[8] To state that a woman whose child had died was a heartless and uncaring mother is defamatory.[9]

It is defamatory to accuse a person of a serious crime which ordinary people do not commit or condone, such as murder,[10] theft,[11] or being a paedophile. Similarly, it is defamatory to say that a person should be in jail since this implies that they are guilty of a crime. It is also defamatory to say that a person was responsible for enabling a person to commit a horrendous crime.[12]

Statements which disparage a person's professional competence or conduct are defamatory, for example, to accuse a doctor of gross professional negligence[13] or a professor of their inability to teach[14] – or write textbooks on delict? Allegations of conduct which is unprofessional in the circumstances are also defamatory: for example, to allege that an athlete refused to play a curling match for Scotland at an international competition,[15] to accuse a solicitor of conducting a case for his own – as opposed to his client's – interests,[16] or to say that a prison warden had sexual relations with a prisoner.[17]

It has been held defamatory falsely to allege that a person is insolvent[18] or is unwilling[19] or unable to pay their debts.[20]

1 *Cuthbert v Linklater* 1935 SLT 94 discussed above at para 15.3. Would this be regarded as defamatory today?
2 *AB v XY* 1917 SC 15, 1916 2 SLT 210; *Kerr v Kennedy* [1942] 1 KB 409, [1942] 1 All ER 412.
3 *Quilty v Windsor* 1999 SLT 346.
4 2012 GWD 37-738. On homophobia see *Campbell v Dugdale* 2020 SC 481
5 *Prophit v British Broadcasting Corpn* 1997 SLT 745, OH.
6 *Stein v Beaverbrook Newspapers Ltd* 1968 SC 272, 1968 SLT 401; *Lord Robertson of Port Ellen v Newsquest (Sunday Herald) Ltd* 2006 SCLR 792.
7 *Carroll v British Broadcasting Corpn* 1997 SLT (Sh Ct) 23. Cf *Watson v Duncan* (1890) 17 R 404. The circumstances will be relevant.
8 *Gilbert v Yorston* 1996 SCLR 1122, 1997 SLT 879, OH.
9 *McCabe v News Group Newspapers Ltd* 1992 SLT 707, OH.
10 *Waddell v British Broadcasting Corpn* 1973 SLT 246; *Berezovsky v Forbes Inc (No 2)* [2001] EMLR 45, CA.
11 *Sutherland v British Telecommunications plc* 1989 SLT 531.
12 *Lord Robertson of Port Ellen v Newsquest (Sunday Herald) Ltd* 2006 SCLR 792.
13 *Simmers v Morton* (1900) 8 SLT 285, OH.
14 *Auld v Shairp* (1875) 2 R 940.
15 *Munro v Brown* [2013] CSOH 117.
16 *McRostie v Ironside* (1849) 12 D 74.
17 *Winter v News Scotland Ltd* 1991 SLT 828.
18 *AB v CD* (1904) 7 F 72.
19 *Outram v Reid* (1852) 14 D 577.
20 *Mazure v Stubbs Ltd* 1919 SC (HL) 112, 1919 2 SLT 160.

(2) Actionability

15.5   The law is a double-edged sword. While it is common to present defamation from the perspective of the wronged pursuer, it must always be borne in mind that litigation, or the threat of it, is not uncommonly used to suppress the publication of unwanted criticism by the powerful against those who cannot afford to hazard the enormous legal costs associated with litigation on defamation. This is known as the 'chilling effect' of the law. While it was always the case that an action could be defended on the basis that the statement was truthful in fact, many ordinary defenders could be facing financial hardship before proceedings reached the stage where they had the opportunity to prove this. The Act seeks to address this issue by imposing various restrictive measures.

The Act imposes a new threshold for litigation of 'serious harm to the reputation' of the defender.[1] English authority on the equivalent provision in the 2013 Act holds that proof of actual or prospective harm to reputation must be established.[2] For litigants other than individuals, effectively businesses, serious harm means serious financial loss.[3] Public authorities have no right to bring proceedings.[4] Natural legal persons, that is private individuals, need to show serious harm to reputation, but need not show serious financial loss. Individuals who discharge public functions or who are employed within public authorities are not prevented from litigating in their capacity as natural persons though they may not do so as office holders.[5]

The Act also imposes a new requirement that the statement is published to a third party.[6] At common law actions required only communication to the party defamed. Publication under the Act means communication by any means that can be accessed and understood and takes place when it has been seen or heard by the recipient.[7] A short limitation period of one year commences from the first publication to the public or a section of the public and any right of action arising from a later publication of the same defamatory material is subject to the same limitation period. Thus, if A publishes a defamatory statement in October 2021 and B publishes the same statement in December 2021 both claims will be limited from October 2022.[8]

1   DMPS, s 1(2)(b).
2   *Lachaux v Independent Print Ltd* [2019] UKSC 27.
3   DMPS, s 1(3).
4   DMPS, s 2. This section also defines public authorities for the purposes of the Act.

5   DMPS, s 2(5).
6   DMPS, s 1(2)(a).
7   DMPS, s 1(4) (b)(c).
8   Prescription and Limitation (Scotland) Act 1973, s 18A as amended by DMPS, s 32.

15.6   At common law each repeat of a defamatory statement gave rise to a fresh right of action. This is no longer the case. Actions can only be brought against the author, editor or publisher of a statement or their employees or agents where they have responsibility either for the content of the statement or for the decision to publish it.[1] The originator is the author provided they intended publication, bearing in mind that publication only requires that the statement is communicated to and seen or heard by a third party. An editor is a person bearing responsibility for content or the decision to publish, for example on a website or in a newspaper. Publishers are commercial operations in the business of issuing material to the public.[2] It should be noted that a person does not fall within these categories simply by providing a means of access such as a hyperlink or signalling approval by 'liking' or sharing, providing in all cases the statement remains unaltered.[3] There is a further qualifier and that is that involvement should not materially increase the harm caused by publication.[4]

This raises the following prospect. Law student A is new to twitter, has only ten followers, mostly classmates, and follows student B. Student B is followed by most of the class and other people within and beyond the university. B tweets a defamatory statement concerning the professor of Scots law. A re-tweets the statement without altering it. One of A's followers, C, is a 'macro-influencer' who also re-tweets the statement and it is seen by 500,000 people across the globe. The professor's reputation is seriously harmed, first in the law school where students now refuse to attend his classes and secondly, among the worldwide academic community. Offers of visiting professorships are withdrawn. B can be sued as the author of the statement as he clearly intended it to be seen. A cannot be sued, but C can, as an agent of B, having materially increased the harm caused. A greater responsibility then, is cast on those whose lines of communication extend further and whose capacity to harm is commensurably more significant.

1   DMPS, s 3(1).
2   DMPS, s 3(2).
3   DMPS, s 3(3)(a).
4   DMPS, s 3(3)(b).

(3) Privileged statements

(a) Absolute privilege

15.7   Absolute privilege attaches to certain circumstances or occasions. The Act does not abolish the common law. Where a statement is protected by absolute privilege, it cannot form the basis of an action for defamation. It does not matter that the statement is defamatory or was made with the intention to harm the victim (malice). The following situations are covered by absolute privilege:

(i)   Statements made in the Westminster Parliament. Any statement made in the Westminster Parliament has the protection of absolute privilege. This includes statements made in parliamentary committees. The statement does not have to be relevant to the proceedings. It is not restricted to statements made by members of either House: it would include, for example, a statement made by a witness giving evidence to a Select Committee. It does not extend to statements made by members of Parliament outside the Houses.[1] Where the conduct of a person in or in relation to proceedings in the Westminster Parliament is in issue in defamation proceedings, that person can waive, for the purpose of the defamation action, the privilege that prevents proceedings in Parliament from being impeached or questioned in court.[2] This is to enable an MP, for example, to rely on his own conduct in Parliament in order to pursue an action of defamation while, of course, retaining the defence of absolute privilege for statements he has made in Parliament!

(ii)   Statements made in judicial proceedings. A statement made by a judge in the course of judicial proceedings is protected by absolute privilege even if it was made maliciously.[3] However, the statement must be made while the judge is acting judicially, ie it must be relevant to the case which is subject to the proceedings.[4] Advocates or solicitors pleading the case also enjoy absolute privilege,[5] provided the statement is relevant to the case. Witnesses giving evidence have absolute privilege as long as the evidence is pertinent to the case.[6] Any findings of fact by a jury are subject to absolute privilege. But parties to a civil action do not enjoy absolute privilege – only qualified privilege.[7] Absolute privilege extends in like way to the participants in quasi-judicial proceedings or tribunals, for example, courts martial, public inquiries, arbitrations, children's hearings, employment tribunals and disciplinary tribunals.[8]

(iii) Reports authorised by the Westminster Parliament. Reports of proceedings and papers etc published by or under the authority of either House of Parliament attract absolute privilege.[9]

(iv) Any statement made in proceedings of the Scottish Parliament and any publication of any such statement authorised by the Scottish Parliament are absolutely privileged.[10]

(v) Miscellaneous. The Lord Advocate is absolutely privileged in respect of what he does in relation to prosecutions on indictment.[11] This protection extends to procurators fiscal and Advocates Depute acting on the Lord Advocate's instructions. Ministers of the Crown are also protected provided the statement is made in the proper exercise of their functions. Reports of the various ombudsmen are also absolutely privileged.

(vi) The Defamation and Malicious Publications Act s 9 accords absolute privilege to fair and accurate reports of court proceedings published contemporaneously. The list of courts covered extends beyond those listed in the Defamation Act 1996 s 14 which the new provisions replaces.

1 *Buchanan v Jennings* [2005] 1 AC 115.
2 Defamation Act 1996, s 13; *Hamilton v Al Fayed* [2001] 1 AC 395.
3 *Haggart's Trustees v Lord President Hope* (1824) 2 Sh App 125, HL; *Primrose v Waterston* (1902) 4 F 783, 10 SLT 37.
4 *Watt v Thomson* (1870) 8 M (HL) 77.
5 *Rome v Watson* (1898) 25 R 733, 5 SLT 377. The privilege extends to written pleadings.
6 *Watson v McEwan* (1905) 7 F (HL) 109. This privilege extends to statements made in precognitions: *B v Burns* 1994 SLT 250.
7 See para 15.8 below.
8 *Thomson v Ross* 2001 SLT 807 (Scottish Solicitors Discipline Tribunal).
9 Parliamentary Papers Act 1840.
10 Scotland Act 1998, s 41.
11 But see *Whitehouse v Lord Advocate* [2019] UKSC 52.

(b) Qualified privilege

15.8 When a statement is protected by qualified privilege, an action of defamation will only succeed where privilege is lost, that is where the pursuer succeeds in establishing malice.[1]

The Act specifies a number of specific types of statement that enjoy this protection,[2] but the common law remains in place and provides the basis for the recognition of qualified privilege in the general case and also the means by which malice may be established.

Qualified privilege arises in the following circumstances:

(i)   Where a person has a moral, social or legal duty to speak, for example, to report a crime or inform a reporter to a children's hearing of child abuse, the statement is protected by qualified privilege. The statement must be made to a person with a reciprocal interest in the information. So, for example, a complaint about the conduct of a police officer is protected by qualified privilege if made to the relevant chief constable but not if made to a newspaper editor. Whether a situation involves a duty to speak which attracts qualified privilege is a question of law to be determined by a court. Generally, complaints and grievances will be privileged where established procedures are followed. Complaints to the chief constable about the conduct of police officers attracts protection if an action of defamation is brought against the complainer by the officer who was the subject of the complaint.[3] Similarly, a letter to the deputy chief executive of the prison service about the unfitness of an employee to serve as an officer has been held to attract qualified privilege.[4] A person who gives a reference enjoys qualified privilege.[5] Qualified privilege may also apply where a person, responds to criticism.

(ii)   Fair and accurate reports of proceedings in legislatures anywhere in the world attract qualified privilege.[6] Although the Act provides for loss of privilege through malice[7] the scope for this must be limited given that privilege applies only to the extent that reports are fair and accurate. Moreover, the subject matter must be of public interest and publication for the public benefit.[8]

        The same points apply to the other instances of qualified privilege listed in Schedule 1 Part 1 of the Act.[9]

(iii)   Parties to a civil action enjoy qualified privilege in respect of statements made in civil proceedings.

(iv)   Under the DMPS, s 10, the publication of statements in peer-reviewed scientific or academic journals is subject to qualified privilege. This is a significant measure in restraining the 'chilling effect' of the law.

(v)   Under the DMPS, s 11 and Schedule 2, Part 2, the publication of certain types of report enjoys qualified privilege. These are various but include for example a fair and accurate report of proceedings at any sitting of a local government committee in the UK. Privilege will be lost where malice is established. The subject matter must be of public interest and publication for the public benefit.[10] Privilege, in instances listed in Schedule 2, Part 2 may also be lost where the defender has neglected or refused to publish a reasonable statement explaining or contradicting the statement complained of having been requested to do so by the pursuer.[11]

As the authorities stand,[12] malice can be established if it can be shown that the defender abused the privileged occasion – as well as proving that he intended to injure the pursuer. Nevertheless, proof of malice is difficult.[13] It may be inferred from extreme language, a previous personal vendetta between the parties or the fact that the defender had no basis for any honest belief in the truth of the statement.[14]

1   But see (v) below with reference to statements listed in DMPS, Sch, Part 2.
2   See ss 10, 11 and the Schedule to the Act replacing now repealed provisions of the 1996 Act and s 6 of the Defamation Act 2013
3   *Fraser v Mirza* 1993 SC (HL) 27, 1993 SLT 527.
4   *Quilty v Windsor* 1999 SLT 346. In *Pearson v Educational Institute of Scotland* 1997 SC 245, 1998 SLT 189, a report on the competency of the pursuer to be head of a college, which the union had sent on to a government department, was held to attract qualified privilege.
5   *Farquhar v Neish* (1890) 17 R 716. However, even if not made maliciously, the writer of the reference may be liable in negligence: *Spring v Guardian Assurance plc* [1995] 2 AC 296, [1994] 3 All ER 129, HL, discussed at para 4.17 above.
6   DMPS, Sch Part 1, 1
7   DMPS, s 11(2).
8   DMPS, s 11(6).
9   Legislature and government documents; Reports of court and inquiry proceedings (not required to be contemporaneous); Court notices and advertisements; Public registers and documents; Reports of international organisations and conferences
10 DMPS, s 11 (2) and (6).
11 DMPS, s 11(4).
12 See especially *Fraser v Mirza* 1993 SC (HL) 27, 1993 SLT 527 at 531 per Lord Keith of Kinkel.
13 For an example of the difficulties, see *Fraser v Mirza* 1993 SC (HL) 27, 1993 SLT 527.
14 *Horrocks v Lowe* [1975] AC 135, [1974] 1 All ER 662, HL.

(4) Defences

(a) Defence of truth

15.9 Defamatory statements are false statements. It is not, however, for the pursuer to prove that they are false. When a defamatory meaning is established, this raises a presumption of falsity. It follows that where the statement or imputation can be shown to be truthful it can be justified and there is a complete defence, but the onus of proof lies on the defender. The common law defence of *veritas* has been repealed and a defence of truth enacted.[1] The defence of truth may be employed when the alleged defamation concerns a statement of fact. Common law authorities may be considered in the application of the statutory rules as the court deems appropriate.

What is necessary to establish truth will depend on the nature of the defamatory statement. To allege that someone is a murderer can be justified by proof of one act of murder; but to say someone is a thief implies that he is currently dishonest and the defence is not established simply by showing he was twice convicted of petty theft 23 years before.[2] It may prove unwise to run the defence where the outcome is doubtful. Protracting litigation may exacerbate the harm suffered by the pursuer which may be reflected in a greater award of damages.[3]

If more than one fact is alleged, *veritas* will operate only if all the facts which are defamatory are proved true.[4]

If more than one fact is alleged, the defence will succeed only if all the facts which are defamatory are proved true. Conversely, if some non-defamatory facts are admitted to be false, then provided these facts have not seriously harmed the pursuer's reputation, the defence will still succeed if the defamatory facts can, nevertheless, be shown to be true.[5]

1   DMPS, ss 8 and 5 respectively.
2   *Fletcher v Wilsons* (1885) 12 R 683.
3   *Baigent v BBC* 2001 SC 281, 2001 SLT 427.
4   *Fairbairn v Scottish National Party* 1979 SC 393, 1980 SLT 149 may be considered.
5   DMPS, s 5(2).

(b) Defence of publication on a matter of public interest

15.10 This replaces the old *Reynolds* defence.[1] This defence had developed as an extension of qualified privilege and was confirmed as a defence of responsible journalism in its own right by the House of Lords in *Jameel v Wall Street Journal*.[2] While the success of the *Reynolds* defence was dependent on the ability of the defender to establish that they had acted responsibly in publishing the material complained of,[3] the focus in the statutory defence is firmly on the question of whether publication was in the public interest and the defender's reasonable belief that publication was in the public interest.[4]

In considering the reasonable belief of the defender, the court must make allowance for editorial judgment[5] and, where the complaint arises from an 'accurate and impartial account of a dispute to which the pursuer was a party', must disregard any omission by the defender to verify any defamatory imputation.[6] Otherwise, the court must have regard to all the circumstances of the case in determining whether the defence has been established.[7]

The development of this defence shows the importance to be given to a responsible free press in a democratic society which is enshrined in Article 10 of the European Convention on Human Rights. Given the shift in focus it remains to be seen how much resort will be made to earlier case law on the *Reynolds* defence. English cases on s 4 of the Defamation Act 2013 which is almost identical to s 6 of the DMPS, seem much more likely be cited as persuasive authority.

1   See *Reynolds v Times Newspapers* [2001] 2 AC 127.
2   [2007] 1 AC 359.
3   Lord Nicolls set out a 10-point list of factors indicating the elements of responsible journalism in *Reynolds* [2001] 2 AC 127 at 205.
4   DMPS, s 6(1).
5   DMPS, s 6(4).
6   DMPS, s 6(3).
7   DMPS, s 6(2). See *Serafin v Makiewicz* [2020] 1 LR 2455 at [72].

(c) Defence of honest opinion

15.11   This replaces the old defence of fair comment and plays the same role in that it affords protection to the expression of opinion, classically, as journalistic comment or in the form of a review. Establishing the defence depends on the defender's ability to show that the statement complained of was a matter of opinion and importantly, the statement must indicate 'either in general or specific terms the evidence on which it was based'.[1] Accordingly, a single-star review on trip advisor which merely states: 'This is an appalling hotel, look elsewhere for accommodation', would not be protected. However, the same statement, accompanied by observations that: 'the beds were damp, the bathroom was filthy, breakfast was served only between 5 and 6am and consisted of cereal that did not require the addition of milk to make it soggy, sleep was disturbed by the sounds of the proprietors fighting with each other', would. The Act does not retain the specific requirement of fair comment that the facts must be truly stated but includes within the definition of evidence facts existing at the time of the statement and 'anything which the defender reasonably believed to be a fact at the time the statement was published'.[2]

The opinion, moreover, must be honestly held and the defence will fail where the defender 'did not genuinely hold the opinion conveyed by the statement'.[3] It would, therefore, appear to be possible to challenge opinions based on the expression of alleged facts that the defender could not reasonably have believed on the basis that they do not constitute the evidence required by s 7(3) or that an honest person could not have held the opinion on the basis of that evidence as required by s 7(4). Just as in the old defence of fair comment, the defence of honest opinion allows for some eccentricity of opinion and does not restrict the terms in which opinions may be expressed, the focus is firmly on the honesty of the opinion.

1   DMPS, s 7 (2) and (3).
2   DMPS, s 7(8)(a) and (c).
3   DMPS, s 7(4) and (5). An exception is made where the defender has published the opinion of a different author: see s 7(6).

(5) Remedies

(a) Offer of amends

15.12   Much potentially expensive litigation has been successfully avoided by the printing of a correction and apology. There has been a statutory basis for offers of amends since the Defamation Act 1996.[1] Under the DMPS, before lodging defences, the defender may make in writing an (unqualified) offer to correct the statement or a (qualified) offer to correct a specific defamatory meaning, to provide a sufficient apology and to pay compensation and expenses.[2] The offer may be accepted or rejected by the pursuer. Acceptance of the offer by the pursuer ends further proceedings and in the case of a qualified offer, ends proceedings so far as the defamatory meaning covered in the offer is concerned. The terms of the offer may be enforced.[3] Where an unqualified offer is rejected, this provides a defence to the action precluding the use of any other defence. This defence is only available where the defender did not know or had no reason to believe that the statement referred to the pursuer and was defamatory of them. The defender, however, enjoys a presumption that this is the case which the pursuer may rebut with evidence to the contrary.[4]

1   Defamation Act 1996, s 2.
2   DMPS, s 13.
3   DMPS, s 14. This section also makes provision for determination where parties cannot reach agreement on the form and substance of the correction and apology, on compensation to be paid or on expenses. See s 14(48).
4   DMPS, s 16. Equivalent provisions in respect of the rejection of qualified offers are found in DMPS, s 17. Offers of amends where multiple persons are responsible for a defamatory statement are covered in s 15.

(b) Statement in open court

15.13 The unsuccessful defender may be ordered to publish a summary of the judgment.[1] Where parties have reached an agreement in settlement of proceedings, whether or not this follows an offer of amends, the Act provides for a statement to be made in open court.[2] Furthermore s 30 empowers the court to order display of a notice, for example on a website, to notify the fact that a statement is subject to proceedings or to remove a statement. The court may also prevent persons who were not authors, editors or publishers from any further sale or distribution of material containing the statement complained of. Publication of a statement that is likely to cause serious harm to a person's reputation may, of course, be interdicted.

1   DMPS, s 28.
2   DMPS, s 29.

(c) Damages

15.14 In an action for defamation the individual pursuer is entitled to an award of solatium in respect of damage to reputation and distress and anxiety. Any patrimonial loss must be averred and proved. Although patrimonial loss, if it has been sustained, is relatively easy to assess, solatium is more difficult because it involves no little degree of speculation. In practice, solatium is usually a modest sum in Scots law.[1] Everyone is assumed to be of good character, so solatium is unlikely to be increased if the pursuer is particularly good. But the more eminent the pursuer, the greater the loss of reputation and more will consequently be awarded as solatium. In general, the worse the allegation, the greater the sum that will be awarded; in particular, the sum may be increased if the defender has persisted in the defamatory allegations against the pursuer.[2] However, at the end of the day, solatium is intended to compensate non-patrimonial loss:[3] a person who brings an action primarily to clear his name will receive only a nominal sum.[4]

A number of factors may serve to mitigate awards of solatium. First, if the pursuer's character or reputation is already tainted before the defamatory statement, evidence can be led by the defender to show that the pursuer did not therefore suffer as much as an ordinary person.[5] An immediate retraction of the statement and an apology will mitigate the loss.[6] This will also be the case if the pursuer provoked the defender into making the defamatory statement.[7] Where an offer of amends has been made this this will also mitigate damages.[8]

1   See, eg, *Gilbert v Yorston* 1996 SCLR 1122, 1997 SLT 879, OH (no evidence that any third party believed the defamatory material: no effect on pursuer's career. Pursuer was awarded £1,500 as solatium).

2   *Baigent v British Broadcasting Corpn* 1999 GWD 10-474 (awards of £60,000 and £50,000 were made against the BBC: the attack on the pursuers' personal integrity and professional ability was very vindictive); *Munro v Brown* [2011] CSOH 117: Kinley v Devine [2014] CSOH 67.

3   *Stein v Beaverbrook Newspapers Ltd* 1968 SC 272, 1968 SLT 401.

4   *Gilbert v Yorston* 1996 SCLR 1122, 1997 SLT 879, OH.

5   *Corrigan v Monaghan* 1923 SC 1, 1922 SLT 634.

6   *Morrison v Ritchie & Co* (1902) 4 F 645.

7   *Paul v Jackson* (1884) 11 R460.

8   DMPS s 16(6) and s 17(5).

C.   MALICIOUS PUBLICATION

15.15   Part 2 of the Act makes certain types of publication actionable. The statements covered in this part of the Act are injurious to reputation but need not be defamatory. The Act provides for the actionability of three types of statement: (1) a false and malicious statement about the pursuer's business or business activities;[1] (2) a false and malicious statement about the pursuer's title to land or other property;[2] (3) a false and malicious statement criticising or denigrating the quality, use or treatment of assets owned, possessed or controlled by the pursuer.[3] These correspond broadly to the old verbal injuries of falsehood causing business loss, slander of title and slander of property, all abolished by DMPS, s 27 along with the problematic category of exposing the pursuer to public hatred, contempt and ridicule which has no new statutory equivalent.

In all forms of malicious publication, the statement must be communicated to a third party and it must have caused (or be likely to cause) financial harm to the pursuer. While at common law, proof of sales opportunities lost presented a major hurdle to the recovery of damages,[4] a more generous approach is taken in the Act which stipulates that financial loss does not need to be shown if the statement is more likely than not to cause financial loss.[5]

There is still a considerable hurdle to surmount in terms of proving that the statement was malicious. It must be established in all three forms that: 'the false imputation conveyed by the statement complained of was presented as a statement of fact (rather than a statement of opinion) and was sufficiently credible so as to mislead a reasonable person … and that [the defender] knew that the imputation was false or was recklessly indifferent as to the truth of the imputation …'[6] In addition the pursuer must establish the defender's motivation for publication and this differs according to the form taken. Liability for statements causing harm to business interests requires that the defender's publication was 'motivated by a malicious intention to cause harm to [the pursuer's] business or business activities'.[7] Liability for statements causing doubt as to title to property requires that the defender's publication was 'motivated by a malicious intention to delay or jeopardise a transaction involving the [pursuer's] land or other property'.[8] Finally, liability for statements criticising assets requires that the defender's publication was 'motivated by a malicious intention to cause [the pursuer] financial loss'.[9]

1   DMPS, s 21.
2   DPMS, s 22.
3   DPMS, s 23.
4   See, eg, *Philp v Morton* (1816) Hume 865; *McIrvine v McIrvine* [2012] CSOH 23, 2012 GWD 9-171.
5   DMPS, s 24.
6   DMPS, ss 21(2)(a) and (b)(i), 22(2)(a) and (b)(i) and 23(2)(a) and (b)(i), corresponding to the three forms of malicious publication, are identical.
7   DMPS, s 21(2)(b)(ii).
8   DMPS, s 22(2)(b)(ii).
9   DMPS, s 23(2)(b)(ii).

Part IV

DAMAGES

INTRODUCTION

The purpose of this last chapter is to give a short account of the law of damages. At the outset it is important to remember that no obligation to make reparation arises unless the victim has sustained constituent harm. As we have seen[1] harm is a constituent part of an actionable wrong: *damnum injuria datum*. Moreover, even if the victim has sustained constituent harm there is no liability unless that harm was a reasonable and probable consequence of the defender's wrongful conduct.[2] If the harm was a reasonable and probable consequence of the defender's wrongful conduct, then there has been a *breach* of the defender's duty of care and the defender's liability to make reparation is triggered. Accordingly, once a wrong has been established, the defender is obliged to compensate the pursuer for the *losses* he or she has incurred as a result of the harm sustained by the pursuer which was constitutive of the delict.

Scots law recognises two kinds of reparable losses *viz* non-patrimonial loss and patrimonial loss.

(a)   Non-patrimonial loss

Solatium is the traditional name given to damages for non-patrimonial loss. Non-patrimonial losses can be regarded as invasions of the victim's personality rights in the broadest sense. Thus, solatium can be awarded in relation to the following: victims of defamation and verbal injury for the affront to their dignity caused by the wrong; wrongful conception; wrongful interference with the corpse of a relative, particularly a child; grief arising from the death of a relative; wrongful imprisonment; assault, in particular non-consensual medical procedures; and for pain and suffering arising from personal injuries. Obviously the assessment of an award of solatium is not scientific involving a degree of artificiality and a considerable element of discretion on the part of the judge or jury.

(b)   Patrimonial loss

Patrimonial losses are the economic losses arising from the harm sustained by the victim. These losses derive from or are parasitic upon the harm that the victim has sustained and which was constitutive of the delict. For example, if A suffers personal injuries, he may receive compensation for past loss of earnings, future loss of earnings, loss of pension rights, past and future medical expenses, ie economic losses which *derive* from the personal injuries. Where A's property is damaged, the derivative patrimonial loss is the cost of repair or replacement and if after repair the property is worth less than before it was damaged, the pursuer can recover the diminution in value. (The owner of damaged property may, of course suffer non-patrimonial loss, for example anger and distress if his papers constituting a lifetime's scholarship are destroyed in a fire.) One of the difficulties with reparation for 'pure' economic loss is that unlike personal injury or damage to property cases, the harm which is constitutive of the delict is itself economic loss.

1   See para 3.16 above: *Rothwell v Chemical and Insulating Co Ltd* [2008] 1 AC 281.
2   See para 3.12 ff above: *Muir v Glasgow Corpn* 1943 SC (HL) 102.

CHAPTER 16

Damages

A. REMOTENESS OF LOSSES

16.1 It will be remembered that Scottish courts once took the view that delictual liability would not be imposed upon a defender if the harm sustained by the pursuer was too remote.[1] However, in the present writer's view, these cases should now be analysed as situations where the court was unwilling to impose a duty of care on the defender, ie the duty of care was being used as a threshold device to deny delictual liability.[2] But even where there has been a breach of a duty of care and the defender is liable to make reparation to the pursuer in respect of the losses arising from the constituent harm he or she has sustained, it does not follow that the defender must compensate the pursuer for every loss arising from that harm. Some losses are 'too remote'. Consider the following example:

As a result of his careless driving, A knocks down a pedestrian, B. B will recover solatium[3] for his or her pain and suffering and damages for derivative economic loss. The latter will include loss of wages between the date of the accident and the date of the action; future loss of earnings from the date of the action, if B is unable to work or can work only at a lower-paid job;[4] the cost of medical treatment and nursing up to the date of the action and the cost of such care in the future. However, if as a result of the accident, B was unable to give instructions to his stockbroker to purchase shares which he had intended to buy, or if B was unable to post his football coupon, the profits B would have made on the shares or the dividend he would have won if the coupon had been posted are not recoverable even though they arise from the fact that B was incapacitated as a result of the accident. These losses are too remote and cannot therefore be recovered.

What criteria do the courts use to determine whether or not losses are too remote? The classic statement of the rule on remoteness of losses in Scots law was articulated by the Lord Ordinary (Kinloch) in *Allan v Barclay*:[5]

'The grand rule on the subject of damages is, that none can be claimed except such as naturally and directly arise out of the wrong done; and such, therefore, as may reasonably be supposed to have been in the contemplation of the wrongdoer.'

However, there is a potential contradiction inherent in this statement. While many losses which are reasonably foreseeable also directly arise from the wrong done, it is possible to envisage situations where a loss directly arises from the wrong but is not reasonably foreseeable and vice versa, ie a loss which is reasonably foreseeable but does not arise directly from the wrong.

This problem has been a matter of particular concern in England. In *Re Polemis and Furness, Withy & Co Ltd*,[6] the Court of Appeal held that the question whether particular losses can be recovered depends only on whether they were the direct consequence of the wrongful act. Provided some harm was reasonably foreseeable so that there was a breach of a duty of care, the defendant is liable to compensate for all the harm directly resulting from the breach of duty even if those losses were unforeseeable.

In this case, stevedores carelessly allowed a plank to fall into the hold of a ship. The falling plank caused a spark which in its turn ignited petrol vapour in the hold. The vapour caused a fire which destroyed the vessel. The court held that while the fire was not a reasonably foreseeable consequence of allowing the plank to fall, some damage to the vessel was. In light of these findings, the court was prepared to hold that since it was reasonably foreseeable that some form of harm would result from the negligent act, damages in respect of losses caused by the fire, albeit not reasonably foreseeable, were nevertheless recoverable as a direct consequence of the foreseeable harm. Although this case is often cited as authority for the proposition that reasonable foreseeability plays no part in determining the extent of recoverable losses, such a conclusion may not be entirely justified. If it had been held that it was not foreseeable that the plank would cause any damage at all, the court might well have held that the consequences of the fire were too remote.

However, it may appear illogical to insist that some harm to the pursuer must be foreseen as a reasonable and probable consequence of the defender's act or omission before there is a breach of a duty of care, ie delictual liability, yet allow the pursuer to recover losses directly arising from that breach which were not reasonably foreseeable. In *Overseas Tankship (UK) Ltd v Morts Dock and Engineering Co, The Wagon Mound*,[7] the Privy Council declined to follow *Re Polemis*. In this case, a ship was being bunkered when some oil being loaded on board spilt into the harbour as a result of the carelessness of the appellant's employees. Morts' employees were welding nearby when the spillage happened. Molten metal from their operations fell onto some debris which caught fire; this in turn set the oil alight, causing substantial fire damage to the wharf owned by Morts. It was found as a fact that it was not reasonably foreseeable that the oil could have been ignited in such a way. Although it was reasonably foreseeable that the oil spillage would cause some harm to the respondent's dock, ie by fouling the dock, nevertheless the court held that the appellants were not liable for the losses caused by the unforeseeable fire. If *Re Polemis* had been applied, it is arguable that the appellants would have been liable for the losses caused by the fire, because some harm, ie the fouling of the dock, was foreseeable and the fire could be regarded as a *direct* result of the breach of duty[8] – albeit that the fire was unforeseeable. However, since harm by fire was not reasonably foreseeable as a probable consequence of the spillage, it is submitted that in this case there was no breach of duty of care, ie there was no delictual liability, and therefore it is not a remoteness of losses case at all.[9]

1   See para 5.10 above.
2   The present writer of this sentence was Joe Thomson. It is in accordance with the view expressed here that the now-present writer has moved the treatment of *Muir v Glasgow Corporation* 1943 SC (HL) 3 and reasonable and probable consequences from Chapter 5 on Breach where it was in the 5th edition to Chapter 3 on Duty in the present edition.
3   For the calculation of solatium, see para 16.12 below.
4   For the calculation of loss of future earnings, see para 16.13 ff below.
5   (1864) 2 M 873. The case was concerned with whether an employer could recover damages for the loss of his injured employee's services. In other words, it was concerned with the defender's liability rather than remoteness of losses. Today it would be analysed as an example of non-recoverability of secondary economic loss. However, the passage has always been regarded as an authoritative statement of remoteness of losses.
6   [1921] 3 KB 560, CA.
7   [1961] AC 388, [1961] 1 All ER 404, PC.
8   Although in this case it is equally arguable that the fire was *indirectly* caused as a result of the molten metal falling on the oil.
9   Cf *Hughes v Lord Advocate* 1963 SC (HL) 31, 1963 SLT 150, where personal injuries caused by fire were reasonably foreseeable: only the extent of the injuries was not.

16.2   The Scottish courts have not given authoritative guidance on the matter; instead, reliance is simply placed on Lord Kinloch's 'grand rule'. In *Kelvin Shipping Co, The Baron Vernon v Canadian*

Pacific Railway Co, The Metagama,[1] Viscount Haldane LC opined[2] that when

> 'a collision takes place by the fault of the defendant's ship, the damage is recoverable, in an action for damages if it is the natural and reasonable result of the negligent act, and it will assume that character if it can be shown to be such a consequence as in the ordinary course of things would flow from the situation which the offending ship created'.[3]

Although there are *obiter dicta* that *Re Polemis* does not reflect the law of Scotland,[4] in *Campbell v F and F Moffat (Transport) Ltd*,[5] the Lord Ordinary (Lord Cameron of Lochbroom) held that the test was not whether the loss was reasonably foreseeable but whether it arose naturally and directly out of the wrong. In that case, the pursuer was injured in a road accident and, as a result, his employment was terminated in 1989. Two years later, his former employer closed the mill where the pursuer had worked and gave the employees working at that date *ex gratia* redundancy payments. In his action for damages, the pursuer sought compensation for the loss of the redundancy payment he would have received if his employment had not been terminated two years earlier as a result of the accident. Lord Cameron took the view that this loss was not so utterly speculative that it could not amount to a natural and direct consequence of the accident.

It is submitted that in Scots law it is too simplistic to see the question of remoteness of damages in terms of reasonable foreseeability on the one hand and direct consequences on the other. The courts use a combination of both tests in assessing whether the loss is a natural consequence of the delictual act. It is only if the loss is utterly speculative[6] that the loss will be too remote and not recoverable in an award of damages. On the other hand, what is clear is that in a case of personal injuries, the defender takes her victim as she finds him. If, for example, A, as a result of her carelessness, burns B, if B has a predisposition to cancer which is triggered by the burn, with the result that B dies, A is liable for B's death even if that was not reasonably foreseeable as a consequence of the burn. In this situation, reasonable foreseeability of death is treated as irrelevant or, alternatively, the defender is deemed to have reasonably foreseen that the pursuer could have been an ill, as opposed to healthy, person.[7] Moreover, as we have seen, where the pursuer is a primary victim, the defender is liable for causing mental or psychiatric illness, even though such illness was not reasonably foreseeable: a case of an eggshell personality rather than an eggshell skull![8]

1   1928 SC (HL) 21, 1928 SLT 117.
2   Ibid.
3   However, this case was clearly concerned with the existence of liability rather than remoteness of losses.
4   See, for example, *Cowan v National Coal Board* 1958 SLT (Notes) 19, OH, per the Lord Ordinary (Cameron).
5   1992 SCLR 551, 1992 SLT 962, OH.
6   As it is submitted is the case in the examples of the loss of profits on the shares and the loss of a football pools' dividend: see para 16.1 above.
7   *McKillen v Barclay Curle & Co Ltd* 1967 SLT 41. This is known as 'the thin skull' or 'the eggshell-skull rule'.
8   *Page v Smith* [1996] AC 155, [1995] 2 All ER 736, HL: discussed at para 4.7 above.

16.3   In *Simmons v British Steel*,[1] Lord Rodger summarised[2] the relevant principles thus:

'These authorities suggest that, once liability is established, any question of the remoteness of damage is to be approached along the following lines which may, of course, be open to refinement and development. (1) The starting point is that a defender is not liable for a consequence which is not reasonably foreseeable. (2) While a defender is not liable for damage that was not reasonably foreseeable, it does not follow that he is liable for all damage that was reasonably foreseeable: depending on the circumstances, the defender may not be liable for damage caused by a *novus actus interveniens* or unreasonable conduct on the part of the pursuer, even if it was reasonably foreseeable. (3) Subject to the qualification in (2) if the pursuer's injury is of a kind that was foreseeable, the defender is liable, even if the damage is greater in extent than was foreseeable or it was caused in a way that could not have been foreseen. (4) The defender must take his victim as he finds him (5) subject again to the qualification in (2), where personal injury to the pursuer was reasonably foreseeable, the defender is liable for any personal injury, whether physical or psychiatric, which the pursuer suffers as a result of the wrong-doing.'

With the greatest respect it is thought that this summary is not without difficulties. In particular it appears to confuse issues of initial liability (factors (3) and (5)) with those of remoteness of losses.[3]

In the present writer's view the law on remoteness of losses can be summarised as follows:

(i)   the victim must have sustained harm which is constitutive of delictual liability: normally this means that the harm sustained was a reasonable and probable consequence of the defender's wrongful conduct.[4]

(ii)   The defender is liable for the non-patrimonial and patrimonial losses for which the constitutive harm is the legal cause provided such losses are reasonably foreseeable. There is therefore no liability to make reparation for unforeseeable losses or losses where the constitutive harm is not the legal cause, ie there has been causative fade.[5]

(iii)   In the case of personal injuries only, the defender takes his victim as he finds him and is liable for unforeseeable non-patrimonial and patrimonial losses provided that the defender's wrongful conduct is the legal cause of these losses. This is known as the 'egg shell skull' or 'thin skull' rule. Thus, for example, where the constitutive harm is a foreseeable physical injury, the defender can be liable for the patrimonial and non-patrimonial losses arising from an unforeseeable mental illness always provided the physical injury materially contributed to the mental illness or its recurrence.[6]

1   2004 SC (HL) 94. The case is an unexceptional example of the application of the thin skull rule in respect of liability for the victim's unforeseeable mental illness following foreseeable physical injuries caused by the negligence of the defender. However, the House of Lords held that both the Lord Ordinary (Hardie) and the Second Division failed to apply the relevant principles!

2   Ibid at 115; the authorities cited by Lord Rodger have been removed.

3   Lord Rodger's *dictum* was followed with approval in *Spencer v Wincanton Holdings Ltd (Wincanton Logistics Ltd)* [2009] EWCA Civ 1404. In the present writer's view that was a case on legal causation and not remoteness of losses. For discussion of the case see para 6.7 above.

4   But where the pursuer is a primary victim, ie is within the area of risk of physical harm, mental illness can be constitutive even if it is not reasonably foreseeable and the victim did not suffer any foreseeable physical harm: *Page v Smith* [1996] AC 155. It is thought that the decision is unprincipled on this point.

5   Where a claimant's suicide was the result of depression caused by a personal injury which was a consequence of the defendant's negligence, the suicide was held not to break the chain of causation; see *Corr v IBC Vehicles* [2008] 1 AC 884. This was an extreme case: normally damages would at least be reduced as a result of the victim's contributory fault. There was no causative fade in *Spencer v Wincanton Holdings Ltd (Wincanton Logistics Ltd)* [2009] EWCA Civ 1404 (plaintiff's fall while filling his car at a garage was still a consequence of losing his leg as a result of an accident at work).

6   *Simmons v British Steel* 2004 SC (HL) 94.

16.4   It cannot be stressed enough that the thin skull rule only applies where the victim has suffered personal injuries. In all other cases the losses must be reasonably foreseeable. Thus where the constituent harm is damage to property, any losses sustained by the owner must be reasonably foreseeable before the defender is liable to pay solatium or compensation in respect of them. In *Yearworth v North Bristol NHS Trust*,[1] for example, on the advice of the defendants the claimants had provided samples of semen which would be put into cold storage by the hospital fertility unit. This was done because the men were undergoing chemotherapy which might render them infertile. Owing to the negligence of the hospital the semen thawed and the sperm died. The men suffered mental distress when they were told that the sperm had been lost and they would therefore not be able to have children as a result of IVF if they became infertile. (Fortunately, they regained their fertility after the chemotherapy ended.) The Court of Appeal held that the sperm constituted property which was owned by the men. The damage to the sperm was the constituent harm. Therefore, the defendants would only be liable for the claimants' non-patrimonial loss if the men's distress arising from the wrongful destruction of their sperms was reasonably foreseeable which in the circumstances the court held it was.

Where the intentional wrongs are concerned, different principles apply and the defender is liable to make reparation for all losses suffered by the pursuer which directly arise from the wrong – whether or not these losses are reasonably foreseeable. The intention to injure the pursuer, which is normally an essential requisite of these delicts, disposes of any question of remoteness of losses.[2]

1   [2009] EWCA Civ 37. In *Attica v British Gas* [1988] QB 304 the plaintiff obtained damages for mental illness caused by seeing her house destroyed by fire due to the negligence of the defendants since mental harm to the owner of the property was reasonably foreseeable as she actually witnessed the fire.
2   *Smith New Court Securities Ltd v Scrimgeour Vickers (Asset Management) Ltd* [1997] AC 254, [1996] 4 All ER 769, HL; *Barry v Sutherland* 2002 SLT 413.

B.   CALCULATION OF DAMAGES

(1) Introduction

16.5   The purpose of an award of damages is to compensate the pursuer for those losses which arose as a result of the delict. It is intended, so far as money can, to place the pursuer in the financial position he would have been if the wrong had not occurred.[1] Where the claim is in respect of damage to property, damages are relatively simple to assess, ie the cost of repair or replacement of the property.[2] If after repair the property is worth less than before it was damaged the pursuer can recover the diminution in value.[3]

It is now settled that if the cost of repair is greater than would reasonably be expected because of the owner's impecuniosity at the time the property was damaged, the pursuer can recover for the increased costs of repair.[4] In *Network Rail Infrastructure Ltd v Conarken Group Ltd*,[5] the defendants damaged the plaintiff's rail infrastructure. This led to the temporary closure of the line. Under track access agreements, the plaintiffs had to pay compensation to train operating companies who had suffered financial loss as a result of the consequent disruption of their schedules. The Court of Appeal held that the cost of repair and the loss of revenue flowed naturally from the damage to the rails. The economic loss sustained by the plaintiff in compensating the operating companies under the agreements was therefore not too remote. As it was in the public interest to have punctual and reliable train services and because the track agreements had been carefully drafted, the defendants were liable to pay damages in respect of the compensation the plaintiffs had paid to the train operators.

Greater difficulties arise in calculating damages in wrongful conception and wrongful birth, pure economic loss and personal injury cases and these deserve fuller treatment.

1   See, for example, *O'Brien's Curator Bonis v British Steel plc* 1991 SC 315, 1991 SCLR 831, 1991 SLT 477 at 480 per the Lord President (Hope); *Cantwell v Criminal Injuries Compensation Board* 2002 SC (HL) 1.
2   The pursuer still incurs a reparable loss even though he could have pursued a contractual claim against a third party to repair the property: *Ford Motor Co Ltd v HLM Design Ltd* 1997 SLT 837, OH.
3   *Hunter v National Specialist Steeplejacks* 2004 GWD 3-49.
4   *Alcoa Minerals of Jamaica v Herbert Broderick* [2002] 1 AC 371; *Lagden v O'Connor* [2004] 1 All ER 277. In these circumstances, the pursuer is not in breach of his duty to mitigate the loss by waiting until he could afford the repairs.
5   [2011] EWCA Civ 644.

(2) Wrongful conception and wrongful birth

16.6   As we have seen,[1] the infringement of a parent's right not to have a child is reparable in Scots law. Applying the remoteness of losses rule, the parents should be entitled to receive compensation for the losses which are reasonably foreseeable as a direct consequence of the wrongful conception. These would include the mother's pain and suffering during the pregnancy and birth of the child; any loss of the mother's earnings during the pregnancy; and the cost of rearing the child. However, in *McFarlane v Tayside Health Board*[2] the House of Lords held that parents could not recover as damages the cost of bringing up a healthy child conceived as a result of medical negligence. Their Lordships did so on grounds of legal policy. Departing from the principle that the function of the law of delict is corrective justice, ie to compensate the pursuer for the losses arising from a wrong, the House held that as a matter of distributive justice compensation for the cost of alimenting a healthy child could not be condoned. To do so would be: (i) disproportionate to the defender's fault; (ii) a further inroad to the principle that pure economic loss is prima facie not recoverable in delict (albeit that the economic loss in such cases is derivative, ie *derives* from the wrongful conception); (iii) to regard the child as a financial liability and nothing else; (iv) to necessitate an attempt to balance the cost of a child's upbringing against the unquantifiable rewards of parenthood; and (v) a potential drain on the limited resources of the NHS which would affect the community's sense of how such resources should be allocated.

The 'principle' in *McFarlane* that the cost of rearing a healthy child could not be recovered in wrongful conception cases was reaffirmed by the House of Lords in *Rees v Darlington Memorial Hospital NHS Trust*.[3] In this case, the child was healthy, but the mother was blind. A majority of their Lordships[4] held that the mother's disability was not a ground for distinguishing *McFarlane*. However, they took the view that an award of solatium did not adequately recognise the wrongful infringement of the mother's freedom to limit the size of her family.[5] Accordingly, she should receive a conventional – non-compensatory – award of £15,000 to afford some measure of recognition of the wrong she had suffered.[6]

McFarlane involved the wrongful[7] conception of a healthy child. What of the situation where a disabled child is born but the mother lost the opportunity to terminate the pregnancy as a result of the defender's failure to carry out the appropriate pre-natal tests? In *McLelland v Glasgow Health Board*,[8] an Extra Division held that in wrongful birth cases the principle in *McFarlane* also applied to exclude the cost of the child's basic maintenance: however, any increased costs attributable to the child's special needs could be recovered. In England, the Court of Appeal reached a similar conclusion in *Parkinson v St James and Seacroft University Hospital Trust*.[9] Accordingly, it would appear that while the basic costs of alimenting a disabled child cannot be recovered, any extra expenditure involved in attempting to make the child's upbringing as normal as possible.

These decisions illustrate once again the readiness of the House of Lords to depart from the application of recognised rules of delictual liability to avoid a result which is not consonant with their Lordships' view of what is desirable in terms of social and economic policy.

1   See paras 4.13–4.15 above.
2   2000 SC (HL) 1.
3   [2004] 1 AC 309, [2003] 4 All ER 987.
4   Lords Bingham, Nicholls, Millet and Scott; Lords Steyn, Hope and Hutton dissenting.
5   *Quaere* whether this also applies to a father's freedom to do so?
6   There can be few more blatant examples of judicial 'legislation'.
7   Ie a conception arising from a failed sterilisation as a result of medical negligence.
8   2002 SLT 446. It should be noted that the father as well as the mother received solatium in respect of the birth of the disabled child.
9   [2002] QB 266. This decision was approved by Lords Steyn, Hope and Hutton in *Rees*.

(3) Pure economic loss claims

16.7   In some situations when delictual liability for pure economic loss has been recognised, it is relatively simple to calculate the loss. For example, in the case of a disappointed legatee, the loss is the value of the lost legacy.[1] Where a surveyor has been negligent and failed to discover defects, the loss to the purchaser is either the cost of repair or the diminution in the value of the property.[2] But difficulties have arisen in quantifying loss when the pursuer has been induced to enter into a transaction as a result of the defender's misrepresentation.

1   *White v Jones* [1995] 2 AC 207, [1995] 1 All ER 691, HL; *Holmes v Bank of Scotland* 2002 SLT 544.
2   *Patel v Hooper & Jackson* [1999] 1 All ER 992, CA.

(a) Fraudulent misrepresentation

16.8   It is well settled that when A has entered into a transaction as a result of B's fraudulent misrepresentation, B is liable for all A's losses arising directly from the transaction, even though some of them might not be reasonably foreseeable.[1] This would include losses which A incurs as a result of a general fall in the market value of the assets involved in the transaction.

1   *Smith New Court Securities Ltd v Scrimgeour Vickers (Asset Management) Ltd* [1997] AC 254, [1996] 4 All ER 769, HL; *Barry v Sutherland* 2002 SLT 413.

(b) Negligent misrepresentation

16.9 What is the position if A has entered into a transaction as a result of B's negligent misrepresentation?[1] When the misrepresentation takes the form of *advice*, ie B advises A to enter into a particular transaction, then B is liable for all the losses incurred by A as a consequence of entering into the transaction, provided such losses are reasonably foreseeable.[2] Again, this could include losses which A incurs as a result of a general fall in the market value of the assets involved in the transaction.

However, when the misrepresentation takes the form of B providing *information* which A uses to decide whether to enter a particular transaction, the House of Lords[3] has imposed a cap on B's potential liability. In other words, B is only liable for that part of A's loss which was a reasonably foreseeable consequence of the information being wrong. Consider the following examples:

(i) B *advises* A to lend £10 million to C, using C's property as security. C defaults. Owing to a general fall in the market value of property, C's property is now worth only £5 million. A can recover from B all foreseeable losses arising from his entering into the transaction with C, ie £10 million – £5 million = £5 million.

(ii) B tells A that C's property is worth £15 million. In fact, it is worth only £12 million. A decides to lend C £10 million, using C's property as security. C defaults. Owing to a general fall in the market value of property, C's property is now worth only £5 million. A's loss is £10 million – £5 million = £5 million. However, B is only liable to the extent that his information was wrong, ie the difference between the negligent valuation and the actual value at the time the information was given: £15 million – £12 million = £3 million.

There are difficulties in defending the judicial reasoning for applying a cap in negligent information cases.[4] Nevertheless, it appears to be settled law. Moreover, where the pursuer has been contributorily negligent in entering into the transaction (which is often the case), the House of Lords has held that the deduction should be made from the pursuer's total loss, not the loss recoverable after the cap has been fixed.[5] So if, in example (ii), A was 20 per cent contributorily negligent, A's damages would be £5 million – £1 million = £4 million: and A would still recover £3 million from B.

318   *Damages*

It should also be remembered that in cases of fraudulent as well as negligent misrepresentation, the pursuer must take reasonable steps to mitigate his loss.[6]

1   Duties to disclose material matters in pre-contract negotiations are discussed in *University of St Andrews v Headon Holdings Ltd* [2017] CSIH 61 (Ex Div).
2   *Bristol and West Building Society v Rollo Steven and Bond* 1998 SLT 9, OH; *Hamilton v Allied Domecq plc* 2005 SC 437. The pursuer's transaction must be within the nature and scope of the defender's duty of care: *Newcastle Building Society v Paterson Robertson and Graham* 2001 SC 734. Where, as a consequence of negligent advice, the pursuer loses a right in land, the potential development value of the land can be recovered: *Paul v Ogilvy* 2001 SLT 171. The time spent by the pursuer in dealing with the problems resulting from the defender's negligence is a recoverable head of loss but not the time spent in preparation for the litigation: *Lomond Assured Properties v McGrigor Donald* 2000 SLT 797.
3   *South Australia Asset Management Corpn v York Montague Ltd* [1997] AC 191, [1996] 3 All ER 365, HL.
4   See, eg, Joe Thomson 'Damages for Misrepresentation' 1997 SLT (News) 301.
5   *Platform Home Loans Ltd v Oyston Shipways Ltd* [2002] 2 AC 190, [1999] 1 All ER 833, HL.
6   *Standard Chartered Bank* v *Pakistan National Shipping Corpn* [1995] 2 Lloyd's Rep 365.

16.10   Difficulties can arise in determining when the pursuer has sustained the loss. In some cases, a loss is sustained as soon as the pursuer enters into a transaction after being given negligent advice. For example, after consulting his solicitor, A agrees to guarantee her son's business debts. She grants a standard security over her house in favour of her son's creditor. The business fails and the creditor enforces the standard security. She sues the solicitor alleging that she had not been advised sufficiently on the nature of the transaction and the standard security. Following the English case of *Foster v Outred & Co*,[1] A's loss would be held to have arisen when she granted the standard security and not when the creditor enforced it: the loss would be the difference in value between an encumbered and unencumbered property. On the other hand, there is no reason to believe that the business will fail. Nevertheless in *Osborne & Hunter Ltd v Hardie Caldwell*[2] the Second Division held that while as a general rule there may be no loss until there is default, each case turns on its own facts: in this case it was negligent to advise anyone to lend money to the borrower and accordingly the client sustained a loss as soon as he parted with his money. In *Law Society v Sephton & Co*,[3] the House of Lords, approving *Foster v Outred*, held that loss occurred when a contingent liability depressed the value of property or led to a party to a bilateral transaction receiving less than he should have done or to be worse off than if he had not entered into the transaction but that the mere possibility of an obligation to pay money in the future does not of itself constitute loss until the contingency in fact occurs.

1   [1982] 1 WLR 86.
2   1999 SLT 153.
3   [2006] 2AC 543.

(4) Personal injury claims

16.11   Where a party suffers personal injuries as a result of the delictual conduct of the defender, he is entitled to obtain solatium in respect of non-patrimonial losses such as pain and suffering and compensation for any derivative economic loss which he has sustained. Again, 'the objective' is, so far as money can, to compensate the injured party for the consequences of the wrongful act.[1] The pursuer can claim in respect of loss, injury and damage suffered. It is now the practice to divide the claim into various heads of losses. Although it is sensible and convenient to do so, it is always important to remember that these are not several discrete claims but a *single* claim which can be regarded as falling into several parts for the purposes of quantification.[2] Compensation for the pain and suffering as a result of physical injury is known as solatium; compensation in respect of derivative economic loss is known as damages.

1   *Admiralty Comrs v SS Susquehanna (Owners)* [1926] AC 655, HL.
2   *Irving v Hiddleston* 1998 SCLR 350, 1998 SLT 912, OH.

(a) Solatium

16.12   It is, of course, clear that no money sum can in effect compensate for non-patrimonial losses such as pain and suffering. In *Wright v British Railways Board*[1] Lord Diplock said that

'such loss is not susceptible of *measurement* in money. Any figure at which the assessor of damages arrives cannot be other than artificial and, if the aim is that justice meted out to all litigants should be even handed instead of depending on idiosyncrasies of the assessor, whether jury or judge, the figure must be "basically a conventional figure derived from an experience of awards in comparable cases"'.[2]

In *McMillan v McDowall*, the judge opined that 'While the assessment of solatium is not a precise science and has frequently been called a jury question, the view of [a Lord Ordinary] in a similar case must be treated with respect.'³

The court therefore approaches the question of solatium on the basis of comparing one case with another and making a determination taking into account the severity and nature of the injuries sustained by the pursuer. The court assesses solatium as at the date of the proof and does not attempt to assess solatium as it would have been at the date of the injury itself.

In making an award of solatium the court takes into account not only the extent of the injury but also the pursuer's awareness of pain.⁴ No award can be made if, as a result of his injuries, the pursuer has been rendered permanently unconscious. Such awards are made not only in respect of physical injury. A person who, for example, suffers from an identifiable psychological condition can be awarded damages where the condition arises as a consequence of a delict.⁵ Where the pursuer had suffered abuse as a child, he was awarded £75,000 as solatium.⁶ In *Maclean v Lothian and Borders Fire Brigade*,⁷ an award of solatium took into account the pursuer's loss of congenial employment.

In making its assessment of solatium, the court takes into account not only the pain and suffering which has been experienced by the pursuer but also the pain and suffering which he is likely to have in the future. A global award is made. The award also takes into account the pursuer's loss of amenity. Everything which reduces the pursuer's enjoyment of life, which has been sustained as a result of the accident, will be reflected in the award of solatium. It has been held in England that the important element in such a claim is the fact of deprivation of amenity and not whether the injured person is aware of such deprivation.⁸ Also included in an award of solatium is the pain and suffering occasioned when the pursuer is, was, or at any time will be, likely to become aware that his expectancy of life has been shortened by his injuries.⁹

1   [1983] 2 AC 733, [1983] 2 All ER 698, HL.
2   [1983] 2 All ER 698 at 699 (Lord Diplock's emphasis). It is submitted that the position is the same in Scots law.
3   *McMillan v McDowall* 1993 SLT 311, OH, at 312 per T G Coutts QC.
4   *Lim Poh Choo v Camden and Islington Area Health Authority* [1980] AC 174, [1979] 2 All ER 910, HL.
5   *Clark v Scottish Power plc* 1994 SCLR 202, 1994 SLT 924; *Lawson v Scotdem Ltd* 1999 GWD 8-393. Distress has, on occasion, been the subject of an award of solatium even in the absence of physical injury or mental illness: *Fraser v D M Hall & Son* 1997 SLT 808; *McLelland v Greater Glasgow Health Board* 2002 SLT 446 (distress to a parent caused by the wrongful birth of a handicapped child).

6   *J v Fife Council* 2009 SLT 160.
7   1998 SCLR 1004, OH.
8   *Lim Poh Choo v Camden and Islington Area Health Authority* [1980] AC 174, [1979] 2 All ER 910, HL. Of course, if the person has been rendered unconscious, he will not obtain compensation for pain and suffering.
9   Damages (Scotland) Act 2011, s 1 (2).

(b) Patrimonial loss

16.13   Having assessed damages in respect of solatium the court must then turn to the question of patrimonial loss. The court first assesses the pursuer's past loss, ie loss incurred between the date of the accident and the date of the proof. It then attempts to assess the pursuer's future loss.

16.14   (i) Damages for patrimonial loss to the date of proof If the pursuer has been out of work since the date of his accident, he will be entitled to be compensated for his loss of income. This loss can take various forms such as loss of wages or salary, a reduction in a share of partnership profits or loss of a dividend in a single-employee company.[1] In addition, the pursuer will frequently have a claim for expenses. The general rule is that reasonable expenses are recoverable. Consequently, reasonable medical expenses can be recovered even if it is shown at a later stage that they are unnecessary.[2] Expenses need not be confined to medical or nursing services. By s 8 of the Administration of Justice Act 1982, when a person has sustained personal injuries or has died in consequence of the personal injuries he has sustained, the defender is liable to pay damages in respect of necessary services which have been, or will be, rendered to the injured person by a relative in consequence of the injuries in question. Section 9 of the Administration of Justice Act 1982 also imposes an obligation upon the wrongdoer to pay to the injured person a reasonable sum by way of damages when he is unable, as a result of the accident, to render gratuitous personal services to his family.

In calculating loss of earnings, the pursuer's income tax must be taken into account and his liability to pay National Insurance contributions.[3] Accordingly, in so far as past patrimonial loss is concerned, the wages which form the basis of the calculation are the pursuer's net earnings.

16.15   (ii) Damages for future patrimonial loss This head of claim is by far the most important in assessing damages in respect of personal injury. The first stage is to assess damages in respect of future loss of earnings.[4] This is done by taking the loss of the pursuer's net earnings at the date of proof and calculating that on an annual basis. The courts do not attempt to speculate on future rates of taxes and National Insurance contributions but base their calculation on the rates current at the date of proof.[5] No allowance is made for possible increases in the pursuer's earnings if he had not been injured. The figure produced is known as the 'multiplicand'.

16.16   The second stage is to find a 'multiplier'. The Ogden tables provide actuarial calculations of lump sums which are required to provide incomes for different persons at different ages. In *Wells v Wells*,[6] the House of Lords laid down that the rate of return on the investment of the damages should be 3 per cent, and that the Ogden tables should be used as the *starting point* for finding the appropriate multiplier. The traditional Scottish approach was to use the Ogden tables as a check on the multiplier which was found by less scientific methods. Nevertheless, the guidelines laid down by the House of Lords in *Wells* have been followed by the Scottish courts.[7] After taking the appropriate multiplier for the tables, there will usually be a deduction to take into account contingencies relating to the pursuer other than death, for example early retirement or redundancy.[8]

In cases where the victim's expectation of life has been diminished, in assessing the amount of future patrimonial loss, the court is to assume that the pursuer will live until the date when his death would have been expected had he not been injured. This is known as the notional date of death. In other words, the multiplier is to be determined on the basis of the notional date of death rather than the date when it is expected that the pursuer will actually die. The period between the expected date of death and the notional date of death is known as the lost period. In calculating the multiplicand in respect of the lost years the court will consider what the pursuer would have earned had he not been injured and what benefits he would have received and then deduct from that amount 25 per cent of the total: the 25 per cent reduction represents what would have been the pursuer's living expenses during the lost period had the injuries not been sustained.[9]

1   *Anthony v Brabbs* 1998 SLT 1137.
2   *Clippens Oil Co Ltd v Edinburgh and District Water Trustees* 1907 SC (HL) 9, 15 SLT 92; *Rubins v Walker* 1946 SC 215.

3   *British Transport Commission v Gourlay* [1956] AC 185, [1955] 3 All ER 796, HL;
    Cooper v Firth Brown [1963] 2 All ER 31, [1963] 1 WLR 148.
4   Future loss of earnings is a matter of chance, not a fact to be proved on the
    balance of probabilities and so the test is one of 'real and substantial chance'.
    Malcolm v Dundee City Council 2017 SLT 1008
5   *British Transport Commission v Gourlay* [1956] AC 185.
6   [1999] 1 AC 345. The House of Lords felt empowered to lay down a 3 per
    cent return because the pursuer would be assumed to invest the damages in
    index-linked government stock rather than in equities which might give a
    higher return but which, of course, are a less safe investment. Under s 1 of the
    Damages Act 1996, the Lord Chancellor and the Secretary of State for Scotland
    have the power to prescribe the rate of return. This has now been reduced to
    2.5 per cent: Damages (Personal Injury) (Scotland) Order 2002 (SI 2002/46),
    art 3.
7   *McNulty v Marshalls Food Group Ltd* 1999 SC 195; *McManus' Executrix v Babcock
    Energy Ltd* 1999 SC 569.
8   Sometimes the multiplier produced by the Ogden tables is not suitable in a
    particular case where, for example, the injured person may be able to return
    to relatively well paid work after retraining: see for example *McGhee v Diageo
    plc* [2008] CSOH 74; *Brand v Transocean North Sea Ltd* [2011] CSOH 57.
9   Damages (Scotland) Act 2011, s 1.

16.17   The third stage is for the court to multiply the multiplicand
by the multiplier to give a lump sum. So, for example, if the
multiplicand is £20,000 and the multiplier is 10, then the total
sum awarded is £200,000. The pursuer is expected to live off the
income and capital, the theory being that the lump sum will have
been consumed by the date the pursuer dies!

Where a pursuer is severely injured, damages can be awarded
for the cost of her maintenance, nursing and medical care in the
future. Again, the multiplicand/multiplier method is adopted.
The court assesses the cost of maintenance and care on an annual
basis and then applies a multiplier based on the Ogden tables.[1]

Loss of pension rights can also be taken into account in assessing
future patrimonial loss,[2] as can the pursuer's general loss of value
in the labour market. In *Hill v Wilson*,[3] damages were awarded for
impairment to earning capacity as opposed to loss of future wages.
It is particularly difficult to assess damages when the injured
person is a child. In such a case, 'it has never been suggested that
damages should be assessed on such a basis, namely on a basis
which provides not only reasonable compensation but in effect a
guarantee of future financial security'.[4] In some cases, the court
will abandon the multiplicand/multiplier method of calculating
future patrimonial loss. This would happen where, for example,
the pursuer has been able to continue working albeit on light work
at a reduced wage, or there is evidence that the pursuer will be

able to resume employment in the very near future, even though the job may be lower paid than previously.[5]

Personal injury cases can be tried by jury. Juries tend to award higher damages than judges, particularly in relation to solatium. Although a court can order a new trial if the sum awarded is excessive, it will not do so unless the damages awarded are beyond what a reasonable jury would award and there is serious injustice: the fact that a judge would have awarded considerably less is not sufficient.[6] In complex cases, particularly those involving future loss of earnings special cause may be shown for withholding jury trial.[7]

1   For the courts' approach before *Wells v Wells* [1998] 3 All ER 481, [1998] 3 WLR 329, HL, see *O'Brien's Curator Bonis v British Steel plc* 1991 SC 315, 1991 SCLR 831, 1991 SLT 477.

2   *Mitchell v Glenrothes Development Corpn* 1991 SLT 284, OH (conventional multiplicand/multiplier method used); *Cantwell v Criminal Injuries Compensation Board* 2002 SC (HL) 1.

3   1998 SC 81, 1998 SLT 69, OH.

4   *O'Connor v Matthews* 1996 SLT 408 at 412, per the Lord Ordinary (Marnoch).

5   *Stevenson v British Coal Corpn* 1989 SLT 136; *McGhee v Diageo plc* [2008] CSOH 74.

6   *Girvan v Inverness Farmers Dairy (No 2)* 1998 SC (HL) 1. Differences between judge and jury awards are discussed in *Young v McVean* [2014] CSOH 13, 2014 SLT 934 and *Currie v Esure Services Ltd* [2014] CSIH 112, 2015 SC 351.

7   See for example *Lewendon v International Paper (UK) Ltd* [2011] CSOH 116.

(5) Interest

16.18   Having assessed the quantity of damages, the court is obliged to consider the question of interest. Interest is payable under the Interest on Damages (Scotland) Act 1958, as amended by the Interest on Damages (Scotland) Act 1971.

Although solatium is awarded as a lump sum, it is important for the purpose of awards of interest to distinguish past and future solatium. Interest is only awarded on past solatium.[1] Past solatium is a sum awarded for the pursuer's pain and suffering until the date of proof. But if the pursuer is experiencing pain and suffering and loss of amenities at the date of the proof, the court will estimate damages to compensate the pursuer for the fact that these may continue in the future. So, for example, a court might award a total sum of £10,000 by way of solatium, made up of £6,000 for past solatium and £4,000 for future solatium. Interest on past solatium is paid at the average court rate for the period between the date of the accident and when the 'pain' diminished:

this could, of course, have occurred before the date of the proof. If the pursuer is still suffering pain at the date of proof, interest will be awarded on past solatium at half the average court rate.[2]

Subject to the court's discretion, interest on damages for patrimonial loss runs from the date of the accident.[3] Again, although a global sum is awarded, damages are divided between past and future loss. In the case of past losses, interest is awarded at one half of the average court rate from the date of the accident to the date of proof. There is no interest payable on awards in respect of future patrimonial loss.[4] The rules applicable to interest in respect of personal injuries operate without prejudice to the general rule which awards interest at the court rate from the date of decree until the date of payment by the defender.

1   *Smith v Middleton* 1972 SC 30; *J v Fife Council* 2009 SLT 160.
2   *Keicher v National Coal Board* 1988 SLT 318; *Preston v Grampian Health Board* 1988 SLT 435.
3   *Macrae v Reed & Mallik Ltd* 1961 SC 68, 1961 SLT 96.
4   *Hill v Wilson* 1998 SLT 69.

(6) Deductions from awards

16.19 Deductions may have to be made from an award of damages for patrimonial loss. Section 10 of the Administration of Justice Act 1982 prohibits the taking into account for the purposes of reduction of damages any benefit the pursuer received in respect of: (a) any contractual pension or benefit;[1] (b) any pension or retirement benefit to which s 2(1) of the Law Reform (Personal Injuries) Act 1948 applied; (c) any benefit payable from public funds in respect of any period after the date of the award of damages which is designed to secure to the injured person or any relative of his a minimum level of subsistence; (d) any statutory redundancy payment;[2] (e) any payment made to the injured person or to any relative of his by the injured person's employer following upon the injuries in question where the recipient is under an obligation to reimburse the employer in the event of damages being recovered in respect of his injuries; and (f) any payment of a benevolent character made to the injured person or to any relative by any person following upon the injuries in question. The section directs, however, that any remuneration or earnings from employment, any unemployment benefit payable from public funds payable prior to the date of the award of damages, or any payment of a benevolent character made by the person responsible for the accident to the injured person, shall be taken into account. Any savings to the pursuer as a result of being maintained in hospital or accommodation provided by a care home service is deducted.[3]

Prior to the introduction of the Social Security Act 1989, in assessing damages for patrimonial loss a deduction was made of only one-half of the value of certain specified benefits, ie sickness, invalidity or disablement benefit, which the pursuer had received during a period of five years from the date of the accident; but in *Hodgson v Trapp*[4] the House of Lords held that the full value of other benefits, such as attendance and mobility allowances, was to be deducted. However, the Social Security Act 1989 made major changes and the law was consolidated in the Social Security Administration Act 1992, Part IV (ss 81–104): Part IV has now been restated, with amendments, in the Social Security (Recovery of Benefits) Act 1997.

When damages are awarded, heads of loss are relevant for the purpose of the Social Security (Recovery of Benefits) Act 1997:

(1)   compensation[5] for earnings lost during 'the relevant period';

(2)   compensation for the cost of care incurred over the relevant period; and

(3)   compensation for loss of mobility during the relevant period.

The following benefits paid over the relevant period are deducted as follows:

From head (1):	disability working allowance, disablement pension, incapacity benefit, income support, invalidity pension and allowance, jobseeker's allowance, reduced earnings allowance, severe disablement allowance, sickness benefit, statutory sick pay, unemployability supplement and unemployment benefit;
From head (2):	attendance allowance, the care component of disability living allowance and any disablement pension increase;
From head (3):	mobility allowance and the mobility component of disability living allowance.[6]

The 'relevant period' is five years from the date of the accident or five years from first claiming benefit as a consequence of a disease. Thus, benefits paid over that five-year period are recoverable from the relevant head of loss. Payments which are paid thereafter are not recoverable. When damages are paid *before* the end of five years, the relevant period ends at the date of payment; therefore, benefits paid after that date but before the five-year period ends are not recoverable.[7] The person paying damages, the compensator, deducts the amount of recoverable benefits from the pursuer's compensation[8] which he then pays to the Secretary of State.[9]

1   *Lewicki v Brown & Root Wimpey Highland Fabricators Ltd* 1996 SC 200, 1996 SCLR 680, 1996 SLT 1283 (payment under employer's long-term disability scheme held to be a contractual benefit and not deducted: cf if it had been treated as earnings or remuneration from employment). Where the pursuer's claim is in respect of loss of earnings and loss of a contractual retirement pension, then s 10(a) applies to the claim for loss of earnings so that his ill-health pension is not deducted but s 10(a) does *not* apply to the claim for loss of a contractual retirement pension so that his ill-health pension has to be brought into account: *Cantwell v Criminal Injuries Compensation Board* 2002 SC (HL) 1.
2   Reversing *Wilson v National Coal Board* 1981 SC (HL) 9, 1981 SLT 67. An *ex gratia* non-statutory payment falls to be deducted: *Duncan v Glacier Metal Co Ltd* 1988 SCLR 320, 1988 SLT 479, OH.
3   Administration of Justice Act 1982, s 11 (a) and (b).
4   [1989] AC 807, [1988] 3 All ER 870, HL.
5   Compensation includes interest on an award of damages for loss of earnings: *Griffiths v British Coal Corpn* [2001] 1 WLR 1493.
6   Social Security (Recovery of Benefits) Act 1997, Sch 2.
7   SS(RB)A 1997, s 3. See *Mitchell v Laing* 1998 SC 342. This case provides an excellent example of literal construction of a statute by the Lord President (Rodger).
8   SS(RB)A 1997, s 6. The compensator obtains a certificate specifying the amount of recoverable benefits paid to the pursuer.
9   SS(RB)A 1997, s 7.

16.20   A major effect of the legislation is to abolish the provision that only one-half of the specified benefits should be taken into account in assessing damages. Under the Social Security (Recovery of Benefits) Act 1997, all the specified benefits received by the pursuer during the relevant period are fully to be taken into account. Benefits received after the relevant period are not affected and are not to be taken into account. The position is therefore that both pursuers and defenders are worse off under the new legislation.

As far as the pursuer is concerned, he is worse off by not keeping half the value of any sickness, invalidity or disablement benefit received during the relevant period. He is, however, better off in that after the relevant period, those benefits which would have previously been deducted in full when assessing damages under the rule in *Hodgson v Trapp*,[1] for example attendance and mobility allowances, are no longer taken into account. Most importantly, awards of solatium are no longer subject to deduction of recoverable benefits. The defender is worse off in that (i) he now pays the specified benefits in full during the relevant period, whereas before he paid only half their value to the pursuer as damages, and (ii) he can no longer take advantage of the rule in *Hodgson v Trapp*, ie that the full value of other benefits paid to the pursuer would be deducted when assessing the damages.

When the compensation is less than a prescribed sum, it will be treated as a small payment, and no deduction in respect of benefits paid during the relevant period will be made.[2]

1   [1989] AC 807, [1988] 3 All ER 870, HL.
2   Social Security (Recovery of Benefits) Act 1997, Sch 1.

C.   PROVISIONAL AND INTERIM DAMAGES

16.21   The normal rule in actions of damages for personal injuries is that the damages are assessed once and for all at the date of proof. As a consequence, pursuers used to delay bringing proceedings for a considerable period until they could ascertain the full extent of their loss. Pursuers often suffered hardship during the period between the accident and the date of proof. The situation was particularly unfair if the pursuer's physical condition was likely to deteriorate as a result of the injuries at some time in the future after the date of the proof. In *Stevenson v Pontifex and Wood*[1] the Lord President (Inglis) observed:[2]

> 'I hold the true rule of practice based on sound principle to be, that though the delict ..., be of such a nature that it will necessarily be followed by injurious consequences in the future, or though it may for this reason be impossible to ascertain with precise accuracy at the date of the action ... the amount of loss which will result, yet the whole damage must be recovered in one action.'[3]

A pursuer's position in these circumstances has, to some extent, been alleviated by s 12 of the Administration of Justice Act 1982, which provides that the court is entitled to make an award of provisional damages in respect of personal injuries. Such an award can be made when it is proved, or admitted, that there is a risk that at some definite or indefinite time in the future, the pursuer will, as a result of the act or omission of the defender, which gave rise to the cause of the action, develop some serious disease or some serious deterioration in his physical or mental condition.[4] Provisional damages can only be awarded where the defender was, at the time of the accident giving rise to the cause of action, either a public authority or an insured person.[5] The purpose of this provision is therefore to give the pursuer an opportunity to claim damages in circumstances where his position is likely to worsen but where he cannot assess the full extent of his loss because the condition will take some time to deteriorate.

Before an award of provisional damages can be made, the pursuer must establish that there is a risk[6] that at some time in the future he will develop some serious disease or some serious deterioration in his physical or mental condition. Although assessment of the risk may be difficult,[7] it is clear that the risk must be more than *de minimis*.[8] There must be evidence that there is the possibility of a *serious* deterioration in the pursuer's condition.[9] If, for example, the pursuer's health or disability will become worse incrementally, there are no grounds for an award of provisional damages because there is no 'clear cut and severable threshold' when the pursuer could apply for damages in the future on the basis that a serious deterioration had in fact taken place.[10] Although the deterioration must be as a consequence of the wrongful conduct of the defender that led to the pursuer's personal injuries in the first place, nevertheless in deciding whether or not the deterioration is serious, account must be taken of the effect of such deterioration upon the pursuer's physical abilities in the context of his ordinary life: '[s]eriousness cannot be assessed in a vacuum'.[11] Damages can only be deferred in respect of the serious deterioration in the pursuer's condition.[12]

1 (1887) 15 R 125.
2 (1887) 15 R 125 at 129.
3 See also *Dunlop v McGowans* 1979 SC 22, 1979 SLT 34 at 39 per the Lord Justice-Clerk (Wheatley).
4 Administration of Justice Act 1982, s 12(1)(a).
5 AJA 1982, s 12(1)(b).
6 Cf the approach of the Lord Ordinary (Dervaird) who suggested (*obiter*) that if there was no risk but a certainty that there would be a deterioration, this would not be a suitable ease for provisional damages: *Prentice v William Thyne Ltd* 1989 SLT 336n, OH, at 337.
7 *Potter v McCulloch* 1987 SLT 308, OH, at 310 per the Lord Ordinary (Weir).
8 *White v Inveresk Paper Co Ltd* 1987 SC 143, 1988 SLT 2, OH, at 6 per the Lord Ordinary (Murray).
9 *White v Inveresk Paper Co Ltd* 1987 SC 143, 1988 SLT 2, OH, at 5 per the Lord Ordinary (Murray). See also *Potter v McCulloch* 1987 SLT 308, OH, at 310 per the

Lord Ordinary (Weir); *Meek v Burton's Gold Medal Biscuits Ltd* 1989 SLT 338n, OH, at 339 per the Lord Ordinary (Prosser). In *Bonar v Trafalgar House Offshore Fabrication Ltd* 1996 SLT 548, OH, the Lord Ordinary (Gill) held that the court must determine what the apprehended deterioration is: contingent liability cannot be imposed on a defender unless the nature and extent of that liability is clear.

10 See also *Prentice v William Thyne Ltd* 1989 SLT 336n, OH ('clear and sensible threshold'); *Robertson v British Bakeries Ltd* 1991 SLT 434 ('recognisable threshold').

11 *Robertson v British Bakeries Ltd* 1991 SCLR 450n, 1991 SLT 434, OH, at 439 per the Lord Ordinary (Osborne).

12 *Meek v Burton's Gold Medal Biscuits Ltd* 1989 SLT 338n, OH.

16.22   Even if the pursuer satisfies the statutory criteria, the court is not obliged to defer the award of damages. The interests of the defender in not being called upon to pay further damages at some indefinite time in the future must also be considered.[1] Accordingly, an application for provisional damages is unlikely to be successful unless the medical evidence establishes that the deterioration is likely to take place in, say, a period of not more than ten years. Moreover, the court has the discretion to stipulate a time limit after which the pursuer is unable to claim further damages for a deterioration in his condition.[2] In *McColl v Barns*,[3] for example, where it was established that there was a risk that post-traumatic epilepsy might occur within seven years of the date of the accident, the pursuer was allowed to apply within that period for a further award of damages if the risk should in fact materialise. In the course of his judgment, the Lord Ordinary (Morison) said:[4]

> 'In my opinion this is a most appropriate case for such an order to be made. An assessment made to reflect the possibility of the condition occurring would be unrealistic and impracticable. If no assessment were made and the risk were to materialise, the pursuer would be unjustly deprived of compensation for a serious injury which would be a result of the accident. Since the additional risk becomes negligible after a period of seven years from the date of the accident I shall restrict the order … to that period …'.

The court is also entitled to award interim damages. Interim damages are to be distinguished from provisional damages in so far as they do not depend upon a pursuer suffering from a continuing disability, the eventual seriousness of which cannot be ascertained. Interim payments can be made in the Court of Session in terms of Rule of Court 89A(1) and will be awarded if the court is satisfied that the defender or defenders have admitted liability or that if the action proceeded to proof the pursuer would succeed in a question of liability without any substantial finding of contributory negligence on his part.[5] The court must be satisfied that it is 'practically certain' that the pursuer will succeed on the question of liability and that any finding of contributory negligence will not be so large as to have a material effect on the assessment of the amount the pursuer is likely to recover as damages.[6] An interim award is taken into account in making the final award and will not be made against the defender unless that defender is either a person who is insured in respect of the pursuer's claim or is a public authority or 'is a person whose means and resources are such as to enable him to make interim payment'.[7]

Lump sum payments are particularly unsuitable in some cases of catastrophic injury, particularly when a child is seriously injured and requires constant care. The sums involved in these cases can run into millions. Yet the victim might live for a long time and the lump sum might prove inadequate to pay for his care. Conversely, the victim may die earlier than expected giving rise to a windfall to his family which in the case of medical negligence will have been at the taxpayer's expense. To avoid these outcomes, in cases of severe catastrophic injuries, the parties have been prepared to settle in agreements which include periodical payments.[8]

1   *Paterson v Costain Mining Ltd* 1988 SCLR 70, 1988 SLT 413, OH.
2   Administration of Justice Act 1982, s 12(2).
3   1992 SCLR 907, 1992 SLT 1188, OH; see also *Lappin v Britannia Airways Ltd* 1989 SLT 181n, OH (five years).
4   *McColl v Barns* 1992 SLT 1188 at 1190.
5   See, eg, *Hutcheson v Ascosmit Co* 1992 SLT 1115.
6   *Cowie v Atlantic Drilling Co Ltd* 1995 SC 288, 1995 SCLR 335, 1995 SLT 1151; *Cleland v Campbell* 1998 SLT 642, OH.
7   Rule of Court of Session 89A(1).
8   *D's Parent and Guardian v Greater Glasgow Health Board* [2011] CSOH 99.

D.   PRESCRIPTION AND LIMITATION

16.23   A pursuer may lose her right to obtain reparation if she does not begin proceedings against the defender within certain prescribed periods. By s 6 of the Prescription and Limitation (Scotland) Act 1973[1] the obligation to make reparation for a delictual act[2] is extinguished after five years. The five-year prescriptive period runs from the date on which the delict is complete, ie when the pursuer suffers *damnum* (harm).

'The right to raise such an action accrues when *injuria* concurs with *damnum*. Some interval of time may elapse between the two … and … in such circumstances time is to run from the date when *damnum* results, not from the earlier date of *injuria*.'[3]

This could cause injustice in cases where the damage suffered is latent and the pursuer does not discover that, for example, his house is unstable as a result of defective foundations until five or more years after the damage was in fact sustained. In such situations, time begins to run only when the pursuer first became or could with reasonable diligence have become aware of the damage.[4] Where the pursuer was the victim of sexual abuse, it has been held that he had sustained injuries, ie the *damnum* had occurred, at the time of the abuse even though he was seeking reparation for a psychiatric disorder which did not present itself until 40 years later: the defender's obligation to make reparation was therefore extinguished by the long negative prescription (20 years).[5]

There are, however, important exceptions to the general rule. First, liability for defective products under Part I of the Consumer Protection Act 1987 is extinguished after ten years.[6] Liability for defamation prescribes after 20 years.[7] Importantly, delictual liability in respect of personal injuries or death no longer prescribes.[8] However, a claim for damages for personal injuries, death, defamation and harassment[9] must be brought within a period of three years. This is known as a limitation period. If the action is not commenced within the three-year period, the pursuer cannot enforce his rights unless the defender waives his right to defend the action on the ground that the limitation period has expired.

In the case of personal injuries or property damage as a result of a defective product, the action is not competent if it is brought after a period of three years from the date when the pursuer knew that it was reasonably practicable for him to be aware that there was a defect in the product, that the injury or damage was caused by the product, that the injury or damage was sufficiently serious to bring an action for reparation and that the defender was liable under s 2 of the Consumer Protection Act 1987.[10] A similar limitation period applies to actions brought in relation to death caused by a defective product.[11] In respect of defamation actions, it is simply stated that the three-year limitation period runs from the date when the right of action accrued.[12]

1 In this section references are to the Prescription and Limitation (Scotland) Act 1973, as amended, unless otherwise stated.

2 PL(S)A 1973, Sch 1, para 1(d). Periods during which the pursuer was induced to refrain from bringing the action by reason of the debtor's fraud or error induced by the words or conduct of the debtor are not reckoned as part of the prescriptive period: s 6(4)(a). See *BP Exploration Operating Co Ltd v Chevron Transport (Scotland)* 2002 SC (HL) 19. Any period under which the original creditor was under a legal disability does not count: s 6(4)(b).

3 *Dunlop v McGowans* 1980 SC (HL) 73, 1980 SLT 129 at 132–133 per Lord Keith of Kinkel; see also *Renfrew Golf Club v Ravenstone Securities Ltd* 1984 SLT 170, OH; *Strathclyde Regional Council v Border Engineering Contractors Ltd* 1997 SCLR 100, 1998 SLT 175, OH; *Osborne & Hunter Ltd v Hardie Caldwell* 1999 SLT 153; *K v Gilmartin's Exrix* 2002 SC 602.

4 PL(S) Act 1973, s 11(3). See for example *David T Morrison & Co v ICL Plastics Ltd* 2013 SLT 413. However, the long-stop 20 years' prescription begins to run from the date the damage occurred: s 7. In theory, therefore, a claim for reparation for latent damage could prescribe after 20 years without the five-year prescriptive period being triggered.

5 *K v Gilmartin's Exrx* 2002 SC 602. The abolition of the long negative prescription in respect of death and personal injuries by the Prescription and Limitation (Scotland) Act 1984, s 6(1) and Sch 1, para 2 is not retrospective.

6 PL(S)A 1973, s 22A, Sch 1, para 2(ggg). In this case the ten years run from the date the product is first put on the market, not the date when the damnum occurs.

7 PL(S)A 1973, s 7(2) and Sch 1, para 2(gg).

8 PL(S)A 1973, ss 6(2) and 7(2) and Sch 1, para 2(g).

9 PL(S) A 1973,s 18B.

10 Prescription and Limitation (Scotland) Act 1973, s 22B.

11 PL(S)A 1973, s 22C.

12 PL(S)A 1973, s 18A(1).

16.24 An action for damages for personal injuries must commence within three years from the date on which the injuries were sustained.[1] However, the three-year period does not begin to run from the date when the injuries were sustained unless it was reasonably practicable for the pursuer to be aware of all the following facts: that the injuries were sufficiently serious to bring an action of damages;[2] that the injuries were caused by an act or omission; and that the defender was responsible for the act or omission.[3] So, for example, where a pursuer sustained personal injury as a result of the defender's delictual conduct but the pursuer did not know that he was injured, as in the case of an insidious disease, the three-year period only begins to run when it was reasonably practicable for him to realise that the illness was attributable to the defender's acts or omissions, ie when he knows he is ill. Similarly, the three-year period will only begin when the pursuer knows that the defender is responsible for the delictual conduct; if this knowledge arises after the date when the injuries were sustained, the three-year period only begins to run from the later date.[4] A similar limitation period applies to actions for damages brought in relation to death which has resulted from personal injuries and actions for damages for harassment.[5] In all these limitation periods, time does not run against a pursuer who is or was under legal disability by reason of non-age or unsoundness of mind.[6]

However, in the case of the limitation periods in respect of actions for damages in respect of personal injuries or death from personal injuries, actions for defamation or verbal injury and harassment, the court has a discretion to allow the action to proceed outwith the three-year period if 'it seems equitable to do so'.[7] All the circumstances of the case are taken into consideration, including the length of time in bringing the action, whether the pursuer was responsible for the delay, whether there is an action available against the pursuer's solicitor if the solicitor was responsible for the delay, the inconvenience to the defender etc.[8] The issue is entirely a matter for the discretion of the presiding judge. In practice, the power is used sparingly in claims for personal injuries or death from personal injuries as a result of the knowledge provisions which have to be satisfied before the three-year limitation period begins to run. An extension, moreover, deprives the defender of a complete defence.[9]

1   PL(S)A 1973, s 17(1) and (2). If the act or omission which caused the injuries was continuing, the three-year period runs from the date when the injuries were sustained or the date when the act or omission ceased, whichever is later: see *Mather v British Telecommunications plc* 2001 SLT 325.
2   *Blake v Lothian Health Board* 1993 SLT 1248, OH.
3   *Kirk Care Housing Association Ltd v Crerar and Partners* 1996 SLT 150, OH. The onus rests on the pursuer to prove when he was actually aware of these facts or did not have constructive knowledge of them: *Agnew v Scott Lithgow Ltd (No 1)* 2001 SC 516; *W v Glasgow City Council* [2010] CSIH 70; *A v Glasgow City Council* 2010 SC 411.
4   This describes the law as understood until *David T Morrison & Co Ltd v ICL Plastics* [2014] UKSC 48. At the time of writing this decision has the effect that the period commences when the pursuer is aware of their loss without the need for knowledge of delictual conduct. *Morrison* is reversed and the law is restored to its previous position by the Prescription (Scotland) Act 2018, but the relevant provisions, s 1(5) and s 5 were not yet in force as of 9 July 2021.
5   Prescription and Limitation (Scotland) Act 1973, ss 18 and 18B.
6   PL(S)A 1973, ss 17(3), 18(3), 18A(2), 22B(4) and 22C(3). No causal connection is required between the period of non-age and the delay: *Paton v Loffland Bros North Sea* 1994 SLT 784. See also *Warner v Scapa Flow Charters* 2018 UKSC 52.
7   PL(S)A 1973, s 19A.
8   For examples, see *McCullough v Norwest Socea Ltd* 1981 SLT 201, OH; *Carson v Howard Doris Ltd* 1981 SC 278, 1981 SLT 273; *Donald v Rutherford* 1983 SLT 253, 1984 SLT 70; *Whyte v Walker* 1983 SLT 441, OH; *Clark v McLean* 1994 SCLR 564,

1995 SLT 235; *Gorrie v Marist Brothers* 2002 SCLR 436; *Harrison v West of Scotland Kart Club* [2008] CSOH 33; *Bowden v Poor Sisters of Nazareth* [2008] UKHL 32, 2008 SC (HL) 146; *Sinclair v Morrison* [2009] CSOH 81; *Chinn v Cyclacel Ltd* [2013] CSOH 17; *A v N* [2013] CSOH 161.

9   See discussion in *Jacobson v Chaturvedi* [2017] CSIH 8; *K v Marist Brothers* 2017 SC 258.

Index

Thomson's Delictual Liability

This edition is dedicated to the memory of
Joseph McGeachy Thomson, 1948–2018.